are in France. Shops are shut
presumably marching in St
... but ... in Deviers ...
... vacance. Eardley and I
1st April by OAP ticket.
Dover and hovercraft, w½ tad
... the air, half beating ...
... to Paris. Taxi to the Prince
where Fear Ok is staying ...
... from him.
... out to dine Ok and C
... neighbouring bistro, and went to
... a palace under the roof ...
... fine view across the
... our Max Jacob painting ...
... wealth, Eiffel Tower to right
... to be a Dwarf's Cell and
American.

Diaries, 1971–1983

The Diaries of James Lees-Milne were originally published as follows

Ancestral Voices, 1942–3 (Chatto & Windus, 1975)
Prophesying Peace, 1944–5 (Chatto & Windus, 1977)
Caves of Ice, 1946–7 (Chatto & Windus, 1983)
Midway on the Waves, 1948–9 (Faber & Faber, 1985)
A Mingled Measure, 1953–72 (John Murray, 1994)
Ancient as the Hills, 1973–4 (John Murray, 1997)
Through Wood and Dale, 1975–8 (John Murray, 1998)
Deep Romantic Chasm, 1979–81 (John Murray, 2000)
Holy Dread, 1982–4 (John Murray, 2001)
Beneath a Waning Moon, 1985–7 (John Murray, 2003)
Ceaseless Turmoil, 1988–92 (John Murray, 2004)
The Milk of Paradise, 1993–7 (John Murray, 2005)

Also by James Lees-Milne

The National Trust (ed.), 1945
The Age of Adam, 1947
The National Trust Guide, 1948
Tudor Renaissance, 1951
The Age of Inigo Jones, 1953
Roman Mornings, 1956 (Heinemann Award)
Baroque in Italy, 1959
Baroque in Spain and Portugal, 1960
Earls of Creation, 1962
The Shell Guide to Worcestershire, 1964
St Peter's, 1967
Baroque English Country Houses, 1970
Another Self, 1970
Heretics in Love, 1973
William Beckford, 1976
Round the Clock, 1978
Harold Nicolson, 1980–1 (Heinemann Award)
Images of Bath, 1982
The Country House: An Anthology, 1982
The Last Stuarts, 1983
The Enigmatic Edwardian, 1986
Some Cotswold Country Houses, 1987
Venetian Evenings, 1988
The Fool of Love, 1990
The Bachelor Duke, 1991
People & Places, 1992
Fourteen Friends, 1996

Diaries, 1971–1983

*Abridged and Introduced
by Michael Bloch*

JAMES LEES-MILNE

JOHN MURRAY

First published in Great Britain in 2007 by John Murray (Publishers)
An Hachette Livre UK company

1

James Lees-Milne's original diary material © Michael Bloch 1994, 1997, 1998, 2000, 2001
Introduction and editorial material © Michael Bloch 2007

A CIP catalogue record for this title is available from the British Library

ISBN-978-0-7195-6682-0

Typeset in 11.5/14pt Monotype Bembo by Servis Filmsetting Ltd, Manchester

Printed and bound by Clays Ltd, St Ives plc

John Murray policy is to use papers that are natural, renewable and recyclable products and made from wood grown in sustainable forests. The logging and manufacturing processes are expected to conform to the environmental regulations of the country of origin.

John Murray (Publishers)
338 Euston Road
London NW1 3BH

www.johnmurray.co.uk

Contents

Introduction

James Lees-Milne is unusual among the great English diarists in that he kept a regular journal during two distinct periods of his life, separated by an interval of more than two decades. The first diary covers the eight years 1942 to 1949. It begins when he was thirty-three, shortly after he had been invalided out of the army and returned to his pre-war job with the National Trust; it ends when he was forty-one, shortly before he left that full-time job to become a part-time adviser. Originally published in four volumes between 1975 and 1985, it forms the basis of the first volume (of three) in the present series, published in 2006. The second diary begins in July 1971, a few weeks before his sixty-third birthday, and continues for more than twenty-six years until a few weeks before his death in December 1997, aged eighty-nine. The first half of this later diary, covering the years 1971 to 1983, forms the basis of the present volume, the second in the series.

Before considering why Jim (as he was known) discontinued his diary in 1949 and resumed it in 1971, one must say something about his early life. He was born at Wickhamford Manor, Worcestershire on 6 August 1908, the second child (he had an older sister and a younger brother) of George Lees-Milne and Helen, *née* Bailey. His parents, who did not work but lived off a rapidly diminishing business fortune, were mainly interested in field sports; they had little time for art, literature or religion, and were puzzled by the fact that, from his earliest years, Jim showed a passionate interest in these subjects. As a child, Jim feared his martinet of a father and worshipped his beautiful but vain mother. At Eton and Magdalen College, Oxford, he failed to distinguish himself. He did, however, develop two qualities which would later be useful to him as a diarist. One was an ability to detach himself from his surroundings and become a dispassionate observer of the world around him. The other was an unusual capacity for romantic friendship: many of the soulmates who feature in this volume – Rupert Hart-Davis, Michael Rosse, Johnnie Churchill, Osbert Lancaster, John Betjeman, Harold Acton, Patrick Kinross, and the Mitford sisters – he got to know during his school and university years.

When Jim came down from Oxford with a third-class degree in 1931, his future did not look bright. Jobs were difficult to come by in the wake of the Wall Street Crash. His family were in financial difficulties, so there was no money to launch him on a career. However, being a handsome youth with pleasing manners, he won the support of several older men and women who were able to help him. These included the proconsul-statesman Lord Lloyd, who employed Jim as his private secretary from 1932 to 1935, and the writer-politician Harold Nicolson, through whose influence he was appointed to the newly created post of Country Houses Secretary to the National Trust in 1936. (The sister of the Trust's leading official was an ex-lover of Nicolson's wife, Vita Sackville-West.) Originally founded in the 1890s to preserve the English landscape, the National Trust had only recently adopted the conservation of country houses as one of its purposes. During the late 1930s, Jim visited hundreds of houses on its behalf; although only a handful of these were offered to, and accepted by, the National Trust at this period, he became adept at both assessing the merits of properties and charming their owners.

On the outbreak of war in 1939, the National Trust suspended most of its activities. Jim was commissioned into the Irish Guards; but his undistinguished military career was cut short when he was injured in a London air raid in October 1940, resulting in a year-long sojourn in military hospitals. As he returned to health, the National Trust was returning to life, as harassed country house owners looked to it for the future salvation of their currently requisitioned properties. It therefore eagerly re-employed him when he was discharged from the army in October 1941.

It was a few weeks after resuming his job that Jim – probably influenced by Harold Nicolson, who himself kept a subsequently famous journal – began his 1940s diary. In the view of many readers, its greatest interest lies in his sharply observed descriptions of visits to the owners – many of them eccentric and almost all living in fairly desperate conditions – of dozens of country houses up and down the land. But it also conveys a vivid sense of life in London during the decade, both during the war, with its hazards and excitements, and afterwards, in the grim atmosphere of 'austerity'. Apart from Jim's descriptive talents and ability to capture mood, it is notable for what it reveals of the somewhat paradoxical personality of the diarist, who appears by turns to be enlightened and reactionary, egalitarian and snobbish, tolerant and disapproving, good-humoured and bad-tempered. It also bears witness to his devotion to many friends of both sexes and all ages. Older friends include Harold Nicolson and Oliver, Viscount Esher, his boss at the National Trust; contemporary friends include the writer James Pope-Hennessy and the war hero Hamish Erskine, men of dazzling charm to whom he looked up with admiration, and Eardley Knollys and 'Midi' Gascoigne, confidants with whom he felt he could discuss anything.

As well as taking a romantic view of friendship, Jim frequently fell in love with both men and women, and had many affairs. At school he loved two boys, Tom Mitford and Desmond Parsons; afterwards, he became infatuated with sisters who reminded him of them, Diana Mitford (future wife of Sir Oswald Mosley) and Bridget Parsons. During the 1930s he admired several women, to one of whom he became engaged; he also pursued various clandestine homosexual affairs, and lived for a year in a discreet relationship with a fellow archi-tectural conservationist, Rick Stewart-Jones. In his wartime diary he describes an affair with an unnamed married woman; it is also fairly clear that he was sexually involved with several of his male friends, such as James Pope-Hennessy.

In 1949, aged forty, Jim – as described in his diary for that year – began a serious affair with Alvilde Chaplin, *née* Bridges, a woman a year younger than himself whom he had known for five years. She was beautiful, elegant, talented, rich, and (for she was a general's daughter) somewhat formidable. She had been married since 1933 to Anthony (later 3rd Viscount) Chaplin, and had a fourteen-year-old daughter by him, Clarissa; but the marriage, while amicable, had always been somewhat hollow, Chaplin being a serial philanderer. (At one moment during the spring of 1949, Jim, Alvilde, Chaplin, and Chaplin's young mistress – and future wife – Rosemary Lyttelton were all living together.) Alvilde was a complex personality, who was both lesbian – she had for several years been the companion of Winaretta de Polignac, the celebrated Parisian patroness of artists and composers, and had inherited part of her fortune – and romantically interested in sexually ambiguous men. She fell in love with Jim, who found her fascinating.

They discussed marriage; but this presented Jim with several problems. First, since 1934 he had been a Roman Catholic, so that marriage to her, who still had a husband living, would cast him out of the Church. Secondly, as a tax exile in France, she could only come to the United Kingdom for ninety days of the year, so that Jim could not live with her while retaining his job, to which he was dedicated, with the National Trust. Thirdly, although he reciprocated her love for him, he was sufficiently aware of her rather possessive personality to foresee that marriage to her would not be easy, and that he might in time fall out of love with her. (When he originally published his 1949 diary in 1985, during her lifetime, he excised the passages in which he expressed these doubts; they have been restored in the first volume of the present series.)

By the end of 1949, these problems appeared to have been overcome. Jim was assured by senior Catholic authorities that, as the Chaplins had lived together so little, it should be possible to obtain a papal annulment of their marriage. And thanks to the benevolence of Oliver Esher, he was able to exchange his full-time post as the National Trust's Historic Buildings Secretary (as the position had been known since 1945) for the half-time post of Architectural Adviser. That he would still have to live in England for six months of the year, for only three of which Alvilde could join him, promised him a measure of independence which was not unwelcome. Meanwhile, he had established a second career as a writer of works of architectural history (the first of which, *The Age of Adam*, had appeared in 1947), which would keep him occupied during the six months of the year that he lived with her on the Continent.

On this happy note, Jim's early diary ends. His reasons for discontinuing it clearly had much to do with his impending marriage. He was writing to Alvilde every day during their frequent separations, and felt that these letters were largely duplicating his diary. At the same time, he did not want to leave an intimate record of his feelings and thoughts lying about for her to read. And from 1942 to 1949 he had led a fairly homogeneous life, working full-time for the National Trust and living in London. Henceforth he would be leading a more fragmented life – spending the winter with her in France, and much of the autumn travelling on the Continent doing research for his architectural books. It would be more difficult to keep a diary under these conditions, especially as he was so busy with his double career.

In 1950 Alvilde divorced Chaplin, and bought a house at Roquebrune near Monte Carlo, where she and Jim spent their winters for the next ten years. In 1951 Jim took up his part-time post with the National Trust, and published his second architectural book, *Tudor Renaissance*. All was not quite well, as the half-promised papal annulment never materialised. Nevertheless, at the price of excommunication, he contracted a civil marriage with Alvilde in November 1951, Harold and Vita acting as witnesses. During the first months of both 1953 and 1954 he kept a sporadic diary (included in the first volume of the present series) which provides glimpses of his married life both in Roquebrune and London: this shows him to be fairly happy and well-occupied, if possibly not seeing so much of his old friends.

The next few years, however, were not happy. Although they led a comfortable life and had many common interests, Alvilde became, as he had foreseen, a possessive, managing wife, disapproving of many of his friends, and tending to scold and nag. An added complication was that she no longer offered him the physical comforts which he had enjoyed during the early years of their relationship. Indeed, from 1955 to 1957 she was absorbed in an affair with Vita Sackville-West, with whom she shared a passion for gardening. Jim affected to overlook this; but when, in 1958, soon after his fiftieth birthday, he in turn fell in love with a young man who shared his literary and architectural interests, she (as he recalled on 18 November 1982) objected strongly, to the point that she decided to give up her French domicile and return to live in England to keep an eye on him.

He found her attitude hard to bear, and their marriage almost disintegrated. That it survived was partly due to the conciliatory efforts of Jim's old mentor Harold Nicolson and Alvilde's recent lover Vita

Sackville-West; partly to their discovery of a lovely Georgian house which they both adored, Alderley Grange in the Ozleworth Valley of Gloucestershire; partly to the fact that neither wished to face the ignominy of a divorce. They established a *modus vivendi* whereby they lived together at Alderley (which was sufficiently large for them to keep out of each other's way) yet led substantially separate lives, staying with separate friends, taking separate holidays, making separate visits to London. Altogether, the early 1960s were a miserable time for Jim: twenty years later, re-reading the occasional diary entries he had written then, he was so pained to be reminded of this wretched passage in his marriage that he destroyed them (30 April 1983).

An added cause of misery was his disillusionment with the two institutions he had loved most, the Roman Catholic Church and the National Trust. His failure to obtain an annulment of his wife's former marriage had already dealt a blow to his faith; the changes decreed by the Second Vatican Council, followed by the papal encyclical reaffirming the Church's prohibition of birth control, killed it completely (as recalled on 9 February 1977). As for the National Trust, he was depressed to see it develop from a cosy organisation of dedicated, gentlemanly enthusiasts into a cumbersome bureaucracy pandering to the tastes of a vulgar age. A battle during the mid 1960s between the 'agents' who controlled the money and the 'aesthetes' who made the artistic decisions, won by the former, led Jim to resign from the staff in 1966 – though he subsequently agreed to serve on the Historic Buildings (later Properties) Committee of which he had once been Secretary. He was also dejected by the countless acts of desecration of England's landscape and architectural heritage at this period, which prompted frequent indignant letters to *The Times*.

However, the 1960s, as they progressed, also produced compensations. His love for Alderley grew with the years, and he took pride in Alvilde's considerable talents as a housekeeper, hostess and gardener – one of several factors which had the effect of rekindling his affection for her. A cause of embarrassment during the early years of their marriage had been that, whereas she was a woman of means (Alderley was her property), he had no money of his own; but the deaths in quick succession of his mother, an aunt and a rich Scottish cousin brought him some capital, along with an interesting art collection. After a short period of religious disenchantment, he rediscovered his former Anglican faith – which he now shared with his wife.

He was also cheered by a late breakthrough in his literary career. Hitherto, he had only published books on architecture. Although these had won him some renown, they had enjoyed modest sales, and as a gifted amateur he began to feel uncomfortable in an art history world increasingly dominated by meticulous academics. In the late 1960s, however, he was inspired to write an autobiographical work entitled *Another Self*. Published in 1970, this was received with rapturous acclaim, and established his reputation as a man of letters.* This success emboldened him to start editing his diary for publication – for *Another Self* dealt with his life up to 1942, the year he had begun it. And at the same time he decided to resume it, after an effective gap of twenty-one and a half years.

To turn from Jim's 1940s to his 1970s diary is a Proustian experience. Many of the characters are still there, but the temporal landscape has changed. The Fifties and Sixties have come and gone. A new world has come into being – brash, secular, sensation-seeking, contemptuous of traditional culture, emphasising the values of the masses rather than the elite, and of youth rather than age. Jim constantly fulminates against this world – and the Seventies, a decade of political and economic turmoil threatening social disorder, will intensify his imprecations. Yet he is intrigued by many aspects of modern life, finds much that is sympathetic about modern youth, and does not miss the 'arrogance and cynicism' of the world in which he was brought up.

In 1949 he is a metropolitan man, long resident in London; in 1971 he has been living for a decade in the depths of the country, and writes about the delights and tribulations – mostly the latter – of contemporary life in a country house. (After a few years, he and Alvilde give up the struggle at Alderley and become tenants of the eccentric Duke of Beaufort in a charming small house at Badminton: henceforth the diary gives a fascinating picture of life on a great estate still run along old-fashioned lines.) In 1949 he is a practising Roman Catholic; in

---

* It remains in print after almost forty years, currently published by Michael Russell.

1971 he has almost completed his reversion to Anglicanism: he is soon to be made a warden of his village church, and sacked from the arts committee of the Brompton Oratory, the final link with his former faith. In 1949 his writing is a secondary career, dedicated to producing works of architectural history; in 1971 it is his main profession, and he has moved away from architecture to become a novelist and biographer. (These 1970s diaries also describe the publication – and the mixed emotions it arouses in the diarist – of the 1940s ones.) In 1949 his working life revolves around the National Trust; in 1971 he is more tenuously associated with it as a member of its Properties Committee, unhappy at the sort of organisation it has become, yet pleased still to be consulted by it, and cherished by former colleagues: this volume ends in a blaze of nostalgia with his retirement dinner in 1983.

Of his earlier friends, many have died. These include Harold Nicolson (whose son asks Jim to write his father's biography), Rick Stewart-Jones (whose sister asks him to write her brother's biography) and Oliver Esher (whose son asks him to write a biography of Oliver's father). Others have changed beyond recognition. James Pope-Hennessy and Hamish Erskine, dazzling personalities in the 1940s, are now wrecks: soon, Hamish will drink himself to death (as will Bridget Parsons, another dazzler of yore), while 'Jamesey' will meet his end at the hands of 'rough trade'. (As Jim reflects [9 May 1975] on meeting another contemporary wreck, who had bullied him as a child: 'How the late worms change places with the early birds.') Only two friends who loom large in the 1940s – Eardley Knollys, with whom he stays in London, and Midi Gascoigne, now his neighbour at Alderley – are as close to him now as they were then, and relatively unchanged. Another link with the past is Diana Mosley, still beautiful and fascinating, with whom he had been in love during the 1920s, and his friendship with whom now resumes after a gap of forty years.

The diarist himself, however, though older and wiser, remains much the same person. He is full of the same paradoxes; he manages to capture the same variety of moods. While frequently grumbling, and old-fashioned in his views, he remains full of curiosity and open to new experiences. He still works furiously hard, determined not to waste a minute of the day. He is amazingly energetic for his age, yet hypochondriacal and given to morbid reflections on mortality, as he was before. He writes in the same elegant, poignant, slightly mischievous style. And the diary, though describing a different life in different times, is surprisingly similar in content to that kept thirty years earlier – an idiosyncratic mixture of reflections on life, faith and nature, descriptions of visits to country houses, accounts of social meetings, musings upon works of art seen and books read, repetition of anecdotes heard, reminiscence of events and remembrance of friends.

He is always candid in writing both about himself and other people – save in one respect. There is almost nothing, in the first years of this diary, to indicate that his marriage, the twentieth anniversary of which he celebrated in 1971, had during the past dozen years been through some violent storms. Clearly, his love for Alvilde, in danger of evaporating in the early 1960s, had been largely reconfirmed by 1971, and he misses no opportunity to stress his admiration and affection for her. (It might be said that his decision to resume his diary was in itself a recognition of their resumption of marital harmony.) Only occasionally does he allow himself to hint at the strains which had until recently come close to overwhelming the marriage, and are still largely present. However, from 1979 onwards, Jim abandons this restraint and writes with far greater frankness about his past and present feelings for her.

As described in this volume, I met Jim in February 1979, when he was seventy and I, twenty-five. I had been fascinated to read his wartime diaries, and found him equally fascinating to meet. I was happy when he in turn became fond of me. We maintained a close friendship for some years: not only was this platonic in character, but (as was the case with many other relationships in his life) we met relatively little, keeping in touch by letter and telephone. I little suspected at the time how much he suffered from the pangs of love: he largely concealed these from me, and not yet having suffered from such pangs myself (an omission since corrected), I was unable to recognise them. And although I was aware that his wife did not altogether approve of me, I was unaware of the extent to which our innocent friendship disturbed his marriage; for her resentful attitude, and his exasperated reaction to it, threatened to revive the marital turmoil of twenty years earlier – though for a relatively short time.

Just after this volume ends, in March 1984, he began to suffer from serious health problems; and the devotion with which she cared for him established a close bond which lasted until her own death in March 1994.

These diaries were originally published by John Murray in five volumes, all bearing titles (in accordance with a whimsical tradition established by Jim in his earlier diaries) deriving from Coleridge's *Kubla Khan*. The years 1971 and 1972 (along with some earlier material) appeared as *A Mingled Measure* (1994); 1973 and 1974 as *Ancient as the Hills* (1997); 1975 to 1978 as *Through Wood and Dale* (1998); 1979 to 1981 as *Deep Romantic Chasm* (2000); 1982 and 1983 (along with 1984) as *Holy Dread* (2001). Jim edited the first three of these volumes himself during his last years (*Through Wood and Dale* appearing posthumously); after his death, I edited the last two (followed by the remainder of the diary, to form the basis of the third volume in the present series). He generally kept these diaries in typed form, except when he travelled abroad: the handwriting sample used as endpapers to this volume relates to a visit to France in April–May 1980, during which I met him in Paris. The original manuscripts of 1971–8 are now (with the bulk of Jim's papers) in the Beinecke Library at Yale, those of 1979–83 in my own possession.

In the abridgement of these diaries to one-quarter of their original published length, difficult choices have had to be made. I have cut out most descriptions of foreign journeys; and I have tended to concentrate on what seemed to me to be the main themes and interests in Jim's life, and the most important friendships. In the interests of concision I have allowed myself every liberty, cutting not just entries but paragraphs, sentences, phrases and words, and tying up loose ends. Those inspired to read the original volumes may still do so, for (with the exception of *Holy Dread*, due to follow shortly) they have all recently been reprinted by Michael Russell in the Clocktower Paperback series. As well as cutting, I have also introduced some new material: scattered through the volume are various entries which Jim originally excised in order to spare the feelings of persons then alive (in some cases, of himself), who are now dead. I have also in some cases restored an original form of words which he altered for similar reasons.

For assistance of various kinds I am grateful to David Bonner, Juliana Deliyannis, Patric Dickinson, Sue Fox, Simon Frazer, Vincent Giroud, Selina Hastings, Bruce Hunter, Jonathan Kooperstein, Harry McDowell, R. B. McDowell, Hugh Massingberd, the late Lady Mosley, Roland Philipps, Liz Robinson, Nick Robinson, Tony Scotland, Moray Watson, Caroline Westmore, and the staffs of the Beinecke Library, the London Library, the Savile Club and the Oxford & Cambridge Club.

One of the delights of editing this volume has been getting to know Theo Richmond, who took the photograph which adorns the jacket and whose meeting with Jim is described on 7 September 1975. He turns out to be my third cousin once removed.

Michael Bloch
mab@jamesleesmilne.com
March 2007

For further information about James Lees-Milne's life and work, visit the Official James Lees-Milne Website at www.jamesleesmilne.com

1971

1971

I am so conscious of the passage of time, or rather the little time left in which to do so much, that I fuss and fret, and waste it rather than save it. For instance this morning I thought to myself, 'What a bore having to review this book, Dorothy Stroud's *George Dance*,* which will occupy three days, and how can I reduce the three to two?' – so that I was not attending to the first five pages, and had to begin again from page 1.

Friday, 2 July

If it were not for the fact that *The Times* never publishes a letter from me on a subject other than historic buildings, I would write one about the Harewood Titian. All this fuss and criticism of the Government for not buying it for the National Gallery for £2½ (or is it 1½?) million. I cannot see that it matters if pictures of this importance (the Radnor Velázquez is another) leave the country. It is not as though they were going to be destroyed, or lost to the world. Whereas important works of architecture which are unique to this country are being destroyed every day. One must get one's values right.

Sunday, 4 July

I hate Bernadette Devlin† as much as I hate the Revd Ian Paisley,‡ if anything worse. Now that she is to have an illegitimate baby and may

---

* Architect (1741–1825).
† Fiery Irish Republican politician (b. 1947); then the youngest Westminster MP (having been elected for Mid-Ulster while still a university student, 1969); although she married her child's father, Michael McAliskey, in 1973, her sex-life cost her support among Catholics and she lost her seat in 1974.
‡ Fiery Ulster Protestant political and religious leader (b. 1927); founder of Democratic Unionist Party and Free Presbyterian Church; Northern Ireland premier, 2007.

be disowned by her beastly, pious Irish constituents, I find that I am pleased, and hope that they may chuck her out. Yet on principle I am all for sex freedom. In other words I, like the rest of the hypocritical world, am ready to seize any stick with which to belabour somebody whom I dislike. That is why buggers are so vulnerable. The moment they get into a fix their enemies will round on them because they are buggers, and not because of the fix they have got into, which may be something quite venial.

Tuesday, 6 July

Attended the Bath Preservation Trust* Committee for the first time – not without embarrassment, for in the past I have been very critical of this Trust and even resigned my membership. When welcomed by the Chairman, Christopher Chancellor,† I thanked them for their forbearance. Unless I am strongly interested by a particular item I find it hard to concentrate on a subject discussed at the meeting. I am riveted by entirely irrelevant matters – the freckles adorning the chest, arms and hands of my handsome but plump female neighbour; the side whiskers of the youngish man opposite which are already grizzled grey; the Chairman's icy politeness and deft parrying of bores; the Deputy Chairman's prosiness and smelly pipe; the Secretary's coyness – and indeed the extreme niceness of one and all, met here to attempt the uphill task of preserving Bath which they passionately love against the depredations of philistine officials who don't care a damn how they spoil the finest city in England.

Thursday, 8 July

I admire people who have no sex life, or at least appear to have none, which is why I approve of circumspection, or hypocrisy if one prefers. For sex should be solely an individual's concern, and speculation by others about it makes for interest. I admire people who are

---

* Vigorous (and faction-ridden) architectural conservation society founded in 1934.
† Sir Christopher Chancellor (1904–89); General Manager of Reuters, 1944–59; Chairman of Bath Preservation Trust, 1969–76; m. 1926 Sylvia Paget.

so original as not to derive pleasure from the same old, over-played game, with its lack of variation, its dreary, repetitive gambits, its inconclusiveness, its vanities and *post coitum animale triste est*. I refer to lust not love, of course.

Monday, 12 July

Dog days. After the wettest, beastliest June on record we are enjoying a July which brings back halcyon memories of those childhood summers which were a perpetual sunshine, of lazing on lawns under the shade of large spreading lime trees. For the past ten days we have had every meal from breakfast to dinner on the terrace. The garden is fragrant with roses which clamber over every wall and intoxicate the senses. People who come here say this is the most beautiful small garden they have ever seen. It is the greatest tribute to Alvilde, for she has created something which, if ephemeral, is a work of art. I have yet to create a work of art.

Nothing gives me more happiness than sitting in the library with the holland blinds drawn down and the bright sunlight filtering through, while the outside world is sizzling and I am cool as a cucumber within.

The dogs* are too silly. In this heat they pant and stalk unwillingly at my heel when I take them out. Yet in spite of this they follow me round the house in the afternoon with looks of expectation and reproach, oblivious of the fact that they don't enjoy walks in the heat. I suppose they have no memories, rather like me in my old age.

Wednesday, 14 July

On Tuesday I lunched with Bridget [Parsons].† On my arrival the French maid said to me half-way up the staircase, 'I am afraid you will find her ladyship rather depressed today', and gave me a knowing look. There was no one in the drawing room. Then I heard a growl and a pair of shoes shot through the door on to the floor, narrowly missing

---

* The L.-Ms' whippets, Fop and Chuff.
† Lady Bridget Parsons (1907–72); o. dau. of 5th Earl of Rosse.

my head. In came Bridget, stumping and complaining. To my surprise she was wearing a very tight pair of black satin hot pants, and a shirt so *décolletée* that her bosom was all but totally visible. When she sat I could see her navel. She was pulling behind her a pair of black trousers which she then put on. We had a delicious luncheon of cold trout and raspberries. Conversation consisted of exaggerated praise of the maid very loudly so that she outside could hear (I suppose poor B. realises that this woman is more important to her than anyone else), followed by complaints of disloyalty of her friends, one after another. I said, 'But Bridget, you are so apt to jump on people that they are rather frightened of coming to see you.' 'What rot!' she exclaimed. We called a cab and with difficulty she hoisted herself in. The Curzon cinema was practically empty, mercifully, for B. fell fast asleep, and snored. After an hour she woke up, said it was a rotten film (which it was), and suggested leaving. I accompanied her back to the flat and left.

Sunday, 18 July

I have often noticed that women who achieve success never cease rubbing it into one. They have no idea of modesty. In fact they are damned pleased with themselves. Nancy [Mitford]* never stops insinuating what a great writer she is. Yesterday Joan Evans† lunched here. She is undoubtedly very clever, and highly respected as antiquarian, scholar and art historian. Yet all her stories redound to her credit. 'I was the first British woman to become a member of the French Wine Tasting Society . . .' 'As the only woman to become President of the Society of Antiquaries . . .' 'I floored him [never her] when I pointed out that I had carried off the Brackenbury Prize in 1909 . . .' Vita Sackville-West‡ was an exception: she never boasted, never spoke of her writing or prowess, and was humility itself.

---

* Hon. Nancy Mitford (1904–73); e. dau. of 2nd Baron Redesdale; novelist.
† Writer (1893–1977; DBE 1976) specialising in mediaeval French art history; neighbour of L.-Ms at Wotton-under-Edge; President of Royal Society of Antiquaries, 1959–64.
‡ Hon. Victoria Sackville-West (1892–1962); writer, poet and gardener; m. 1913 Hon. (Sir) Harold Nicolson (1886–1968), diplomatist, writer and politician.

Thursday, 22 July

I thought I would visit Chavenage [House] near here, now open one afternoon a week. A pretty Elizabethan manor with nothing whatever inside. Had to join a party which was shown round by the butler, a nice man who has been with the family since the 1920s. He read every word from a large sheet of paper attached to a board, and his ignorance after all these years was remarkable. At the door into the garden the butler passed us on to Major Lowsley-Williams,* the owner, a happy, plump, friendly man, who showed us the chapel, over-restored in the last century and badly pointed. While our party of twelve slowly dissolved, one member, an anglicised German, and I were left behind feigning an interest in the carved altar front which the Major was extolling, obviously made up from a James I bedback or overmantel. The German got down on his knees to examine it, and said, 'There is only one man who could give an opinion on this, and he is James Lees-Milne. Now in his book *Tudor Renaissance* . . .' I foolishly put my hand on his shoulder and said laughing, 'You had better be careful what you say, for I am he.' The poor man had a shock. The Major kept repeating, 'It is the most extraordinary coincidence I have ever known.' It was fairly extraordinary. The German said he had once met me with Hiram Winterbotham,† and that he was the author of a book on Baroque architecture for which I wrote a preface more than ten years ago.

Friday, 23 July

My happiest mornings are those when I wake up to the realisation that I have no plans at all for the day, not even a meeting with the Diocesan Architect at the church, not even a visit to the tailor in Bath – nothing.

---

* Major Philip Savile Lowsley-Williams (d. 1986).
† Businessman and aesthete (1908–90); well-known figure in the Cotswolds until recently moving to France with his ex-guardsman servant Ball.

Saturday, 24 July

On my walks I don't look around or above enough. My eyes are too fixed on the ground, or rather are looking within myself. I am too introspective. I don't consider the natural world around me as I should. Yet I am tremendously susceptible to my surroundings, and could for that reason never be happy living in ugly country. I think this also goes for Raymond [Mortimer] and Desmond [Shawe-Taylor],* who love Long Crichel yet – unlike me – never go for walks, never set foot outside their garden. A. asks me why they bother to live so far from London when they would be just as happy in Surbiton, since the country means nothing to them. The fact is, it does. Something of the Dorset landscape sinks in. Just the same with me here. My walks are of course made by the dogs, without whom I would be even less responsive to nature.

Monday, 26 July

I suppose the reason I have never been invited to join the Historic Buildings Council† is my sullenness and despair. It is the only committee I have ever wanted to be on, and I used to feel deeply over the slight, like Lewis Namier,‡ who was not given a fellowship at All Souls because, Raymond [Mortimer] tells me, he was the most egregious bore of all time – not I think my worst failing, which is possibly sheer dullness. I was one of the first people in the movement to save country houses. In an indirect way I instigated the foundation of the HBC through Esher§ when I was secretary of the [National] Trust's Historic Buildings Committee. I believed I could not be left out, and dire was my disappointment when I was, and some with a tithe of my

---

* Raymond Mortimer (1895–1980), literary critic; Desmond Shawe-Taylor (1907–95), music critic; co-tenants of Long Crichel, Dorset.
† Quango set up in 1953 (following report of Gowers Committee, which had been much influenced by J.L.-M. and other N.T. figures) to disburse government grants for the upkeep of buildings of outstanding historic or architectural interest.
‡ Oxford historian (1888–1960).
§ Oliver Brett, 3rd Viscount Esher (1881–1963); leading figure in N.T. and for long years Chairman of its Country Houses/Historic Buildings Committee of which J.L.-M. was Secretary, 1936–50.

experience were put on. Oliver Esher and Jack Rathbone[*] several times approached the chairman, that odious Alan Lascelles,[†] on my behalf, with no results.

Friday, 30 July

Going for a walk I rang the Gascoignes' bell. Midi [Gascoigne][‡] not back from London yet. Bamber and Christina[§] were sunbathing in the garden and made me talk for five minutes. I noticed that the figures of both were the same, slim, slender, with small hips. Bamber's waist as narrow as mine was five years ago (*eheu!*); she has no bust. They are very alike also in their points of view. Before dinner they came and sat with us on our lawn. Pity we had not known they were alone or we would have asked them to dine, without their parents, and possibly have *talked*; for Bamber is a highly intelligent boy although I have not yet got beyond expressions of jocular esteem, skimming the very surface of things, and not down to earth. This is often the case with children of old friends. Seldom conversation.

Friday, 6 August

My birthday. I woke oblivious of it, concerned only with a pain in my left eye. While I was shaving A. came in and kissed me. She did not believe I had forgotten, and I believe it is the first time I ever have, because now a birthday means little to me. I am sixty-three. I used to despise, yes, despise people who had reached that age because physically they were repugnant to me. They still are. A. overwhelmed me with presents – a suitcase with initials, an ink-wash by Charles

---

[*] John Francis Warre Rathbone (1909–95); Secretrary of N.T., 1949–68.

[†] Sir Alan ('Tommy') Lascelles (1887–1981); Principal Private Secretary to King George VI and Queen Elizabeth II, 1943–53; Chairman, HBC, 1953–63; friend of Harold Nicolson who later refused to help J.L.-M. with his biography of H.N.

[‡] Hon. Mary ('Midi') O'Neill (1905–91); m. 1934 Frederick ('Derick') Gascoigne; friend of J.L.-M. since 1930, who for the past decade had been his neighbour at Mount House, Alderley.

[§] Bamber Gascoigne (b. 1935); writer, broadcaster and publisher; m. 1965 Christina Ditchburn.

Tomlinson* of dragonflies, two ties and a brown pullover. A. loves giving as much as receiving.

Saturday, 7 August

Horrible things happen to the body. Weakness of valves, etc. Greater care must be taken to be clean. I hate admitting to wearing plates; and because on Tuesday next I have to surrender my bottom plate to Mr Plowman the dentist for adjustment, and shall not have it returned till the following day, I am reluctant to go to the theatre with Freda Berkeley† on Tuesday evening. A. thinks this absurd, saying that it is not as though I had no front teeth, and it is only some teeth at the back which are missing.

Tuesday, 10 August

With Eardley [Knollys]‡ to Berkeley Castle [Gloucestershire] yesterday. Ten years ago when I went as a visitor I thought it ghastly. That opinion was confirmed yesterday. The rooms are badly arranged, the contents indifferent and badly looked after. The Stubbs picture badly in need of repair. Horrible shapeless rooms; and bare stone walls a poor background for gilt furniture. The best furniture, with sofa, chairs and mirrors *en suite*, splendid in themselves, have been badly regilded with oil, not water gilding. The late Earl§ fudged up the place by introducing Gothic doorways, galleries and even windows brought from France. Much of the outside is badly restored. Bad, bad, bad nearly all the way round. The only good thing is the terraced garden. This is beautiful. The situation is not impressive. Yet seen from across the meadow at twilight the Castle does look like a crouching tawny lion, about to spring.

---

* Poet and lecturer in English at Bristol University (b. 1927); m. 1948 Brenda Raybould; neighbours of the L.-Ms.
† Freda Bernstein (b. 1923); m. 1946 (Sir) Lennox Berkeley, composer (1903–89); old friends of the L.-Ms with whom A.L.-M. often stayed in London.
‡ Painter (1902–91); formerly on staff of N.T.; close friend of J.L.-M. since 1941.
§ Randal, 8th and last Earl of Berkeley (1865–1942); uncle of Lennox Berkeley (who would have succeeded him but for his father's illegitimacy).

Had a horrid nightmare last night. Some schoolmaster or don was correcting my Latin prose. He was devastating me with sarcasm about my illiteracy. I was feeling miserable and humiliated. At the back of my mind I was thinking, 'This beastly man does not realise that I am capable of better writing than this. If he only knew, and would take the trouble to find out my potentialities. I know I can write, I know I can. Damn him!' In fact I was retrojecting myself to my Oxford days [1928–31] when I had nothing to show for myself, when my education was neglected, and I resented this neglect, and yet fostered secret and intensely passionate ambitions to write.

Thursday, 12 August

Mrs Golda Meir,[*] the Israeli Prime Minister, interviewed on *Panorama* on Monday, came across as a transparently sincere woman, astute, tortured, but honest. Impossible not to like and admire her. In the course of the hour she said she did not want to be remembered, didn't want any place or prize to be named after her. She had never kept a diary. Which remark made me ask myself why on earth I did. No doubt I explained why in 1942. Then no doubt the reason, even if I was not honest enough to give it, was, partly at least, a contemptible, vain desire for a vestige of immortality, idiotic though such a craving was.[†] Now it is different. I am going to keep this diary only for six months, just to see if I can make a book out of it, out of everyday events, thoughts, nothing much, nothing at all perhaps. But one must be candid. That is the first absolute necessity. Unfortunately one cannot always publish candour.

Friday, 13 August

No, the chief purpose in keeping a diary is to keep one's hand in. It keeps the fingers flexed, and the mind. Even so, I pay not the slightest regard to style, syntax or grammar. I forge ahead without any consideration of good prose. I wonder if Harold Nicolson, whose

---

[*] Israeli premier, 1969–74 (1898–1978).
[†] J.L.-M's wartime diaries had not yet been published at this time.

diaries are impeccably written, took trouble, or even rewrote. I believe not. He was a disciplined, trained and professional writer, who simply could not go wrong, even when improvising. I remember him typing his diary at the end of the day, and early in the mornings. He did not use all his fingers, and his typing was not fast, but he never wavered, never hesitated, and went straight through like cutting butter. So it seemed to me listening to the click, click in the next room at King's Bench Walk. That was in 1934–5, when I was a paying guest.

I know no greater agony than having a manuscript turned down. It has happened to me several times, and the pain, humiliation and disappointment are always devastating. This past winter I suffered from acute depression because my novel* was rejected by literary agent David Higham,† and publishers Hamish Hamilton‡ and Jock Murray.§ Yesterday I began to read through it again after a break of nine months. It is worse than I had supposed, stilted and old-fashioned. I have a dreadful belief that old writers today, unless tremendously distinguished, are simply not wanted. Look at the way Leslie Hartley¶ is now treated by reviewers, as an old, fuddy-duddy reactionary without an original idea to convey.

Saturday, 14 August

Yesterday was A's birthday. As we get older I think with dread of the awful possibility that she may die before me. Pray God it may not be. Yet I wonder what she would do without me, because she has not many intimate friends. Nor indeed do I have many left, but I think I could make new friends more easily than she somehow.

---

* Eventually published by Chatto & Windus in 1973 as *Heretics in Love*, the novel concerns an incestuous relationship between nobly-born twins, resulting in a son with whom the father later falls in love.
† Literary agent (d. 1978).
‡ Publisher (1900–88); m. 1940 Countess Yvonne Pallavicino (d. 1993).
§ John Murray VI (1909–93); head of publishing firm; Eton contemporary of J.L.-M. who eventually became his publisher (from 1990).
¶ L. P. Hartley (1895–1972); novelist, author of *The Go-Between*.

Sunday, 22 August

At dinner with Sally Westminster,* Nigel Birch,† now Lord Rhyl, talked of Tom Mitford,‡ dead these twenty-six years. Nigel said he was no good as a barrister, but good as a Judge Advocate. Said he doubtless would have given up his indiscriminate sex life, married and borne many children, become a model husband – and, I added, probably a disciplinarian father. Talked of his beauty, and Randolph [Churchill]'s;§ until Randolph was twenty-one, he was the most beautiful creature one could imagine. He had magnificent eyebrows and deep-set eyes, like Lady Randolph Churchill,¶ to judge from her photographs. Nigel said he and Tom were Randolph's best and indeed only friends; and R. died as much from excessive eating as drinking.

Tuesday, 24 August

Went for a walk with Desmond [Shawe-Taylor] through the fields and Foxholes Woods. He is the sweetest fellow, entertaining, funny and extraordinarily quick. Very affectionate too. But his fussiness is a disease. He can't enjoy himself for worry whether his shoes will get dry before departure, whether he will leave them behind in the boothole, whether we would forward them if he did so. He has to have a simple statement of fact – the sun rises at 5.30 today – explained and argued over before he can accept it. But when one can steer his mind away from these worries he is immensely stimulating.

One sad thing about advancing years is that old friends become, with few exceptions, more trying to live with, some too trying to be with for more than a day. *Ergo*, one should love but not live with them.

---

* Sally Perry (1911–91); m. 1945 Gerald Grosvenor, 4th Duke of Westminster (1907–67); neighbour of L.-Ms at Wickwar Manor.
† Conservative politician (1906–81); cr. life peer as Baron Rhyl, 1970.
‡ Hon. Thomas Mitford (1909–45); only brother of the Mitford sisters; contemporary of J.L.-M. at Lockers Park and Eton, and the great love of his adolescence; killed in action in Burma.
§ Journalist and politician (1911–68); o.s. of Sir Winston Churchill; Eton contemporary of J.L.-M. and of Tom Mitford (whose cousin he was).
¶ Jennie Jerome (1854–1921); m. 1874 Lord Randolph Churchill (1849–95); American mother of Sir Winston.

Friday, 27 August

One false illusion in my life has been that sweet reason will win through, and that in no circumstances need man resort to force. On the contrary, events since the war have taught me at last what wiser men than I discovered years ago, namely that force is essential to uphold right. Right must be might, even if might is not right. Violence has reached such a pitch that only violence can restrain it. The thugs of this world cannot be checked by light sentences and comfortable cells, but by being executed, got rid of by the quickest, least offensive means, a prick in the arm and a gentle slipping away to God decides where.

Sunday, 29 August

I believe that one ought to pay the utmost respect to old people who have been clever, successful or distinguished. At least, I was brought up to do it. It is not now generally accepted. Indeed, why should one pay the same measure of respect to the ex-distinguished person of today as to the distinguished person of yesterday, who may be foolish, drooling, useless, ugly and an encumbrance, for the last is no longer the same person as the first? You do not treat the callow child the same way as you will treat him when he becomes distinguished years ahead. You treat him as he deserves at the time, roughly perhaps, crossly, chasteningly if he demands it. Therefore you should treat the old, gaga person with disdain, disregard. That is the rational corollary. Thank God I was brought up the way I was, I can only say.

Monday, 30 August

When Midi [Gascoigne] told me that Bamber's novel had been accepted,* my immediate reaction was envy. I contained it, and said jubilantly how splendid the news was. That I should be even slightly envious of this charming, successful young man is preposterous and reprehensible. How can any good be expected of humans who are subject to such degrading instincts?

---

* See 21 May 1972.

14

Sunday, 5 September

Midi spoke to Bamber about my novel and told me to ring him up because he had advice to offer. I did so last night and was just slightly nettled. I expected him to say he would give me an introduction to his friend at Cape's who had taken his novel. Instead he said he could not bother the friend without first reading my novel himself to see if it was good enough. I did not say, 'The hell you won't', but did say I would not bother him, and had already decided, since his mother had spoken to him, to submit it to Norah Smallwood* at Chatto's.

Wednesday, 8 September

All day suffering from terrible *Angst*, a gnawing in my vitals and a terrible dread that something ghastly is about to happen. What is the cause? Maybe the fact that today I have packed and posted my typescript to Norah Smallwood. Am I making a fool of myself by persistently hawking this bloody novel around? Am I too insecure to write about incest, homosexuality, bestiality, necrophilia, coprophilia and the divers little nasty habits that flesh is heir to?

The L.-Ms went on a motoring holiday to Scotland, during which J.L.-M. researched his history of the later Stuarts. Ten days into their trip, A.L.-M. was assailed by toothache and returned home to see her dentist, while J.L.-M. continued to Edinburgh, booking into 'a horrid commercial hotel'.

Sunday, 26 September

I had a ghastly experience. Depressed by my miserable little bedroom, and having telephoned to A. in London, I decided since it was not yet dark (6.15) to venture outside the city in search of the site of the Battle of Prestonpans.† Found it and then dined early at a road-house. Motoring back, already within the outskirts of the city, I was stopped for rather a long time at some traffic lights. A man in a dusty blue

---

* Dragon-like chairman of Chatto & Windus (1909–84).
† Victory of 'Bonnie Prince Charlie' against the forces of King George II in September 1745.

raincoat, sallow-faced, about thirty-five, not a hippy, not apparently labour-class, called out, 'Are you going to the City Centre?' Yes, I said, jump in. He did. Immediately I regretted it because he stank of whisky. He kept repeating that he wanted a drink, and asked me to stop so that we could drink together. I said I would not have a drink, but that if he wanted one that was his affair, only I suggested that he had had enough drinks already. This made him very cross and disagreeable. He questioned me, Who was I, where did I come from? I was reticent, but said that I came from England, which must have been apparent. When we got to Princes Street I tried to stop and get rid of him. But he would not get out, the cars behind me became impatient and blew their horns, so I was obliged to drive on. In one of those residential streets behind Princes Street I drew up along the pavement. The man asked for money. I said I was damned if I would give him any, and said 'Get out immediately.' He wouldn't. For a second or two I sat and thought, what do I do now? The street was fairly empty. Suddenly he seized a coat of A's from the back seat and threw it over my head, while he rifled my pockets to the left side. Took two or three pounds. Luckily the rest of the money I had cashed that afternoon was in another pocket the far side from him. I managed to grab hold of the door handle by feeling for it and got out to the pavement. Through the open door I launched a blow at him, but could not hit him hard enough because of the distance. He then slipped into my driver's seat and began starting up the engine. I managed to blow the horn violently, to no avail. Then there was a tussle for the key. He struck me on the nose with the book I had been reading over dinner. My nose poured with blood. In this tussle he broke off the keys in the ignition lock. In a rage he then got out and started pummelling me on the pavement. A young man and girl friend approached. I beseeched them to help me. 'I gave this bloody man a lift. He has attacked me. He is trying to steal my car.' 'On the contrary,' the man shouted, 'he has assaulted me.' The couple walked off. Another man in bowler hat and swinging a furled umbrella merely said, 'Compose your differences, my good men.' It was only when a larger group of youths approached that the man ran off, saying, 'I have got your keys. I have taken your number. You'll hear more of this.' Bewildered, shocked and miserable I got back into the car. What was I to do, with no ignition key? By some miracle the stump, though broken, remained in the ignition, although the boot and car keys had gone. I started up and drove off I knew not where. Eventually I found a lock-up garage, because the car was full of my and A's luggage. I walked back to the hotel. A sweet young waitress gave me plaster for my nose which bled like a pig's. I took two Mogadons before I could get to sleep. Next morning I was so upset that I drove straight home within the day.

Monday, 27 September

I think it is as much the realisation that the majority of the human race are savages, and that we in this country have reverted to jungle society, as the personal indignity, that has upset me.

I have read Kay Hallé's* book about Randolph Churchill. What comes out vividly from the accounts of him by some thirty friends is that he was a resounding personality, positive and not negative. All admitted his brutish and offensive manners. But his great qualities were honesty and courage. Had Randolph had my adventure in Edinburgh he would have acquitted himself with gusto. He would have pursued the man, bashed him, brought him to justice; not slunk off as I did, feeling myself lucky to be rid of the skunk.

Monday, 4 October

Bruce Chatwin† lunched with us yesterday. Came in like a whirlwind, talking about himself. He has no modesty; shows off. A. complains of this. But Bruce is an attractive young man of a different generation, Birmingham, ambitious, bubbling with enthusiasms, still very young, feeling his way, not self-assured, and on the aggressive. I like him. A pity he is already losing his looks. We talked hilariously and seriously of the young's revolt against the establishment. Bruce, having listened to my views – surprising that he can listen – declared that I was basically an anarchist too. I am not quite sure of that.

---

* Pre-war American friend of J.L.-M. and Randolph Churchill (d. 1992).
† Travel writer and novelist (1940–89); m. 1964 Elizabeth Chandler (from whom he separated, 1979); they were neighbours of the L.-Ms at Holwell Farm.

He and I went for a short walk with the dogs through Foxholes Woods. Then he was enchanting, and all his bombastic social manner left him. He talked enthusiastically, sensibly, unaffectedly. I am certain that in another ten years he will have ceased to be bumptious. He said he felt happy only in the natural wildernesses of the world. Feels constricted in England, lonely in Holwell Farm – not surprising – and is very conscious of today's lack of opportunity for exploration and getting away from the madding crowd. Told me that, being a war baby, he was his mother's darling. He only saw his father on his rare leaves from the Army, and when he appeared in the home Bruce resented his intrusion. His mother, an unwise woman, doted, even dressed him up in her clothes for fun when he was only six. He hates transvestism in spite of this silly treatment, but is inevitably homosexual. Said that homosexuality is nothing whatever to do with genes, but solely upbringing. I don't altogether agree. He admitted it was odd how homos are on the whole more intelligent, certainly more sensitive, than heteros. Said that in many primitive tribes the homosexual becomes the wise man, the healer, the oracle and often the leader, and is greatly revered. I asked what would happen if a white man descended and fell in love with the healer. Would the tribe regard him as hostile Martian, or a divinity of wisdom and light, their union a mystic, wonderful blessing for them? All depends on the tribe, he said.

Saturday, 9 October

I am constantly amazed at the historical ignorance of people who should know better. For instance, in the beautiful *Go-Between* film,* motor cars dating from the 1930s were allowed to appear in Norwich Close in what was meant to be Edwardian times. In the short excerpt shot at our house in May for *The Search for the Nile,*† the coachman's livery did not date from the 1860s, as was intended, but the 1820s. Furthermore, the director persisted, in spite of my friendly remonstrances, in making the coachman bring the carriage up to the front door at breakneck speed, the coachman whipping the horse in a frenzy. I pointed out that carriages

---

* Film by Joseph Losey based on L. P. Hartley's novel (1970).
† Award-winning TV drama series broadcast in 1971.

walked slowly to front doors. I can remember this when I was a child at Ribbesford.* Furthermore, in a ludicrous way the carriage was halted with the horse's head before the door, whereas of course the carriage door should have been opposite the front door.

Monday, 11 October

We dined at Moorwood. Prue [Robinson]† as cheerful as ever; never once alluded to her illness, or allowed a suspicion that she was under the threat of recurrence of cancer. I admire her courage. The three boys‡ home on leave from Winchester. Nicky the second is about the most handsome boy I have ever seen. He is sixteen and a half, but looks eighteen. A sidelong smile has taken the place of a rebarbative scowl. I talked after dinner with Ted, the father, about them in the way the old do the moment the children's backs are turned. He said that Nicky alone was an introvert, and might surprise them yet. He clearly is the intellectual of the three. I tremble for him on account of his superlative looks.

Sunday, 17 October

The Somersets§ dined on Friday. David a moody man, and very restless. One would suppose he was born with a handful of silver spoons sticking out of every corner of his mouth. Heir to a dukedom, rich, handsome, successful, courted, blessed with a heavenly and beautiful wife and four children. He also has good health, strength, guts, and above all charm, that often fatal gift of the gods. What more could a man want?

---

* During J.L.-M's childhood, Ribbesford House near Bewdley, Worcestershire had been the residence of his paternal grandmother, who lived there in Victorian style.
† Hon. Prudence Arthur (1932–76); o.c. of J.L.-M's sister Audrey (1905–91) by her 1st marriage to Matthew Arthur (later 3rd Baron Glenarthur); m. Major Edwin ('Ted') Robinson (1921–85) of Moorwood House near Circencester; she had been diagnosed with breast cancer.
‡ Their sons Henry (b. 1953), Nicholas (b. 1955) and Richard Robinson (b. 1957).
§ David Somerset (b. 1928); art dealer; cousin and heir of 10th Duke of Beaufort (whom he succeeded as 11th Duke and owner of Badminton estate, 1984); m. 1950 Lady Caroline Thynne (1928–95), dau. of 6th Marquess of Bath; they lived at The Cottage, Badminton.

Yesterday afternoon a woman came for an interview as house-keeper. She was half an hour late. During the wait I worked myself into such a state of nerves that I could easily have run away, or created a diversion, like setting the house on fire. I hate interviewing people, perhaps because I remember hating being interviewed, when I was searching for jobs in vain, years ago. One's *amour propre*, one's pride, one's sense of inferiority and of the interviewer's superiority, one's inadequacy, are too painful to be witnessed in others now. The lady came, was perfectly self-possessed, rather noisy, absolutely in command of herself, confident, and superior. My nerves evaporated within two minutes, and I found myself becoming first prickly, then a little indignant that she was so much at ease.

Tuesday, 19 October

Leslie Hartley came for dinner last night. His is a terrible decline. He is enormous like a blown-up bull-frog who gnashes his ill-fitting false teeth. He tottered in, not knowing what he was doing. With him there came the most appalling smell of fish. I said to A., 'What can that ghastly smell mean?' She said, 'I know only too well', for she had nursed old people in the war. Throughout the evening she sprayed scent at him, without his having the slightest idea why. At dinner he made no sense. His memory has entirely gone. He drank whatever was given him, vodka, wine, port and more port, and appeared less drunk as the evening proceeded. For after dinner I was able to talk to him about books, while he sank from the sofa, with the cushion, on to the hearth rug. I am so fond of him, and his condition is very sad indeed. Why must one's friends ruin themselves with 'that nasty Bottle', as the Cardinal of York said apropos his brother, Prince Charlie?*

Monday, 1 November

Particularly when I am abroad [he had just visited Italy for Stuart research] I glance through the list of deaths and am always secretly

---

* Prince Charles Edward Stuart (1720–88) and his brother Prince Henry, Cardinal Duke of York (1725–1807); Jacobite pretenders.

disappointed when there is not one of someone I have known. Not that I want my friends to die, the very reverse, but I suppose like most sub-educated people I get pleasure out of being able to mourn.

I no longer enjoy aimless sightseeing. I must have an objective in view. As soon as I had exhausted what I had come to investigate for my book, I did not know where to turn. On my last day I wandered from one church to another not observing anything in that particular manner which is essential for profit.

Wednesday, 3 November

Last night I dined with the Chatwins at Holwell Farm up the Ozleworth Valley. The moon was full, so I walked there with the dogs. The scene was serenely beautiful, absolutely quiet. A mist rose from the bottom of the valley. The moon scurrying through faint clouds illuminated the Newark woods. The bells of Wotton church started pealing. I have not experienced so Samuel Palmerish a scene for ages. I might have been plunged back into 1820. Shelley's lines came ringing in my ears –

> And like a dying lady lean and pale,
> Who totters forth wrapped in a gauzy veil,
> Out of the chamber . . .

although the moon was not tottering, but scurrying like a boisterous well-fed cheeky cherub. Bruce could not continue them. I don't believe he has read a word of Shelley. He was not very nice to Elizabeth who cooked a marvellous dinner; he was very abrupt and discontented; whereas when he came to tea with me the day before he was all charm. I have seldom met a human being who exudes so much sex appeal with so comparatively little niceness. What does this boy want? He is extremely restless. He hates living at Holwell, wants continuously to be on the move, and is off to South America. When the '*or*' has worn off the '*jeunesse*', how much substance will be left beneath?

Thursday, 4 November

Never has there been such a beautiful autumn. One golden day after another. I took the dogs across the field below and to the south of

Foxholes Wood. The damp leaves from the hedgerows smelt more acrid than I remember for years, and the cowpats sweeter. As children we loved the smell of horse droppings. We had a pony trap which we were allowed to drive along the lane from Evesham for shopping and to Bretforton to tea with the Ashwins.* Audrey would drive, aged twelve or thirteen; Dick† and I, aged eight and ten respectively, were passengers. Miss Wood, the governess, being overweight, was not allowed by Mummie to join us, and was obliged to bicycle, which she greatly resented. Whenever the pony did its business, which involved first a premonitory raising of its tail over the crupper, then pouff, pouff, out would come the fresh, green buns. We children, relishing the delicious aroma, and entirely without any Freudian guilt or repressed sex instincts, would rush to the back of the trap, Audrey even relinquishing the reins, lean over the door and inhale the fallen droppings in the road. Miss Wood thought this behaviour disgusting and reported it to Mama, who reprimanded us, not for being disgusting – it never occurred to her that we were – but for being unkind to the pony in that our action tilted the trap backwards so that the shafts were raised in the harness, and thus caused the pony discomfort. I am amazed now that such young children could drive a pony trap along main roads, but we did, and often without the governess bicycling alongside.

Sunday, 7 November

Isn't it better that we should all be forgotten? We are, of course; even Winston Churchill, even Byron, Shakespeare will be forgotten when our civilisation has passed, and a new one dawns after the atomic disruption of the world. There is something infinitely pitiable in the way human beings can't face up to mortality. The rich buy themselves memorial tablets, which get destroyed by time and vandals. The

---

* Squires of Bretforton Manor (neighbouring Wickhamford Manor where J.L.-M's parents lived from 1906 to 1947) from the sixteenth to the twentieth century; the last of the line was Harry Ashwin who died there in 1983 (see 15 June 1983).
† J.L.-M's younger brother Richard L.-M. (1910–84); m. 1935 (as her 2nd husband) Elaine Brigstocke (1911–96).

ambitious make names for themselves, although totally undeserving of immortality because most of them are second-rate. The deserving unambitious are too modest or too idle to produce anything which will keep their names before the public eye after they have gone. I think of people like my Aunt Deenie,* so good, simple, un-evil, unambitious, without guile, without intelligence, dead these nineteen years and totally forgotten. She has no memorial tablet, no gravestone. She left nothing behind her that is memorable, except a flickering, diminishing love in the hearts of Audrey, Dick and myself. Her contemporaries are all dead. There is not a soul beyond us three who even remembers that she existed. I suppose children are the best memorials, because in them and their children one never quite dies. In a hundred years' time not one soul will know that I existed, for my books will not be read. All I can be sure of is that, had I never existed, the future of the world, or should I say of our civilisation, would not be quite the same for the following paltry reason. However unimportant I may be, I have said something, uttered some word which, overheard by another, has even in an infinitesimal degree influenced his life, which has in turn influenced another's for good or evil. The fact that one has existed means that one has trod on and killed an insect which has deprived another insect or bird of sustenance, which has affected another bird or insect, and so on ad infinitum. In these attenuated hypotheses lies our chance of immortality. Nevertheless once this world is destroyed I doubt if an individual's existence on it will have any remote bearing upon the existence of an individual in another solar system. So there is no hope of immortality except through the grace of God and His word, if only one can have faith. Faith is essential to man's happiness. But who has unquestioning faith? Peasants used to. But they are dying out. I only hope that by growing simpler and better I may enhance my wavering faith. Yet I suppose one should not sit back and expect this to happen. Every good requires inexhaustible effort, and waiting for faith to come is not the way. Prayer, prayer, prayer the theologians answer. Yes, but I have never known how to pray. I can only meditate, and worship, and communicate, and thank. Is this enough?

---

* J.L.-M's mother's sister Doreen Cunninghame (188?-1952), widowed during the First World War.

Monday, 8 November

A., who came back [from Cyprus] last night, has an uncanny way of arriving at telepathic truths, or near-truths.* For instance, if I have invited someone she does not like to dine with me in London, she will say, 'Have you seen So-and-So lately?', when in fact I may not have mentioned his or her name for months. When she saw the little heart I took from the Rome church – incidentally it is made of tin, not silver – she admired it, and said, 'Such things can only have been stolen from churches.'† She is a suspicious character, and hates things being concealed from her. Yet she will not understand that no one, certainly not a husband or wife, is obliged to tell all; that husbands and wives are not one flesh, one soul, indivisible. This is just what I dislike about the married state and shall never reconcile myself to.

Thursday, 11 November

I had four shocks yesterday afternoon in London. In Brooks's, Ralph Jarvis,‡ now a little, bent, hollow-chested old man. I only recognised him by his deprecating laugh. Quite cheerfully he told me he was suffering from a tired heart from which he could never recover. I met Francis Watson§ walking into Christie's. Lined and the shape of his face turned from an oval to a circle, plump body, tiny steps and absurd. Am told he now has a boyfriend, since his ugly wife's death, who treats him abominably; and this pleases. Then in the London Library Patrick Kinross,¶ thin and blotched with dark blue spots. Freda [Berkeley] says he sleeps all day, cannot get on with his history of the Ottoman Empire, and talks about his will. Lastly John

---

* Not entirely uncanny: she was in the habit of steaming open his letters and listening-in to his telephone conversations.

† On his recent visit to Rome, J.L.-M. had purloined a votive heart from a heap of discarded objects littering a disused altar in the Church of Santa Maria Minerva; he was afterwards consumed with guilt.

‡ Colonel Ralph Jarvis of Doddington Hall, Lincolnshire; Eton contemporary of J.L.-M.

§ Sir Francis Watson (1907–92); Director of Wallace Collection, 1962–74; Surveyor of Queen's Works of Art, 1963–72; m. 1941 Mary Gray (d. 1969).

¶ Patrick Balfour, 3rd Baron Kinross (1904–76); writer.

Summerson* approached me, with a rather sweet smile and wearing a beret on one side of his head. Has become an old man. I said, 'Only last week I was looking at the monument to Pius VII in St Peter by Thorwaldsen. He always reminds me of you, majestic, handsome and holy.' He said, 'I have not enjoyed a book [*Another Self*] so much for years. Can't you write a sequel?' No, I replied, I don't dare. 'I expect you are right. It is not a thing that could be repeated.'

Wednesday, 17 November

The whole question of our leaving Alderley has arisen again, because of this tiresome woman giving notice.† For some months it has been happily dormant. But it does seem as though we shall never get a single woman to settle, and we cannot afford more. A. secretly wants to move to London in spite of her protestations that she prefers the country, and has taken a small flat for herself which she is furnishing and decorating. London has changed so much for the worse since I lived there ten years ago that I couldn't bear to live in it again permanently.

Saturday, 20 November

Dined with the Somersets. When the women left the table, David, Peter Quennell,‡ Derek Hill§ and I talked about the everyday things people take for granted and don't write in their diaries, such as going to the lavatory and how much and where they wash themselves. Even Pepys, Peter said, doesn't mention how he washed and what with. He did mention that he had a place of easement on the leads of the roof in one house, and in the basement in another. In the eighteenth century grand people living in the country sent to London for washballs. David said, 'I never wash at all. I have two baths a day, but never wash.' He is the cleanest, sprucest man I know. I said one did not have

---

* Sir John Summerson (1904–92); architectural historian; curator of Soane Museum, 1945–84.
† Miss King, the woman interviewed by J.L.-M. on 18 October, had resigned after a week in the job.
‡ (Sir) Peter Quennell (1905–93); writer and editor.
§ Landscape and portrait artist (1916–2000).

a bath to wash but for relaxation, that one washed much better without a bath. All one needed was a washbasin and a bidet. The latter is essential but the English still for some idiotic reason find bidets funny. In my youth they thought them immoral. I wash myself thoroughly after I have soaked in the bath. It means standing up and soap-washing neck and ears, rather perfunctorily, then chest, under the arms, stomach and groin, and lastly legs. With a sigh of relief I return to the water, and lying wash the toes, and scrub the finger-nails with a brush. In the height of summer in the Mediterranean I don't need a bath. I stand upright and naked, and slosh in front of the basin.

Sunday, 21 November

A. found an advertisement in the *Wotton Gazette* under 'Situations Wanted' by a gardener-handyman with three children. Suspects it may be our gardener Mr Müller, with or without the missus. The terrible truth is that one cannot trust anyone today. One is suspicious of them all. They have no loyalties, no morality, no gratitude, no decency – all those virtues for which *one* is so conspicuous. They think only of themselves and of money, and more money, and employers are 'they', to be rooked, tricked and deceived. It is a sad state of affairs. After the dozens of experiences we have encountered since we have lived here these past ten years, no bad treatment will ever surprise us again.

Thursday, 25 November

To the Bath Preservation Trust annual meeting in the Guildhall. The huge room was packed. Christopher Chancellor a bad chairman, couldn't be heard. Several people spoke with rage in their hearts. One young man, a self-confessed Communist, said, irrelevantly but with venom, 'Damn the elegant buildings, it's the people's needs that are at issue, and not the privileged people either.' I thought to myself, with Miss King's troubles in my mind, is the world today mostly evil, or just stupid? I went away having decided for evil. Then this morning Miss King, having packed and said goodbye, confessed to me that she was going to a doctor to discuss her 'instability'; something was the matter with her, she did not know what. I did. She is a lonely, crotchety old spinster going through what Tony Gandarillas* would call 'the time of her life'. Now I decide the world is mostly stupid. Then, reading the papers, and the way in which the marchers outside the House of Commons injured policemen and horses and smashed Members' cars, I am certain that these people's motives *are* evil. So was that young anarchist's last night. They are anti-everything, positively destructive. I have no sympathy for them. Let them burn.

Thursday, 2 December

Last night I read the book on F. L. Griggs[†] which Harry Horsfield[‡] lent me weeks ago. Griggs was Harry's wife's brother-in-law. I had not before realised what a great etcher he was. His landscapes, his content with poverty, his generosity, make me feel humble. His adoration of England, the England of smocks and hayricks, was touching. Why, when we lived at Wickhamford [Manor, Worcestershire], did we not know people like Griggs, instead of those idiotic, arrogant, stupid good-timers with their contemptible standards of what was right for people of their class to do and say, their abysmal ignorance of art and intellect, and their pride in ignorance? Answer – Griggs would not have wanted to know us.

Griggs's etchings bring back to me the nostalgic cosy beauty of Broadway and Chipping Campden and the Cotswold villages of my boyhood in the 1920s. I relish the memory of winter in these little villages, the smell of wood smoke, the empty streets, grass growing down the humped middles of the roads, animals straying, the inhabitants all belonging and knowing one another, the hounds wandering among all, the clip-clop of horses and occasional bulb horn of some old-fashioned motor car. Oh the bliss departed! Every sortie by car was an adventure. My father putting the Minerva into reverse half-way up Fish Hill, and our just reaching the top one

---

[*] Rich bisexual Chilean diplomat prominent in London and Paris society (d. 1970).
[†] Artist and architect (1876–1938).
[‡] J.L.-M's stepfather; Worcestershire gentleman and First World War aviator who married J.L.-M's widowed mother in 1953, though they lived together but briefly (see 16 November 1973).

frosty afternoon on the way to the Knoxes' children's party at Springhill. I suppose we skidded downhill later in the dark, but I don't remember.

Monday, 13 December

There is really no one whom I like kissing or being kissed by on the mouth. I notice that certain women will try to do it to me, old retainers such as Mrs Haines[*] and Irene Staveley, who make for my mouth a bee-line which I endeavour, usually in vain, to parry. In sophisticated circles no one does this. All my women friends put their faces aslant to mine barely touching; usually first one cheek and then the other is proffered. To kiss, say, Eliza Wansbrough[†] or Diana Westmorland[‡] any other way would be unthinkable. Very few men kiss me, only some very old friends like Raymond [Mortimer], Eardley [Knollys], Desmond [Shawe-Taylor], and then with token rather than actual embraces. I remember Emerald Cunard[§] embarrassing Lord Wavell[¶] at dinner at the Dorchester by asking, 'Field Marshal, do you like kissing on the mouth, or where?'

Thursday, 16 December

The Lennox Berkeleys had their silver wedding party on Tuesday. About forty people to a stand-up dinner. Many old friends, yet I did not enjoy it. I never enjoy parties of this sort. I have no small talk – precious little big talk either. I only went because A. said I must. However I did enjoy the entertainments because I didn't have to make

---

[*] A maid at Wickhamford Manor who married Haines the chauffeur.

[†] Elizabeth Lewis (1897–1995); dau. of Sir George Lewis, 2nd Bt (and granddau. of Sir George Lewis, 1st Bt, late Victorian solicitor); m. 1928–38 George Wansbrough.

[‡] Hon. Diana Lister (1893–1983), yst dau. of 4th and last Baron Ribblesdale; m. (3rd) 14th Earl of Westmorland; neighbour and close friend of J.L.-M.

[§] Maude Burke of San Francisco (1872–1948); m. 1895 Sir Bache Cunard, 3rd Bt; London hostess.

[¶] Field Marshal Earl Wavell (1883–1950); wartime commander, Viceroy of India, and poet.

conversation. These consisted of, firstly, a piece for four hands, commissioned by Burnet Pavitt,* composed by Lennox, and played by Lennox and Burnet. Very charming it was too, a waltz in the Poulenc† manner. A. said afterwards that it was light – which explains why I enjoyed it. Then John Betjeman‡ read a short poem he had composed for them – too light by half. Paul Dehn§ read a sonnet he had composed. Arthur Marshall¶ gave two recitations, one the funniest I have ever heard, of Queen Wilhelmina** broadcasting to the British people in the war in broken English. And John Julius Norwich†† sang to his guitar, plangently. There is no doubt the Berkeleys are greatly beloved by a host of friends, and Freda was very moved by the testimonies of their love.

Sunday, 19 December

June at the Berkeleys' party told me she and Jeremy [Hutchinson]‡‡ had recently dined at Chequers. Ever since her marriage there had been coldness from Heath.§§ She had sent him a message through a mutual friend on the eve of their wedding. After all, she explained, he had never so much as held her hand, far less breathed a word of love. The Hutchinsons motored to Chequers from London. There

---

* Businessman with musical interests (1908–2002); intimate friend of J.L.-M. since 1948.
† Francis Poulenc (1899–1963); French composer whom A.L.-M. had known before the war.
‡ Sir John Betjeman (1906–84; ktd 1969); poet (Poet Laureate, 1972–84) and architectural conservationist; m. 1933 Hon. Penelope Chetwode (1910–86).
§ Film and television scriptwriter (1912–76).
¶ Schoolmaster and humorist (1910–89).
** Queen of The Netherlands, 1890–1948 (1880–1962).
†† John Julius Cooper, 2nd Viscount Norwich (b. 1929); o.c. of Alfred Duff Cooper, 1st Viscount (1890–1954) and Lady Diana Manners (1892–1986); writer and broadcaster; m. 1st 1952–85 Anne Clifford, 2nd 1989 Hon. Mary ('Mollie') Philipps.
‡‡ Jeremy Hutchinson QC (b. 1915); m. 2nd 1966 (as her 2nd husband) June Osborn, *née* Capel (d. 2006), daughter of J.L.-M's friend Diana, Countess of Westmorland; cr. life peer, 1978.
§§ (Sir) Edward Heath (1916–2005); Prime Minister, 1970–4 (Leader of Conservative Party, 1965–75); possessed musical interests.

was a small dinner party of mutual friends exclusively. I asked if Heath was cosy. No, for he shuns all conversation, all intimacy. He is terrified of talk which is not about national or international matters. But he was proud of Chequers and showed them the Nelson and other relics. They saw his bedroom. June said she supposed this was always the Prime Minister's bedroom. No, he said, it was not the last PM's bedroom. He and Wilson* do not just dislike, they detest each other.

Monday, 20 December

Dined at Badminton. David away. Cecil Beaton† staying. He has much aged, very white in face and hair, and scalp covered with light red blotches. A slight paunch. He has lost the old exuberance, but is mellower, and has for me great charm and sweetness.

Cecil said he could not see more of Jamesey [Pope-Hennessy].‡ He took him to the theatre a month ago. James kept screwing up his eyes, focusing them on something unseen while making the most excruciating faces, and stretching out an arm in a mad fashion. Was distant and nagging. Kept on pitching into Cecil, and expecting him to admit guilt for the malpractices of our ancestors 200 years back. 'Well,' said Cecil, 'the truth is that I feel no guilt whatever for the fact that in 1771 my ancestors may have been slave traffickers.' He is sure James was 'high' and doped. 'Why', he asked, 'must he write books on such boring subjects' (as slaves)?

Cecil does nourish some hates in his life still. I suppose that any-one who has once done him an injury is never forgiven, like Anne Rosse§ of whom some truly horrifying caricatures exist. Or has he

---

* Harold Wilson (1916–1995); Labour Prime Minister, 1964–70 and 1974–6; cr. life peer, 1979.
† Artist and society photographer (1904–80).
‡ James Pope-Hennessy (1916–74); writer and bohemian, former intimate of J.L.-M. to whom he had not spoken since they had quarrelled during a visit by J.P.-H. to Alderley in January 1967.
§ Anne Messel (1902–92); m. 1st Ronald Armstrong-Jones, 2nd 1935 Michael Parsons, 5th Earl of Rosse (1906–79).

an objective view of right and wrong? I can't make out. Charming, disarming as I find him, he is the archetypal Twentyish man. And the Twenties mean cynicism.

Wednesday, 22 December

Every single night I am woken up at about 4.30, occasionally later. I have dreams, nightmares, and then lie half-awake, aware that some-thing is wrong, but not sure what. It is strange how our subconscious lives are governed by the dictates of the bladder. And the bladder affects presumably the behaviour of the adjacent sexual organs. Why in God's name were they put so close together? This ridiculous march of events, or non-events, takes place every night until I am awake enough to rouse myself and stumble down the five steps to my bath-room. With care, I can, on returning to bed, fall asleep again fairly soon, the elusive tranquil sleep I always long for but which invariably turns out to be a battle. But if I have been unwise enough to open or shut a window, even pat Fop in his armchair, I become wide awake and do not fall asleep before it is time to get up. Then I hear my little tortoiseshell clock on the shelf beside my bed give its silvery strike of 8. I turn on the news from Radio 3 and listen to the summary. I get out of bed, and stroke or have a word with Fop who may by now have jumped on the bed. I draw the heavy wine-red curtains and drowsily descend the steps to the bathroom again, carrying the wire-less with me.

Thursday, 23 December

To the strains of Couperin and Rameau, conducted by Raymond Leppard,[*] that charming, boyishly attractive man whom I wish I knew more intimately, I shave, cutting myself whenever the blade is a new one. Before the glass I feel awful, sway a little as though I had a hangover, whereas the previous evening I drank one glass of wine. Nevertheless I sing in accompaniment to Rameau and expulsions of wind accumulated during the night. In winter I like

---

[*] Conductor and harpsichordist, who pioneered a revival of Baroque music (b. 1927).

to keep an ear open for the school bus which descending from Tresham slows down before reaching the corner to pick up the Alderley schoolchildren. Since it is high in the chassis I try to duck to prevent the Tresham children getting a glorious glimpse of me standing half-naked and scraggy with soap on my face. Having shaved and washed my teeth (I am inclined to eat digestive biscuits during the night), I soap my neck and ears. Sometimes Fop comes down to the bathroom with me, flop, flop, flop, and when I return up the steps he whines because he is frightened of slipping on the polished boards, so I have to lift him. Strange how after all these years he never thinks ahead. Back in my bedroom I think swiftly – what do I wear today? Nothing is happening, no one is coming, therefore another old pair of trousers, the yellow corduroys, yesterday's dirty shirt and a polo sweater to cover it up, thus avoiding the necessity of choosing a tie. Hastily I pull back the bedclothes to air them, ruffle the pillows and, carrying book and papers, descend the main stairs with Fop in wild excitement because he longs to go out and to greet Chuff who meets him in the hall. A mutual examination of pudenda ensues and they part company, satisfied. By 8.35 I am ready for breakfast.

Friday, 24 December

The stairs are the greatest joy to me, indeed are the part of the house I admire the most, so spacious and generous. The stairwell is huge for the size of the house, which when rebuilt in the middle of the eighteenth century was a smallish middling sort of house. Before the two downstairs rooms were extended about 1810 they were exactly the same size as the centre stairwell. The actual staircase is of oak, with turned and twisted balusters, three to each tread, and a comfortable handrail. Ramped at the newel posts the handrail swoops switchback-like down to the bottom, where the balusters swirl round in the curlicue. The dado echoes the height and rampage of the handrail and the balusters. I could write about the merits of this staircase for ever.

Our Christmas with the Droghedas* at Parkside, Englefield Green [near Windsor], much the same as in past years. Present-giving, effusive thanks, cries of gush as we unpack expensive parcels which we don't always want, much over-eating of too rich food, walks in Windsor Park – which I do like – ending on the third day with frayed tempers on the part of the overstrung Joan who picks little quarrels with Garrett, who in turn bends over backwards to make amends for nothing wrong he has done, but she likes to make him suppose he has done. Derry† looking Byronic having lost weight, and picturesque with thick, bushy dark hair and a white face. He and I on Christmas morning stride down the Long Walk back from St George's Chapel to Parkside exchanging harmless confidences. We wonder why Parkside, which is a nice, white, once-Regency house with pretty things inside, good taste, is yet without much character, and like any Ascot tycoon's villa. It does not seem lived in, has no knick-knacks. The rooms have that vacancy which rooms have when used for company and not by the family.

---

* Garrett Moore, 11th Earl of Drogheda (1910–89); businessman, Chairman of Royal Opera House, and childhood friend of A.L.-M.; m. 1935 Joan Carr, pianist (d. 1989). Since their marriage in 1951, the L.-Ms had spent most of their Christmases with the Droghedas at Parkside.
† Dermot, Viscount Moore (b. 1937); photographer; son and heir of 11th Earl of Drogheda (whom he succeeded as 12th Earl, 1989); m. 1st 1968–72 Eliza Lloyd, 2nd 1978 Alexandra Henderson.

1972

1972

Thirty years ago today I began my diary which I continued for some eight years, then broke off. My first entry expressed worry that, in my thirty-fourth year, middle age was not distant.[*] Now old age has come. The resumption last July was to be for six months only. I shall continue for another six months.

Tuesday, 4 January

Two of the three Robinson boys came to luncheon. We asked Joanie Harford[†] to join us to help with the ordeal. It was the very opposite of an ordeal. They were both absolutely charming. They are interested in everything, have perfect, easy manners, are not the least gauche or awkward, are already men of the world. Henry is eighteen, Nick seventeen. Nick is better looking than words can describe, tall, good figure, carries himself erect. Is writing a thesis for his A-level on David Cox[‡]. I telephoned Audrey to congratulate her on her grandsons and she asked, 'Did Nick tell you what his ambition of the moment was? It is to go to Rome with you.' I told A. this who said, 'Let's take him tomorrow. I would like to adopt him.'

Cheered this morning by a letter from Norah Smallwood saying she will gladly re-read my novel. But she will first of all give it to another to read and form a fresh, unbiased opinion.

---

[*] Cut by J.L.-M. from the published edition.
[†] Joan Wylde (d. 1973); m. Charles Harford of Ashcroft, ancestral estate near Alderley; leading personality of the neighbourhood.
[‡] English artist (1783–1859).

Wednesday, 5 January

My only criticism of the two boys is that they both have that fashionable cockney accent which is so odd in children of their upbringing. Winchester of all correct schools too. Why do upper-class boys have to speak like the lower classes? Do they do it on purpose, in submission to the classless age, in protest against their elders? I don't think so. I think they hear it spoken all around them, and imitate it like parrots.

While beginning Proust's *Captive* in bed last night I listened to the 11.30 news. It was a shock to hear the announcement of Gerry Wellington's* death. For a moment I let the book fall to my lap, and thought about him. Then picked it up and resumed. Thus we take note of the passing of our oldest friends. Because of their old age we accept it with hardly a demur, thinking, 'Well, it is not quite my time yet.' This sounds hard and unsympathetic. But for the past few years Gerry had changed into a querulous, unhappy, indifferent old man. This morning I still feel fairly sad. No man was better qualified to inherit a dukedom. Not a wholly estimable character, for he was selfish, unforgiving and cruel. He nevertheless was the best companion in the world, highly informed, and great fun.

Thursday, 6 January

Gerry had the memory of an elephant, and never forgave an injury, intended or supposed. When in 1937 I and George Chettle of the Ministry of Works together compiled a list of the three hundred most important country houses in England and Wales – an absurd undertaking, as I knew at the time – we rather naturally did not include Stratfield Saye [Hampshire]. Gerry, in those days a valued member of the Country Houses Committee, never trusted my judgement thereafter, and I know he bore me a slight grudge, notwithstanding his kindness and hospitality to me always.

---

* Lord Gerald Wellesley (1885–1972); yr s. of 5th Duke of Wellington; architect and member of N.T. committees; s. nephew 1943 as 7th Duke; m. 1914 Dorothy ('Dot') Ashton, poet and sometime lover of Vita Sackville-West.

I counted the list of books read in 1971. They amount to 142 – not including articles, or parts of books. No wonder Agatha Christie[*] dissented when I said few people read as many as a hundred books in one year. 'I always do,' she protested. 'I read over two hundred.' I wish I could remember half my total.

Saturday, 8 January

At the Bath Preservation Trust committee we voted on the Bath Tunnel. The strange result was that the old trustees were in favour and the young ones against the proposal, they protesting that it was bound to cause harm to the amenities of the city. In bed I read my diary of January 1942, the year in which I began it. How immature I was then in spite of my thirty-three years, how censorious and absurd. Yet I find it difficult to believe that all the experiences of my past life, good and bad, the thoughts thought and the things (not deeds) done, have not been to some purpose, to be gleaned in a later time.

Friday, 14 January

A person cannot deceive others about his origins. Alec Clifton-Taylor[†] said he had little opinion of poor Derek Sherborn.[‡] 'He pretends to be grander than he is. He pretends that his house is an old manor house of the Sherborns. He buys ancestors.' I don't know whether these strictures are justified for I barely know Derek Sherborn. But if they are, what an ass the man must be. He ought to know that others will see through the façade. It is easier to know whether a man has ancestors than it is to know his age. How extraordinary that people can so deceive themselves. I believe it is the

---

[*] J.L.-M. had met the celebrated mystery writer (1890–1976) at a dinner party in the 1960s.

[†] Writer and broadcaster on architectural subjects (1907–85).

[‡] Architectural conservationist (1924–2004); Inspector of Historic Buildings, Department of Works, 1948–82 (Inspector-in-Chief, 1978–82); born of modest origins in South London, he later lived at Fawns Manor, Middlesex, which he claimed as the historic seat of the Sherborns (and which had in fact been bequeathed to his father in 1950 by an owner of that name).

romance in men which leads them to fabricate illusions about themselves; it is something not reprehensible but foolish.

Saturday, 15 January

The *Ecologist* has come out with a strongly worded declaration signed by some thirty distinguished scientists, and Peter Scott,* to the effect that the population/pollution problem is so grave, so urgent that the signatories may found a new political party. In my totally ineffectual way I have been labouring on about this very subject, only to be considered a crank. Now letters are written daily to *The Times*, and everyone who thinks at all realises that the future of the earth is literally at stake. The Conservation Society is quoted every week. And when it was founded ten years ago and I was on the founding committee, I was actually invited [though declined] to be the principal speaker at its first annual meeting. Now established scientists like Professor Fraser Darling† are its speakers, and Presidents of the Royal Society to boot.

Friday, 28 January

Saddened but not distraught to read the announcement of Bridget [Parsons]'s sudden death. Thirty years ago this would have been a cruel blow, but she had died some years ago to me and most of her friends. When I think of the amorphous, hideous, querulous lump of flesh which had been that bright vision, identical with Desmond‡ whom I so dearly loved, I rail against life. I was, in the war days, in love with Bridget because she seemed an incarnation of Desmond with whom I had been deeply in love. Both were in my mind when I wrote my novel [about the amorous twins]. It is dreadful how one can be

---

* (Sir) Peter Scott (1909–89); o.s. of Captain Robert Scott 'of the Antarctic' and Kathleen Bruce (whom J.L.-M. befriended during her 2nd marriage to 1st Baron Kennet); artist, naval officer, naturalist and writer; m. 1st 1942–53 Elizabeth Jane Howard, 2nd 1951 Philippa Talbot-Ponsonby.

† Sir Fraser Darling (1903–79); ecologist.

‡ Bridget's yr bro. Hon. Desmond Parsons (1910–37), whom J.L.-M. loved at Eton.

unmoved by the deaths of those to whom one was deeply devoted in years gone by.

Saturday, 12 February

After the Trust meetings on Wednesday I went to Chesterfield by train; was met and driven to Chatsworth [Derbyshire] for two nights. Three Mitford sisters staying, Debo,[*] Diana[†] and Pam.[‡] Together they seem very affected until one gets 'into' the Mitford swing, and then it's difficult to get out of it. When I left on Friday morning Debo said, 'Diana is a saint nowadays. I am the first to admit that previously she was anything but.' I do not forget her ruthlessness and pro-Nazi sentiments – but then Tom Mosley has changed from the bombastic pseudo-Mussolini to the calm, wise elder statesman. Diana told me that somebody was writing his life[§] and they were giving him help. Then she said with a seraphic look, 'He is inserting that disobliging piece you wrote about Kit.'[¶] All I did was to make a face. I was not going to excuse myself. Thought it best to change the subject. Did not want to cause offence by having to say that what I wrote was what I felt then. Time is not always the enemy. Diana said, 'I look upon you as a brother.' What forgiveness.

She had flown from America the day I arrived at Chats. One American said to her, 'What did your father do to produce such brilliant children?' Diana said he did nothing. Tom Mosley told her she should not have said this. She should have said that her father, because he was a landowner, was a farmer.

---

[*] Hon. Deborah Mitford (b. 1920); m. 1941 Lord Andrew Cavendish (1920–2004), who s. 1950 as 11th Duke of Devonshire.

[†] Hon. Diana Mitford (1910–2003); m. 1st 1929 Hon. Bryan Guinness, 2nd 1936 Sir Oswald ('Tom') Mosley, 6th Bt (1896–1980); lived at Orsay near Paris.

[‡] Hon. Pamela ('Woman') Mitford (1907–94); m. 1936 (as 2nd of his 6 wives) Professor Derek Jackson (d. 1982).

[§] Robert Skidelsky (b. 1939; cr. life peer, 1991) – see entry for 20 July 1977. His biography of Mosley appeared in 1975.

[¶] In *Another Self*, J.L.-M. paints a lurid picture of Mosley's demagogy and raffish entourage (then deployed on behalf of his 'New Party') as witnessed by him during the 1931 general election. (Mosley – known to intimates as 'Tom' and to his wife as 'Kit' – was a family connection of J.L.-M., his aunt Dorothy Edwards-Heathcote having married J.L.-M's uncle Alec Lees-Milne.)

Saturday, 19 February

With these repeated blackouts when the electricity is cut off for hours at a time* we are reduced to candles. How beautiful the golden light they shed. How mysterious and solemn the flickering shadows they induce. While we walk up and down our stairs the big shadows of the banisters move against the white walls of the hall softly and across the portraits. Suddenly a white face is looking at you, then retreats into the shadows. I find reading by candlelight difficult, and A. finds it impossible. How did they manage in the old days? Those over thirty didn't, couldn't.

Tuesday, 22 February

A prospective lady housekeeper came yesterday afternoon for an interview. The conversation and ritual are always the same. Please come into the library, we both say. Did you find your way all right? Idiotic remark because otherwise they wouldn't be here. After asking the same questions we receive the same answers. Yes, I don't mind dogs, so long as I am not expected to take them for walks. I don't mind a little cooking. Where have you been? At Mrs So-and-So's for six weeks, Mrs X's for five months, Mrs T's for three months (they have never been anywhere for long). And why are you leaving Mrs So-and-So now? Because I never have five minutes to myself. Am never off my feet. I have to take breakfast up to people in bed, nurse Mr So-and-So who is incontinent, wash him, dress him, take him for walks, etc. 'If I may interpose' (a favourite expression), 'I would like two days a week off for hunting. Yes, I would bring my own horse. And then if I may have my two step-children for weekends. They're no trouble.' The moment the applicant has gone we telephone the So-and-Sos. They say, 'Don't quote us', and after a pregnant pause add, 'Don't touch her. She drinks, is a thief, is bone idle, complains ceaselessly.' Actually yesterday's lady we quite liked and she seemed to want to come to us. Looking out of the window she said, 'What lovely lilies of the valley you have.' 'They are snowdrops, actually.' 'Oh, is that what they are? I love the country and country

---

* Owing to industrial action by power station workers.

things. What a lot of books you have. Have you read them all? And do they require dusting?' Oh God, the boredom of the conversation.

Saturday, 26 February

We stayed two nights with the Graftons* at Euston [Hall, Norfolk]. What a good, decent, public-spirited pair they are. She with her juvenile courts, her family, and royal waitings. He with his endless committees and chairmanships. Billa [Harrod],† likewise staying, says he never refuses an invitation to address an amenity society. He is great fun to be with and has a wry, not un-sly humour. Yet disapproving. Architecturally, Euston is a mess, made so by the clumsy way his father demolished three-quarters of it. The family portraits make a superb collection.

I ponder, do I like pornography? In literature, honestly hardly at all, because I find the written word unexciting. But in photography, I am afraid Yes, so long as it is not vulgar, or subversive – by which I mean that I don't approve of obscene photographs calculated to corrupt, or lead to violence; those which are of beautiful people and merely titillate the appetites strike me as harmless. If the participants are ugly and the actions vile, then I am revolted. Do I write contradictory cant?

Monday, 28 February

I am finishing the last Proust novel, thank goodness. It is a great struggle to keep the attention fixed. Sometimes I feel on the verge of inspiration to write a work of genius myself, such is the effect Proust has on me. But the wave disappears without my quite realising what the inspiration is about. The trouble is that, difficult though Proust be, he has expressed practically every thought that has occurred to me, with a thousand others besides.

---

* Hugh FitzRoy, 11th Duke of Grafton (b. 1919); Chairman of Society for the Protection of Ancient Buildings; m. 1946 Fortune Smith, Mistress of the Robes to HM The Queen from 1967; J.L.-M's colleague during 1950s when, as Earl of Euston, he had been N.T. Historic Buildings Representative for East of England.
† Wilhelmine Cresswell (1911–2005); Norfolk conservationist; m. 1938 (Sir) Roy Harrod, economist (1900–79).

I think at times of my callous unkindness to Mama during the closing years of her life, with much remorse. I recall walking with her from La Meridienne to Roquebrune village and her making what I considered heavy weather in climbing the gentle slope under the archway.* Now I puff when I have jumped off the sofa and run upstairs for something. On returning to the sofa my heart thumps and I am breathless. It is difficult to summon sympathy for others when one is feeling well and normal. When Harold [Nicolson] was in his dotage I did feel profoundly sorry and distressed to see him in that condition, and even humble that I, so far his inferior, should be all right; yet I did not sympathise to the extent of not forgetting his misery by the time I had left Sissinghurst and was back in the train to London and having a jolly evening with J[ohn Kenworthy-Browne].†

Friday, 3 March

Before I left for London on Wednesday *The Times* telephoned. Would I write an appreciation of Violet Trefusis‡ who was dying? I am trying hard to get out of this for I did not know V. very well, or really like her. She was an opinionated, self-praising person, very mischievous and even cruel. It will be amusing to learn to whom she bequeathed her possessions. She adored teasing us all with promises. The last time we were at the [Villa] Ombrellino [Florence] she told me she would leave me the Prince Regent's snuff box. Her chief claims to fame cannot be included in an obituary, namely her elopement with Vita, and her appalling conduct towards her friends. What in her favour? Wit, yes, and puns. Could be very funny. Vanity engaging. 'Do you admire my shoulders?' She was a romantic, living in a world of special

---

* When the L.-Ms lived in the South of France during their early married life – the episode described in J.L.-M's diary for 13 February 1953.

† John Kenworthy-Browne (b. 1931); expert on neo-Classical sculpture, formerly on staff of N.T. and Christie's; intimate friend of J.L.-M. since 1958.

‡ Violet Keppel (1894–1972); daughter of Edward VII's mistress, Hon. Mrs George Keppel; lover of Vita Sackville-West, with whom she eloped soon after her marriage in 1919 to Major Denys Trefusis (as described in Nigel Nicolson's *Portrait of a Marriage* – see 14 March and 14 October 1973).

fantasy, a sort of Ronald Firbank[*] world, like Daisy Fellowes.[†] People who live fantasy lives are not usually estimable, but given to deceit.

At *The Flying Dutchman* last night with Joan Drogheda in the Royal Box. Act I most tedious. Rosamond [Lehmann][‡] kept whispering, 'When will it end?' I said, 'When will it begin?', for as yet there had been no incident and the Dutchman was rambling on with a boring soliloquy. The second and third acts were however enjoyable. Senta was a Swede called Caterina Ligendza, with a splendid voice to raise the roof, a very beautiful woman like Diana Mosley. So alike that all my inhibited love for Diana when I was nineteen and she seventeen surged within me. It is interesting how an operatic performance can revive emotions experienced nearly half a century ago.

Sunday, 5 March

I said to Ros[amond], it is a terrible thing to realise that adventure can never happen to one any more. One used to go out to dinner with a faint, sweet anticipation that possibly one might meet someone with whom one might go home, even to bed, and with whom one might have a lasting affair. She sighed and said, You still might, darling. Not on my life, I answered. She said she had no one in her life, now Jim Mossman[§] was dead, whom she deeply loved. 'Of course I love my friends,' she said, 'but I am not in love with any of them. Whereas you still love J., don't you?' 'Yes,' I said, 'I certainly do, deeply, devoutly, though the first fine careless rapture has passed.' After fourteen years I am still in love with him. A measure of my love is that, when I have not heard from him for a week, I get anxious and unhappy.

Rory [Cameron][¶] has written to A. from Cap Ferrat that he is wretched because of his French lover leaving him and feels as though

---

[*] Novelist (1886–1926).

[†] Marguerite, dau. of 4th Duc Decazes; m. (2nd) Hon. Reginald Fellowes; Anglo-French society figure, notorious for her malice.

[‡] Novelist (1901–90); friend of J.L.-M. since 1950s.

[§] Television reporter; committed suicide, April 1971.

[¶] Anglo-American garden designer and travel writer living in South of France (1914–85); old friend of A.L.-M.

his inside were filled with concrete. A. is not the best person to elicit sympathy from in this particular case. She thought the lover a dreadful creature, as I did when I met him at Rory's two years ago, an ignorant, second-rate peasant. But R. loves him and is utterly miserable. Like all people in love he is mad, not responsible for his feelings or actions. Nevertheless he makes a mistake in telling all his friends, male and female, about his prostration.

Tuesday, 7 March

I said to Brian Gascoigne* that the spring still upsets me – 'that detestable spring', as Constantia Fenwick† called it. He said it upset him too; that it reproached him. I said, presumably you feel, here is this old earth which has rejuvenated itself, and is ready again, whereas you, etc. He said, Yes, that's the reason. He must be about 25 or 26. He wears his hair below shoulder length, which infuriates his silly old father who gets puce with rage at the mere sight of him.

Saturday, 11 March

Penelope Betjeman telephones to say they are leaving Wantage. Says John will never tear himself away from London and would rather she took a small house miles off, possibly in the Welsh Marches, where he could retire for months on end. Poor Penelope, surely she must realise that John does not want to live with her at all, that he goes off with Elizabeth [Cavendish]‡ weekend after weekend, and to his Cornish house for weeks at a time. (I did not tell her that they are both staying with us next weekend.) I suppose it is pride which makes women cling to delusions of this sort rather than face the truth. Yet P. is eminently sensible, and likes her independence.

---

* Yr s. (b. 1943) of Derick and Midi Gascoigne.
† Constantia Fenwick (1905–93); m. 1936 Ralph Arnold (1906–70) of Cobham, Kent.
‡ Lady Elizabeth Cavendish; dau. of 10th Duke of Devonshire; lady-in-waiting to Princess Margaret; close friend of John Betjeman since 1950s.

Monday, 13 March

There is a grossness in drinking which I dislike. Robin Fedden[*] came to stay last night. He drank in the course of the evening half a bottle of whisky, quite one bottle of red wine, two glasses of port and one of brandy. Not only is it extremely expensive for the hosts, but uncivilised. It simply means that we do not want to have him to stay again. Yet I am fond of Robin and I admire his intelligence and great ability. This morning he was down to breakfast at 8.30 fresh as a daisy. How does he do it?

Friday, 17 March

Am asked to write an article on Bath for *The Times*, illustrated with photographs by Tony Snowdon.[†] I rang him up at Jeremy Fry's,[‡] where he is staying, to consult. He had spent the day going round Bath, seeing for himself the recent devastation and meeting the Mayor, Planning Officer, Chancellor of the University and the bag of tricks. He said, 'I hope this line is not bugged, but Stutchbury[§] is a fiend, and Casson[¶] has no taste whatever.' Went on to say that they had got Adam Fergusson in his article to criticise Stutchbury for not mentioning the work of Colen Campbell[**] in Russia in his boring book on Campbell. I said, 'Boring the book may be, but Campbell never worked in Russia that I am aware of. Are you sure you don't mean Charles Cameron?'[††] 'God,' Tony exclaimed, then

---

[*] Writer and mountaineer (1909–77); J.L.-M's successor (1951–68) as Historic Buildings Secretary of N.T.
[†] Anthony Armstrong-Jones (b. 1930); son of J.L.-M's friend Anne, Countess of Rosse, by her 1st marriage; photographer; m. 1st 1960 HRH Princess Margaret, 2nd 1978 Lucy Davies; cr. Earl of Snowdon, 1961.
[‡] Inventor and businessman (1924–2005), then living at Widcombe Manor near Bath; m. 1955–67 Camilla Grinling.
[§] Howard Stutchbury; Bath City Planning Officer; author of *The Architecture of Colen Campbell* (1967).
[¶] Sir Hugh Casson (1910–99); architect, whose plans were opposed by the Bath Preservation Trust.
[**] Scottish architect (1676–1729); author of *Vitruvius Britannicus*.
[††] Scottish architect in service of Catherine the Great (1743–1812).

turned to Jeremy who came on the line. 'Have we really made this mistake?' Their two voices sounded much alike on the telephone. 'Who am I talking to now?' I asked. 'Charles Cameron,' came the answer. 'Now it's Campbell speaking.' 'Stutchbury here,' I said. All rather foolish.

Saturday, 18 March

John Betj. and Eliz. Cavendish to stay the weekend. John now shuffles instead of walks. We tease him about it. Feeble [Elizabeth Cavendish] and I walking with the whippets saw hounds the other side of the valley. A still and beautiful afternoon, we could hear the voices of the huntsmen clearly, that high-pitched, querulous note. She said, 'That's David Somerset's voice, swearing at someone or something.' Half an hour later, back in the house, I heard his aeroplane buzzing us over-head. I ran out to the front and waved my paper. I saw David's profile clearly as he circled over us a second time. He and Caroline and Jeremy Fry dined. An enjoyable evening. We talked about drugs until midnight. Caroline and David smoked one evening a whole marijuana cigarette each. She said she had no heightened sensations at all. She heard David say, Take off all your clothes. Which she did. He was then sick.

Tuesday, 21 March

I asked John if he ever saw Lionel Perry[*] these days. He recited:

> Literary Lionel while sitting in his den
> Was visited by lots and lots of homosexual men.

My love for J.B. is very deep. I am sure that hundreds of his friends like to believe that they are the chief confidant and the one person with whom he is most happy. I don't kid myself to this extent. But I am sure that I am one of his fairly intimate friends. With him

---

[*] Intimate friend of J.B. from their days as fellow undergraduates at Magdalen College, Oxford.

confidences pour out, fun, folly, tears, wisdom, recitation, readings of extracts from the *DNB, Burke's Peerage,* shouts of laughter, jokes about Irish peers, his friends, fear of the after-life and God's retribution, total disbelief in the whole thing, genuine deep devotion to the Church, hatred of Papistry – what a mixture. What torments he suffers, what enjoyment he extracts from life. I wish he were not so physically collapsed. He has a huge paunch, which means shrunken everything else; and the shuffling! He and Feeble no longer keep up the pretence that they are not totally and permanently attached. She does not ever seem to get bored, or irritated by his fantasies. Just worships him.

Walking to church he said, I wonder what the bell-ringer will look like. I said boy bell-ringers should be plain, spotty and wear spectacles. Yes, he said, men don't make passes at boys wearing glasses. We were mistaken, our bell-ringer was a very pretty little boy with a cream complexion. After Matins, Gilbert Wheat the Headmaster button-holed John who was made to go to Rosehill* for coffee. The boys came up with autograph books. J. is pursued wherever he goes. At Westonbirt,† where I took him during the afternoon, he was sent into ecstasies by a girl with flaming red hair and blue jeans who was lolling lasciviously over a table in the library. These thrills and what he calls 'letchings' are sheer fantasy, I presume.

Friday, 7 April

This morning at breakfast a letter from Chatto & Windus. Well, I say to myself, there is nothing to be gained by deferring the opening of it. And at least the envelope doesn't contain the returned typescript. So I open it gingerly. Norah has accepted my novel and offers me terms. Blessed be God for being so good to me. And about time too.

---

* Rose Hill Preparatory School occupied the neo-Jacobean Alderley House.
† Gloucestershire girls' school, formerly the seat of the Holford family: A.L.-M. had lived there in childhood, the widow of her uncle Graham Menzies having married George Holford.

Thursday, 13 April

John [Kenworthy-Browne] took me to a film at the Curzon which I realised was a good film but which I disliked. Called *The Last Show** of something or other, it was set in a provincial oil town in Texas. The squalor of the shacks and the inhabitants, the total, absolute lack of culture and refinement turned my bourgeois stomach. It upsets me that such societies can exist in Western countries. J. says this is the wrong way to look at such a film, and he is probably right. Certainly I was appalled by the message that sex was the exclusive recreation of these people. J. thinks me very puritanical and he passes no moral judgements on works of art.

On Tuesday I went to Chatto & Windus and was greeted by Norah Smallwood. She is an immensely impressive woman. Extremely intelligent, obviously most capable; knows her own mind and would never compromise or be weak, yet is always polite and charming – to all outside the office I mean. She looks delicate with an absolute scone-white face. After some preliminary compliments she passed me on to Enright, the poet,† who having read my typescript, went through it with me, or rather pointed out a few lapses of style. When these are pointed out to me I invariably agree, and am left with little confidence that the rest is all right.

Wednesday, 19 April

I often wonder why it is that the old look forward so greedily to the newspapers, or the radio news, considering that their lives will soon be over, and future events must concern them so little. Whereas the young are indifferent to the news. During the war my parents listened to the radio news five times daily and infuriated me by rushing into the house to listen. Usually both fell fast asleep before it was over.

---

* *The Last Picture Show*, based on a novel by Larry McMurtry. This entry caused much amusement to McMurtry, a fan of J.L.-M's diaries who wrote a celebrated article in their praise in the *New York Review of Books*, November 2002.
† D. J. Enright (1920–2002); poet and schoolmaster.

Saturday, 22 April

At Abinger's* request I asked John Betj. if he would give an address in Westminster Abbey in July to mark the hundred and fiftieth anniversary of the death of Shelley. He said No, for he did not like Shelley. He agreed with Tennyson in declaring that Shelley was not worth Keats's little finger. Life like a dome of many-coloured glass staining the white radiance of eternity – it made no sense at all. All that rot about the Skylark. Besides he was silly as a man, and wrong-headed. Leigh Hunt was a far better poet. So I have had to disappoint the Keats–Shelley Committee. J.B. said Anthony Blunt† was a great Shelley fan. Would he not do? Or the Poet Laureate?‡ But the latter had already been asked and declined because of poor health.

Monday, 24 April

Lunching at Michael Astor's§ at Bruern [Abbey, Oxfordshire] yesterday was Boofy Arran,¶ as jumpy, nervous and funny as ever. He reminded me of incidents which happened years and years ago, of how Harry d'Avigdor-Goldsmid** wore such tight trousers that his enormous parts were protruberantly in evidence. Boofy also reminded me of the evening when the three of us dined together and went by prearrangement to a brothel with a red light over the door in the little Georgian square beside the Hyde Park Hotel, next door to Kathleen

---

* James Scarlett, 8th Baron Abinger (1914–2002); chairman of Keats–Shelley Committee.

† (Sir) Anthony Blunt (1907–83); Surveyor of the Royal Pictures, 1945–72; officially disgraced in 1979, when it was revealed that he had been a Soviet agent (see 17 November 1979).

‡ Cecil Day-Lewis (1904–72); Poet Laureate, 1967–72. He died the following month, to be succeeded by Betjeman.

§ Hon. Michael Astor (1916–80); 3rd s. of 2nd Viscount Astor and Nancy, Viscountess Astor MP; writer, patron of artists and member of N.T. committees.

¶ Arthur Gore (1910–83); Oxford contemporary of J.L.-M.; s. 1958 as 8th Earl of Arran; best known as the peer who introduced into Parliament the Sexual Offences Bill which decriminalised homosexuality and became law in July 1967.

** Sir Henry d'Avigdor-Goldsmid, 2nd Bt (1909–76); Oxford contemporary of J.L.-M. who often entertained him at Somerfield, his house in Kent; MP (C) Walsall South, 1955–74.

Drogheda's house – now all demolished. When we got there Boofy
and I got the giggles and escaped, leaving Harry. Next morning we
telephoned Harry to apologise for letting him down. His reply was,
'It didn't matter at all. I had the three of them.'

Saturday, 29 April

Actually began writing my Stuart book yesterday, having spent the
earlier part of the week roughing out the section on James II. Already
I see that this is going to be a long book.

Thursday, 4 May

At a meeting of the Bath Preservation Trust last night several people
referred to my article and letter to *The Times*. The last, they said, had
effectively demolished Casson. Afterwards I had supper with Michael
and Isabel Briggs* at Midford. They are enchanting alone. A most
intelligent, civilised and amusing couple. Isabel, who in company
holds herself like a spirited horse on the curb, when she decides to
release herself sparkles at a spanking gallop. She has no small talk
which makes her dinner-table companion nervous until he knows
her. She never says a foolish thing. How I love them for the contribution they make towards a civilised world.

Friday, 5 May

In the evening to three plays given by the Wotton-under-Edge players
as part of the Wotton Festival in the Town Hall. Two of the plays
were drivelling, the third, Shaw's *Great Catherine*, splendidly acted by
Howard Mann the greengrocer who gave a truly professional performance as Prince Patiomkin. He is a tragic figure, tied to Wotton and
the little shop which he hates by a philistine, tyrannical old father.
Howard Mann goes to Rome for his holidays and takes photographs
of Bernini fountains, reads voraciously, is a gentle and enlightened

---

* Michael Briggs, businessman and aesthete, later Chairman of Bath Preservation
Trust, of Midford Castle near Bath; m. 1953 Isabel Colegate, novelist.

solitary in a small, provincial town, a square peg in a round hole. And the citizens of Wotton all say how clever Howard is; he is made for better things. Now it is late. He must be fifty-five.

Friday, 19 May

Johnnie Churchill* telephoned during dinner to say he was at the new Berkeley Hotel with Kay Hallé, 'on the crack', he said, after forty years. So next day at noon I went to the Berkeley to see Kay and Johnnie. He is enormous, but mentally the same as when I first met him, the eternal adolescent. Kay has blonde hair, her face still youthful and sweet. She said that Martin Gilbert† who had taken over Randolph's life of his father came upon a packet of passionate love letters written by Sir Winston to Lady Goonie Churchill,‡ Johnnie's mother. I had often been told that Sir W. was in love with her, but at what stage of their lives I don't know. Johnnie does not think he is Winston's son.

I have bought at Sotheby's for £45 a scrap of a letter of Byron, but without his signature; in fact it is only three lines, without date, having been cut from a page with scissors. Such is the scarcity of any word written by B's own hand.

Sunday, 21 May

Bamber Gascoigne's novel, *Murgatreud*,§ is out. Almost unreadable, although by a great effort I did get through it. Schoolboyish and unmelodious. Allegorical, and unfeeling. Yet I have no doubt his contemporaries like it, judging by the reviews they have given it. And he is so clever, good and nice.

---

* J. G. Spencer-Churchill (1909–92); nephew of Sir Winston; friend of J.L.-M. since they had crammed together for Oxford in 1928; artist.
† (Sir) Martin Gilbert (b. 1936); historian; Fellow of Merton College, Oxford.
‡ Lady Gwendeline Bertie (1885–1941); m. 1908 Major John Strange ('Jack') Churchill.
§ *Murgatreud's Empire*, Quartet Books.

Thursday, 25 May

Yesterday at 1.30 – A. being away in London – the whippets and I boarded the car and motored to Moccas [Court, Herefordshire]. I had not visited the Scar since May 1962 when I scattered Mama's ashes there. Although it was speckling with rain when we arrived, the place was as beautiful as I remembered. Indeed I can think of no area of the British Isles more beautiful. It is still unspoilt, although there were wheelmarks of cars which had recently driven up, indicating that the brutal public has discovered the sacred precincts. The precipitous cliff above the Wye, so steep that I have vertigo looking down upon the swirling river, the wonderful aged Spanish chestnuts and oaks, the curve of the grassy banks from Bredwardine, the flat meadow spattered with veteran trees like shaggy tea-cosies and the deer park rising beyond, the oblique glimpse in the left foreground of the red brick Court, all vindicated my decision of twenty years ago that this is the loveliest view of England. And it is England not Wales, although on the Marches. And although I only once took Mama to the Court and she had no connection with Moccas, yet the Baileys* came from Brecon and Herefordshire, and I could think of no place more worthy of her ashes. Standing on the turf I thought as hard as I could about her, remembering how she enjoyed a jolly view. The deathly silence broken only by the distant purr of the river below, the exotic cackle of pheasants in the wood behind me, the dogs gambolling on the turf. This is praying, I presume, this intensely thinking about, and wishing for the peace and happiness of, somebody very beloved who is dead and and when alive had no belief in a future survival whatsoever.

Monday, 29 May

St Phi. Neri day at the [Brompton] Oratory, beginning with Solemn Mass. A fine performance, and in the old style, Latin ritual which was

---

* J.L.-M's mother's family, descended from Sir Joseph Bailey, 1st Bt (1783–1858), who made a fortune from iron and railways in Wales; he himself was born in Yorkshire, but sat for much of his life as MP for Breconshire and had his seat there at Glanusk Park.

impressive. Yet I was strangely unmoved, no longer belonging to this Church,* in spite of the theatricals of the high altar, the Cardinal† donning and doffing his mitre, my friend Father Michael Napier,‡ tall and distinguished, declaiming, and censers swinging. Went round to the dinner, all the guests already assembled. The first person I came upon was Adrian Jones to whom I hurriedly whispered, 'Do I genuflect, or is it no longer done?' 'Certainly, to the ground, *if* you are presented. They hate it now, but you must.' I was presented, and did genuflect to the ground. In fact I heard my knee make a resounding crack on the floorboards. The Cardinal tried to prevent me but I wouldn't be prevented. But I had no opportunity of kissing his ring. Don't think he wore one. He has charm. He said, 'You were on the Pope's Commission investigating the chair?§ Was it St Peter's, do you think?' I told him what he doubtless knew already, that it was ninth-century, Charles the Bald's, and explained the radio-carbon test. He laughed, and said, 'A pity, but it's just as well our Faith does not have to depend on such relics.' I thought he would be shocked if he knew of my lapse from *our* Faith. Excellent dinner, with champagne which I don't like, served by men in some sort of uniform. Adrian explained that the qualification for joining the Oratorians used to be a personal income of £400 a year, which was more than the Foreign Office's. The evening took me back thirty years to such occasions as the Wiseman¶ dinners with Mrs Belloc Lowndes.** Although intelligent and awfully jolly, these Catholics are unreal. There is a pretentious sexlessness about these people, which is false, and makes for unease.

---

* J.L.-M. was received into the Roman Catholic Church in 1934, and 'lapsed' during the 1960s for reasons explained in his diary on 9 February 1977.
† John Heenan (1905–75); Archbishop of Westminster, 1963–75; Cardinal, 1965.
‡ Michael Napier (1929–96); Roman Catholic convert, who as an Oratorian priest fiercely upheld the old rites. He was not to remain J.L.-M's friend for long: see 28 March 1974.
§ During 1968–9, as described in *A Mingled Measure*, J.L.-M. was one of a commission of six set up by Pope Paul VI to investigate the provenance of St Peter's Chair.
¶ Nicholas Wiseman (1802–65); first Archbishop of Westminster (1850–65).
** Novelist (1868–1947) whom J.L.-M. befriended in the 1930s.

Tuesday, 30 May

Caroline [Somerset] very funny about the Duke of Beaufort's* rage against Tony Snowdon who, having been invited to Badminton for the horse trials, refused because they bored him. The refusal (not the reason) was all right, and pleased the Bs. But two days before the trials he said he *was* coming, which entailed much alteration of rooms and putting old ladies in the attics, etc. He infuriated the Duke by saying that hunting was cruel. Then he said, 'The competitors in the horse trials must be terrified.' 'Equestrians are never terrified,' the Duke said, 'only cissies are terrified.' He began belabouring the fire with a poker. Princess Margaret wanting to calm his rage said, 'Tony doesn't mean terrified, really, he means nervous.' 'No I don't, I mean terrified,' Tony insisted. Whereupon the Duke, completely out of temper, shouted as he banged away at the fireplace, bending the poker. 'Damn this fire, I tell you, damn it, damn it!' Tony thereupon left that afternoon while the party were at the trials, without saying goodbye.

Friday, 2 June

Wednesday being a stinking afternoon I decided to make a dash for Badminton which is now open on Wednesdays in the summer. I wanted to see the portrait of the Countess of Albany† which is reproduced in a book on Prince Charlie published in 1900. Caroline said it was no longer there. Having bought my ticket and passed through all the state rooms I saw no sign of it. In each room a 'lady' steps forward, says with a sweet, sugary smile, 'Good afternoon, this is the dining room. Such a pleasant room I always say. The portrait on the left of the fireplace is Queen Henrietta Maria, on the right King George I by Holbein. Now this is such a pretty piece of needle-work. In the olden days they always did things so beautifully I always think', and so on,

---

* Henry Somerset, 10th Duke of Beaufort (1900–84), of Badminton, Gloucestershire; m. 1923 Lady Mary Cambridge (1897–1987; niece of Queen Mary, consort of King George V); Master of the Horse, 1936–78; leading figure of the hunting world, known as 'Master' from the age of eight, when he was given his own pack of harriers.
† The title by which Princess Louisa von Stolberg (1753–1824) was generally known after her marriage in 1772 to Prince Charles Edward Stuart.

maddeningly, getting all wrong. At any rate in the last room there was the Duchess as usual, talking to people as she likes to do. I went up and said, I am J.L.-M. 'Yes,' she said, 'I know you very well of course,' and promptly introduced me to someone as Mr Milnes-Gaskell. However, when I told her what I was searching for, she dived under a rope and dragged me upstairs. At the top of the grand staircase was the portrait, quite small, rather dirty, and enchanting. The Princess Stolberg sitting on a Baroque chair, wearing feathers in her hair, holding a domino, a dog bounding at her feet, a northern view – France or the Low Countries? – in the background. The Duchess said she was sure she would have been a Jacobite. Said she hated Cromwell more than Mr Wilson. That the Duke of Windsor* reminded her of Prince Charlie, which was shrewd. She is a simple, yet not stupid woman, uneducated, pathetic, and, I assume, gnawed by jealousies. Can't listen to what one says; no one over fifty can, and has to chatter. Is immensely shy.

Wednesday, 7 June

The sentimental indignation over the way the Duke of Windsor was treated, exhibited mostly by leftists and others who wish to do away with the monarchy, is hard lines on poor George VI. He never wanted to become King and only consented out of a sense of duty. People today who were not alive thirty-six years ago do not understand the very real distress caused by the affair. The truth is that the majority of British people and all the Dominions would not have Mrs Simpson as Queen. Possibly in a similar circumstance today they would. But then, they would not. I think I realised this at the time, if reluctant to admit it, for I rebuked Harold Nicolson for being a party to hoofing the King off his throne. I was wrong. My indignation was caused by my being a believer in divine right. When the other night I heard a repeat of the King's voice during the abdication speech about 'the woman I love', I so well recalled the actual occasion. I was staying the night with Diana [Mosley] at Wootton Lodge in Staffordshire. The tears poured down our cheeks as we sat spellbound.

---

* The ex-King (1894–1972; reigned as Edward VIII, January–December 1936) had died on 28 May.

Yesterday I lunched at the Travellers with Hugh Montgomery-Massingberd,* who is now editor of *Burke's Peerage* and *Landed Gentry*. With him his assistant Andrew Walls, who must be all of twenty-three. They were perfectly charming, but so deferential and polite, the younger one calling me Sir, that I was put in a state of acute nervousness. I could hardly bear it I was made so shy.

Tuesday, 13 June

John Pope-Hennessy† has invited me to join the organising committee of the Byron Exhibition which he is to stage for the death anniversary in 1974. Very kind of him, and done because I put the suggestion to him for such an exhibition.

Billa Harrod stayed last weekend. A. found her irritating and was cross because Billa dared to criticise her food. I told A. it was a joke but she did not see it in this light. I admit Billa is often sharp, and her chief failing is inordinate jealousy of others whom she considers to be in competition with herself.

Wednesday, 14 June

I almost shocked A. with the vehemence with which I said this morning that I would betray my best friend and go to any lengths short of murder if I thought he proposed desecrating the landscape or an old building.

Friday, 16 June

Such unwonted quiet last night that reading in bed I could hear the Bristol trains, a sound I associate with Wickhamford, when as a boy lying in bed I sometimes listened to the expresses on the Honeybourne–Evesham track, which conveyed to me a romance and mystery and freedom when I was stuck at home, fretting. I suppose I

---

* Hugh Montgomery-Massingberd (b. 1946); writer, journalist, publisher, genealogist, and future author of a play – *Ancestral Voices* – based on the diaries of J.L.-M.
† Sir John Pope-Hennessy (1913–95); art historian; Director of Victoria & Albert Museum, 1967–73; brother of J.L.-M's former close friend James P.-H.

pictured rich and beautiful young creatures in first-class carriages on the way to my adolescent vision of paradise.

Sunday, 18 June

Peterborough of the *Daily Telegraph* telephoned. They had heard I had written a novel. Yes, I said; but when asked what it was about, I hedged. I can't bring myself to say, incest and sodomy. So I said, a simple romantic tale. A. says Grace* will give notice when she reads it. But she probably doesn't read, like the majority of mankind.

Friday, 23 June

A. in the car said that we owed more to Harold and Vita than almost any of our older, now dead friends. I said Yes, undoubtedly, and that I missed them more than any. A. said she owed what gardening success she now enjoys entirely to Vita, who taught her all she knows. I thought of what I owed to Harold. In writing *Another Self* (which is not an auto-biography, but autobiographical sketches, which I regret I did not make plain) I was inspired by Harold's *Some People*.†

This morning I received a letter from Richard Stewart-Jones's‡ sister Elizabeth [Pulford], suggesting that I write a biography of Rick. She says he has become a legendary figure, and a life ought to be written while people who knew him are alive. I could certainly not write it for Rick had no life that needs recording, although his was a remarkable personality, wayward, idealistic, generous to a fault, intuitively intelligent, philanthropic. Besides, he was one of the chief loves of my life. I suffered more on his account than anyone else's, almost. I could not write a life of this Sir Galahad without dealing with this aspect of our relationship, and that would not suit his family, I dare say. Elizabeth says that his tiresome widow, Emma, has destroyed all his boyhood letters to his mother, that sweet woman.

---

* The recently appointed housekeeper.
† Harold Nicolson's celebrated work of semi-fictionalised autobiography, first published in 1927.
‡ Architectural conservationist (1914–57), with whom J.L.-M. was in love for some years after their first meeting in March 1938 (see 31 October 1975).

Wednesday, 28 June

We motored to London for the première of John Betj's film on Australia, and dinner after. While we were having drinks at the bar of the cinema Tony Snowdon arrived, ran up to us and talked about Bath. Full of vitality and cheer. Then Princess Margaret arrived, followed by the Prince of Wales. I was taken aback, not having expected such. Elizabeth Cavendish presented us one by one. Then Princess Margaret came up to Tony and, small though he is, she almost tiptoed to kiss his ear, and whisper. Tony said, 'You know Jim?' 'Yes,' she said, and moved away. After the film we went to Rules Restaurant in Maiden Lane where John had hired an upstairs room with a single table. We were a party of ten, including Princess Margaret, Prince Charles and Tony. I sat next to Mary, Duchess of Devonshire,* and a nice youngish man who I afterwards learned was Patrick Garland.† Opposite him sat the girl he is living with, a film star, placed next to the P. of W. on Elizabeth's right. Then Tony, then A. on John Betj's left, John, Princess M., John Drummond‡ who had produced the film, the Duchess, me, Garland. I hardly spoke a word to the royals, but watched them closely. Prince Charles is very charming and polite, shook hands with us all and smiled. P.M. is far from charming, is cross, exacting, too sophisticated, and sharp. She is physically attractive in a bun-like way, with trussed-up bosom, and hair like two cottage loaves, one balancing on the other. She wore a beautiful sapphire and diamond brooch. She smoked continuously from a long holder, and did not talk to John once. At 11 Prince Charles asked Elizabeth if he might leave, for he had to motor to Portsmouth. He said he was tired, and looked worn out. E. patted his hand and said, 'Of course, love, Sir,' and beckoned to John. We all rose. He shook hands with us. Princess M. kissed him and Tony called out, 'Good-night, Charles.' 'Good-night, Tony.' E., who had taken her shoes off under the table, walked barefoot downstairs and into the street to see the P. off. She said to the driver, 'Mind you drive carefully.' P.M.

---

* Lady Mary Cecil (1895–1988); dau. of 4th Marquess of Salisbury; m. 1917 10th Duke of Devonshire; mother of Elizabeth Cavendish.
† Writer, broadcaster and theatre director (b. 1935).
‡ (Sir) John Drummond (1934–2006); Executive Producer BBC2 Arts Features, 1969–77.

while she was out of the room picked up E's shoes and put them on her plate. This annoyed Tony who said, 'It's unlucky, I don't like it.' So P.M. took them off, put them on her chair, and walked to the window. A. said to me, 'You must go and talk to her,' but I knew she didn't want me to. She was in a cross mood and twice said she wanted to leave. Indeed it was time, but Tony said he wanted to wait another five minutes. Finally she induced Tony to take her, after E. had said that I would drive her in my Morris. Thank God I didn't have to. In following her, Tony made us promise to come back to Kensington Palace. Which we debated. I did not want to go because I thought Princess M. would not be pleased. The Duchess said to me as we left – 'Well!'

However we went to the Palace since the Duchess accompanied us, and we knew she would not stay long. Tony met us in the courtyard and explained the architecture; what was Wren's work, what his. Their apartments are very well done by Tony in mock William Kent style. P.M. more gracious to me in her own house and took me into the dining room. But I did not find conversation very easy or agreeable.

I told A. that, after Prince Charles left, Elizabeth told me to sit next to her in his place. This I did, and drank water out of his glass, which I enjoyed doing. I said I would not have drunk out of P.M.'s. A. said, yes, she had gone to the loo with P.M. and sat on the seat after her, but would rather have sat on the one Prince Charles had just sat on.

Saturday, 1 July

Exactly a year ago I restarted this diary, meaning to continue for six months. And here we are. Diary has not turned out the kind I meant. It is too factual, too gossipy, too introspective, and lacks cognition.

Monday, 3 July

Dining at the Somersets' sat next to George Weidenfeld.* For years I have harboured a grievance against this man. He once asked me to edit a book on European palaces, and I agreed with some reluctance, being

* Austrian-born publisher (b. 1919); co-founder, with Nigel Nicolson, of Weidenfeld & Nicolson, 1948; cr. life peer, 1976.

in the middle of another book. Everything was settled, including advantageous terms, but I heard no more. Then I heard from Sachie that he had been asked and accepted. Tonight Weidenfeld was charming to me. Flattered me over *St Peter's* [1967], and suggested I might write for him a book on Bernini and his times. Asked me what I was now writing and said he would gladly accept the Stuarts. I said, 'But you haven't seen it.' 'I will take it on trust,' he said. But would he? He is extremely well-informed. Talked of the Baroque and eighteenth-century popes. Knows each one. Then talked of Palestine and the Israelis. Says he is a deeply sympathising Jew, but has no belief. I did not suppose he had.

Friday, 7 July

Have been pondering over what someone said the other day: that when one is awake at 3 a.m. then one sees life, and death, as they truly are, in their stark, terrible, hopeless reality; that at all other times of the day, one sees these infinite things through rose-tinted spectacles; that everyday life is a delusion, is the occupational opiate which deceives us into optimistic speculation.

Saturday, 22 July

At Oxford on my way to London on Wednesday to look up inventories of James II's belongings in the Bodleian. While waiting the customary hour or more for the MSS to be produced I wandered round the town. Looked at 63 High Street in which I had lodgings for two years, and wondered whether my room had been on the first or second floor (I think the second), when a round-faced jolly youth pushing a bicycle into the door asked if I wanted anything. I thanked him and said I was merely looking at the house where I lodged more than forty years ago. 'Good Lord!' he said, and laughed heartily. He must have been all of twenty. I was horrified by Oxford, so down-at-heel, streets filthy and shabby, undergraduates worse than shabby, hippy to a man, beards, bare feet, hair in the wrong places, stinking; walls daubed with slogans, 'Why are the workers penalised?', 'Fuck Sparrow!',* etc. Crowded,

_____

* Sir John Sparrow (1906–92); Warden of All Souls, Oxford, 1952–77.

steaming and beastly. Hideous, unsympathetic new buildings beyond the university town, and by the station a wilderness of car park, the station itself demolished and replaced by sheds which look as though put up in an afternoon for a week's duration. Walked into Magdalen. Much the same. My rooms in College, No. 6 Cloisters on ground floor, looked as lugubrious as ever. Peter Acton[*] had No. 5 next door and I remember him standing at the cloister entrance grinning superciliously. Gardens well maintained in an urban fashion, corporation bedded-out flowers in regiments in the borders.

William Plomer[†] gave a lecture at the Royal Society of Literature. What he said did not have deep significance, but the way he quietly and humorously delivered the lecture was a work of art. In reading some funny passages from Kilvert he briefly stopped to laugh, which enhanced the audience's pleasure. Still, he did not impart why Kilvert is such a superlative diarist, beyond his being a poor curate living in the country who noticed life's small contingencies. There is more than that to him. He was a prose poet, he looked at natural things, and he saw deep meaning in little events. He understood human nature like a god and sympathised with simple people. William has become a beautiful man with his white hair and sharp, gentle features, and his beautiful manners.

Sunday, 30 July

On Friday evening we motored to Ditchley[‡] to hear a lecture by K. Clark[§] on the Universal Man. Very suave, very balanced, plenty of food for thought. No lecture by K. disappoints. He told me the other day that the preparation of this lecture had given him infinite pain,

---

[*] Grandson of the Whig historian; killed in air crash, late 1940s.

[†] South African born writer (1903–73), whose edition of the 1870s diary of the Revd Francis Kilvert appeared in 1938.

[‡] Ditchley Park, Oxfordshire, where Sir David Wills had established a foundation in 1958 to 'advance international learning' and 'promote Anglo-American understanding'.

[§] Sir Kenneth Clark (1903–83); art historian; Surveyor of the King's Pictures, 1933–45; a national celebrity through his *Civilisation* television series (1969); cr. life peer, 1969.

and it was the last he would deliver. So I am glad I heard it. The Universal Man is someone who gives fresh answers to the ancient, timeless questions – Alberti, Leonardo, Newton, Franklin, Jefferson. Lord Perth[*] in giving thanks suggested that K. was one such himself. I think this may be so. A. said as we came away that everything this man has to say is worth pondering.

An extraordinary foundation, this, at Ditchley. Why we were invited I don't know. Most of those present were distinguished ambassadors, artists, dons, the Cheethams,[†] Adrian Daintrey,[‡] John Sparrow, etc. Diana Cooper[§] came late into the marquee and stood myopically at the entrance. We made her sit with us. She looks an ancient woman now, with sunken eyes and taut skin. Said she was involved in yet another motoring contretemps with the police. Her foot got stuck under the clutch, mercifully not the accelerator. Asked her age, which is eighty, she replied 'A certain age', which they interpreted as seventy. This pleased her. K. came up most graciously – he is always gracious. Said he had come straight from Houghton [Hall, Norfolk], which he thinks less beautiful than Ditchley. Does not like the state rooms being on the *piano nobile*. I find Houghton perfection. Ditchley is spoilt by iron cages over the chimney stacks. I find the outside of this house a little too stiff and gaunt, but the inside[¶] wonderful. After an excellent supper we walked on the west terrace. A mown lawn gives way to a field of cut hay which slopes down to the lake. Nothing could be more serene on a warm summer night, the air perfumed with sweet smells. Mrs Lancaster's planting of hedges with statuary a masterpiece, more French than English.

---

[*] John Drummond, 17th Earl of Perth (1907–2002).

[†] Sir Nicolas Cheetham (1910–2002); kinsman and Eton contemporary of J.L.-M.; HM Ambassador to Hungary, 1959–61, and Mexico, 1964–8; m. (2nd) 1960 Lady Mabel Brooke.

[‡] British artist (1902–88).

[§] Lady Diana Manners (1892–1986); officially dau. of 8th Duke of Rutland, though she supposed her father to have been the journalist and politician Harry Cust; m. 1919 Alfred Duff Cooper (1890–1954; cr. Viscount Norwich, 1953), diplomatist, politician and writer.

[¶] Decorated by Nancy Lancaster (1897–1994), who lived there between the wars while married to Ronald Tree MP.

Friday, 4 August

Motored to Beckley Park. It is a small house, very high, with at the back three square, projecting garde-robe flues and a staircase, the latter a twisting spiral of oak treads carved underneath into soffits and the ends set squarely into the wall. Was perhaps built as a hunting lodge. You approach down a long, wooded lane and it stands with feet on Otmoor. A most romantic, timeless old house like the end of a delicious dream, a harbour one longs to get to. A shaded garden of clipped box pyramids and curlicues, and tight yew hedges. Semi-moated still. Red brick on a stone base. Inside, plastered walls studded with timber, ancient furniture and general atmosphere reminding me of Westwood, Ted [Lister]'s* house, *délabré* too as though it had just survived Cromwell's civil war. The bedrooms looked very uncomfortable and before central heating was installed it must have been the coldest house in Oxfordshire. I liked the Fieldings, dedicated to the place as to a delicate and precious child. They are threatened with a motorway fifty yards from the front door *and* by a reservoir which will submerge not only Otmoor, the oldest moor in the world, but Beckley House as well. View from an upstairs window of a far-away fen-like landscape, uneventful, seemingly isolated, yet beastly Oxford suburbs just two miles off.

Thursday, 10 August

Geoffrey Houghton-Brown,† with whom I dined in London, asked what my novel was about for he had read the *Daily Telegraph* paragraph on it. When I told him briefly he remarked caustically, 'Your friends will say it is wishful thinking.' Will they really?

Just as I was boarding a bus opposite St Stephen's Hospital yesterday Babs [Johnson]‡ rushed up, enfolded me in a voluminous embrace on the pavement, jumped the queue and followed me. I paid for her ticket

---

* Edward Graham Lister (1873–1956) of Westwood Manor, Wiltshire; diplomatist and art collector; bachelor admirer of J.L.-M.

† Artist, country house restorer, antique dealer and ardent Roman Catholic convert (1903–93); friend of J.L.-M. since 1930s.

‡ English writer (as Georgina Masson) of books on Italy (1912–80).

to Green Park. We sat on the top deck for she is a chain-smoker, all the daily workers silently reading their papers or gazing into space – until we arrived. Babs without the least concern or consideration for others talked at the top of her voice a spate of highbrow stuff. She began with praise of A's article in the *RHS Journal* and of her garden. I politely asked *sotto voce* what book she was working on. 'The courtesans of Italy,' she bellowed. 'There is nothing, simply nothing I don't know about Italian brothels,' she said. People looked over their newspapers at this elderly British spinster. Then she rattled on about Aretino,* how permissive yet how poetical he was. His descriptions of gardens were so cerebral. And she proceeded to quote him for ten minutes. I thought she was praising our garden at Alderley. I heard her saying, 'Your pleached lime walks, your fanciful box hedges, your topiary yew hedges. May we come again to enjoy the exquisite calm and solace of your garden in spring?' I said, 'Well, Babs, the garden is not up to much in the spring. You really ought to come next June.' 'What are you talking about?' she asked. 'I was quoting Aretino.' Women writers can be terrible bores about their own books.

Monday, 14 August

On Friday A. and I motored to Long Crichel [Dorset]† for the weekend, the first for many a year. We enjoyed ourselves immensely. A. found Raymond [Mortimer] very gentle and sympathetic, always having been frightened of him before. Indeed he has mellowed. Desmond [Shawe-Taylor] excitable as though on the verge of discovering a new Maria Callas. Pat [Trevor-Roper], our other host, silent and withdrawn, as if in awe of the others' intellects – but the real reason is that Raymond and Desmond talk so much that he cannot be bothered to compete unless his opinion is asked for.

---

* Pietro Aretino (1492–1556); Italian poet, known for his licentious satires.
† Three English aesthetes – Eardley Knollys, Eddy Sackville-West and Desmond Shawe-Taylor – had gone to live in this house in 1945, and made it a haven of civilised hospitality. Eardley left during the 1950s, his place taken by Raymond Mortimer; Eddy left in the 1960s, his place taken by the ophthalmologist Patrick Trevor-Roper (1916–2004).

On the way we visited the garden at Cranborne Manor, that romantic house. Garden poetic like a missal illumination or a series of verdure tapestry panels. We then visited the Anthony Hobsons[*] at Whitbury. Highly civilised pair, sharing our apprehensions about the world. And yesterday we lunched with the Reynolds Stones[†] [Litton Cheney, Dorset]. After luncheon Reynolds conducted us round his wilderness garden, from which he seeks exclusive inspiration as an artist. The wilderness is beautiful but uncontrolled. He will not even have a fallen tree removed, but allows it to remain a rustic archway covered with moss across a tangled path.

All the people we met this weekend were highly intelligent aesthetes, all deeply apprehensive about the dire threats to the landscape, in fact to the whole earth. Yet not one of them has the authority to help right matters. These people representing the highest standards of civilisation are powerless to stop the devastating flood of spoilation. The flood is hastened by those who have the power, namely the vast, mindless, faceless majority with no principles but personal greed.

Thursday, 17 August

On Monday to luncheon at Corsham [Court, Wiltshire] for a meeting of the Methuen Trustees, with Robin [Fedden] and Fred Bishop[‡] representing the National Trust. A strange position to find myself in, trustee of a large country house confronting N.T. officials. Paul's[§] nephew John[¶] present. He and Paul make thinly veiled attempts to be polite to each other, but are poles apart, waves of mutual antipathy washing around the room. When I was leaving, John met me getting

---

[*] Anthony Hobson (b. 1921); bibliographical historian; m. 1959 Tanya Vinogradoff.
[†] Reynolds Stone (1909–79); designer, wood engraver and artist, Eton contemporary of J.L.-M; m. Janet Woods (1912–98).
[‡] Sir Frederick Bishop (1915–2005); Private Secretary to Prime Minister, 1956–9; Director-General of N.T., 1971–5.
[§] Paul, 4th Baron Methuen (1886–1974); artist and member of N.T. committees, who after inheriting the Corsham estate in 1932 made repeated efforts to donate it to the N.T., which never felt able to accept it owing to lack of endowment.
[¶] John Methuen (1925–96); scouting enthusiast; inherited Corsham estate from his uncle, 1974 and Methuen title from his father, 1975.

into my car and said that his uncle did not know it, but he had fixed the settlement all right. By which I understood him to mean that when Paul re-settled the Estate's future he, John, made his solicitor insert a clause whereby he can bar the entail when he succeeds. An unwise thing to confide in me, who am Paul's friend and only anxious to tie things up so that future heirs shall not dissipate the property.

Saturday, 19 August

Went to talk with Joan Evans last evening. She visibly older in that she has developed that skinned look, taut and shiny face, straight falling hair like rain; but she is as talkative as ever. Her chest rather more hollow and she has a tiresome, ticklish little cough. She told me her father was born in 1823, her grandfather in 1781. That she hated Ivy Compton-Burnett* ('That ——ing, ——ing woman,' she hissed) because Ivy made mischief between her and Margaret Jourdain,† once a very great friend of Joan; that jealousy was the reason, but unjustified because 'my friendship with Margaret was completely unemotional'. 'Then,' I asked, 'hers with Ivy was emotional?' 'Oh yes.' The subject arose when Joan took me into the dining room to show me for the tenth time the porphyry head, a lovely thing bought in Italy by her brother Arthur Evans.‡ Asked my advice what to do with it on her death. I could not well say 'Leave it to me', so I said, 'Don't, whatever you do, leave it to a museum.' 'Yes, I think I shall leave it to the Ashmolean.' 'Where it will be put in a cellar and forgotten,' I added. Why does she ask me these things? Is it to tease?

Joan's other great hate is Winston Churchill. She would not watch his funeral on television. She is almost the only person to agree with me that Churchill was responsible for the widespread destruction of European works of art in that he refused to consider conditional surrender. Had he done so the war would have ended long before it did and before the nations sought to release their rage in needless carnage

---

* Dame Ivy Compton-Burnett (1884–1969); novelist, whom J.L.-M. befriended during the war.
† Friend (1876–1951) of Ivy C.-B.; expert on furniture and decoration.
‡ Sir Arthur Evans (1851–1941); archaeologist; half-brother of Joan Evans.

and destruction. Besides, Churchill so evidently enjoyed the war that I could never like him. I merely acknowledge him, like Genghis Khan, to have been great.

Tuesday, 22 August

I do not often look at my body closely. I did so today in the glass. It is becoming like that of St Jerome in Old Masters, the old man's, bulging at the waist in a roll, elsewhere creased, dented and scrawny, like stretched elastic.

I motor to Marston in Lincolnshire to stay with the Squarson, Henry Thorold.* He looks as Rory Cameron might look under torture: a profile like George III's and a stomach like George IV's. Is extremely greedy and hogs his food. An enthusiast. Madly keen antiquarian. His passionate interests are architecture and genealogy. Knows Lincolnshire backwards, and all the families that ever were, they being to a man his relations. Is fervently right-wing and deplores all that I deplore. Is in fact a most sympathetic being. He motors around the country in a large old Bentley and wears a dog-collar, an unexpected combination. Belongs to the school of Wyndham Ketton-Cremer† and Gyles Isham,‡ who is a close friend. Is one of the last county historian squires. Should be an archdeacon. Marston Hall, his house, is not very interesting, being the fragment of a once larger medieval mansion, reduced in size in Georgian times. Crammed with Thorold portraits. Henry has recently imported and set up a whole room from a family house, Burston near Dulverton, namely a 1699 plaster ceiling and wainscot, grained and painted with coats of arms, and over the fireplace a portrait of a country house, possibly Burston at that date.

---

* The Revd Henry Thorold (1921–2000); sometime housemaster at Lancing College; bachelor antiquarian and author of guide books; he and J.L.-M. developed a sparring relationship.

† R. W. Ketton-Cremer (1906–69); squire of Felbrigg Hall, Norfolk (which he donated to the N.T.); county historian and man of letters.

‡ Sir Gyles Isham, 12th Bt (1903–76); squire of Lamport Hall, Northamptonshire; actor.

Friday, 1 September

Yesterday being Audrey's birthday, I took her to luncheon at the Bay Tree in Burford and on to Wickhamford to see the old Haineses.* But before calling we walked into the orchard and talked to the gardener of the present owners of the manor. He said they were away and we might walk in the garden. We went into the church and both agreed it had been too tarted up. All the oak pews which used to be silvery grey now varnished a black treacle. A hideous red carpet covers the chancel. In our day the church was very simple and slightly down-at-heel. I am so pleased with Reynolds Stone's slate tablet I had put up to our parents, a beautiful thing worthy of the monuments in this old church. The garden much changed. Nice that an opening has been made in the trees the far side of the pond so that a distant view now had from the house across the field opposite to the hills beyond Broadway. Found in the spinney the dogs' cemetery, little stones carved with the names and dates of the departed, with sentimental inscriptions and even verse quotations, rather touching. The drain at the deep end of the pond, still emitting a clear, resonant note of falling subterranean water, brought back ambivalent memories of adolescence. Peered through the windows of the downstairs rooms, all pitch dark and melancholy. Commonplace furniture and subfusc stuff quite without taste, and the most ghastly glass door leading to the terrace. Hideous bedding-out, reds and yellows. In fact the house struck me as the most melancholy place imaginable. No wonder it was an unhappy one.

Beautiful sunny day, but driving back across the Cotswolds the sky darkened behind a pitch-black cloud caused by stubble burning, which takes place at this time of year all across the country. It destroys much animal and all insect life, little voles and spiders. Makes one sick. At Wickhamford all the elms dead, and every surviving tree has some disease. The pear trees, apple trees and prunus in the village gardens all dying. A sort of death pall has descended. What can be the meaning?

---

* J.L.-M's parents' old chauffeur and his wife, formerly a maid at Wickhamford Manor.

Tuesday, 5 September

Penelope Betjeman came to luncheon and I took her to Hawkesbury to look at some derelict cottages. Which she liked but has already found something in Radnor which she wants more and has made a bid for. Truly I hope she does not come to live within a mile of us. I don't think I could bear it. I love her dearly, but she is impossible to be with for longer than two hours at a stretch. No wonder John cannot endure. She bulldozes one, is utterly self-centred, she overwhelms and overbears. Strange thing is that she makes excuses for John always. Says he has to go to Scotland, or he has to stay in London for a film. She never admits that he prefers to be with Elizabeth [Cavendish], and is with Elizabeth the greater part of the time.

Wednesday, 6 September

Having watched the Trades Union Congress on the television I am more and more convinced that Communism must come to this country within twenty-five years.

Tuesday, 26 September

Received a very sweet letter from Eardley today, saying that I am the easiest person for him to be with, that he never has to think before he talks, and can be as happy either talking or remaining silent. I have replied that I regard him as far and away my most intimate friend. Indeed it amazes me how I can be with him all day and every day for a fortnight [they had just visited Austria] and never tire of his company, and always have something to communicate to him.

Friday, 29 September

A. has lately found that notes have been disappearing from her wallet, and suspicion flies at once to one person. It is nearly confirmed by her finding out from her bank in Wotton that another bank received from our milkman a £20 note with the consecutive number to two others which she had in her wallet. So we are waiting to learn from the milkman by whom he was given this particular note.

Tuesday, 3 October

Things which others take in their stride reduce me to a state of nervous collapse. Such as facing the suspect this afternoon with the theft of a £20 note from A's bag, one of several which have disappeared over the months. We had proof from the bank and the milkman. Of course she was tearful, denied positively that she had taken others, or any object, which I knew was untrue, said that her husband would kill or leave her out of shame at what she had done, their children would disown her and the whole bloody lot would starve. She contradicted herself as all liars do, saying first that she was so desperate she was driven to steal the one note, and in the next breath denying that she had any debts or was in need of cash. Didn't know what had come over her, etc. I sat watching the agony across her face, the plausible gestures, the acute embarrassment, and disliked her. I merely said that I would not tell her husband or the police.

Had a letter from some art historians in New York, asking if I would give them a photograph of my picture of St Peter's, Ben Nicolson[*] having assured them I would. But I have no photograph and cannot get someone from Bristol to come all this way to take one. I saw Ben two days ago, looking lean, cadaverous and extremely scruffy. His friends are fond of him, but I dislike his political views, his beastliness to his wonderful mother, and his narrow-ranging art historicism. I have no patience with art historians. Give me amateurs any day – by which I mean unpedantic lovers of art, not soulless machines, computers which tell the date of a picture or piece of furniture and its maker by rote.

Cecil Beaton was lunching with the Somersets on Sunday. He said that all writers should make money. I said there were far too many books published and I felt little sympathy with authors of unwanted books. They ought to do something else for a living, sweep streets or become bus conductors. I hastened to add, before he had time to say

---

[*] Benedict Nicolson (1914–78); er s. of Harold Nicolson and Vita Sackville-West; Deputy Surveyor of the King's Pictures, 1939–47, subsequently editor of *Burlington Magazine*.

it himself, that I did not exclude any of the books I had written from the unwanted category, but that I had hitherto earned my living by other means and now had some private means.

Wednesday, 8 November

Poor Lady Berwick[*] has been killed in a motor smash, crossing the main road from the Mytton and Mermaid, where she had been dining with her best friend, to the Attingham Park gates. Christopher Wall[†] tells me she was eighty-three, very lonely, with creeping arthritis and subject to bronchitis; that it was a mercy she had no pain and died quickly. I think fondly of when I first met her and Lord Berwick before the war, discussing with them how to make over Attingham to the National Trust. She was then very beautiful, young middle-aged, stately, unhappy with her old eccentric husband, wanting romance. I always admired her, but found her too much of a *grande dame*, too much the tragedy queen. After Lord B. died how she mourned!

Thursday, 16 November

Yesterday morning I went to St James's Palace through the Lord Chamberlain's entrance. Met by Oliver Millar[‡] – always so polite and dignified – and directed to the huge Queen Anne Room at the south-east corner of the place, which he affirmed was the room in which James III was born. But I can't believe this. It is far too large, that is to say if the original birth-room corresponded with the dimensions of this one, which dates from the nineteenth century after a fire.

---

[*] Edith Hulton; m. 1919 Thomas Noel-Hill, 8th Baron Berwick; she encouraged her husband to donate Attingham Park, Shropshire, to the N.T., a bequest which took effect on his death in 1947.
[†] N.T. Historic Buildings Representative for Thames & Chiltern Region, 1956–94 (b. 1929).
[‡] Sir Oliver Millar (1923–2007); art historian; Surveyor of the Queen's Pictures, 1972–88 (Deputy Surveyor, 1947–72).

Thursday, 23 November

I am reading Volume II of Quentin Bell's[*] excellent life of Virginia Woolf.[†] Her genius strikes me each time I read a sentence of hers, often written between bouts of madness or even during them. Which makes me question how mad anyone ever is. But I am tired of the Bloomsberries and their squalid little incestuous relationships. They were an inestimable lot, really. During the greatest war of carnage known to civilisation they played no part in relieving suffering. Neither V. Woolf nor L. Strachey[‡] once refers to the horrors of the war, to which they deliberately blinded themselves. I believe they were right to be pacifists, for that war was totally unjustifiable. But their bitchy conduct at Garsington, enjoying the fleshpots of Lady Ottoline Morrell,[§] whom they all abused and mocked behind her back, does not commend them. Lady O. was the most stalwart of the lot. I once saw her at a picture exhibition, prancing into the gallery and out again like an ill-disposed rocking horse.

Saturday, 25 November

I lose battles all along the line. The Rural District Council has decided – I knew of course that they would – to allow the erection of an enormous cow factory in the Ozleworth Valley behind this village, in spite of the valley being within the AONB (which stands for Area of Outstanding Natural Beauty). These designations mean nothing. There is always a reason, venal or financial – same thing – for the local authority to give way. Let us face it, beauty of landscape is absolutely at a discount in England and the world. The most beautiful country of northern Europe in my youth will before I am dead

---

[*] Art historian (1910–96); son of Clive Bell (1881–1964), critic, and Vanessa Stephen (1879–1961), painter and interior designer, leading lights of the Bloomsbury Group.
[†] Virginia Stephen (1882–1941); novelist and publisher, aunt of Quentin Bell; m. Leonard Woolf.
[‡] Lytton Strachey (1880–1932); writer and critic.
[§] Lady Ottoline Cavendish-Bentinck (1873–1938); m. 1902 Philip Morrell MP; hostess who offered hospitality to writers, artists and intellectuals (with several of whom she conducted love affairs) at Garsington Manor near Oxford.

be irredeemably ruined, damned and finished. Within one lifetime –
it is a terrifying thought.

Thursday, 30 November

St Andrew's Day, on which Bonnie Prince Charlie successively disgraced himself by getting drunk, finally so disgustingly drunk that his
wife flounced off to a convent; and over fifty years ago I was wont [at
Eton] to sit on the wall beside the Slough Road, wearing a scug cap,
striped blue and white, and cheer the Oppidans in their match against
the Tugs* at the Field Game, wondering how the the perspiring mass
beneath me could be so tough, so brave, so splendid.

Saturday, 9 December

At the British Museum Reading Room I ordered two books containing Benedict XIV's† letters, and scanned the index for references
to the Cardinal Duke. There were dozens. It is as clear as day that he
was, poor man, homosexual. He had infatuations for young, handsome clerics. The Pope was surprised, but thought there was nothing
criminal in it. Nor was there, I should say. But his old father was very
upset, and gave the lovers the sack. There were sulks, non-speakers
and the Cardinal flounced off twice. The father said, I never want to
speak to you again, and when the son left, wept and begged his return.
Not one word is mentioned about love, or sex. Yet there it is, and no
book has suggested it that I am aware of, until muck-raker Milne
comes along. It all started with Raymond [Mortimer] apprising me of
a disparaging remark in Mrs Thrale's diary‡ about the Cardinal's
footman leaning too closely over the Cardinal's chair, which might
lead to other clues.

---

* The 'Tugs' are King's Scholars living in College, as distinct from the 'Oppidans'
living in boarding houses. 'Scug caps' were worn by boys who had not won school
or house colours.
† Pope, 1740–58 (1675–1758).
‡ Reflections by Mrs Hester Thrale (1741–1821) on her friendship with Dr Samuel
Johnson (1709–84).

Friday, 15 December

John [Kenworthy-Browne]'s criticism is always sound. I have told him
he is a sort of young sage. He has read *Heretics* and says that the end is
confusing. He is right. J. who cannot always decide what is the right
course for him to take knows what others should take, and when and
how they go wrong. He would be a splendid proof-reader, like Eddie
Marsh,* for he pinpoints errors and queries ambiguities. In fact he is
an extremely perceptive person, because he is super-sensitive.

Sunday, 17 December

Last night a young man, a doctor of history from Liverpool University,
came for the night.† He is writing a book about Princess Winnie.‡
Came to see A. not me, and plied her with questions. Sensitive, intelligent and earnest. Not handsome, but a fine face, and very long,
white, nervous fingers. Rather bedint,§ pronounces Italian *Itarlian* and
holds his fork in that ungainly way as if it were a dangerous instrument. Kept saying things like, 'Did the Princess really know
Lady Diana Cooper, Lady Cunard, Lady Colefax,¶ Miss Rosamond
Lehmann?' We almost felt apologetic for knowing them ourselves and
all the others he mentioned. Finally A. said, 'You see the circle was
small. All these people knew each other.' One wonders what he can
and will make of such a circle. How can he, born towards the end of
the war, and living in a genteel villa in the outskirts of Liverpool, have
a clue? But then how can anyone writing about a past age, and a circle

---

* Sir Edward Marsh (1872–1953); civil servant and man of letters; friend of poets
and writers (including J.L.-M. from 1935).
† The visitor called himself Michael de Cossart.
‡ Winaretta Singer (1865–1943); heiress to sewing machine fortune; m. (2nd) Prince
Edmond de Polignac; Paris social figure and patroness of artists and composers; close
friend, during the last decade of her life, of A.L.-M., then married to the aspiring
composer Anthony Chaplin. Cossart's study of her – *Food of Love: Princess Edmond de
Polignac and her Salon* – was published by Hamish Hamilton in 1978.
§ Word from the private language of Harold Nicolson and Vita Sackville-West,
meaning 'common'.
¶ Sibyl Halsey (1872–1950); m. 1901 Sir Arthur Colefax QC (1866–1936); London
hostess and founder (1933) of decorating firm.

of society he has never been in, have a clue? It is audacity to write about anyone from the past. One can never know what their jokes were, their sophisticated nuances. One will take seriously what they laughed at and laugh at what they felt seriously about.

Saturday, 30 December

The Rector said on Christmas morning, 'When I have ploughed through services at Alderley, Tresham and Hillesley I am going to bed with' – I didn't know what he was going to say – 'a large, a LARGE, Jim . . . bottle of port and my pipe.' Ploughed through!

We are having the shortest days now. By 4 it is too dark to read by daylight. I love it, the drawing of curtains, lighting of fires and back to the cosy womb. So long as we don't have social engagements I am happy here, as the days are short and the evenings long. Today I have finished the section on the Cardinal of York. I have the final section on the Countess of Albany ahead. Then I shall have finished, or rather finished getting the Stuarts down on paper – before tackling the polishing, the typing, the pruning, the correcting of publisher's corrections, the retyping, the prefacing, the acknowledging, the illustrating, the jacketing, the indexing and the whole seemingly endless appendiculating which every book (other than a novel) calls for.

1973

1973

Robin Fedden has been appointed CBE. I immediately sent him the most congratulatory letter of affection I knew how to write. I would simply hate him or anyone to suppose that I am not delighted. What are my feelings? No resentment at all, and only the faintest envy. Such honours mean very little to me, which sounds disingenuous, but truthfully isn't; also I *know* that Robin has done far more for the National Trust than I ever did. I had my years of glory, a long time ago, twenty-five years or more, but did not sustain them. No, I am happy that Robin's services have been recognised. These are honest sentiments.

A. and I went to Leslie Hartley's memorial service in Holy Trinity, Brompton. Congregation large, all old friends, most of them with one foot in the grave. The young seldom go to such services, and when they do their youth shines out like a good deed in a naughty world. We sang the first hymn, which had a phrase reminding us, the singers, how short a time we had to go. Not very tactful, I thought.

Thursday, 11 January

Hugh Montgomery-Massingberd lunched at Brooks's. Told me news of the plans for Burke's which he is fostering. Thinks that Weldon, part owner of *Bryant's Index*, may edit *Burke's Guide to Country Houses*. Hugh definitely intends to tackle this formidable task, with the help of a committee of people like John Harris,[*] John Cornforth,[†] and me. Is producing next month *Burke's Guide to the Royal Family*, which won't

---

[*] Expert and writer on architectural subjects (b. 1931); curator of RIBA Library and Drawings Collection, 1960–86; rented a weekend cottage at Ashcroft near Alderley.
[†] Architectural historian on staff of *Country Life* (1937–2004).

interest me much. He had to see Mountbatten,* who is writing the preface. Mountbatten told Hugh he must in the *Guide* call the children of the Queen Mountbatten-Windsor. Hugh said he supposed the name had already been settled by the College of Heralds when the Queen and Prince Philip were married. Mountbatten explained that Sir Winston, then Prime Minister, told the Queen the Cabinet would not allow this double name, but Windsor only, and that the Queen was so upset that she did not have another child for six years.† It is bad news, Hugh told me, that there is not to be another *Burke's Peerage*.‡ Finished, because of the expense; they cannot be sold under £20 now.

Sunday, 14 January

Nancy Mitford is still in the Nuffield Fitzroy nursing home, where she has been since A. arranged for her to fly to London in September. I have long dreaded seeing her. However, having received messages that she would like to see me, I went last Tuesday. She received me sweetly, lying in bed, her head over the sheets like a tiny marmoset's. '*Jimminy*, do sit down!', etc. She much brighter than I expected, but deaf and gets cross if she can't hear. But I was conscious that she barely took in what I said. I felt I was boring her. She says she reads all day, and since being in this home has read all Henry James and Trollope as well as every new book which is sent her. Nancy is still sharp and tart. Complained that Lady Monckton§ came and told her about the ailments of their mutual friends, the last thing she wished to hear. Helen

---

* Louis, 1st Earl Mountbatten of Burma (1900–79); last Viceroy of India (1947) and first Chief of the Combined Defence Staff (1959–65); as a great-grandson of Queen Victoria and uncle of Prince Philip, he saw himself as the power behind the throne.

† Hugh Massingberd writes about this extraordinary conversation in greater detail in his memoirs *Daydream Believer: Confessions of a Hero-Worshipper* (2001).

‡ At that time, it seemed unlikely that there would ever be another edition after the 105th which had appeared in 1970; but the publication was revived by Morris Genealogical Books which bought the rights in 1989, a 106th edition appearing in 1999 and a 107th in 2003.

§ Hon. Bridget Hore-Ruthven (1896–1982); eldest dau. of 9th Baron Ruthven of Freeland (whom she succeeded, 1956); m. (2nd) 1947 (as his 2nd wife) Sir Walter Monckton (1891–1965), cr. Viscount Monckton of Brenchley, 1957.

Dashwood,* of all people, is the favourite. She brings her food every day, and is always full of cheer and good news. I felt most inadequate. The truth is that when one is as ill as she is one only wants to see the same persons, and I suspect that seeing an old friend like me, after intervals, is exhausting. She said how pleased she was that Violet Trefusis was dead. They had a row, and V. wrote her 'such an awful letter'. A month or two later V. telephoned N. and said, 'Did my letter give offence?' 'No,' said N., 'only a glorious excuse,' and rang off. 'That was the end of that. It is so seldom one is able to say the right thing at the right time.' I made conversation like mad, as one does in the company of royalty, because one fears, possibly wrongly, that during a short, infrequent encounter one should not allow silences. Complaints that Raymond Mortimer was disloyal, never came now. I said he was abroad.

Friday, 19 January

A. and I drove on Monday to Wilderhope Manor in Shropshire, via Kidderminster. What used to be unviolated Shropshire country around Kinlet is now dotted with modern bungalows. Kidderminster is of course quite unrecognisable and has been bulldozed and rebuilt, like Plymouth after the Blitz. Bridgnorth and Bewdley are becoming a ghastly mess. The first, perched on its delightful acropolis, now overlooks an ocean of factories and horrors. The little narrow Georgian street at its feet is about to come down. Bewdley's outskirts are fringed with caravan sites along both ends of the river; and houses are now to be seen on the crest of Blackstone Rock from Ribbesford. Lax Lane in Bewdley, leading from the river quay to High Street, has every single house boarded up. These are charming little two-storeyed artisan houses, which one might suppose could serve instead of the caravans. The house in High Street in which Mr Baldwin† was born – a plaque

---

* Helen Eaton (d. 1989); m. 1922 Sir John Dashwood, 10th Bt (1896–1966); châtelaine of West Wycombe Park, Buckinghamshire, wartime HQ of N.T., whose foibles J.L.-M. (to her indignation) described in his wartime diaries.
† Stanley Baldwin, 1st Earl Baldwin of Bewdley (1867–1947); friend of J.L.-M's grandparents, who owned the neighbouring Ribbesford estate; succeeded father as Conservative MP for Bewdley, 1908; Prime Minister, 1923–4, 1924–9, 1935–7.

has been put on the wall recently – has had the Georgian porch wrenched off by a lorry. The conglomeration of wires, pylons, ill-placed factories and execrable villas is so horrifying that I utterly despair of the landscape. I know that people say there has always been change which is resented by the old. But never, never has there been such dev-astating change as during my lifetime, change always for the worse aesthetically, never for the better. The public *en bloc* are blind to hideous surroundings. I prefer to stay at home in my ivory tower and never go on expeditions rather than be affronted at every familiar turn with a substitute architectural monstrosity.

Monday, 22 January

At my age dread of death governs all thought.* Each fresh symptom of my decay, physical and mental, and the passing of contemporaries, are clockwork reminders of annihilation. In reading biographies I always assess the lives of others in relation to the span I have reached, the measurement permanently asserting itself. I don't believe any old people aren't frightened of death. All the ones I have talked to admit the fear.

Saturday, 3 February

Yesterday I met John Betjeman at Bath station at 12.20. He wanted to see the horrors perpetrated by Casson and Dr Stutchbury. I motored him round the city. He was appalled. Thought the worst offences were the new Balance Street blocks and the University. Agreed the latter was one's vision of hell. We lunched beautifully at The Hole in the Wall. Here the waitresses recognised him. So did Seagar's book shop. So did the cashier in the Midland Bank, who at once informed the manager, who rushed out. So did the attendants in the Pump Room. In walking through Queen Square I saw a man turn round and stop before a house in the square. John, hestitating on the pavement, said, 'In one of these houses there used to be the finest staircase in Bath.' Hardly were the words out of his mouth when the man rushed

---

* He then had another twenty-five years to live.

up, exclaiming, 'It was this house, Sir John. Come in.' We did, and admired the stairwell, all that is left, and the splendid stucco relief work on the walls. In an instant the manager of the firm, a gent with a purple face and breathing fumes of alcohol, ran from his office down the back stairs, eager to talk to the poet. Just as well I had not told the Bath Preservation committee that he was coming, for he would have been mobbed. J. says it is worse since he was made Laureate. That people all over the world send him their poems, seldom with stamped and addressed envelopes; that people appear on his doorstep at eight in the morning asking to read their odes to him. To everyone who approaches him he speaks courteously; and his humility is touching. After dinner last night he said to Burnet Pavitt, 'After you, please. You are so distinguished. I am only a fraud who has got away with it.' A trifle disingenuous?

Wednesday, 14 February

It snowed in the night. The garden looked as though sprinkled with icing sugar, the rich cake showing through, not by any means deeply covered. Went for a walk with the dogs this afternoon around Badminton, from Shepherd's Cottage to Worcester Lodge, and thought I should never leave this place, I am so fond of it. A pale blue sky overhead, bright sun, and although a thaw, very beautiful. Dogs did not much enjoy themselves. Nowadays they do not like the wet, or the cold. They are dreadfully cissy. It is our fault, we have made them so by treating them like humans.

I am reading Robin Maugham's* autobiography. Very readable and courageous. Yet I feel these homosexuals enjoy parading their adventures. On every occasion he introduces some affair he has had, with a boy at school, or in the Tank Regiment. All great fun, but minorities become bores when they parade their grievances. There is a book out, I see, by a member of the Gay Club, indicating that the Government of England should be handed over to the queers. God help us! Where would we be, for the temperament, the unreliability?

---

* Robin, 2nd Viscount Maugham (1916–81); his autobiography published that month was *Escape from the Shadows*.

Maugham is also very severe with poor Willie.* I dare say what he tells is true, but it is certainly unkind. Who am I to speak? If I poke fun at my poor father [in *Another Self*], I don't, I hope, malign him.

Thursday, 15 February

Robin Maugham is, I believe, a nice man, but he is vain. He is too pleased with his own writing. This is a feminine streak, *vide* Nancy M. and so many women. He has descriptive ability. Tells a story well, and at times is very funny. But he compares himself with Willie. This should not be. Willie was a first-rate writer – I don't mean man – with an incisiveness which no one else possessed. A cold, steely, cruel style, but clean as a whistle. Robin is nothing to him. I only once met Robin, with Harold [Nicolson], who was fond of him. Robin had a friend whom he brought to see Harold in Albany. He made the boy take down his trousers and show Harold the size of his cock. H. somewhat puzzled.

Saturday, 24 February

Thursday was publication day [of *Heretics in Love*]. Only one review so far, in last Sunday's *Observer*, apparently very unfavourable. I lunched with Norah Smallwood and Hugo Brunner.† Iris Murdoch‡ was to have come too, but had influenza. Before arriving at the office I worked myself up into a frenzy, and had to sit in St Martin's church trying to calm down before I could even enter Chatto's office. In the London Library I skulked to avoid friends. Even so two came up to say, 'What about this novel?' I can't bear any reference to it. Luncheon was however enjoyable. Norah is a most sympathetic woman, calm too. Says I am not to worry for I am bound to get horrid reviews, and counsels me not to read them. Even so, kind friends tell me about

---

* William Somerset Maugham (1874–1965); novelist, playwright and short story writer; uncle of Robin Maugham; a friend of the L.-Ms in the South of France in the 1950s.
† Director (later Managing Director and Chairman) of Chatto & Windus, 1967–85 (b. 1935).
‡ (Dame) Iris Murdoch (1919–99); philosophy don and novelist; m. 1956 John Bayley (b. 1925), Professor of English at Oxford.

them. Someone wrote today condoling about the *Observer's*. It is extraordinary how as a publisher Norah takes the 'permissive' for granted nowadays; thinks a book without it lacking, like an egg without salt.

Monday, 25 February

Yesterday's *Sunday Times* had such an excellent, understanding review of *Heretics* that I was induced to read it. How dishonest one is. I vowed not to read any more reviews, because the unfavourable ones hurt so, and because I am assured one is favourable, I read it. Yet this review has restored my confidence a little. At last someone has recognised that the book is not contemptible, but a serious effort. What I mind is that it should be dismissed for the wrong reasons – because it is about a vanished world which is realer than the hideous, squalid world we are living in.

Thursday, 1 March

Although I inveigh against motorways, I confess to getting some satisfaction in buzzing along them in my little Morris. The car simply purrs and whizzes, and the country often is so clean and exciting as one slashes through it. There is no doubt that the sense of speed uninterrupted is stimulating, and arouses ruthless instincts.

Spent £5 on a Byron dinner in the House of Lords, thinking it would be fun. But not a single old friend, no one I knew, and the dinner filthy. Began with pale soup made of stickfast; dry fish in rolls, also in stickfast sauce; overcooked beef with stringy leeks; and what is called a sundae, *i.e.* a tinned peach covered with synthetic cream squatting on ice. Coffee undrinkable. I sat next to a Dutch woman married to the head of the Italian Institute in London, and a member of Nottingham Council. Not inspiring. At the top table lords – Lytton* in the chair, Bessborough,† Longford,‡

---

* Noel, 4th Earl of Lytton (1900–85); great-great-grandson of Byron, who also inherited the Barony of Wentworth through Byron's wife Annabella.
† Frederick Ponsonby, 10th Earl of Bessborough (1913–93).
‡ Francis ('Frank') Pakenham, 7th Earl of Longford (1905–2001); Labour politician, publisher and humanitarian campaigner; m.1931 Elizabeth Harman, writer.

Strabolgi,* Abinger – and two commoners, Mrs Langley Moore†
and Professor Somebody. The lords were gracious to us poor everyday folk. They were courteous, slick and capable. I thought how
these hereditary peers still count for something. But how snobbish
the English still are. Bessborough read very well Byron's second of
three speeches delivered in the Lords, advocating Catholic emanci-
pation. An excellent sentiment behind it, but the speech of a drama-
tist. Then discussion. Tributes were paid to Byron as poet, prose
writer, champion of the downtrodden. I meant to stand up, and
then didn't because of my absurd shyness, to draw attention to
Byron the sage, of whom his contemporaries – Scott, Moore,
Rogers – spoke with awe, and whom Goethe who could not read
English considered a prodigious intellect. For whereas Shelley was
silly, and Keats adolescent, Byron however provocative never said a
foolish thing, and his every utterance was noteworthy. He was a
giant among men. This distinguishes him from his contemporaries.

Monday, 12 March

We got back from Morocco at three in the morning, having stayed
nine days with David Herbert‡ in Tangier, three of which we spent
at Meknès, motoring into the Atlas and hinterland. A most beautiful country of infinite landscape variety, like England. Beautiful
people, cheerful and sympathetic and picturesque, wearing their
national dress, all the women veiled. Keen sense of colour in their
clothes.

David is an engaging figure. He is adored by all and sundry.
Wherever we went he was greeted with affection. Hall porters and
waiters in hotels and restaurants kissed him on both cheeks. People on
the road wave to him in his car. He is unguarded and cares not a fig
who knows that he is homosexual; rather he revels in it. I was sur-

---

* David Montague de Burgh Kenworthy, 11th Baron Strabolgi (b. 1914).
† Doris Elizabeth Langley (1903–89); m. 1926 Robert Sugden Moore; author of
books on Byron.
‡ Hon. David Herbert (1908–95); yr. s. of 15th Earl of Pembroke; Eton contemporary of J.L.-M.

prised to find on Sunday morning that he goes to church in time to show the congregation their pews. He takes the offertory bag round, not like most of us discreetly looking away as he hands it to a member of the congregation, but peering in to see how much has been given, nodding, smiling and cracking jokes. At the airport we duly kissed each other on both cheeks.

Wednesday, 14 March

A. and I lunched with Nigel Nicolson* at the Café Royal. I knew what he wanted to tell us. Sure enough, he has written a book, called *Portrait of a Marriage*, including Vita's autobiographical story of her elopement with Violet Trefusis, and amplified it with the story of her lesbianism and happy marriage with Harold. When he asked our opinion five years ago we thought this idea a mistake. Now we both feel that so much has been revealed about her, notably in Q. Bell's biography of V. Woolf, that it no longer matters. I said he ought in fairness to say that Harold likewise led his own life, and was not an aggrieved but a complaisant husband. Nigel agreed, but said that his father was never *in love*. His affairs were like a quick visit to the National Gallery between trains. Both Eardley [Knollys] and John [Kenworthy-Browne] to whom I told this think Nigel ought not to cash in on his parents' love life, and that it is no one's business. Both strongly disapprove. I am not sure. I think the book, which is going to be *the* book of 1973, will enhance V's reputation.

Nigel is a ball of fire. He has his *Alex*† coming out now, having been serialised. Then *Portrait*. He is going to the Himalayas in the autumn, to write about them; he has been commissioned to edit Virginia Woolf's letters, and the life of Lord Curzon which Philip Magnus‡ is abandoning. He is a fearsome worker, just like Harold.

---

* Soldier, politician, writer and publisher (1917–2004); yr son of Harold Nicolson and Vita Sackville-West; inherited Sissinghurst Castle from his mother, 1962, and donated it to N.T.
† *Alex: The Life of Field Marshal Earl Alexander of Tunis.*
‡ Sir Philip Magnus-Allcroft, 2nd Bt (1906–88); historian; m. 1943 Jewel Allcroft of Stokesay Court.

Monday, 19 March

On Friday I was taken by Tony Mitchell,[*] the N.T. representative, to Charlecote [Park, Warwickshire] to help put some of the finishing touches to the arrangement of the rooms for the forthcoming season. To think that I did this with Alice [Fairfax-Lucy][†] and Clifford Smith[‡] in 1947. I was appalled to find, looking behind a picture which I had hung in the drawing-room then, that the strip of damask fabric was there a deep gold, whereas the rest of the hangings are now a straw colour. Since this house has been in the Trust's care the light has faded these hangings. Found dear old Alianore[§] wandering round the stables. She is seventy-nine, much changed. The new custodian apparently said, after I left, how charming I was. 'Of course he is,' said Alianore, who is simple but truest blue. 'He was at Eton and in the Guards.' Brian rang me up to tell me this, with much merriment.

Tuesday, 20 March

My figure has completely gone. My waist is non-existent. Two straight lines from the shoulders to the ankles. I remember noticing this sudden change of figure in my grandmother, and later my father. Both had superb figures, as mine was. After this change both went very quickly. Mummy never lost hers. When I told A. this, she reminded me that in Paris last year, trying on dresses, she complained that none of them looked right on her. '*Alors, madame, vous êtes pareille de haut en bas*', the shop woman remarked in that charming French way.

---

[*] Anthony Mitchell (b. 1931); N.T. Historic Buildings Representative 1965–96; m. 1972 Brigitte de Soye.

[†] Hon. Alice Buchan (1908–93), dau. of 1st Viscount Tweedsmuir (the novelist John Buchan); m. 1933 Brian Fairfax-Lucy (1898–1974), who lived at Charlecote following its donation to the N.T. in 1947 and s. brother as 5th Bt, 1965.

[‡] H. Clifford Smith; N.T. furniture expert.

[§] Alianore Fairfax-Lucy; unmarried sister of Sir Brian who looked after the gardens at Charlecote.

Wednesday, 28 March

I find myself breathless these days for no apparent reason. This does not prevent me from taking fairly long walks – though I doubt if I would wish to walk more than ten miles now. Sometimes I feel as if a weight were on my chest. Some mornings rising from bed I feel stiff all over and frangible as though a loud noise might break me in two. Indeed, noises send me into great distress. Quiet is more and more necessary to keep me together.

I have lately been thinking that perhaps I shall never be able to cry again. Another emotion freezing up? But when this morning Schubert's *Impromptu in G Flat* was played on the wireless, I was moved to tears. Glad of this.

Thursday, 5 April

Yesterday I visited Ockwells in Berkshire. The first time I went there was in 1936, the then owner being Sir Edward Barry.* The result was covenants over the house and estate, but no gift to the National Trust. Sir Edward wanted to give, but could not afford to do so. He had two married daughters, as I remember, neither of whom was very rich. Even so, their agreement to their father giving the covenants was a generous concession. In those days Ockwells was generally considered a very important house indeed. It was written up in all the architectural textbooks, as a mid fifteenth-century manor house of the earliest non-fortified sort, of much importance. Sir Edward extensively restored it before the First World War with the help and advice of people like Lutyens, Edward Hudson and Avray Tipping. No one disputed its merits. Yesterday however John Cornforth and Christopher Wall, who accompanied me, expressed the view that Ockwells was an over-restored fake, beastly in every way, and not worthy to be held by the National Trust. Thus I have lived to see taste change. Ockwells was never the sort of house

---

* Sir Edward Barry, 2nd Bt (1858–1949); J.L.-M. describes a visit to him at Ockwells on 22 February 1942, at which time he hoped to sell the house to a rich philanthropist who would donate it to the N.T.

I cared for, yet in the 1930s I did not dream of questioning its importance.

Saturday, 7 April

Set forth in my tiny Morris by the motorway for Tabley House [Cheshire]. Left at nine and arrived Tabley dead on time at 11.45 a.m., getting off the motorway at Knutsford. Met Eardley and Merlin Waterson,* the enthusiastic young representative. Object, to look once more at Tabley House and estate which John Leicester-Warren[†] intends to bequeath. He greeted us at the door. Reminded me that I last visited the place in September 1945 when his father and mother living there. He was at Eton with me, a ridiculous figure with absolutely no chin and a bewildered expression. Merlin says he looks like an old pheasant, with behind slightly sticking out, and nose like a pheasant's beak. At Eton he was cruelly mobbed. Now very old and rather less undistinguished, with a gentle, courteous manner. He has a slight stammer. Has turned Tabley into a school for what he calls slow developers – like himself. Curious how men who themselves at school were bullied cannot in after-life get away from the school aura. Obviously this a good school, and the house very little injured by it. Full of interesting things, not least the Regency picture gallery built for the first Lord de Tabley, all the pictures hanging as originally hung, on chains from lion masks. These gold masks in most of the rooms. No rooms arranged now and furniture merely dumped. House could be made something very splendid, if we put back proper glazing bars, removed outside stink pipes and tidied up generally. Yet not a magical house, and a clumsy design. The sweeping perron on the great south front, instead of drawing the eye upwards to the *piano nobile* as it should, drags the eye down the sweep – to nothing. Perhaps a great statue between the claws would satisfy, in providing the focus needed. From across the mere, with Turner's tower to the water's edge, it makes a splendid scene. I truly hope we eventually get it.

---

* N.T. Historic Buildings Representative for West Midlands and Wales, 1970–81 (b. 1947); later Historic Properties Director from 2002.

† Lieut-Col John Leicester-Warren (1907–75).

Thursday, 26 April

On the 12th I went to Rome with Henry and Nick Robinson. Alvilde joined us on the 15th. She had a nasty experience the evening before. Went to dinner with the Chatwins at Holwell Farm, returned at 10.45. On walking into the kitchen smelled cheap cigarette smoke. Saw the door into the garden open. Walked into passage and saw the dining-room upside-down, all drawers open and cupboards. Feared burglars might still be in the house. In fact they had been disturbed by her car lights on the drive, and had just bolted with all our china which hung on the walls, plus one pair of my Copenhagen fruit dishes. They had not set off the alarm or ventured beyond the dining-room. Strange thing that the keys of the silver cupboard had been found by them and actually put in the lock, but the door not opened. Had it been, the alarm would have gone off. Until 1 a.m. A. was engaged with police and CID men. Left next morning at ten to join me. We knew this was bound to happen sooner or later. Dining-room window smashed to pieces, one very small boy presumably having forced his way through the glass and cut himself in the process, for blood was found. Not enough blood unfortunately. They escaped over the garden wall. Two of our napkins found under the wall. All the rest and some table cloths were used for wrapping the china in A's shopping bag. China must have been broken in the wall climb, we suppose.

Rome was dreadful. My relations with Rome are love-hate, love of the Rome I used to know just after the war, hate of it today. The traffic, the crowds abominable. The Minerva Hotel filled no longer with cardinals, monsignors and old English governesses, but with hippies. Each evening a charabanc-load of students from everywhere, America, Europe, Asia, unloaded, and left next morning after breakfast, rendering the nights hideous with pop music and shouting.

The boys most strange. Sweet they were and polite, but never expressed enthusiasm for anything. Never read the guidebook I gave them, seldom knew what they were looking at. Everything I told them was greeted with 'H'm!' Nick moderately interested in paintings, but Henry not apparently interested in anything. Neither used his eyes. Never looked at a building or discriminated between one church and another. Architecture quite out; ditto history, it seemed to me. At meals when well oiled with wine they unfolded a bit, but I did not get beyond polite terms with them any more than with their buttoned-up mother. Their clothes ghastly, and they never changed in the evening, never once changed their shirts. Scruffiness unbelievable. Nick rather spotty and teeth not clean. Henry the picture of cleanliness in his person, white teeth and rosy skin. Yet Nick's beauty undeniable. Faultless features, eyes, nose and hair (unbrushed, the pity of it). Aged only eighteen, he may improve. Can I tell his doting mother? Certainly I shall tell Audrey.

Don't want to return to Rome ever again. A. and I flew to Munich, from delicious cold sunshine to Siberian winter. Stayed with Liz and Raimund von Hoffmansthal* in their mediaeval castle of Prielau on the edge of Zell-am-See. Also staying Loelia Lindsay,[†] Angus Menzies,[‡] Ali Forbes,[§] Diana Cooper. I did not enjoy this visit, too jet-settish for me, conversation about people, people; and Ali, though very bright and clever, loquacious, shouting everyone else down. Liz not easy to communicate with; the best is Diana Cooper, who is very well educated, well-read. But I can't hear what she says in spite of her bell-like Edwardian voice with its beautiful pitch.

One evening at dinner, Loelia and Raimund told Diana on my right that she was drinking less and they hoped she was drinking less elsewhere. No, she said, she was not. They said, 'Why on earth do you get drunk? You are much nicer when you are sober.' 'I have to,' she said, 'out of shyness.' 'Rot!' they shouted. 'It's not rot,' she said. Her reason is she fears, before appearing at a party or meal, that she will not be able to shine in the way expected of her. On others saying, 'But when you are drunk you don't shine at all', her reply was, 'I believe I am shining and that's all that matters to me.' Loelia went on that it was absurd, because she (Diana) had been brought up to know she was the wittiest, most beautiful, most desirable person in England – which she

---

* Lady Elizabeth Paget, dau. of 6th Marquess of Anglesey; m. 1939 Raimund, s. of the librettist Hugo von Hoffmansthal.

[†] Hon. Loelia Ponsonby (1902–91), dau. of 1st Baron Sysonby; m. 1st 1930 (diss. 1947) 2nd Duke of Westminster, 2nd 1969 Sir Martin Lindsay of Dowhill.

[‡] Bachelor cousin and intimate of A.L.-M. (1910–73); interior designer.

[§] Alistair Forbes (1918–2005); American-born journalist resident in Switzerland, famous for his social knowledge and his long and eccentric book reviews.

is, or was – whereas she (Loelia) was brought up by her parents to believe she was stupid, hideous, hopeless and generally undesirable. 'So if I behaved like you there might be some excuse for me.'

Sunday, 6 May

Complaining like mad I accompany A. to the Gloucestershire Society ceremony today. But it is really a charming affair, quite anachronistic and rather fun. This year Sally Westminster is President and she invites us, because I seem not to be a member. Church 11.30 at Wickwar. Procession up the nave. All very county, upper class and ducal. Sally reads the first lesson from Genesis, about the creation of the world. With her pretty voice she reads well. The Duke of Beaufort reads the second lesson, increase and multiply, which we thought unsuitable for these two.* Duke and wrong Duchess – for Mary Beaufort conspicuously absented herself – walked arm in arm to their car and drove off. ('Didn't she read it beautifully?' Master said.) Drinks in Sally's house and luncheon in a tent on the lawn. Bitterly cold day and I froze. At the end of the meal we drank the Queen's health, and finally sang the extraordinary colloquial song about Charles I composed when the Society was founded in 1657. It has been celebrated and the song sung every year since that date.

Sunday, 13 May

A. and I gave Lennox [Berkeley] for his seventieth birthday a very prettily-bound almanac of poems, circa 1830, with a lyre engraved on the cover, and also an autograph letter from Gounod to John Broadwood dated 1871. Lennox delighted. We all went to dine at Helen Dashwood's pretentious flat next to the De Vere Hotel. Fourteen persons, stiff affair, and it did not go with a swing. Only champagne to drink, before, during and after dinner. Only alternative orange juice. Patrick Kinross was furious and called for wine. I pointed out that we were Helen's guests and not in a restaurant. I drank nothing. Sat between Freda Berkeley and Charlotte Bonham

---

* Sally Westminster was known to be one of the Duke's many mistresses.

Carter,* who is as bent as Sibyl Colefax used to be. Had to lower my head into my soup plate, then skew it sideways in order to be on a level with hers and make her hear. She has however all her wits about her. Diana Cooper is an exact contemporary of Charlotte, but whereas the latter is an old woman, Diana is not. Looking splendid in a powder-blue and gold dress.

I do not like Helen Dashwood in spite of the years I have known her. She is infinitely affected and brash. Said to A., 'I told the PM yesterday that he must make Lennox a K[night].' She still claims to know all important people, and to wield influence through them, which is patently absurd.†

Wednesday, 16 May

Two boys from Oriel, Oxford came to see the house. One an architectural student, pupil of Howard Colvin‡ whom he venerates but does not like. This boy with flaming red hair and beard looked like the young Swinburne; the other very handsome and nice, white teeth, looked like Desmond Guinness§ used to look, and rather affected, but charming. The first called John Martin Robinson,¶ the second Colin McMordie.**

Sunday, 20 May

John Betj. and Feeble came last night *en route* to London from Cornwall and left today. We looked at his film *Metroland* on the telly with Mrs Barratt our wretched old housekeeper who was thrilled with the

* Charlotte Ogilvy (1893–1989); idiosyncratic social figure; m. 1926 Sir Edgar Bonham Carter (1870–1956), civil servant and member of N.T. committees.
† In fact, on Heath's recommendation and much to his own surprise, Lennox Berkeley was knighted in the New Year's Honours of 1974.
‡ (Sir) Howard Colvin (b. 1919); architectural historian, then teaching at Oxford.
§ Hon. Desmond Guinness (b. 1931); yr s. of Diana Mosley by her 1st marriage to 2nd Baron Moyne.
¶ John Martin Robinson (b. 1948); later a Herald at the College of Arms, Librarian to the Duke of Norfolk, Vice-Chairman of the Georgian Group, and a writer and consultant on architectural and genealogical subjects.
** Colin McMordie (1948–1985); later an art dealer in Paris.

honour, and dined late afterwards. Rather shocked at how old John has become, though worse on the film made some months ago than he looks now. Took them to lunch at Cerney House [near Cirencester] with Quentin Craig. Never have I seen a Regency house more mauled within. No words can describe the horror of it. A. drove there with Elizabeth, John with me. He told me Penelope, though she had wanted to marry him, probably was never in love with him; that she is quite impossible to live with; that he does not know if his son is alive or dead, for his last letter was returned from a dead-letter office in New York. He is worried over lack of money. His secretary costs him £50 a week and he does not earn enough to cover this item of expense. The demands made on him now he is Laureate bring no financial return, and much work. Showed us a letter he has just received from the Duke of Kent who offers his services in preventing London being totally transformed. John must go and see him. Another letter, from Heath, asking him to translate a Portuguese poem into English to be put to music by Arthur Bliss* and played to the Portuguese President on his visit to the Queen. And so it goes on. His poem published in Adam Fergusson's *Sack of Bath*, out tomorrow, has been written for nothing but love of Bath. As we drove past Malmesbury John said, nodding to a signpost, 'In that village I had my first experience of sex with the son of the vicar. It was in a punt on the river. I was quite spent. That night the brother came into my room, but I was too shocked by what I had done with the other during the afternoon, and so lost a second opportunity.' He was then fifteen. We agreed that no subsequent escapades have eclipsed those early schoolday ones.

Tuesday, 22 May

In the evening I went to the Archdeacon's Visitation and was sworn in as a church warden. Such a splendid old boy, so humorous, clever and holy, just what a high-up dignitary of the English Church should be, a true descendant of a Trollopian cleric. He gave the assembled wardens a little pep talk on their duties, and the importance of this ancient office. Not the least pi, yet serious and impressive. Our

---

* Sir Arthur Bliss (1891–1975); composer.

assembly of church wardens was a musty, subfusc lot. While waiting for the Archdeacon I looked at them and wondered if there was one I would consent to go to bed with without being paid £50,000. I badly need £5,000.

Saturday, 26 May

The Lambton–Jellicoe scandal makes me sick.[*] It's a witch hunt. And what the hell does it matter to anyone on earth that these men have slept with whores? Thelma Cazalet[†] said, 'I do not condone; and I do not condemn.' And she added, 'I do not understand.' That may be true. I do. Lord Lambton, interviewed by Robin Day[‡] last night, gave one of the most poignant and splendid performances of candour and guts. He was marvellous. Not that I hold him in high esteem as a public figure, from all I hear. I am far more sorry for Jellicoe, who is a quiet, un-raffish man. I wrote him a letter of condolence, in fact a second-class fan mail.

Wednesday, 30 May

Debo and Woman came to dinner. Their news of Nancy dreadful. She knows she is dying, and they think she has two months to live; her legs all swollen with water. Otherwise she is a living skeleton and cannot move her body or even her head, and is always in pain. Her pursuit is making her will with her sisters' help. This gives her much pleasure and causes merriment.

---

[*] A newspaper article alleged, with photographic evidence, that Viscount Lambton MP (1922–2006; s. as 6th Earl of Durham, 1970, and disclaimed peerages but continued to use courtesy title) had smoked marijuana with two call girls. He thereupon resigned both as a junior defence minister in the Heath Government and as MP for Berwick-upon-Tweed. Heath demanded to know if any other members of his Government had used the services of call girls. The Lord Privy Seal, 2nd Earl Jellicoe (1918–2007), an otherwise blameless man and a war hero, confessed to having done so, and was sacked.

[†] Thelma Cazalet-Keir (1899–1989); Conservative MP for Islington East, 1931–45.

[‡] (Sir) Robin Day (1923–2000); television interviewer. Lambton had asked that his eleven-year-old son be present during the interview, which inhibited Day (as he wrote in his memoirs) from employing his usual pugnacious technique.

Debo asked to go round the garden before dinner. Torrents of praise, and congratulation over the tidiness, the growth of everything, the blueness of the ceanothus. 'Oh no, damn it, it's too much. Let's go home, Woman, don't look. I can't bear it, I've never seen anything like it', etc.

Thursday, 31 May

By this morning's post I receive a letter from Nancy, still in her firm hand, but misspelt and shaky, and piteous. It begins, 'It's very curious dying and would have many a drole amusing & charming side were it not for the pain. We had screams over the Will. The Dame's [A.L.-M's] share. "But she'll be furious if she only gets *that*." ' Then she says the doctors are so tiresome, they will not give her a date for her death. They merely say, 'Have everything you want', meaning as much morphia. I have been haunted by this letter all day. Extraordinary that someone on the threshold of death can write like this, and still make jokes.

Monday, 4 June

Flaming June. David Herbert, his sister Patricia* and Michael Duff† lunched. The first time any of them has been here. All most appreciative and raving about the garden and house. Whiffs of patrician fun. The overriding quality of these people is a complete lack of seriousness, which is refreshing. Conversation may lack depth but it scintillates with the ludicrous.

Tuesday, 5 June

Stuffy old Alec Clifton-Taylor lunched with me at Brooks's. Very affectionate as always. Said, 'You may appear to strangers to epitomise

---

* Lady Patricia Herbert (1904–94), dau. of 15th Earl of Pembroke; m. 1928 3rd Viscount Hambleden.
† Sir Michael Duff, 3rd Bt (1907–80); Welsh landowner and Lord-Lieutenant of Carnarvonshire; m. 1949 Lady Caroline Paget, dau. of 6th Marquess of Anglesey.

the conventional; but you are thoroughly unconventional. This is
what your friends discover.' Spoke disparagingly of 'the de Trafford
man of Hill Court [Herefordshire]' as 'one of those', the first time I
have ever heard him acknowledging homosexuality as existing. De
Trafford has withdrawn his offer of Hill Court because, he alleges,
the N.T. returned his loans of furniture from Montacute [House,
Somerset] damaged, and refused to pay for their repair. I wonder if
this is true.

Monday, 11 June

Burnet [Pavitt] had A. and me to Covent Garden, *Trovatore*, and dinner
during the intervals in the little closet, King Edward's smoking room,
below the Royal Box. It is minute and decorated in Edwardian Adam
style, very *gemütlich*. Splendid cast and divine music. Yet throughout
the witch's passionate arias I was working out the theme for a novel:
that of two sisters, one with young son who is a paragon of virtue;
the unmarried sister was in love with the boy's father, now dead.
Father would never look at the spinster and married the other. So
spinster sets out to corrupt the son, teaches him to smoke pot, drink,
and finally tries to seduce him. Failing, resorts to drugging him, and
then ravishes him. But having administered an overdose, she kills him.
Is this plot too like that of *Heretics*? And shall I get the reputation of
being obsessed with incest? Worse still, would I be identified with the
spinster?

Wednesday, 20 June

Yesterday afternoon we went from London to the Queen's party at
Windsor Castle. Was honoured to be asked, but reluctant to go. A. on
the other hand delighted, and looked forward to it like mad. Why we
were invited I could not guess. A. wore her diamond necklace and
diamond bracelets and looked spendid in an uncrushable Indian dress.
I, as 'commanded', in black tie. We went to Robin Fedden's house
where a hired car came to fetch the three of us at seven o'clock.
Consequence was we reached Windsor too early and circled round
the town and park. Then joined a stream of motors to the Castle.

Drove through St George's Gate to the State Entrance Tower. Beautifully organised, polite policemen, servants in scarlet livery. A. discarded her shawl downstairs. Up the Grand Straircase at the head of which a man and woman, may have been Master of the Household and wife, greeted us. Passed into the State Ante-Room, where drinks handed round and we saw many friends, Ken Davison,[*] the Verneys of Claydon. Long talk with Ralph Verney[†] who said my views on traffic control proved useful to his Traffic Commission. Admired the Gothic fan tracery ceiling of this apartment, by Wyatville. Then passed into the Waterloo Chamber.

We three sat in the third row; behind us a space and row for the royals, one armed chair for the Queen. An orchestra in front. A door from St George's Hall thrown open, and the Ascot house party trooped in and took their seats. After a pause the Queen entered, followed by the Queen Mother, Duke of Edinburgh, Princess Anne, Princess Margaret and Tony (in scarlet Household dress and medals, looking like a Ruritanian prince), beautiful Princess Alexandra, Ogilvy.[‡] Yehudi Menuhin[§] entered the platform, and 'God Save the Queen' played. Then a most suitable and delightful concert, Mozart, Schubert, Handel (all pieces chosen by the Queen, Yehudi said afterwards), and one piece specially composed for the Queen by a young man, who conducted, Edmund Roxburgh, consisting of songs from Burns's verse set to music, one Jacobite song. By now it was ten o'clock or later. We walked out of the Waterloo Chamber – the best of the Lawrences are of two Popes, Pius VI and VII – through the King's State Drawing Room, and there lined up to shake hands with the Queen and Duke, who were standing in the Guard Chamber. Our card was taken up by a liveried servant, names announced and we advanced. A. curtseyed deep; I bowed, perhaps too deep, but my loyalty is deep. The Queen smiled very sweetly, the Duke wearing

---

[*] Hon. Kensington Davison DSO, DFC (1914–2005); yr s. of Sir William Davison (1872–1953), Mayor of Kensington, 1913–19, MP for South Kensington, 1918–45, cr. Baron Broughshane, 1945; s. brother as 3rd Baron, 1995.

[†] Sir Ralph Verney, 5th Bt (b. 1915), of Claydon House, Buckinghamshire.

[‡] Hon. (Sir) Angus Ogilvy (1928–2004); m. 1963 HRH Princess Alexandra of Kent.

[§] Violinist (1916–99; cr. life peer, 1993).

Household uniform, Prussian blue Garter and sash, said something like, 'Oh yes, how are you?'

We proceeded into St George's Gallery, a wonderful apartment. There were little tables along the south side, and a long buffet table along the north-east side. John Sparrow, when I asked him whether we were to be placed or not, said, 'I don't know about you, I am sitting next to Queen Elizabeth.' A. pushed her way straight to a table where John Pope-Hennessy was sitting with a tiny little old lady dressed in white. Only half-way through supper I realised she was Ava Waverley.[*] Delicious supper of cold vichyssoise in cups, cold meat and salads, chocolate mousse or strawberries and cream. Champagne or red wine. I sipped at one glass of champagne (horrid drink) throughout the evening. A regiment of attentive footmen in tailcoats of scarlet. Looking down the great length of the room I was reminded of one of those coloured lithographs in *Pyne's Royal Residences*.

Supper was finished after midnight, when we were supposed to go home. But no. The Royals came into the Gallery. I avoided Tony Snowdon and Princess Margaret. In passing close to her I overheard her saying to Angus Ogilvy who happened to brush her arm in passing, 'Must you do that?' in her snappish voice. I didn't want to get into conversation. Hugh Grafton said, 'Well, fancy you being here, you *are* getting on' – a snide little jab I thought.

We were conducted by the Queen round the staterooms which are not usually open to the public, beginning with the Queen's Presence Chamber and ending with the Rubens room. It was difficult to look at all the treasures on account of talking. Celia McKenna[†] kept running up to me and asking 'What was that?', as though I could possibly know. But I did recognise two cabinets made for Henrietta Maria. Wonderful silver-on-ebony furniture. The wall hangings nothing like as pretty as they were in George III's time, and some carpets very unworthy. The Vermeer had been brought from London specially for us. A. rushed up to me in the Queen's State Drawing

---

[*] Ava Bodley; m. 1st Ralph Wigram (d. 1936), 2nd 1941 (as his 2nd wife) Sir John Anderson, member of War Cabinet (cr. Viscount Waverley, 1952; d. 1958); J.L.-M. had met her at the tables of London hostesses in the 1940s.

[†] Lady Cecilia Keppel, dau. of 9th Earl of Albemarle; m. 1934 David McKenna.

Room to say, 'You must come and see the Cardinal Duke's canteen in the Library.' As we walked through the door the Queen was standing in the doorway talking. So we flattened ourselves against the wall. Until she passed on everyone stood stock still. I remarked how obsequious most people look on talking to royalty, bowing and scraping ingratiatingly. How impossible to be natural. I am sure one must try to be. Yet when it came to saying goodbye to the Queen at the head of the staircase, all I could murmur was, 'It has been the greatest treat, Ma'am.' Really, how could I? She smiled wanly. It was 1.30. We got back to London in pouring rain at 2.15. I stayed the night at Brooks's.

I wanted to take in everything I saw, but could not. The salt on our table was of gilt, of a putto and shell, as though it were by Cellini; the sugar caster of silver weighed a ton. Pair of gold mandarin jars on the chimneypiece, portrait by Honthorst of Charles I as a boy, Canaletto of Murano unlike anything by Canaletto I have seen; the Wyatville ceilings, the would-be Grinling Gibbons work reminding me of what the Bachelor Duke did at Chatsworth. A. tells me the Queen was dining in our room. I had my back to her so did not see. Q. had a special footman in blue livery behind her chair, at a decent distance so he could not overhear conversation. He waited upon her only. Every now and then she turned and gave him a message or a note.

Saturday, 23 June

I have decided that the reason one keeps a diary is the compulsion to write something, anything. Secondly, all intending writers are advised to keep diaries for practice, like playing scales. No doubt diary-writing is also a kind of vanity. One has the sauce to believe that every thought which comes into one's head merits recording.

Yesterday I went with Bloggs Badwin* to Ribbesford churchyard. I noticed on the way that the elder is more splendid than I ever remember it. We went into the church, Bloggs with a pair of binoculars to read the inscription in small letters at the bottom of the Burne-Jones west window to his great-grandparents, I to look at a tablet to my grandfather and the over-varnished pews which he

---

* A. W. Baldwin, 3rd Earl Baldwin of Bewdley (1904–76); yr s. of Prime Minister.

constructed for himself in 1905. Then we advanced in search of the graves of Bloggs's great-grandparents and my grandparents. He donned a pair of waders, though it was a fine day and the grass was dry, and a pair of thick leather gloves; he took up a billyhook and I a scythe. By chance our two graves were practically adjacent at the top of the hill in this huge churchyard. We hacked away and revealed the inscriptions on the stones; mine were quite obliterated by moss, the graves choked by long grasses. Bloggs very cross because his grave is endowed and he had written to the vicar who had never answered his letter. Instead they have spent the money on planting hideous lobelias and geraniums round the church. I told Bloggs they ought to scrap all this nonsense and put sheep in the graveyard.

We lunched at The Hundred House, Abberley. Bloggs talked a lot about his father whom he worships. While Prime Minister he used to walk from Astley to Rock church, some ten miles. He walked everywhere, talking to yokels as he went. Nothing he liked more in Downing Street than to hear Bloggs tell him stories in broad Worcestershire, which he speaks fluently. He said that his father in old age steeled himself by means of his implicit religious faith, his love of literature and art, against the ferocious criticism of his neglect to re-arm before the Second World War.

Sunday, 24 June

We had Diana Cooper to stay the weekend. I met her at Chippenham station. Saw her at far end of the platform struggling with a suitcase and a large basket. Embraced her, took the suitcase, and would have taken the basket, but she insisted on carrying it, because inside was her Doglet, under a coat. A dog's ticket is as much as a child's, and she won't pay for one. We got through the barrier all right. In the car chat about this and that. Easy. It is when others are present that I find her less sympathetic. For she *must* be, no, *is*, the centre of attention and she will talk so much. I find her constant drinking merely a bore. Fill up, fill up, with gin, vodka, anything it seems. The garden was open this afternoon and she sat with me at the gate, taking the money because it amused her to talk to the people. Some recognised her under her hat, those unmistakable, God-given features. Who would guess she is over eighty? And Doglet on her lap was an object of attention. She has little balance and wobbles perilously. With the least prompting she spouts scenes from Shakespeare. She eats nothing; pecks at spoonfuls on her plate, and leaves most of that. She is indifferent to comfort and possessions. Doesn't mind what happens, whom she sees, so long as it is somebody interesting.

Saturday, 30 June

After breakfast Pam telephoned to say that Nancy is in a coma and sinking fast. This evening before dinner she telephoned again that N. died at 1.30. She is to be cremated and her ashes buried at Swinbrook churchyard next Saturday. Difficult to imagine that bright spirit silenced.

Wednesday, 4 July

I wonder what Nancy has left to A., and also I wonder just a little if she has left me some small thing. I try hard not to think anything of the sort, but I do not succeed.

Cecil Beaton who came to tea here on Monday said that Jamesey [Pope-Hennessy] ought to be set up now, for he has two commissions for money-spinners – lives of Noël Coward* and the Duchess of Windsor.† I said I did not envy him the last one. 'Oh, but just think of the poor little Cinderella who made good,' Cecil said. C. looks immensely distinguished. We all went to Claverton [American Museum near Bath] to listen to Desmond Guinness lecture on Jefferson. He did it well, with much confidence, all the jokes, the grimaces, the flirtatious mannerisms carefully rehearsed. Cecil said afterwards that Desmond is beautiful, but not nice. He certainly is handsome, with piercing, clear, cold blue eyes. Reminds me of [his uncle] Tom [Mitford], without the straightforwardness.

---

* Actor, playwright, songwriter, poet and possessor of other talents to amuse (1899–1973).
† Bessie Wallis Warfield (1896–1986); m. (3rd) 1937 HRH Edward, Duke of Windsor (1894–1972); Beaton had taken the photographs at their wedding in France.

Saturday, 7 July

Have received a snub from the Librarian of Windsor Castle to whom I wrote asking permission to see the Stuart papers. Was given to understand that anyone reputable was given permission. But no. R. Mackworth-Young* replied that unless I was an accredited biographer of a Stuart I could not visit the library. To my questions about the Cardinal King's jewels I got no answer at all.

Are all handsome men narcissistic? During these dog days all the young and not so young doff their shirts and work naked to the waist. They love exposing their bodies. The other day I met Mervyn the Badminton keeper in his jeep, naked to the navel. Had a chat with him. All the time he was caressing his torso, running his hands affectionately across his breasts and navel, and under his arm pits, like a lover with his mistress. Does this mean that he is in love with himself? I have often noticed this behaviour by men who are not at all homosexual, the moment they are naked. They do not make love to themselves when they are clad. Perhaps it is shyness because they are naked in public. But I think not. Men are more interested in titillating themselves than women are.

Monday, 9 July

On Saturday A., Helen Dashwood (who invited herself for the night) and I motored to Nance's funeral. We were bidden to lunch by Rosemary Bailey† at Westwell at 12.30. It was a family affair. The Beits,‡ the Gladwyns,§ the young Redesdales¶ gathered. All dressed in black. I in a dark suit for I no longer have a black suit, and morning dress is no

---

* Sir Robert ('Robin') Mackworth-Young (1920–2000); Royal Librarian and Assistant Keeper of The Queen's Archives, 1958–85.
† Rosemary Mitford (b. 1911); first cousin of Mitford sisters; m. 1932 Commander Richard Bailey.
‡ Sir Alfred Beit, 2nd Bt (1903–94); m. 1939 Clementine Mitford (sister of Rosemary Bailey).
§ Gladwyn Jebb, 1st Baron Gladwyn (1900–97); diplomatist and Liberal politician; m. 1929 Cynthia Noble (she d. 1990).
¶ Clement Mitford, 5th Baron Redesdale (1932–91); m. 1958 Sarah Todd.

longer worn. Lord Redesdale who was chief mourner *was* so dressed. We motored to Swinbrook church. It was a most lovely day, sunny with clouds which rendered the Windrush landscape blue. Greeted at the church door by Peregrine Hartington.[*] I wore dark spectacles to conceal the tears. We were put, with Geoffrey Gilmour[†] who had come from Paris, in a front pew. In front of us were only Rosemary Bailey and Clementine Beit who wore a black straw hat perched becomingly on the top of her head, tilted over the nose. C. kept turning round watching who came in. Before us on the chancel steps, raised on a small blue velvet covering, a tiny, common little wooden box, one foot by one foot, containing all that is left of Nance. The utter nullity of existence and fame overwhelmed me as I gazed at this piteous object. Such a beautiful church, with the fine Fettiplace monuments and Tom's tablet, and the clear windows with the sun filtering through, the west window framing the great fountain of green trees beyond the churchyard. Lord Redesdale carried the box on its little cushion down the aisle. We all followed. Close to the tower a tiny, shallow hole was surrounded with wreaths and bunches of flowers. The tiny box was lowered, not very far. Then Lord Redesdale beckoned the three sisters to file past. Diana, Debo and Pam, all three wearing black scarves over their heads like three classical Graces. Tom Mosley bowed to the grave in passing. We were all directed to file past. A. was so upset by the cards to Nancy from the sisters, the inscriptions with their pet names for her, that she burst into tears. I wanted to escape by the back gate but we were obliged to stop and chat. I merely kissed Diana and Debo and Woman, and avoided Tom Mosley out of shyness. He looks like an old, old rabbi. A very harrowing experience.

Sunday, 22 July

What we have dreaded for months, no years, has now happened. One of the dogs, Chuff, died yesterday evening. We had to take him to the

---

[*] Peregrine Cavendish, Marquess of Hartington (b. 1944); o.s. and heir of 11th Duke of Devonshire (whom he succeeded as 12th Duke, 2004); m. 1967 Amanda Heywood-Lonsdale.
[†] Anglo-Argentine art collector resident in Paris (1907–82); Oxford contemporary of J.L.-M.

vet, whose advice was to let him go. I suppose we did right. Neither of us could face watching him die, for which I feel guilty. Vet said in an extremely kind way, 'Wait in the car and I will tell you when it is over.' We managed to get out of the surgery, both sobbing, and in the car gave way completely. Suddenly I laughed at the spectacle of two elderly people sobbing together in a small car. But tears keep returning and have flowed ever since.

Saturday, 4 August

On Thursday we went to picnic with Penelope [Betjeman] in her tumbledown hovel near Cusop on the Breconshire–Herefordshire border. She told us that John's shuffling was not a trick he had subsided into, but was caused by hardening of the arteries [in fact by Parkinson's Disease]. She is having to build a shower in her cottage because he can no longer get into and out of a bath. She deplores the amount he drinks. Told A. she was hugely grateful to Elizabeth for looking after him. Penelope has no running water, no light and no telephone. Water has to be fetched from a neighbour – God knows where there is one – and the lavatory tank must be filled before the plug can be pulled. This operation is restricted to once a day. P. doesn't mind these deficiencies the least bit. She is fearfully bossy. 'Now Jim, you are to put the horses in the field. When you have done that I want you to put up an old door so as to prevent the puppies escaping from the stable. Alvilde, get the cider from the barrel in the woodshed.' At first one thinks one cannot stand it. But one falls into her ways. She is so good-hearted. When she laughs, which she does at all jokes against herself, she roars. Over coffee I was handed a bowl of sugar, brown mixed with white. I said, 'Darling, are you quite certain this mixture is not worm powder for the horses?' Penelope looks much older, lined and yellow. This is 'Inja' for you.

Monday, 6 August

Today I become an old age pensioner. If I wished to get a job I couldn't. Henceforth I receive a pension from the State. A. gave me a new radio, very small, chic and pretty with an excellent tone. The old one which was Aunt Dorothy's[*] still works but is becoming a trifle senile.

Friday, 10 August

On Wednesday A. telephoned me in London that she had seen her doctor, Allinson, about the throbbing in her head. He told her she had come to him just in time. She was suffering from temporal arteritis; he has given her Cortisone and performed a slight operation, removing a small fragment of the artery wall under local anaesthetic. Had this not been done she might have been struck blind in both eyes. This has upset me greatly. I immediately telephoned the Sitwells[†] with whom we were to stay this weekend. Georgia commiserated about A., which reduced me to tears. I wish I were not so uncontrollably melted.

Saturday, 11 August

Yesterday I lunched with Joanie Altrincham[‡] and the John Griggs[§] to meet Iris Murdoch and husband, latter a gnome-like sprite, bald, plain with bad teeth, an impediment of speech, quick and very clever. Iris Murdoch and I sat together. She is a little forbidding. Has short cropped hair *à la* Penelope Betjeman, whom she somewhat resembles. Is stocky, wearing a maternity gown of flowered muslin, and trousers. She made a few trivial remarks of politeness about my novel which she intended to read. I was able to riposte by saying I had read and enormously admired *The Black Prince*. Asked if she ever wondered what her hero was now doing and thinking in prison. The asinine

---

[*] Dorothy Edwards-Heathcote (1884–1965); m. 1912 Alec Milne Lees-Milne (1878–1931). J.L.-M. was devoted to this eccentric, pipe-smoking relative, who lived with another woman in the Scottish highlands, and inherited her property when she died.
[†] Sir Sacheverell Sitwell, 6th Bt (1897–1988), of Weston, Northamptonshire; m. 1925 Georgia Doble (d. 1980).
[‡] Hon. Joan Dickson-Poynder (1897–1987); o.c. of 1st Baron Islington; m. 1923 Sir Edward Grigg MP (1879–1955), cr. Baron Altrincham 1945; she lived at Tormarton near Badminton.
[§] Writer (1924–2001), official biographer of Lloyd George; succeeded father as 2nd Baron Altrincham 1955 but disclaimed peerage 1963; m. 1958 Patricia Campbell.

things one says because of one's upbringing not to allow silences when in the company of strangers. She said, of course, that once she had finished a novel she never dwelt on the characters again. Enjoyed talking to John Grigg at luncheon. He has splendid manners, is attentive to fools, very intelligent, and the quintessence of a gent, which he may not care to be thought. We talked of Baldwin and Lloyd George. I told him of my one and only meeting with Lloyd George in a committee room at the House of Commons.* He was offhand, autocratic and unsympathetic, a fussy, florid little man with an over-endowment of white hair.

John agrees with Philip Magnus that verbal recollection and anecdotes of the subject of a biography one is engaged in are practically valueless. People's memories are coloured by what they think the listener wants to know, and usually faulty. I asked because that morning I had received a letter from Jamie Hamilton pressing me to write a biography of Nancy Mitford. Me, of all people. Diana Mosley is the literary executor and apparently wants me to. I am amazed. First impulse to say No, No. But on re-think I am not so sure. Oh God, what a perplexity. I really want to finish my eccentric country house owners book.

Friday, 17 August

Much to our surprise we were invited to lunch at Badminton in order to meet Horatia Durant, an ancient cousin of the Somersets, and a great-great-granddaughter of Nelson. Only us and the Duchess, four in all, Master mercifully away fishing in Scotland. Duchess is always friendly, simple and child-like. Took A. and me round the downstairs once again and said exactly the same things I have now heard her repeat four times, some good little jokes too. Occasional touching remarks like, 'When I was little I was a Teck.' And 'Queen [never 'Aunt'] Mary insisted on buying that Garter ribbon when it came into the market and put it into Windsor, although it was really ours.' Showed us the travelling George† which is said to have belonged to Prince Charlie, and dozens of Garter

---

* J.L.-M describes this meeting with David Lloyd George (1863–1945; Prime Minister, 1916–22; cr. Earl, 1945) in his diary for 23 April 1942.
† The jewel of the Order of the Garter.

ribbons and seventeenth-century Georges which didn't, and William IV's hair, 'cut off his head and given by Queen Ad'lid to my grandmother.' Mrs Durant evidently bores them stiff with her interminable stories of Somersets. 'I say, "What about my family for a change?" But it might not exist for all she cares. Let's be on Christian-name terms.'

Thursday, 23 August

Yesterday went to London re the proposition of the book on Nancy. Talked first to Eardley who said, 'I hope you won't do it; but I am sure you will.' Then went to Albany where I lunched with Roger Machell and Jamie Hamilton. They were very friendly and talked politenesses. Asked what book I had finished. I said the Stuarts, 'which you turned down'. Half-way through luncheon I raised the matter I had come about. They asked what were my reservations. I said the chief one was that I did not admire Nancy's prose style; never had. They took this badly and were, I could see, amazed. Anyway Jamie had received that morning a letter from Diana saying that on no account must mention of Palewski* be made. I said then no book could be written, because he was the inspiration behind N's writing and the cause of her going to live in France and her pro-French and anti-British outlook. He need not be mentioned by name, but the great and only affair of her life could not be omitted. Diana also now favours a symposium, not a straightforward biography. I said these sorts of commemoration were seldom satisfactory. I suggested that her letters should be published. Rather unsatisfactory meeting. I said that Raymond [Mortimer] was dining with me and they gave me permission to discuss the matter with him.

At Brooks's, Raymond said nothing would induce him to write N's life; that there was little life to write about. Said N. might be classed with E. F. Benson† by future generations. He did say that the best thing

---

* Colonel Gaston Palewski (1901–84); wartime aide and peacetime minister of General de Gaulle, then still active in French public life as President of the *Conseil Constitutionel* (1965–74); he only briefly reciprocated Nancy Mitford's enduring love for him; m. 1969 Violette de Talleyrand-Périgord.

† Novelist (1867–1940).

would be to publish a selection of her letters, carefully edited with connecting passages, and a longish introduction about her. I entirely agreed, and after he had left me, telephoned Jamie and told him this. I think I shall hear no more of the proposition.

Thursday, 30 August

On the point of leaving for Scotland at eleven when the telephone rang. It was Jamie Hamilton to tell me that he saw Diana [Mosley] in Paris yesterday, and explained my reluctance to write Nance's life; and he and she agreed to ask Harold Acton.* I am sure Harold will be far more suitable than me, for he belonged to N's sophisticated, scratchy young Twenties generation. Besides I am sure N. would not have wanted me to write her life. Had I not turned down the offer I might have written the one best-seller of my lifetime, or at least had a chance of doing so. Am certain my decision has been the right one. Poor A. disappointed however.

Sunday, 9 September

Yesterday the telephone bell rang and a voice said, 'I am Dorothy Hobhouse, Christopher's† sister. May I come and see you?' I invited her to tea today. A charming, tall, distinguished, un-smart typical English spinster, which is what I expected. Christopher used to be ashamed of her. She reminded me that they were brought up in Gloucester Cathedral Close, their father being a Canon. In 1920 he lost his mind, their mother died, and they were passed on to a parson uncle who could not make head or tail of Xtopher, Kit she calls him. She is immensely proud of him. Said at once on shaking hands, 'You will see at once that I am unlike Kit, neither good looking nor brilliant.' This drew me to her from the start. She wanted to know what I could tell her about his young days (not that he ever reached middle

---

* Sir Harold Acton (1904–94); writer and aesthete, resident in Florence.
† Christopher Hobhouse (1910–40); bisexual barrister and writer, author of a biography of Charles James Fox; J.L.-M. saw much of him in the 1930s when they were both lodgers in Harold Nicolson's rooms in King's Bench Walk.

aged ones). I said we all admired without revering him; that we laughed not at, but about him. We would say to one another, 'Have you heard this outrageous thing Hobvilla has said or done?' That he showed incipient signs of greatness in his keen curiosity, his determination to try everything at least once. I said if he had lived and stuck to the Bar he might have been Lord Chancellor today. That he was no romantic; was a realist. Was sarcastic, and his pomposity was assumed. We found it funny. He was arrogant, and would speak in slow, measured terms with his head thrown back and a contemptuous curl on his lips. He was paradoxical, brilliant, absurd, amusing and conspicuous. I see him very clearly with his handsome face and lithe figure. He must live like a prince without a penny; must be an MP at the age of twenty-one; that he might well have made and lost several fortunes. She said her cousin Sir Charles warned her never in any circumstances to lend him money from her slender capital. Sure enough he asked her to. She had the strength to resist, and refuse. I showed her the copy of his *Fox* which he gave me, with his immature, terse inscription, and told her I somewhere had a photograph of him. This I could not find. A nice, touching woman. What I did not tell her was that Christopher had little use for me; and that I did not really love him. Nor did I tell her that Harold [Nicolson] did love him very dearly. She made no mention of his tiresome wife and the child. Jock Murray was extremely kind to them after C. was killed.

Monday, 17 September

Midi asked me to walk with her this evening down the lane. She said she was in a quandary. Brian her younger son announced a month ago that he had an illegitimate son, aged three years, by a black girl. He is no longer living with the black girl, who has another love. The two parents are now merely friends. The way the bombshell fell on Midi was aptly chosen. She was tending Derick's grave in the churchyard here, with Brian. In a moment of happy recollection she remarked to Brian, 'Father loved this place. He was so happy in his last years, so proud of you and Bamber and Veronica. I think his only disappointment was there being no Gascoigne grandson.' 'Well, there is one,' came the reply. 'He's black.'

Wednesday, 19 September

Eardley and I lunched. I think I shocked him by saying airily I would quite like to die now; that I hated the world which had left me by, and had no future to look forward to. And future was all that mattered to a man. I did not go into particulars, the millstone dragging me into the abyss of annihilation. It is the certainty that I have been a failure as a son, brother, lover, husband, conservationist, committee member, friend, writer, and what else? Everything really. I suppose most people have a similar millstone tied to the neck.

Sunday, 14 October

Today was an occasion which might have happened forty years ago – no, a hundred and forty years ago. The Bishop of Gloucester* visited our church and gave a sermon. Afterwards, escorted by the Rector, he came to luncheon here. To meet him we had Gilbert Wheat, the headmaster of Rosehill School, Rachel Savory, the good woman of the village, Midi [Gascoigne] and her brother Terence[†] who was staying with her. The Bishop, charming to talk to, human and understanding, looks and behaves like a Prince of the Church, which is a nice change. In church he wore a splendid scarlet chasuble with gold tassel hanging over his surplice at the back. When he came to us he wore a purple soutane with double-breasted top-piece of embroidered buttons, a fine silver cross suspended on a chain round his neck, and snow-white starched dog-collar. We filed into the dining-room, and when we reached our places A. said, 'And now, my Lord Bishop, will you please say grace?' The Bishop told us that he was one of those in the House of Lords who had pressed for the amendment that Alderley and Berkeley villages should remain in Gloucestershire, and not go to Avon.[‡] Referring to empty churches, he poignantly

---

* The Rt Revd Basil Tudor Guy (1910–75); Bishop of Gloucester, 1962–75.
† Hon. Terence O'Neill (1914–90); Prime Minister of Northern Ireland, 1963–9; cr. life peer, 1970.
‡ The local government reforms promulgated by the Conservatives in 1974 created a new County of Avon based on Bristol, to the dismay of those residents of Gloucestershire who were swallowed by it.

remarked that no clergyman of the Church of England today could claim spiritual success. He said that in his city eighty per cent of the inhabitants had never heard of him and didn't care tuppence for his office. As a young man his first cure was in Cornwall. At his first service one person attended, at the second two, at the third three. At the fourth, none. The loneliness and desolation of the spirit of the sincere priest were devastating today.

Nigel [Nicolson] has sent us a copy of *Portrait of a Marriage*, which I have read. It is very well done and will I am sure eventually enhance Vita's reputation in so far as she was a vindicator of extra-marital liberties of the Lesbian kind. Vita loved with passion. She was a passionate woman. I think Nigel exaggerates in making Harold out to be a saint. He barely mentions Harold's peccadilloes which, in contrast to V's, were casual fly-by-nights. Vita's affairs were all love ones. She was monogamous, not promiscuous. She loved, not merely lusted. Of course, the starry section of the book is Vita's memoir of her elopement with Violet. I find something a little comical about this; and something almost disingenuous about the endless expressions of her and Harold's mutual adoration. As Frankie Donaldson* said last night, surely married couples do not keep on reiterating their deep devotion to one another after forty years. Were H. and V. writing with an eye cocked on posterity? In thanking Nigel I somewhat impertinently put to him all these points except the last. I did not want to suggest that the letters had been intended for future publication, like Horace Walpole's, lest he might suppose I questioned their sincerity, which I don't. But I did say Harold was not an immaculate saint.

Thursday, 25 October

Received a letter from Norah [Smallwood] yesterday which should have rejoiced my soul. To my amazement she says the foremost American publishers of paperbacks have taken my *Heretics*, mentioning the possibility of sales of 150,000 and dollars galore. This

---

* Frances ('Frankie') Lonsdale; writer; m. 1935 'Jack' Donaldson (1907–98), Eton contemporary of J.L.-M., cr. life peer as Baron Donaldson of Kingsbridge, 1967, Minister for the Arts, 1976–9.

astonishes me for I imagined the book had been a complete flop here. What odd fortunes one's books do have. But she continues to say that because of the recent publication by some woman of another book on Prince Charlie, and because of the great length of mine, she fears, etc. This information has depressed me far more than the other gist of the letter has impressed me. I have replied that once my books have been launched I take little further interest in them. Before they are born I am extremely sensitive and solicitous about them. After three years of sweat, blood and tears over the Stuarts I shall be in despair if it is rejected. I make a mistake in telling people what I am writing about. It invites bad luck.

Saturday, 27 October

Drove to meet the 6.20 train at Kemble this evening, to pick up Pat Trevor-Roper. As I turned off the Cirencester road, the sun was setting below a bank of rising mist, throwing upon the twilit sky a pinky primrose light. Against this backcloth a row of elms, their feet in the swirl of mist, their arms drooping against the skies, looked tranquil and serene as though they must endure for ever in this setting, a promise that England would remain as I had best loved it. Whereas of course it is a miracle that the row of elms has survived, and doubtless by next year these divine trees will be dead. The disease has not yet exterminated every elm in this part of Gloucestershire, as it already has in Worcestershire. This morning Alastair Finlinson showed me what happened to the elm. On Fry's land by Wotton, he tore the bark from a dead elm. It came off like parchment. Underneath, the bole was covered with a film of sticky white foam, like castor sugar. This is the fungus which the beetle brings. The fungus throttles the tree so that it cannot breathe.

Monday, 29 October

At dinner on Saturday, Pat Trevor-Roper professed not to know the difference between a bounder, a cad and a shit. The older ones among us explained that the first two terms were common in our youth, whereas 'shit' was a term we did not use, and approximated to 'cad'.

Caroline [Somerset] in her outspoken manner said, 'I know what a shit is,' and turning to David said, 'David's one.' She thought it a complimentary term. Since David has frequently been called one,[*] we were amused. I don't think he was.

Thursday, 8 November

Yesterday I spent at Uppark [Sussex] with the NT Arts Panel. What is certain is that nearly everyone connected with the Trust is 'decent'. Sitting round the dining-room table, on which incongruously Emma Hart[†] once danced, there were some twenty of the most understanding, cultivated, earnest men of good sense and taste it were possible to find – Robin Fedden, Brinsley Ford,[‡] Johnny Walker from the Metropolitan Museum, Roddy Thesiger,[§] Lord Plunkett,[¶] not to mention the staff – Bobby Gore,[**] young Martin Drury,[††] Gervase Jackson-Stops[‡‡] and Merlin Waterson. Could they be a bettered lot?

A horrid thing happened last night as I was driving back from the station. Beyond Little Badminton and Shepherd's Cottage, not going very fast before a corner, in the headlights I saw rushing sideways from the verge an enormous fox. Before I could stop there was a bang against the front wheel, and a bump, and I had run over it. What was I to do? One cannot kill a fox without a large stick or an instrument. One cannot touch it with bare hands. Hoping it might be dead, I turned in a gateway and anxiously drove back. There in the middle of the road

---

[*] Notably by the satirical magazine *Private Eye*.
[†] Better known as Emma, Lady Hamilton (1761–1815), mistress of Horatio Nelson.
[‡] (Sir) Brinsley Ford (1908–99); Hon. Adviser on Paintings to N.T.; Eton contemporary of J.L.-M.
[§] Roderic Thesiger (b. 1915); antique dealer and member of N.T. Historic Buildings Committee.
[¶] Patrick, 7th Baron Plunkett (1923–75); equerry to HM The Queen, and Trustee of Wallace Collection.
[**] Francis St John Gore (b. 1921); N.T. Adviser on Pictures, 1956–86; Historic Buildings Secretary, 1973–81.
[††] N.T. Historic Buildings Representative for S.E. of England, and adviser on furniture, 1973–81 (b. 1938); subsequently Historic Buildings Secretary, 1981–95, and Director-General, 1995–2001.
[‡‡] Architectural historian and adviser to N.T. (1947–95).

in the distance I saw reflected from my headlamps two huge eyes which moved slightly, pitiably. I was so stricken, so revolted by myself, so at a loss, that I backed away, turned and drove on. I am sure the poor thing must have been nearly dead. Ought I to have run over it again? Oh the horror! And the shame! A real countryman like the Duke of Beaufort would have known what to do. Not so a cissy from the suburbs.

Friday, 16 November

The morning of Princess Anne's wedding* I walked from Eardley's flat in West Halkin Street through Green Park. It was a fine, brisk November morning, the sun out. There was an unusual atmosphere of festivity and expectation. Crowds of women were scurrying from Hyde Park Corner down Constitution Hill towards the Palace to catch a glimpse. The newspaper posters on the other hand contained the gloomiest portents in their headings, fuel crises, more strikes, Bank Rate rising to unprecedented heights, the stock market falling to the plumbiest depths. Yet the public were determined to enjoy the spectacle of the Princess, who is ugly, marrying a handsome boy who is barely a gentleman. It seems to me that royalty forfeits its mystique, its pointfulness when it becomes like you and me. It should marry only other royalties, and not nice, healthy, sporting, silly commoners who are common. I meant not to view the wedding, but at Brooks's saw members and staff gathering round the television set brought downstairs into the bar. Curiosity impelled me to look; the sheer beauty of the glass coach, the scarlet trappings, the Baroque pageantry, the beauty of Princess Anne's white dress and the slimness of her waist, the beauty of the bridegroom's uniform and the back of his well-shaped head with glossy chestnut hair, riveted me for an hour.

Harry Horsfield lunched and I asked him if marriage to my Mama had been unadulterated hell for him. He said, not unadulterated. He contradicted my surmise that drink was the cause of her tiresomeness. He said she did not drink so very much; her fits were the principal cause. At times she became possessed of demons, threw rages which

---

* Princess Anne (b. 1950) married her equestrian friend Captain Mark Phillips (b. 1948) on 14 November.

were dreadful to witness. When finally he told her that he thought it best for him to leave her, she brightened and said she agreed absolutely. 'And then, Harry,' she said, 'we can go back to being the friends we were before we married.' But they never did. It was too late. The truth is that Mama was not made to live with others. She could not bear having the same person about her for more than a few hours. Like me she was a recluse, or more accurately a solitary.

Harold Acton lunched with me at Brooks's yesterday, the first time I have had him alone for years. Undeniably his charm is limitless and his wit contagious. We talked much of Nancy. I have offered him all her letters to me, and felt sure A. would let him have hers which are far more numerous. He said he hadn't asked Raymond [Mortimer], who he knew disliked him, for his. I said I would ask Raymond, which I have done. R. said it involved labour on his part searching through trunks, sorting and re-reading. But he told me to convey to Harold that he would let him have some letters, if not all. Harold is mischievous without being malicious.

Friday, 23 November

The Osbert Lancasters* stayed last weekend. Osbert, whom I nowadays see once every two years at most, remains the same as he was at Oxford, only he – unlike another unchanged Oxford survival, Johnnie Churchill – was highly sophisticated at the university. A little greyer, Osbert is no whit less plain, or rugged, or facetious. That is his pity, he is more facetious than funny. And the text of his latest book which he brought for us, *The Littlehampton Bequest*, bears this out. The incomparable illustrations (and they are marvellous) are far more amusing than the text. It was strange to be reminded by Osbert that he stayed with me at Wickhamford with my parents and brother Dick, in I suppose 1930. Very few of my friends were invited to the manor. The idea of them bored my parents. Anne Lancaster is extremely tall, with a splendid lissom figure, very pretty face, dresses admirably and is elegant. Is the exact opposite to Osbert in looks, demeanour and behaviour,

---

* (Sir) Osbert Lancaster (1908–86); cartoonist, humorist and dandy; m. 1967 (as her 2nd husband) Anne Scott-James (b. 1913), journalist and horticulturist.

although O. is always neatly dressed, too neatly for the country. She told me that Osbert is not the least bit interested in individuals, only in people in the mass. He knows nothing, she asseverated, whatever about the heart, a piece of anatomy which bores him stiff. Talking of novels, Osbert said he enjoyed all Anthony Powell's* and looked forward eagerly to the next. We three said they left us colder rather than warmer, because they are about people without hearts.

Poor Angus [Menzies] was run over last weekend while walking down a country lane near Basingstoke on one of his rambles, by a motor-bicyclist. A. and I were told by telephone and on Monday drove to Basingstoke Hospital to see him. He has broken both legs and his head is badly battered.

Saturday, 1 December

When I was a boy in the 1920s, old photographs of my father and mother, their relations and friends, taken in the 1890s at the age I then was, looked to me incredibly archaic, with their antediluvian clothes and fusty fashions. Whereas today when I look at photographs of myself and my family taken in the 1920s they look slightly different, but by no means archaic. In fact, were I now to see people on the street wearing these clothes I should pass them by without astonishment, merely thinking them rather square. Yet the difference in time is fifty years, compared with thirty. Can it be that the change in dress style during the last half-century has been less momentous than during the first period? Or is this another indication of ageing?

Tuesday, 4 December

We were lunching with Audrey today, ostensibly to meet the Wingfields† in the hope that they might let me see Barrington Park

---

* Anthony Powell, novelist (1905–2000); m. 1934 Lady Violet Pakenham (1912–2002).
† Charles Talbot Rhys Wingfield (b. 1924); m. 1954 Hon. Cynthia Hill, dau. of 6th Baron Sandys. J.L.-M. finally succeeded in seeing their house a year before his death, on 20 September 1996.

[Gloucestershire]; but they never turned up, or even sent a message of excuse. Theirs is the most inaccessible house in England, and all attempts at entry fail. All the art historian boys like John Harris and Gervase Jackson-Stops have received a flea in their ear, if any acknowledgement of their requests. Prue and Ted [Robinson] however also lunched, and just before leaving at three we talked about Angus's accident, for Prue knew him. On our return to Alderley the telephone rang and Angus's niece, in a great state, informed A. that Angus had suddenly died an hour ago. Presumably from a clot, or the wrong drug, for he was being treated for pneumonia. Angus who was so healthy, vital and beloved, almost a brother to me (as he certainly was to A.), for I had grown to love him dearly. He was the only one of our relations, of our age, who was on our beam, with similar interests, similar friends, similar sense of fun and understanding.

Monday, 10 December

We went to Angus's funeral at Golders Green, arriving early. A uniformed and urbane attendant asked which funeral we were attending. A. said Mr Menzies at 1.15. 'No, no, my dear,' this horrid man said, 'always at twenty minutes past the hour, twenty to the hour, and the hour itself.' We were ushered into the most bad-taste waiting room I have ever entered. Brown brocaded wallpaper such as you get in the Bewley Pipe Shop, frosted glass windows, blue serge chair covers. Another official rushed in to say, 'Are you attending the Oppenheimer funeral? If not, please pass along.' The coffins as though on a conveyor belt. Derek Hill joined us. The actual service took ten minutes. There was a poignant incident. When the coffin started to slide, Piero, Angus's Italian servant, ran forward and placed some small token, which I could not see, on the coffin lid, retired to his seat and broke into heart-rending sobs. We were quickly ushered out, past the clergyman who shook hands, round a corner, through an arched passageway into the garden of rest, or whatever it is called. Looked at the wreaths. Those of the previous funerals already stacked within the cloister. A. said she must lunch with the family, Angus's brother Michael and his children. So Derek and I left together. We wanted to go out by the way we came in. The door under the arched passageway had been shut. We tried to open it, and saw through the cracks of the boards a coffin being wheeled on a bier. Retreated immediately and passed through the garden into the street. Derek and I lunched in Hampstead. Alone Derek is always charming and sympathetic. With people, and above all at parties, he is insufferable. I went to his house and he showed the small head of K. Clark which he is now painting for Murray's. Since he asked for my opinion, I said the nose was too hooked and the chin too defined. Also a portrait of Walter Buccleuch* in robes of the Thistle or Archers, with a plumed hat. Derek's likenesses sometimes fail with the mouth of his subjects. This is commonly the feature which portrait painters get wrong, I notice.

Wednesday, 12 December

Sachie [Sitwell], who read a short address at Angus's memorial service in St Peter's, Eaton Square, lunched alone with me at Brooks's afterwards. Full of gloomy forebodings. Influential City friends warn him that 'we' have only three months to clear out of England. Another tells him to hoard his cartridges, for there will be shooting within that time.

J.L.-M. is here referring to the national crisis which had arisen during the autumn. The Arab–Israeli war in October had led to an Arab oil embargo against the West; in the wake of this, industrial action by the National Union of Mineworkers, supported by the railwaymen and power station workers, created a fuel shortage which threatened to bring Britain to a halt.

Sunday, 16 December

Yesterday we lunched with Diana Westmorland. She was blazing with fury against the Trades Unions, and Mr Gormley† in particular, for

---

* Walter Montagu-Douglas-Scott, 8th Duke of Buccleuch and 10th Duke of Queensberry (1894–1973).

† Joe Gormley (1917–93); President of National Union of Mineworkers; cr. life peer, 1982.

saying over the air that he did not care a damn about the inconvenience he was causing the public, and he was going to have a jolly
good Christmas. She wanted to write him a letter. What should she
write? I said, 'The Dowager Countess of Westmorland presents her
compliments to Mr Gormley and begs to inform him that he is a shit.'
Her retort was, 'No. I will write, "Fuck off to Russia!"'

Wednesday, 19 December

Now I see in *The Times* that Hamish [St Clair Erskine]* has died after
a short illness. I suppose it was cirrhosis of the liver. The last time I
saw him was in the Droghedas' box at Covent Garden into which he
and his sister Mary [Dunn]† gatecrashed during an interval, somewhat to Joan's displeasure. He was then purple in the face. For years
I had not wanted to see him, and when he last stayed here he was
very boring with interminable stories of the 1930s and his archaic
juvenile jokes of our undergraduate days, for he never grew up and
his values remained those of his Edwardian father, the spendthrift
Lord Rosslyn. Yet if ever there was someone who began with every
silver spoon, except money – this he always got hold of through his
looks, charm and desirability – and frittered away his life, it was
Hamish Erskine. At Oxford he had the most enchanting looks – mischievous, twinkling eyes, slanting eyebrows. He was slight of build,
well dressed, gay as gay, always snobbish however, and terribly conscious of his nobility, which came solely from his father's side, not
his attractive mother's. The toast of the university, he was tossed from
one rich limousine to another. Somehow I don't think tossed from
bed to bed, for he was not very sexy. He loved being admired and
given expensive presents, which he casually left lying around and
lost. I still have one of these no doubt ill-gotten presents, the gold
wrist watch with initials engraved on the back which I wear now; I
hasten to add it was in part payment of money lent him and never

---

* Hon. James Alexander ('Hamish') St Clair Erskine (1909–73); yr s. of 5th Earl of
Rosslyn.
† Lady Mary St Clair Erskine (1912–93); m. 1933–44 & 1969 Sir Philip Dunn, 2nd
Bt (d. 1976).

returned to me. At Oxford he was everything I, then a simpleton, would have liked to be and now despise, namely a shallowly sophisticated, lithe of mind, smart society figure. For long I distantly loved him and was attracted by him. Then I grew out of him. He had natural intelligence which he never cultivated, though he had a smattering of erudition and would talk about books, music and art in an amusing superficial way. He had an affected, mincing, screwy little manner, dancing on the tips of his toes, smoking endless Balkan Sobranies and always boozing. Latterly he was completely superannuated and to the young must have seemed a primordial little Edwardian monkey, something left over from a past age, not to be taken seriously. Oh dear, the sadness! He who was envied and admired by hundreds will be utterly forgotten in ten years, as though he had never lived at all.

The present crisis is most upsetting. Having listened to Barber's[*] excellent broadcast I then heard Healey,[†] who had the mendacity to maintain that Barber's budget was aimed against the working man, whereas it merely taxed the rich man, not altogether a bad thing. The calculated lies of politicians! Then the simultaneous news of the Arabs shooting and killing over thirty innocent travellers in Rome airport, the three bombs in London planted by the IRA, the squabbles of the European Community meeting, everything is so atrocious and evil that it is a wonder we do not all go raving mad or commit suicide.

Little Hamish had his glorious hour, or year. He was incredibly brave during the war, escaped from prison camp, walked across Italy to rejoin the Allied troops, and won the Military Cross. Like Mummy's Jock Hume-Campbell[‡] he was the decadent aristocrat *par excellence*, easily adapting in a crisis to standards of living hitherto beyond his ken and, one would have supposed, wrongly, beyond his endurance. And he descended to taking the jobs of *dame de compagnie* to Daisy Fellowes

---

[*] Anthony Barber (1920–2005); Conservative politician, Chancellor of the Exchequer, 1970–4; cr life peer, 1974.

[†] Denis Healey (b. 1917); Labour politician, Shadow Chancellor 1970–4 and Chancellor of the Exchequer, 1974–9; cr. life peer, 1992.

[‡] Sir John Home-Purves-Hume-Campbell, 8th Bt (1879–1960); J.L.-M's godfather, and his mother's lover from about 1915 to 1930; born to affluence, he ended his life in penury in Newfoundland.

and Enid Kenmare.* Even these jobs he could not hold down, because he was incapable of rising before midday. Daisy told me once that Hamish's first duty was to blow out the spirit lamp of her tea kettle through a little silver trumpet at 5.30 p.m. He could not be depended upon even to fulfil this degrading function.

While still at Oxford Hamish was engaged to Nancy [Mitford]. She was very much in love with him – she was five years older – and he presumably not in love with her. I remember them now, dining with me in the George restaurant when we were undergraduates, Hamish drunk and indifferent, Nancy gazing at him with adoring eyes. The engagement petered out, and Nancy soon recovered, but not to the extent of not being contemptuous of Hamish ever after.

Thursday, 20 December

This morning I took my poor old dog, Fop, to the vet to have more teeth out and his anal troubles investigated while under the anaesthetic. I begged the vet, if he found he was beyond recovery, to let him go. I was quite calm. I never said goodbye, or patted him. I merely took off his lead. The vet, Riley, a nice man, took him in his arms. I just cast one quick glance at Fop's old grey head which was not looking at me. The vet said, 'I quite understand,' and left hurriedly. He said he would telephone. During the afternoon A. and I drove to Badminton to collect dead bracken. I thought that because the vet had not telephoned Fop had come through the operation. Late in the afternoon while I was out he rang. A. said to me, 'The vet had to let him go.' I followed her into the house and said, 'What I must do immediately is remove all the dog baskets to the attics,' and started to do this before taking off my heavy coat. While carrying his special basket from the library I burst into tears. A. was angelic,

---

* Enid Lindemann of Sydney NSW (d. 1973); m. 1st 1913 Roderick Cameron of New York (d. 1914), 2nd Gen. Hon. Frederick Cavendish (d. 1931), 3rd 1933 (as his 3rd wife) 1st Viscount Furness (d. 1940), 4th 1943 (as his 2nd wife) 6th Earl of Kenmare (who d. same year); South of France society figure, known as 'Lady Killmore' owing to the *canard* that she had murdered her husbands; mother of A.L.-M's friend Rory Cameron.

comforting and sensible. I recovered quickly, and now merely have the ache of sadness at losing the companion of twelve years, day and night. This house is cheerless without the two dogs, and their departure marks the end of an era, the heyday of Alderley with which they have been so intimately, so essentially associated. *Eheu!* you darling old friends.

1974

1974

The first weeks of 1974 were dominated by the national crisis. Faced with a fuel shortage and continuing industrial unrest, the Heath Government introduced emergency measures in the New Year, including a three-day industrial week. When the National Union of Mineworkers called a national strike in February, Heath called a snap election to decide 'who governs Britain' – which he narrowly lost. The belief of the L.-Ms and many of their friends that Britain was about to 'go communist' explains their unfortunate decision, at a time of plunging values, to sell Alderley Grange and most of their possessions and move to the confines of a maisonette in Bath.

Tuesday, 1 January

So ends one of the saddest years of my life, as far as the death of friends is concerned. Henry Yorke,[*] Hamish Erskine, Angus Menzies, Nancy Mitford, Joanie Harford, Ralph Jarvis, William Plomer, Bob Gathorne-Hardy[†] and Don Nicholas[‡] have gone. And, by no means least, beloved Chuff and Fop. Also I think the year has been even more infamous than the war years, because barbarities of a kind far less excusable than wartime barbarities have happened in endless succession, the assassination of perfectly innocent people at the hands of the Irish and the Palestinians. The morale of the British Mr Average has never been lower, his values more debased, his covetousness, greed and lack of self-respect more conspicuous.

---

[*] Novelist (1905–73), under the pseudonym of Henry Green.
[†] Hon. Robert Gathorne-Hardy (1902–73); 3rd s. of 3rd Earl of Cranbrook (and brother of Lady Anne to whom J.L.-M. was engaged in 1935); bibliophile, adviser on books to N.T.
[‡] Donald Nicholas; expert on the House of Stuart.

Last night before going to bed I had a blazing row with A., who insisted I was going to London next Monday instead of Tuesday, as I had previously told her, because I wanted to enjoy myself, whereas she knew perfectly well that the only reason for going was a dentist's appointment I have for 10 o'clock on Tuesday morning. I lost my temper, stamped, threw my slipper on the floor because I could not throw it at her, and cursed and swore. Anyway, why the hell shouldn't I want to enjoy myself? Slammed the door and went to bed without saying good-night. How infinitely foolish old people can be. This morning I went to her room, apologised profusely, and we embraced tenderly.

Sunday, 6 January

Yesterday we lunched with Eliza Wansbrough. Gavin Faringdon* was there. I have not seen him in a long while. He must have had a stroke because he shuffles slowly into the room, then stands immobile, as though unable to continue, or to sit. And his legs start shaking. He is rather pitiable. His mind is as sharp as ever, although he does not volunteer subjects of conversation. Those cat-like eyes are now benign. He almost purrs, and is gentle. Such a contrast with the old Gavin, his lithe, panther movements, his dangerous eyes, wit, and his forked cruelty. He was a most dangerous man, evil I think, and malevolent.

Eliza said after luncheon that she was incurably pessimistic about affairs. Indeed never have affairs been worse in my lifetime. In an unboastful way I want to record how often I have been right in foreseeing events. I foresaw the present confrontation between Government and anarchy, and wanted it to happen three years ago when the Conservatives got in. It would have been better then. Feebleness has been this country's undoing. No national service, the exaltation of godlessness, cynicism, the terrorism unchecked except by another form of lawful terrorism. I think it very possible that there may be fighting within four months. If Heath gives way to the Unions this time, the moderates who make up eighty per cent of the population

---

* Gavin Henderson, 2nd Baron Faringdon (1902–77); rich and raffish peer supporting the Labour Party.

will be in despair. The extremists will press their demands and have to be resisted with force by a super-leader.

Monday, 7 January

A. is shocked that Olive Lloyd-Baker,* that highly respectable, respected county lady, lately High Sheriff of Gloucestershire, and dressed soberly and becomingly, has suddenly transformed herself. She now has short, closely cropped grey hair like a man, and wears a man's jacket, trousers and tie, in fact Radclyffe Hall rig. I say that her inhibitions of a lifetime have been released after seventy-one years because she has overlapped the age of permissiveness. She was always a secret lesbian and has now thrown her cap over the windmill.

Saturday, 12 January

Paul Methuen's funeral at Corsham today. I attended a trustees' meeting at Ivy House, where the heir Captain Methuen† – very old and decrepit – lives, and the nephew John. The latter has a wild look in the eye and may be 'retarded', if not mad. My trusteeship unfortunately ends with Paul's death, although I still have to help clear things up. We were talking about the rare plants in the hothouses, suggesting that Kew might be consulted, or even presented with those they wanted. John Methuen remarked, 'You can leave that to me. I will consult the Bath Corporation Parks Supervisor for advice.' Those municipal philistines! And when we were making a date for the next meeting, George Howard,‡ whose wife Cecilia is dying of cancer, said, 'I will certainly come if I possibly can. But owing to Cecilia's illness you will understand if I am unable to.' At this John Methuen, his cousin, remarked in a jolly tone, 'I dare say our next family reunion will be at Castle Howard.'

---

* Owner of Hardwicke Hall near Gloucester (d. 1975); a 'spirited, tough, old-fashioned spinster' from 'a good old county family' (2 June 1975).
† Anthony Paul Methuen, 4th Baron Methuen (1891–1975); brother of Paul Methuen, 3rd Baron, and father of John, 5th Baron.
‡ George Howard of Castle Howard, York (1920–84); a trustee of the Corsham estate; m. 1949 Lady Cecilia FitzRoy; cr. life peer, 1980.

Saturday, 19 January

How extraordinary Charlotte Bonham Carter is. When after Paul Methuen's funeral we had tea with Diana Kendall* in the library at Corsham, there was Charlotte sitting in one of Paul's large Chippendale armchairs, holding a plate on to which Alvilde was piling cakes and sandwiches. She had missed the funeral and come for the tea. Unlike most of the guests who pecked at a cake and drank half a cup, she was tucking into a huge meal, saying she had not eaten since dinner the previous evening. I think she was quite unaware why she had come. She was about to motor herself in the dark and through the fog to Hampshire.

Friday, 25 January

Alvilde came into the library at six to tell me that the wireless announced the death of Jamesey Pope-Hennessy – killed most foully by three young men while sitting in his flat at eleven o'clock this morning. His young servant was out shopping, returned, was attacked in his turn and, badly wounded, rushed into the street, his hand cut to ribbons. The police station is opposite James's flat, a thing I have often wondered wryly about, I mean whether they were aware of the strange comings and goings. But this is a hideous tragedy. My first fears are about what may be disclosed. One man has been arrested, bleeding in a bus at Marble Arch. I think it must be a case of drug addicts, or something extremely sinister. Although I have not seen James for seven years, when he last stayed here in 1967 so disastrously, yet I always loved him, albeit I did not wish to see him again. I sent him a postcard from Italy in October to remind him of my existence and my affection. Lately he has been much in my thoughts because in 1942 and 1943 [the years for which J.L.-M. had been editing his diaries] I saw or spoke to him practically every day. We were inseparable. He was one of the most brilliant creatures I have known, but alas, he was a bad friend.

---

* Paul Methuen's devoted secretary.

Thursday, 31 January

I went up specially for Jamesey's Requiem Mass. It was strange to be attending this memorial to Jamesey, who I remember saying to me that we could never die. When it was over I stayed behind to avoid the usual crowd of gossiping friends at the church door. I lit a candle for James, then left. His brother John was still on the pavement, his face as swollen as though he had wept for a fortnight. Walking away I ran into Patrick Kinross, who complained that all the funerals and memorial services he had to attend were a great interruption to his writing.

Wednesday, 6 February

Dined with Seymour Camrose* and Joan Aly Khan† at a house in Hobart Place which I was not certain to be his or hers. The Michael Trees‡ present. Anne Tree told me she was the happiest person in the world, born rich and upper class, and married to the only man she ever wanted, a man who had a host of women at his feet. The man, Michael Tree, is a very nice, very brainy bumble-bee who sucks a pipe and is the best friend of David Somerset. No doubt he harbours hidden depths. Anne Tree said she regretted that, as children, she and [her sister] Elizabeth [Cavendish] were never allowed to learn about the Devonshire treasures for fear of their becoming 'swanky' with other children. The consequence was she lacked education in the arts, which she is now deeply interested in. The two girls were never given proper allowances for the same reason. Her father laboured under a lifelong regret that he had no regular profession. I told her I remembered him saying that he wished he could have been a dentist, which she confirmed was true.

These immediate days are perhaps politically the most critical of my lifetime. Much talk about the devastating situation, and Seymour thinks anything might happen overnight, like a Communist takeover.

---

* John Seymour Berry, 2nd Viscount Camrose (1909–94); newspaper magnate.
† Hon. Joan Yarde-Buller (1908–97), dau. of 3rd Baron Churston; m. 1986 2nd Viscount Camrose (having formerly been married to Loel Guinness and Prince Aly Khan).
‡ Michael Lambert Tree, painter (1921–99); m. 1949 Lady Anne Cavendish, dau. of 10th Duke of Devonshire.

Thursday, 7 February

I was formally admitted to the Society of Antiquaries. The ceremony involved being called before the President, a distinguished man with a beard, bowing to him, having my hand shaken and being told I was admitted, bowing and retiring to my seat amidst applause. Five of us were admitted. I believe the applause for me was a little louder than for the others, but I will not swear to it. While drinking tea before the ceremony I felt completely out of sympathy with the Fellows I found myself among. A lot of old fogies of the dreariest description. Why did I join this dank association?

Went to the Lucian Freud* exhibition. Only a few of his pictures are beautiful. Among these a small head of Jamesey [Pope-Hennessy], his hand to his chin. I remember this in his flat. I wish it were mine. The over-lifesize heads are revolting, namely Debo and Mary Devonshire.

Sunday, 10 February

William Rees-Mogg† telephoned this morning. We had a long conversation about the situation. I said I applauded the attitude of *The Times*. He asked what were the views of the people round here. I said the shop-keepers in Wotton were strongly against the Unions. I asked why, instead of holding an election,‡ Heath had not tried for a coalition government. He said Heath and Wilson would never work together. Then why not Whitelaw§ and Jenkins?¶ He thinks Heath may just get back. I asked how he would be any better off in this case. William said if he increased his majority he would have renewed authority; if he scraped through he would reach a compromise, face-saving solution to the miners' dispute.

---

* Artist (b. 1922).
† William Rees-Mogg (b. 1927); editor of *The Times*, 1967–81; cr. life peer, 1988.
‡ The general election had been announced on Thursday 7 February, to take place on the 28th.
§ William Whitelaw (1918–99); Conservative centrist politician, then Secretary of State for Employment; cr. Viscount, 1983.
¶ Roy Harris Jenkins (1920–2003); Labour centrist politician (later co-founder and leader of Social Democrat Party); Deputy Party Leader, 1970–2 (resigning over the party's hostility to British membership of European Economic Community); m. 1945 Jennifer Morris (b. 1921; DBE 1985; Chairman of N.T., 1986–90).

If Wilson scraped through he would be bound to press for a coalition, because no foreign power would advance him the money we have got to get. This is encouraging. I said I thought this crisis as serious as in 1939, because the enemy we were fighting was a hidden enemy.

Sunday, 17 February

Last night we dined at Westwood Manor with the Denys Suttons.[*] The Tony Powells and Roger Manners[†] the other guests. Lord Roger is a stockbroker. He says the City has come to a standstill. It expects a complete economic collapse any day, when we shall be in the same condition as Germany in 1923. We must expect chaos, the £ to be worth 1 penny, if we are lucky, and the oil sheiks buying up our industries. A jolly prospect. All agreed that no single politician dared tell the people the truth about the ghastly situation. The English will not face up to a crisis such as they have never experienced since 1066.

Wednesday, 27 February

Looking at a photograph of some anonymous mid-Victorian gent with long hair, bushy mutton-chops and fuzz around his inscrutable patriarchal chin, I can for the first time in my life envisage him as a human being, instead of a stuffed, insalubrious dummy, as heretofore. Because so many people today look like this, all facial hair in the wrong places. In the same way, two years ago, one could see a Donatello youth, a Bronzino youth, in the tube train every day. Unfortunately that style of haircut is already obsolete. Such a pity. The tendency today is to readopt the grizzly aspect and do away with the Florentine Renaissance long hair devoid of beard and side whiskers.

Friday, 1 March

We are finished. We may as well pack up. We have left it too late. We were warned we had three weeks to clear out of England. That was

---

[*] Art historian and dilettante (1917–91); editor of *Apollo*, 1962–87.
[†] Lord Roger Manners (b. 1925); yr s. of 9th Duke of Rutland.

three weeks ago. Labour has got in. The consequence is a victory for the Unions who are the dictators of the Labour Party. I see nothing but total disaster ahead.

We have made a bid for a maisonette in Lansdown Cresent in Bath. It consists of ground floor and basement floor, and is hardly big enough. The ground floor however has one huge library which was made for Beckford,* and one room behind which A. will have as a bedroom. Below will be my bedroom, looking into a north court, cellar-like. When we move we shall have to get rid of seven-eighths of our beloved possessions.

Monday, 4 March

Walked with Midi through the fields and Foxholes Wood. She said laughingly that all her life she had been an outsider. In the Twenties she did not belong to the Twenties set; she was not accepted by her husband's sporting friends, nor by intellectuals as one of them; she was not accepted by county people, as owing to her being a Socialist and not a Tory, they regarded her as a bit of a traitor to her class. I said I had always considered myself an outsider too.

Monday, 18 March

I motored to Sufton Court near Mordiford in Herefordshire, arriving at 2.45. This house has been offered to the Trust and those who have seen it were undecided whether we ought to take it, and asked for my opinion. For me the conundrum resembled several I encountered in the old days. I fear the house is not important enough, although the exterior is fairly decent and the surroundings overlooking the confluence of the Lugg and Wye and the meadows towards Hereford, of which only a cluster of houses and spires and the cathedral tower are delightfully visible, have great merit. The most interesting thing about Sufton is Repton's original Red Book with the water-colour slides of what existed and what he intended doing. Today Repton's improvements

---

* William Beckford (1760–1844); writer, traveller, builder and collector, who lived in two houses in Lansdown Crescent during his later years.

can be detected, although a good deal smudged. The owner, Major Hereford, is a nice old bumble-bee, although younger than me. His deference to his wife, formerly headmistress of the school which occupied the house during the war, loquacious and didactical, saddened me. 'My wife who has such knowledge, such taste, such wisdom, etc.' There is a son by a former marriage, and a grandson. The Herefords have owned Sufton since the thirteenth century in unbroken descent, with a single kink through the female line. A wonderful territorial name and connection. Sad too that on his father's death, while this one was serving overseas, the trustees sold all the furniture. The remains are what the French would call *quelconque*, upholstered armchairs in jazzy plush and beaten Benares ware in evidence.

Talking to these people made me realise that, whereas among my intellectual superiors I am a rather stupid person, among ordinary minds I am fairly (only fairly) bright. The impercipience of the Herefords going on and on, without sensing the irrelevance of their chatter, was amazing. I was in a considerable hurry to get to tea with the old Poës* at Leominster. With great kindness Major Hereford insisted on putting me on the route. He drove ahead in his car at a snail's pace, stopping every five minutes to get out and show me some famous landmark. When he finally reached the Leominster road he descended from his car once again, clinging to my open window so that the knuckles of his fingers went white. Nevertheless I had an affection for the major.

I reached the Poës' house late, at five. They were sitting like Buddhas with the tea on a trolley in front of them, impatiently waiting. I had telephoned this morning asking if they would care to see me. Answer in the affirmative. I thought I would bring pleasure into their old lives (Frida is a little older than Mama [1884–1962] would have been). I don't think I did a bit. First of all they gave me a message to telephone *The Times* urgently. This was the editor asking me to allow them to cut out of my letter a reference to the Pope's attitude to birth control as 'moronic and downright wicked'. Moronic I agreed was a bit strong. They would not have either adjective. I then

---

* Frida Lees (a first cousin of J.L.-M's father, at whose home in Derbyshire J.L.-M's parents had met in 1904); m. 1913 Colonel John Hugh Lovett Poë DSO.

said I was miles from home, had not a copy of my letter on me, and suggested they scrap it altogether. But no, the editor wanted to print it. So I capitulated. Returned to the Poës. Frida with quivering hands started pouring tea and slopping it over the silver tray. So I asked brightly if she would like me to pour for her. She threw me a look like a dagger-thrust. Jack said crossly, 'You know Frida has poured out tea since long before you were born.' I accepted the reproof. Then the telephone beside Frida rang. I thought, I am damned if I am going to interfere again. Awkwardly the poor old thing tried to reach the receiver. Jack said, 'Aren't you going to help Frida?' So I picked it up and answered it for her. A voice said, 'This is Dorothea speaking. Who are you?' 'Oh, I'm just a cousin,' I said, and handed the thing to Frida. I heard Frida say, 'Dorothea, I'm afraid I can't speak to you now. We have an interruption. But when the six o'clock news is over, *if we are allowed to watch it*, I will ring you back.' For the next half-hour I talked brightly, senselessly, and left them. Not a great success I fear.

Thursday, 28 March

Yesterday I received a letter from Fr Michael Napier of The Oratory, strongly deprecating my *Times* letter, and pointing out at some length that overpopulation is no problem, and underpopulation in many countries is. His letter is so ill-judged, so blinkered and stupid that it has merely confirmed the views I expressed that the Catholic Church is lamentably at fault in its fatuous anti-contraception attitude. He ends by saying that doubtless I intend to resign from The Oratory Arts Committee, and coldly thanks me for my past services!

Healey's budget has come and gone. It penalises the rich. This ex-Communist announced his intention of penalising them further. His motives are wholly political. They do nothing to save the economy, nothing to boost industry. Everything this new government has done and said is intended to placate the Trades Unions. My worst fears are being realised. The Unions brought down the Tory government. Now they are cock-a-hoop. The Unions are dominated by Communists, whereas there is not a single Communist MP today.

Thursday, 4 April

Norah Smallwood has just telephoned that they want to publish my [1942–3] diaries. Apparently Ian Parsons* is mad about them, and read out passages to the weekly board meeting. However, thinks that they should be a little pruned. I agree that much trivia can come out, so long as someone else does the pruning and I am allowed to approve. But I don't want the spice taken out. The publishers are frightened of libel always.

Friday, 5 April

This morning Simon† telephoned that Haines had had a further stroke and was in Evesham Hospital. A. with her usual sense and rapid decision said we must go at once. While I waited in the familiar cottage hospital lounge I recalled those dismal visits to Mama who was here before her death in 1962. The moment I saw Haines in the men's ward I knew there was no hope for him. Very clean and pink he was, half sitting up in bed, wearing coarse striped linen pyjamas. He kept picking with his hands under the sheets, always a bad sign. Eyes not glazed, but unseeing and bloodshot, tears welling and nose running. I think he knew who I was, but am not sure. Nothing I said registered. He rambled incomprehensibly. I could barely hear what he was saying, but I think it was in praise of the nurses. I was deeply saddened to watch beside the bed of this old man who has all my life been a pillar of our family well-being. It was always Haines who was sent for in an emergency, always Haines who solved every crisis, burst pipes, electric light fuses, car not starting, Haines who knew where my mother had put her rings for safety, Haines to whom we children when in disgrace turned for comfort and advice. The first person on return for the school holidays we dashed to see was Haines.

---

* Managing Director of Chatto & Windus (d. 1981).
† J.L-M's nephew Simon Lees-Milne (b. 1939), o.c. of his brother Richard ('Dick') and Elaine *née* Brigstocke; m. 1st 1962–74 Jane Alford, 2nd 1976 Patricia Derrick.

Tuesday, 9 April

David Somerset was told by Lord Rothschild,* who is still the head of the Government Think Tank, that undoubtedly this government is determined to finish off the capitalists. David met Lord Balogh† and asked him why he did not work for the economy of his native Hungary, which was Communist, and live there instead of in England. Balogh replied that he was not a Communist and did not wish to live in a Communist state. But that is precisely what he is reducing England to.

Saturday, 13 April

Alex Moulton‡ and I were to have started on our tour last Tuesday, but owing to Haines's funeral I had to postpone it for one day. Alex called for me in his 1973 Rolls, an exquisite travelling carriage which glides whether cruising at 40 m.p.h. or darting at 90 m.p.h. We stayed two nights at Portmeirion [Gwynedd], a delightful Italian Baroque fantasy village until you look at the buildings, which are shoddy and will not endure. I was touched to be handed a note from Clough Williams-Ellis§ asking me to be sure and call on him. Alex and I went on Thursday evening at six. The old man – he is ninety-one – met us at the door of Brondanw and took us round the garden, which is laid out on Hidcote lines, in compartments. This evidently the fashion of that generation, Sissinghurst another example. He knows nothing about plants and shrubs. Says he is a frame-maker, which is true. Lady W.-E. came forth to greet us. We sat and talked for an hour and a half. He is a marvel. Dressed in the usual fancy dress, of breeches and yellow stockings, and odd folded-over blue tie. In full possession of every faculty, only slightly deaf with an aid. He stood showing me plans of various buildings of his

---

* Victor, 3rd Baron Rothschild (1910–90); banker, zoologist and government adviser.
† Thomas Balogh (1905–85); political economist and adviser to Harold Wilson; cr. life peer, 1968.
‡ Dr Alexander Moulton (b. 1920) of The Hall, Bradford-on-Avon, Wiltshire; engineer, inventor of the Moulton bicycle and motor-car suspension; friend of J.L.-M. since 1944.
§ Sir Clough Williams-Ellis (1883–1978); architect and architectural conservationist; m. 5 Amabel St Loe Strachey.

which he complains are being demolished, houses he built before the first war. He is outliving his own creations, which depresses him. Said Lutyens had a great influence upon him. No one taught him. Said he was an amateur. This is too obvious for his architecture bears it out. It is flimsy stuff. What a charmer, so friendly and forthcoming. 'You and I', he says, 'share the same sympathies and antipathies.' She is a beautiful lady, quick, perceptive and very clever. Also very left-wing. Her eyes are blank. They do not appear. She misses nothing so they must be there, but they seem to be blank orbs, steely, expressionless.

Tuesday, 23 April

Norah [Smallwood] has given her verdict. They do not want the emasculated, rewritten Stuart book.* She asked if I was prepared to have another go at it. I said No, not on any account. She asked if it might not be better after all to go over the original book, which had embraced all the exiled Stuarts. I told her that it was impossible. I had destroyed it in cutting it up for the second version. Then she said how much Chatto's were looking forward to publishing the diaries, wondering what title we should give them, and suggesting that certain passages should be omitted, such as those likely to give offence to the Trevelyan family which includes one of their partners. I said, 'Norah, I had planned that a serious book of mine should appear next. I have already published an autobiography, and a novel which has not been a success, and which people thought, wrongly, was also autobiographical. I will not now have my diaries published unless I can get the Stuart book or some other published in between.' She looked astonished and we sat in embarrassed silence. A. says I am cutting off my nose to spite my face. This may be true, but it is how I feel. I just cannot reconcile myself to the fact that I can no longer 'write', and have to fall back on old material — rubbish like the diaries, written thirty years ago.

---

* As a biography of Bonnie Prince Charlie had recently appeared, J.L.-M. had been persuaded to rewrite his history of the exiled Stuarts as 'the Countess and the Cardinal', concentrating on Prince Charlie's wife, the Countess of Albany, and his brother, the Cardinal Duke of York.

Friday, 3 May

On Tuesday David Pryce-Jones[*] came to see me. He telephoned a few days before to ask. I said Yes, in spite of the fact that Debo had warned me that his reason might be to pump me about Bobo[†] whose life he wants to write. Debo, Pam and Diana are dead against it. Decca[‡] whose friend he is has urged him to do it. I expected to be irritated by an intrusive manner. Not at all. He could not have been more understanding, more charming. However I began straight away by saying I surmised he had come to talk about Bobo, that the three sisters were among my oldest friends, and therefore I could not discuss this subject. He looked crestfallen, but the ice having been broken we discussed biography generally. At the end he begged me to write to Debo and point out that if he did not undertake the project, somebody else would, somebody very hostile, which he was not. How anyone could want to write about Bobo in the first place beats me.

At last the maisonette of 19 Lansdown Crescent is ours. We have signed cheques for £19,000 each and sent them off. Neither of us wants to go to the place in the least. And the irony is that this evening I saw in Bath a small house for sale in Darlington Place which I know would suit A. down to the ground. I am overcome with guilt about Lansdown Crescent for it is my selfishness which has pushed her into this project. Beckford's library is what got me.

Thursday, 9 May

On Tuesday went to London for the day to see David Higham who lunched with me. The long and short is, he persuaded me that I was foolish to withhold the diaries from Chatto's, and he felt sure some publisher would take the Stuarts.

---

[*] Writer (b. 1937); son of J.L.-M's Eton contemporary Alan Pryce-Jones (1908–2000; editor of *Times Literary Supplement*, 1948–59).

[†] Hon. Unity Mitford (1914–48); fourth of the Mitford sisters, who became enamoured of Hitler and shot herself in Munich when Great Britain declared war on Germany in 1939.

[‡] Hon. Jessica Mitford (1917–96); m. 1st Esmond Romilly, 2nd 1943 Robert Treuhaft; satirical writer living in USA; the 'Communist' Mitford sister.

To my pleasure I had a letter from Colin McMordie at Oriel asking if he might come and see me. Arranged for him to dine with me last night as A. was in London. He is twenty-four, bright, very intelligent, rather affected, queer I should guess, sympathetic and very pretty. I had to restrain myself from patting him, and was discreet and avuncular. I try so hard to be natural with the young. Anyway, it is flattering when they ask to come forty miles for the pleasure of one's company and advice. He talked about his thesis and his future when he leaves Oxford. He was very clean and tidy, wearing a blue pullover with silk scarf and bell-bottom trousers, absurdly like skirts, and not becoming. The tightness of modern trousers round the knees causes creases.

Thursday, 23 May

A. and I went to Bath. No. 19 Lansdown Crescent maisonette is now ours. We came away pleased, and think we can make it quite cosy. Even though it was raining heavily today the semi-basement room was light and cheerful.

Sunday, 26 May

We lunched with Ann Fleming[*] at Sevenhampton. A pastichy sort of house, nearly all new in correct Georgian or Regency taste. What's strikingly beautiful is the contour of park gently sweeping down to a lake, with two urns well placed against the trees. Robert Kee[†] was there, an intelligent, civilised man whom I met on the only occasion I stayed at Ham Spray with the Partridges.[‡] This was when he was married to Janetta. Also present the Stephen Spenders.[§] He has lost the last vestige

---

[*] Ann Charteris (1913–81); m. 1st 1932–44 3rd Baron O'Neill (brother of Midi Gascoigne), 2nd 1945–52 2nd Viscount Rothermere, 3rd 1952 Ian Fleming (1907–64; creator of James Bond).
[†] Robert Kee (b. 1919); writer and broadcaster; m. 1st 1948 Janetta Woolley, 2nd 1960 Cynthia Judah, 3rd 1990 Hon. Catherine Mary Trevelyan.
[‡] Frances Marshall (1900–2004); painter and diarist, survivor of Bloomsbury Group; m. 1933 Ralph Partridge (d. 1960); they had lived at Ham Spray, Wiltshire, formerly the home of Lytton Strachey and Dora Carrington.
[§] (Sir) Stephen Spender (1909–95); poet and critic; m. 1941 Natasha Litvin.

of good looks. At Oxford he was a radiantly beautiful seraph with a shock of golden hair. Now he is a collapsed pudding, bluff, untidy, badly dressed, square in figure and deportment, reminding me of Ralph Vaughan Williams* in old age. We talked of the Mitfords and he referred to Jessica as a Communist bitch. I should have said to him, 'You were a Communist dog once.' We all agreed that it was rare for young people to know what they wanted to be when they left university. Stephen said, 'I always knew from my earliest boyhood that I wanted to be a poet.'

Tuesday, 28 May

Charlotte Bonham Carter asked us to dinner before we went to the Byron party given by Roy Strong at the V. & A. There were 6 people when we arrived at eight, and 20 by nine, eating in two rooms, balancing plates on knees. Filthy food. I sat next to Cynthia Gladwyn, who told me how distressed Nancy had been when she discovered that Hamish, to whom she was engaged, was 'what he was'. Charlotte a gallant old thing, organising and drilling this huge party. Apparently she gives about one a week, usually on Mondays. The Mondi Howards† there, and we shook hands. Then she hugged me and said, 'How can you be so formal?' The truth is I had forgotten I once knew Cécile so well. She reminded me of walks in Hyde Park when 'you were the most handsome man I had ever known, I was thrilled by you', and I had not the faintest idea at the time. Then the Byron party. A magnificently arranged exhibition, one compartment a supposed reproduction of Byron's room in the Palazzo Mocenigo, Venice – you look into it and it is dark save for a few taper candles, filled with cats, dogs, books on the floor, walking sticks, etc., just as the poet might have had it.

We have definitely decided to sell this house. The last straw was to be told by the nice woman who puts her cows in our paddock that the Müllers told her, and the man who does the mowing, that they intend to leave in September. So we have written to the agent who

---

* Composer (1872–1958), who in 1944 had arranged with J.L.-M. to donate his family estate in Surrey to the N.T.
† Hon. Edmund ('Mondi') Howard (1909–2005); yr s. of 1st Baron Howard of Penrith; diplomatist; m. 1936 Cécile Geoffroy-Dechaume.

has been badgering us for months, to say we will definitely sell. Feeling heartbroken.

Friday, 31 May

We went this afternoon to Glanusk [Park, Breconshire] to lunch and tea with Peggy De L'Isle.* It was fun to be eating off silver with the Bailey crest, the same as my forks and spoons. Saw the portrait of Sir Joseph painted about 1830, still youngish, with firm little mouth, and his pretty second wife with their child, my great-aunt Spearman. Also bust of Sir Joseph in the private chapel where all the Baileys are buried. Bust of him taken later in life. He is ugly in the mouth and jowl; strong resemblance to photographs of my grandfather whose lower face is similarly simian. Not an engaging countenance. He must have been immensely rich and besides building Glanusk in 1828 owned a dozen other seats. He also collected pictures, one Velázquez at least, which Toby Glanusk sold during the war for nothing. I also noticed several Charles II and James II mugs, like the tankard I possess, with heavy Baroque chasing, which I have been told was put on by the Baileys in Victorian times. Peggy De L'Isle very friendly indeed, bluff and benevolent like Dreda Tryon† and Betty Hussey.‡ Her daughter Shân Legge-Bourke§ turned up for tea, a pretty girl with golden hair and fair skin. We had tea in the nursery. Shân's child of nine was the centre of attention. To it we had to address our conversation. At its puny jokes we laughed. At its boastful remarks we marvelled. Adult conversation ceased entirely. I cannot believe this is the right way to treat children. Had we been in France this child,

---

* Margaret Shoubridge; m. 1st (as his 2nd wife) J.L.-M's cousin Wilfred ('Toby') Bailey, 3rd Baron Glanusk (1891–1948), 3rd 1966 (as his 2nd wife) William Sidney, 1st Viscount De L'Isle VC (1909–91; Eton contemporary of J.L.-M. and Governor-General of Australia, 1961–5); hunting personality and friend of 10th Duke of Beaufort.
† Etheldreda Burrell; m. 1939 2nd Baron Tryon (he d. 1976).
‡ Elizabeth Kerr-Smiley (d. 2006); m. 1936 Christopher Hussey (d. 1970), architectural historian and sometime editor of *Country Life*; she lived at Scotney Castle, Kent.
§ Hon. Shân Bailey (b. 1943); Lady-in-Waiting to HRH Princess Anne; m. 1964 W.H.N. Legge-Bourke.

if present at all, would be seen and not heard, and certainly not addressed. It would remain inconspicuously in the background, demure and unnoticed and, if looked at, it would curtsey.

Monday, 10 June

We lunched on Saturday with the Downers* at Oare [House, Wiltshire]. I had a long talk with Alec. He is an intimate friend of Heath (in so far as anyone can be intimate). Said Heath was 100 per cent good, whereas Wilson was a man of no convictions, though a skilled parliamentarian. Alec sees no ray of hope for this country which is rapidly on the Marxist slopes to perdition. When he told me that Lord Carrington was staying with him next week, I begged him to give him a message that we Conservative voters in the country are desperately frustrated that our leaders are too timorous, and that the time has come when the Conservatives must no longer be afraid of offending the susceptibilities of the Left.

Today we had the Rupert Loewensteins[†] and Denys Suttons to lunch. Whereas Downer is a Tory of old-fashioned integrity and honour, these two are of the tough, unscrupulous sort. Both very clever men, they said that the Conservative shadow government ought to bribe the Liberal MPs, that every man had his price.[‡] Rupert, a merchant banker, advises against having any stocks and shares, only cash.[§] All very fine; but if everyone had cash what would happen to the economy? Denys says – watch the art market. When the bottom falls out of that, you may be sure the end has come. But how does one recognise the bottom's impending dissolution?

---

[*] Sir Alexander Downer (1910–81); Australian politician and diplomatist, High Commissioner to London, 1964–72; m. 1947 Mary, dau. of Sir James Gosse. (The Gosses and the Downers were leading families in South Australia where A.L.-M's father had been Governor during the 1920s.)

[†] Prince Rupert zu Loewenstein (b. 1930), financial adviser, of Biddestone Manor, Gloucestershire; m. 1957 Josephine Lowry-Corry.

[‡] Heath had already tried to bribe the Liberals with a coalition offer in March, without success; in any case, he would not have had a parliamentary majority even with all the Liberal votes.

[§] Stocks and shares were to stage a tremendous rally early in 1975.

Monday, 17 June

We stayed at Parkside for the Garter Ceremony this afternoon at St George's Chapel. We were given front seats in the nave and were within touching distance of the procession. The beauty of it! The Queen looking radiant because her horse won a French race yesterday. Prince of Wales smashing. Garrett [Drogheda] of course the most elegant of the Garter Knights. Opposite me Shân Legge-Bourke, wearing a turban and pretty dress. Everyone else a frump except A., very smart in white dress with little black spots and black sequin hat. Derry in a mustard suit, all wrong. What a moving ceremony. The prayers appropriate, being exhortations to withstand evil and have courage – much needed in view of the House of Commons being bombed this morning by those bloody IRA.

After the ceremony we returned to Parkside for a cup of tea on the lawn. Sir Gerald Templar* told Garrett while they were robing that the revolution would undoubtedly come before twelve months had elapsed. Everyone is abysmally depressed.

Friday, 21 June

This morning I endeavoured to get a Bath number for three-quarters of an hour. Three times I rang the exchange, three times the supervisor. Finally I was driven so mad with rage that I shouted abuse down the mouthpiece and smashed the telephone to smithereens on the hearthstone. Pieces of it flew across the room. Instead of feeling ashamed I felt greatly relieved. I only wish the telephonist who had been so obstructive and impertinent to me had been the hearthstone.

Sunday, 30 June

Loelia Lindsay, with whom we stayed at Send this weekend, told me she had sold most of the Westminster jewellery and deposited the proceeds in a Swiss bank – 'in case', as she put it. How many wise people have not taken similar precautions?

---

* Field Marshal (1898–1979); Gold Stick from 1963.

Wednesday, 3 July

June and Jeremy Hutchinson gave a musical party in their divine house in Abercorn Place. Christopher Osborn[*] played Schubert, correctly without intense feeling; then Menuhin, accompanied by his son Jeremy, played Beethoven. This son is attractive and gifted; Menuhin's other son is plain and has no apparent gifts. During the performance the latter had to leave the room, ostensibly overcome by the heat (it was cold), and during supper spoke to no one. Poor boy, I felt sorry for him and understood his predicament, which no one else did.

I was placed next to Rhoda Birley[†] and Diana Westmorland at the end of a long narrow table for thirty. Mr Heath sat exactly opposite me. I was unable to have one word with him, the noise was terrific, but I watched him like a lynx. When he meets you, greets you, he does it with cumbersome affability; that is the end of the matter. June introduced me. He shook my hand warmly (his is podgy), smiled and said, 'Of course, yes.' He has no social graces whatever. For this I like him. He is not faintly interested in women, probably not in men either. He talked across June with Yehudi Menuhin about musical scholarships. Has no small talk, and when at the end of supper June left and made Christopher's little Burmese friend sit next to Heath, he did not address a single word to her, and went on talking with Yehudi. The poor child could not bear the honour beyond five minutes and discreetly left. Mr Heath seemed not to notice her departure. June then came up to me, gave me a great shove in the back, and said, 'Now's your chance. Ask the leader all the questions you want to put to him.' And to Heath, 'Jim's a great supporter. He's madly right-wing, and really supports Enoch,'[‡] at which Heath gave a wry smile and turned away. Left his place in fact. No wonder, perhaps.

---

[*] Concert pianist; son of June Hutchinson by her 1st marriage.

[†] Rhoda Pike; m. 1921 Sir Oswald Birley, portrait painter (1880–1952).

[‡] J. Enoch Powell (1912–98); writer and politician, fiery opponent of Commonwealth immigration and British membership of EEC; sacked by Heath from shadow cabinet after his 'Rivers of Blood' speech, 1969, and avenged himself in 1974 by advising his supporters to vote Labour; Ulster Unionist MP for South Down, 1974–92.

Monday, 8 July

A. was in London today. The evening was so still and beautiful that, as I wandered round the garden, inhaling the smell of rose petals in the golden light, I wept at the prospect of parting with this place. I could not bring myself to look at the advert in the *Sunday Times* yesterday. I feel positively sick with sadness. Then A. returned and was so full of orders, enquiries, bustle and fidgets that I longed to get away from her, and be alone with my melancholy.

Tuesday, 9 July

Nigel Nicolson lunched with me at Brooks's. He has only received four really rude letters from strangers about *Portrait of a Marriage*. The book has sold 100,000 copies in the USA already. He has received dozens of letters, mostly from American lonely hearts, asking for his guidance as though he were a marriage advisory bureau. He is now editing all Virginia Woolf's letters which will take six volumes. He is to spend two months in the year on each. He works with a fine discipline, and one American woman scholar to help him. V.W. never dated any letters; always headed them Thursday or Monday, without giving the month or year. He explains some of the difficulties he encounters. For example, V.W. wrote an exemplary letter declining the offer of marriage from a friend called Sydney Waterlow,* phrased with impeccable tact, kindness, understanding and firmness. It was lent Nigel by Waterlow's son. The same day V.W. wrote to Lytton Strachey: 'Sydney Waterlow has just left. I detest him. He entered the room bringing with him a smell of stale semen.' Now how can Nigel quote this one? She makes several unkind references to Raymond [Mortimer], saying he is a hopeless character, like a kitten playing eternally with a skein of wool.

I told Nigel about my diaries and he gave some advice. Don't put in the day of the week and do put in square brackets the surname of a person whom you refer to a second time by his christian name. Don't print anything unkind about a living person, and beware of wounding relations, etc.

---

* Sir Sydney Waterlow (1878–1944); writer and diplomatist; British Minister to Athens, 1933–40.

James [Pope-Hennessy]'s case is reported in today's *Times*. The disclosures are horrifying. He was choked to death by a hairnet down his poor throat. James, who was in his way highly fastidious and extremely nervous; James, young and attractive and fascinating, referred to by the thugs as 'the old bloke'. Nigel, who asked to see the account, turned away with tears in his eyes. 'Awful, just awful,' he said.

Thursday, 11 July

Debo who stayed last night said that the two saddest events in her life were the selling of Swinbrook [House, Oxfordshire] when she was fifteen, and the elopement of Decca with her first, Communist husband. Strange, when one reflects that she lost two or three babies soon after birth, lost Nancy, her mother, brother Tom and others.

Jeremy Fry who dined said that leaving Widcombe [Manor] was ghastly, but the relief of being free from the burden of the house was now immense. Thought in a year's time he might start minding again dreadfully. He said he could never let a house of his because it would be a defilement. He invests his houses with human attributes. I like this. He says his business is all but ruined by 'the situation', and all the money he got for Widcombe has gone to pay the bank for his business deficits. A year ago his business was flourishing. When I said goodbye to him beside his car on the drive he gave me a warm kiss on the mouth. Debo found him fascinating. She and he talked about Snowdon and Princess Margaret. P.M. told a friend the other day that she so hates her husband now she can hardly bear to be in the same room as him.

Sunday, 14 July

Alfred and Clementine Beit stayed this weekend. She told me about their recent ordeal. The two of them were listening to the gramophone together after dinner at Russborough [Co. Wicklow]. Suddenly the door burst open and three men, without masks but with revolvers, entered. They immediately pinioned the Beits and tied their arms behind their backs, and their feet to their arms very tight so that it hurt. Then made them lie face downwards on the floor. One man stayed with them as a guard with his revolver pointed at their heads. The other two fetched the staff of six, brought them into the same room as the Beits and tied them, not so tightly, and laid them on the floor. It was then that Alfred turned up his head and was hit so that he bled profusely. Clem thought he was injured worse than he actually was. When Clem stretched out a hand to hold that of the cook to comfort her she was sternly ordered to take it away. Abuse was shouted at them. Clem was carried off by one man, held in front of him, half shoved half carried – very painful. As she passed down a passage she saw the back of a woman in a blue and white, neat tailored suit, with a head of black hair. The man piloted Clementine down some stone steps to the basement, saying, 'This is where you belong, you capitalist pig.' Clem warned him that the steps were uneven, and he might fall with her. He cursed her and told her to shut up. He threw her, bound, face down on a stone floor and left her. She waited seemingly for ages, then heard movements upstairs and voices. Didn't know whether it was the gang or the household, so remained quiet. Finally James the footman discovered her, and on releasing her burst into tears and embraced her. The others thought she had been abducted. The little housemaid had managed to untie her bonds and release the others upstairs. Alfred in a great state, thinking that Clem had been taken away, was at the telephone when Clem came into the room. His reaction was to say to her, 'Where the hell have you been?'

After the stolen pictures had been recovered and Rose Dugdale[*] caught the Russborough household were taken to the farmhouse one by one to identify things. Immediately Clementine recognised the blue and white suit and the black wig worn by the woman in the passage. She undoubtedly was Dugdale. Dugdale's mother was my harmless friend Carol (erstwhile Timmins).

Friday, 19 July

I hate the people who come to look at this house. I regard them as desecrators. One lot complained that the house was no larger than their own in Solihull. I was inclined to retort, 'Then why not stay in

---

[*] Dr Rose Dugdale; radical civil rights leader with IRA sympathies; she received a prison sentence of 18 years (of which she served 9) for her involvement in this and other episodes.

Solihull?' Another said the drive was not long enough. I felt like answering, 'But you can easily extend it by making it twist and turn round the paddock.'

We went on Wednesday night to the Gala at Covent Garden to celebrate Garrett [Drogheda]'s retirement from the chairmanship after seventeen years. It consisted of snippets from opera and ballet, which are always tiresome. Yet I was impressed by the dancers. Thought Anthony Dowell* a most beautiful creature, his dancing the perfection of discipline, his compact drawing-board figure like an ephebe's on a Greek amphora. Antoinette Sibley† the quintessence of delicacy and desirability. A perfect pair. Then Nureyev‡ and Margot Fonteyn§ danced together. Nureyev is already beefy and has lost the gloss of youth. Yet I have seldom seen a head carried more proudly. Fonteyn is far past dancing at fifty-four. Yet what poise and confidence in her movements, and how winning her manner. When the performance was over a large sheet descended upon the stage outlining and magnifying the familiar slender figure of Garrett. He was introduced by Jennie Lee¶ in gold spangles who made a long and tedious speech in what sounded like Esperanto. Then Garrett spoke. He was not the least sentimental, but the perfect paradigm of patrician ease. Every word was audible, and to the point. He was his usual mischievous self; quite cheeky to the Queen, telling her that now she had found the way he hoped she might make a habit of patronising the opera, yet respectful at the same time.

We went to a champagne party in the crush bar. Agony. I could not hear one word. Could not bear to go on to the buffet supper on the stage. Left A. with the Berkeleys and escaped to my car. Got it out of its parking place and started off, but was stuck in a jam with Garden lorries in front of and behind me. The hold-up was caused by the police

---

* (Sir) Anthony Dowell (b. 1943); English dancer; Director of Royal Ballet, 1986–2001.
† Prima Ballerina at Royal Ballet (b. 1939).
‡ Rudolf Nureyev (1938–93); outstanding Russian dancer who defected to Great Britain in 1961.
§ Dame Margot Fonteyn (née Peggy Hookham; 1919–91); doyenne of English ballerinas.
¶ Labour politician (1904–88); Minister for the Arts, 1964–70; m. 1934 Aneurin Bevan; cr. life peer, 1970.

stopping all traffic until the Queen had left. I had one and a half hours' wait. Could neither advance nor leave to return to the supper party. Served me right, I suppose. I talked to the porters and lorry drivers. They were furious about the poor Queen. 'It is always the same whenever *she* comes here. Why can't *she* stay away?', etc. So I said, 'I don't suppose she wanted to come any more than you would. She has come out of duty, because the performance has been organised for charity. And what's more she has been working all today.' I knew this, because Lennox in the interval told me he received his accolade this morning with the other award winners. 'Anyway'— I said — 'if you had a President, just the same thing would happen.' 'All right, squire,' they said. I am not sure how derogatory this term was meant to be. Before the queue could move, one of the men brought me a tin mug of disgusting tea with, 'Here you are, chum.' They really are nice, but so self-motivated.

Saturday, 20 July

Motored Geoffrey Gilmour, who stayed the night, to lunch with Woman at Caudle Green. English farmhouse luncheon specially prepared by Woman for her Parisian guest, of roast chicken and summer pudding. She has no help whatever, does housework and gardening, and looks after the heifers. Finds it too much and means to let the house to her godson and build herself a bungalow for £30,000. Then I motored Geoffrey to Ronnie Greville's* new house, Cubberley, near Ross-on-Wye, by Claud Phillimore† in 1972. It must be the last country house to be built. Derivative but charming. Walls white-harled over. Inside a long passage from end to end, rather like a gallery. One huge saloon with high-coved ceiling. Cork walls, the cork laid out in thin strips like wallpaper, and dyed mauve and pink, very pretty. Dining-room walls of orange felt; sounds hideous, and is bold and arresting. Lovely furniture. Altogether a most comfortable and desirable house. At the far end of the gallery is a colonnade or orangery, not used as such but as a sun room. The stairwell has a domed ceiling from which is suspended a huge chandelier, made to Ronnie's design. He, who used to

---

* Ronald, 4th Baron Greville (1912–87).
† Architect in classical tradition (1911–94); s. nephew as 4th Baron Phillimore, 1990.

be extremely handsome, is now sixty-two, suffering from heart failure. His face a wreck of its former self. Hair thin and dyed ginger. Eyes tiny and rather sinister. Only his old, wicked smile recalls the Ronnie I remember. And of course his camp manner and gestures.

Saturday, 3 August

The Filipina on being paid her wages this morning revealed that in spite of her promise to us a month ago to stay until we moved in the autumn, she was leaving in ten days' time, when her holiday was due. We told her this was dishonest. All she did was to snigger. Then I paid M. and got nothing but growls and complaints from him. I now long to get away from them all. I loathe and detest them. All they want is less work and more money. They have no decent feelings, no regard for truth. They are spoilt and rotten. I hope unemployment leaps to astronomical proportions, and that they are humiliated and come begging cap in hand for work. I shall be prepared to undergo every personal deprivation for the satisfaction of seeing them reduced to starvation.

Saturday, 10 August

Last night we dined with Ian [McCallum]* at the American Museum. He had staying Michael York and wife.† A charming pair and apparently our greatest film stars. I saw him impersonating Christopher Isherwood‡ in a recent film [*Cabaret*]. A clear complexion, so youthful that there is no difference between skin of the face and the neck. Golden hair not very long and thin-spun, with slight sideburns. Curious nose, slightly beak-like and intriguing, fine wide eyes and large, provocative mouth. Shop-window figure, and well-dressed. An exquisite. Quiet, modest and unspoilt. Takes an intelligent interest in things of the mind. Does not drink alcohol. Smiles sweetly and seems surprised when addressed. Wife Pat, a little gushing, much older, with

---

* Curator of the American Museum at Claverton near Bath (1919–87); a friend of J.L.-M. since the Second World War (in which I.McC. was a conscientious objector).
† Michael York-Johnson (b. 1942); actor; m. 1968 Patricia McCallum, actress.
‡ Novelist (1904–86).

son of twenty-two she said. Includes husband in conversation in a possessive manner. He defers to her sweetly, but may be irritated by her anxiety. Says he may be obliged to become an expatriate because he is taxed so high that he cannot make money. They were brought over to Alderley this afternoon, and we were enchanted with both.

Wednesday, 14 August

I am reading Jan Morris's* *Conundrum*, decently told tale of her change of sex. I now remember as a child desperately wishing that I were a girl, and feeling desperately ashamed of my wish. But on reaching adolescence my wish totally vanished, and I have never ceased being glad I am a man. But during childhood I certainly was passive. Ever since fifteen or sixteen, say, I have on the contrary been active. The girl-wish stage may have been caused by funk, for I feared the first war might last so long I would have to be in the army, and the trenches.

Thursday, 15 August

The Acloques† have bought this house for £102,500. This is the figure agreed upon after gentlemanly bargaining through the intermediary of agents. I am no longer heart-broken, but relieved. A. is so relieved that she is able to sleep again. Had we waited three months longer we might not have sold at all, and been landed with Lansdown Crescent in addition. As things are, we shall not be certain that the deal is clinched until contracts are exchanged, documents signed and money handed over. The financial situation is so dicey that events might occur within the next few weeks, a complete national collapse, and the purchasers not be able to pay. Then where would we be? We begin to be excited about our new dwelling. If only A's room were not underground. Her bedroom will be charming, I think, although facing north. But what will she do in Bath with a pocket-handkerchief of a garden?

---

* Writer (b. 1926), known as James Morris prior to a much-publicised sex-change in 1973.
† Guy Acloque; m. 1971 Hon. Camilla Scott-Ellis, yr dau. of 9th Baron Howard de Walden.

Motored to lunch with Rosamond [Lehmann] at Yoxford [Suffolk]. Her cottage in the village street incongruously tiny. It had been an antique shop. It reminded me of the shop in *Alice*, and Ros of the old woman who turned into a sheep. She was dressed from neck to ankle in flowered chiffon and walked heavily leaning on my arm down the village street, a strange spectacle in such rural surroundings. When I said A. and I might be visiting Australia with a view to emigrating, she was shocked that I could contemplate leaving my friends. 'Do you really think you could leave me, for instance?' she asked rather rattily. Airily I replied, 'I suppose so – now.'

Reached Holt Rectory [Norfolk] in time for dinner. Stayed three nights with Billa. Roy Harrod is now senile, laughs and gets cross at a whim. Forgets everything. Has to write things down. Billa can never leave him for more than a few hours at a time, for he would get lost or set the house on fire. She wonders if he may have a tumour on the brain. Billa does far too much, with her Norfolk churches, her preservation work, the cooking, her children, grandchildren, and Roy. Dom[*] and his recent wife, who is Christopher Hobhouse's posthumous daughter, came for the weekend. She, whom I have never met before, is now older than Christopher was when he was killed. She exactly resembles him, the same arrogant carriage of the horsy head, handsome, good figure, clever girl. It was fun to see her. I much liked 'Our Economic Correspondent'. He is humorous, jolly, and gentle with his father.

Saturday, 14 September

This place is already going to seed, becoming down-at-heel, since our selling it. Windows unclean, the garden a mess – Müller being away ill or feigning illness, we cannot be sure which. My emotions now are of one to whom a love affair has become sour. He wants to get clear of the old lover and the memories as quickly as possible.

---

[*] Dominick Harrod (b. 1940); Economics Editor of BBC, 1979–93; m. Christina Hobhouse.

Monday, 16 September

After a Sudbury committee meeting,* Debo asked me to stay the night at Chatsworth. I always take the precaution of carrying a toothbrush, comb and razor. She said Decca was coming to stay. So I did not resist. Andrew [Devonshire] was also at home. He was extremely friendly and welcoming. I was touched by his charming, open manner. Yet the rapidity of his intensely clever, quickly changing mind does not always induce ease, and I feel shy with him. He showed me a host of pictures he has just bought, innumerable Lucian Freuds, of whom he is a notable patron. Decca still resembles Nancy in face, although hers is rounder, and less fine. She has a double chin, and wears ugly large round spectacles. Was dressed less chiclessly than I expected, but not well. Has a deep ginny voice, which was explained by the amount she drank and smoked. So un-Mitfordy, this. She is undoubtedly clever and, like Nancy, sharp. Affectionate towards me without much feeling behind the manner. Sophie Cavendish† almost grown-up, but still a child, rather touching, with leanings towards architecture, provided it is Victorian or grotesque.

Before dinner I walked with Debo. She visited the cows, the bulls, the stallions, the new additions to Rowsley Inn, the gardens, the farm, talking to all and sundry and giving instructions. I said to her, 'How are you able to cope with all this?' She said, 'It is my passion. Stupid, I know.' I said, 'It is far from stupid. It is marvellous, and right.' Both Devonshires are like everyone else deeply depressed by events. In saying good-night Andrew remarked, 'If I am driven away from Chatsworth, which is likely, I shall never return. I shall never set foot in Derbyshire again.' Asked what was going to happen with large establishments like his, I said the only hope of survival seemed to me the National Trust. 'Um!' was all he muttered. Yet here they still are surrounded by works of art of the greatest rarity, living in this enormous house, with old retainers, servants and butler and footman, and private telephonists on duty all day and night; and providing access to the public practically the whole year round. Long, long may it last.

---

* J.L.-M. and Debo Devonshire both sat on a small N.T. committee to advise on the redecoration of Sudbury Hall, Derbyshire.
† Lady Sophie Cavendish (b. 1957); yr dau. of 11th Duke of Devonshire.

The L.-Ms devoted much of September and October to the depressing task of removing the contents of Alderley Grange before vacating the house in November. Much was given away to relations, or stored by friends and neighbours; much was taken to London to be sold.

Sunday, 22 September

The Filers,[*] new purchasers of The Mount House, lunched. Arrived late which infuriated us, then stayed till six. But the reason of our submitting to this ordeal is that they are going to borrow much furniture from us, and so store and maintain it free. He is an extraordinary pushing young man, full of self-confidence, a bald-headed (though with all his own hair) thruster, like John Harris, only he is a business tycoon. He goes up to things and examines them with close scrutiny, remarking on their appeal, or otherwise, to him. Peers into the pewter mats, commenting on their motto and crest. Peers into the portraits, asking who they are of. Is anxious to buy anything and everything. Wants to have ancestors. Has the money. Such people deserve to get on. He has already bought a farm near Hillesley with the object of winkling the owner out of the barn which faces The Mount House and installing him as tenant of the farm. There is no impertinence beyond his ambition. I wish him well in his venture.

A. and I have been dismantling in earnest. Are sorting out our books, and are disposing of hundreds and hundreds.

Friday, 27 September

Went to Christie's. A ghastly young man with outrageously gushing good manners begged me, if not inconvenient, to step into a waiting room. No, sir, I am afraid it is occupied. If you don't mind, sir, stepping *this* way. 'It is like being shown a cubicle in Simpson's in which to change one's trousers,' I reflected. 'Oh, sir,' etc. Then I began unpacking. Diffidently I presented the first of my wares, an oriental vase of A's. With much tittuping and smirking the young man went off, came back to say that Mr So-and-So was, he regretted, too busy

---

[*] James Filer, entrepreneur; his wife Britta.

to see me. 'I am afraid, sir, very much afraid, it is Korean, mid nine-teenth-century.' He did not need to tell me it was no good, and I must take the lousy thing away. Inwardly I vowed that never again, never, would I so prostitute myself at Christie's or Sotheby's, at least in person. Then the English porcelain. A very polite, natural, middle-aged man called Hudson appeared, looked at them, advised which I had better sell in Bath and which bring up to him. Most helpful. Felt that much better. Off in pelting rain to Brooks's, to fetch the panel portrait. No taxi available, and the distance really too short. So I walked holding my overcoat over the picture, myself getting soaked. Michael Tree rescued me in the foyer and directed the supercilious, queenly young man to send Mr Somebody to me directly. I felt more important. Mr Somebody expressed considerable interest. 'By Miervelt,'* I suggested. 'Not improbable,' he said. 'There is an identical one at Blair Castle,' I said. 'Yes, this may be a contemporary copy.' 'Or the Duke of Atholl's may be a contemporary copy of mine,' I ventured. Picture taken away for detailed examination by experts. A. and I are pooling our proceeds to pay the exorbitant bills for decorating the Bath premises.

Sunday, 6 October

I often think I am far-seeing and correct in my political judgements. Am certain I was right in 1970 when I said Heath ought, when the Tories were re-elected, at once to have a confrontation with the Unions, at the risk of civil war. Even today I believe that a confronta-tion (which would undoubtedly entail civil war) would result in an eventual victory for common sense, though it is no longer a foregone conclusion. As it is, this week's election may be a complete victory for Labour and the Unions, and so Marxism within two years.† I was right about the danger of the intellectuals flirting with Communism in the Thirties, right about favouring Munich in 1938 because we were not ready to fight the Germans, right in knowing that Communism was a worse evil than Fascism, and right in deploring Churchill's insistence

---

* Dutch artist (1567–1647).
† In fact the election on Thursday 10 October was disappointing for the Labour Government, which was returned to office with a majority of only three.

upon unconditional surrender and the consequent acceptance of the Russian occupation of Eastern Europe. Oh God, the pace things are running downhill now is sickening.

We cart packing-cases of china and objects and books to Newark Park.* The packing seems endless. I counted the total number of meat dishes of my Crown Derby dinner service, which alone amounted to forty-five. We have dozens of others. Most of the old services have cracked and broken dishes and plates, very many ruined by soda and detergents. I think the Edwardian days were the worst for damage by servants ignorant of good china.

Wednesday, 16 October

Met Peter Tew, the hearty old architect who worked for Paul Methuen at Corsham; also for Moley Sargent† who lived with his mother at 19 and 20 Lansdown Crescent. He said that he repaired the library at number 19 after the bomb damage during the war. There was very much damage, and he spent £4,000 on the library alone out of War Damage Commission money. The ceiling was down and most of it had to be restored; much of the scagliola pilasters had to be repaired by Jacksons. He assured me that the mirror doors over the bookshelves at the north end of the room were not there when he restored the room. They must be post-war innovations. I am much relieved and have decided that I can with clear conscience have them removed. This assurance has come just in time, for the painters have finished in this room and we hope to move in on 11 November

Tew said that when the bomb fell on the road outside number 19 (the bow front of 20 collapsed and had to be rebuilt) the tenant had a lot of Beckford's books which he had collected. The only shelves which were quite unharmed were those containing the Beckford books, and they were behind the glazed doors. Tew also told me that the bay to the

---

* The American architect Bob Parsons (1920–2000) had recently become the N.T. tenant of this Elizabethan shooting-box with splendid views over the Ozleworth Valley; having been befriended by A.L.-M., he offered to store the L.-Ms' possessions.
† Sir Orme Sargent (1884–1962); Permanent Undersecretary for Foreign Affairs, 1946–9.

right of the fireplace contained a secret recess. I said I guessed this when I saw his original plans of the two houses made for Sargent, for there is an unidentified space marked on them. He could not remember how one had access to the space, but his partner (who was another tenant of number 19, before the Strathconas*) used to keep his silver in it. Tew is going to ask this man to meet me and show me.

Sunday, 20 October

It is curious to recollect how, when I was a small boy, my greatest pleasure in life was to steer my father's car, especially when he left me in control of the wheel, which was often for minutes on end. There was so little traffic on the road when I was ten to twelve. At a slightly later age, when sitting beside him on the front seat, I used to slip my hand surreptitiously under his left thigh. He never seemed to notice. How I dared I can't think. To my inner self I said I was exploring.

Tuesday, 22 October

We motored to Renishaw [Derbyshire] on Friday for the weekend. My first visit. For years I have longed to see it. I wish I had done so during Osbert's† regime, for then it must have been more Gothic and gloom-filled than it is now. Reresby‡ and Penelope have brightened it up. For instance, the large drawing-room curtains, sky blue with no pelmets, and tweaked together along the tram-line in the French style, are innovations. An 1850 water-colour in this room shows curtains with bold pelmets. The room is dominated by the portrait, by Fosburgh, of Osbert seated like a doge with a staff, his cane. Excellent likeness, and formidable. 'The eyes follow you round' in menacing fashion. The famous Adam commode beneath the Sargent conversation piece is about the most beautiful piece of furniture in all England. The house still has much atmosphere, and is filled with family things

---

* Donald Howard, 4th Baron Strathcona and Mount Royal (b. 1923).
† Sir Osbert Sitwell, 5th Bt (1892–1969).
‡ Eldest son (b. 1927) of Sir Sacheverell Sitwell, whom he s. 1988 as 7th Bt (having earlier inherited Renishaw from his uncle Osbert); m. 1952 Penelope Forbes.

and treasures, in the same higgledy-piggledy way as at Weston. A. and I were given one room with a double bed. Because of its immense size it was all right and we slept happily until A. started, as is her wont, thrashing around at 3 a.m.

Ten people were staying. Delicious food, and an old family butler who obliges for house parties but will accept no recompense, no gratuity. Other guests were Elizabeth Longman* (pretty and whimsical); Felix Kelly† (right-mindedness and sense of humour); Sir Henry Lawson-Tancred‡ (baronet and widower, intelligent, friendly); Lady Bowker§ (Levantine, glossy, gossipy, nice); Patrick Forbes, youngish (after dinner looking at Reresby's slides on the screen I caught him raising his head in order that a sagging chin should not be observed – but I did observe), a vintner; Rosie Forbes, our hostess's sister, jolly, slightly boozy, smoky, glowing. Penelope is beautiful, stately and sharp. I don't understand why Sachie and Georgia hate her. Their hate is returned.

In the car Reresby told me that when Osbert began suffering from Parkinson's, David Horner¶ (whom he calls Blossom) had an affair which upset Osbert, entirely dependent upon him for dressing and generally ministering. Later David Horner fell down the stairs at Montegufoni and was incapacitated worse than Osbert. So Osbert turned against David and treated him cruelly. David was intensely jealous of the Maltese who came to Osbert as handy-man, turned secretary and confidential adviser. Sachie refers to him as 'poor Osbert's catamite'. Reresby affirms that his father is very conventional and a strict observer of the proprieties. This is, I think, true. Reresby does not criticise his father and mother, and speaks sweetly of them in the face of much provocation.

Indeed Reresby is a very sweet fellow. The shape of his round face is Georgia's, but all the features are Sachie's. The voice is Sachie's. He has wide knowledge of many subjects, but is not creative. We can't all

---

* Lady Elizabeth Lambart (b. 1924); er dau. of Field Marshal 10th Earl of Cavan; m. 1949 Mark Longman (he d. 1972).
† New Zealand-born artist (d. 1996), specialising in paintings of country houses in their landscapes.
‡ Sir Henry Lawson-Tancred, 10th Bt (b. 1924), of Aldborough Manor, Yorks.
§ Elsa Vidal; m. 1947 Sir James Bowker, diplomatist.
¶ Companion of Sir Osbert Sitwell.

be, alas. He tells long stories, explains matters at inordinate length, expecting attention. Has a coarse streak. For example, in showing us to our bedroom he said to A., 'If Jim gets too randy you can always put the bolster in the middle', and to Lady Bowker, 'This strange tap with two handles can be used by two lesbians at once.' These sorts of remark make one squirm a little.

After dinner the first night we were shown a film of safari, R. supplying commentary with a host's good-natured relish. One by one the company, headed by Penelope and followed by A., slunk off to bed, Penelope having given us a signal of permission, but unnoticed by R. Before undressing I realised that I had left my reading spectacles downstairs. Descended and quietly re-entered the drawing-room to hear R. droning on, 'And in this slide you will notice in the far distance a giraffe with what appears to be two heads.' There was not a single soul in the audience. I snatched up my specs and while mounting the stairs heard R. still declaiming and chortling with satisfaction to himself. I find this aspect of Reresby lovable.

Monday, 28 October

J.K.-B. met me at Brooks's before we left for a play. My old friend Betty, the accountant, took us into the bombed ante-room round by the back premises, for it and the coffee-room are boarded up.* She was emphatic that the bomb was not thrown through the window, because as she explained no one could throw something as small as a hand grenade through thick plate-glass windows and thick velvet drawn curtains. Whereas this bomb exploded in the middle of the room. I talked to the nice wine waiter, Michael, who was in tears. He held himself responsible for the injuries to one of the two apprentice waiters, whose parents are friends of his. He said he persuaded these people to let their boy work at Brooks's, they being country people reluctant to let their

---

* A bomb had exploded in the club dining room (traditionally known as the coffee room) on 22 October, part of an intensive IRA bombing campaign on the British mainland. The possible intended victim was the ex-premier Edward Heath, who had spent the early part of the evening at the club; but he had dined elsewhere, and by the time the bomb went off, all diners had left the room and only staff remained.

son go to London. I overheard Edward Mersey* say to another member that if it was proved that Brooks's were responsible (e.g., for allowing a stranger to enter the building), then the compensation payable by the club would be about £10,000, which he called a pretty good sum for a boy of seventeen. It seemed to me that it was little enough compensation for the loss of a leg. During the war I was in constant fear that Brooks's would be injured by German bombs. It is true that it had its windows blown out and it escaped several nearby fire bombs. But it did escape, only to be severely damaged by an anarchist's bomb thirty years later.

Sunday, 1 December

On 11 November we moved out of Alderley, and stayed the inside of a week with Sally Westminster at Wickwar. We came daily to Lansdown Crescent. Actually moved in on the 15th to sleep. By now we are nearly settled. There are still things like curtains which we await. On Friday the 22nd we said goodbye to Alderley for good, having removed the last remaining objects in the house. Left it quite empty, and vastly melancholy. In parting with the Müllers I had no regrets that I might never see them again but a pang of intense sadness struck because this moment was the final break with the house, which I dearly loved and in which I had hoped to end my days.

Wednesday, 4 December

Cyril Connolly's† death is a shock. He was about the cleverest and most literary of my generation. His knowledge of the classics was prodigious. His wit, his style were highly entertaining. About the best critic of his time, better than Desmond MacCarthy‡ or Raymond Mortimer. I used to see a lot of him and his first wife Jeannie when they lived in King's Road during the early Thirties. But Cyril always frightened me. He could be devastatingly rude, and snubbing. He had

---

* Edward Bigham, 3rd Viscount Mersey (1906–79).
† Author, journalist and critic (1903–74).
‡ Sir Desmond MacCarthy (1877–1852); critic.

a very seductive voice, and when amiable could be enchanting. Like other brilliant men to whom literary ability comes too easily – Alan Pryce-Jones is another – he was idle, and never fulfilled himself.

Friday, 13 December

I dined with Patrick [Kinross] on Monday. He told me Cyril was very attractive as a young man, as I saw for myself from a snapshot P. has of him. P. has framed a host of photographs of his friends in a corner of his working room. He said Cyril was the first person he slept with, at Oxford. The next day Cyril left him a note in the porter's lodge, merely saying 'Alpha and Omega'. However he repeated the performance. He was a great bibliophile, and advised Christie's on books. But his knowledge of porcelain, on which he prided himself, was less sure. He had a valuable collection of first editions, all kept wrapped in cellophane, and so never read or even touched.

Friday, 20 December

The Badminton estate agent told us on Tuesday that he had just read the new Finance Bill from cover to cover. The measures to be taken against large estates are far worse than he had imagined. Discretionary trusts are to be particularly penalised. Every ten years a transfer tax will be levied on them, and retrospectively. For example, 1975 will be the tenth year since Badminton was put in trust, therefore it will be subject to this appalling penalisation. He said the Duke hardly realised this, and thought it better he should not. Caroline Somerset said to me that it meant the end of their hopes to live in Badminton.

Monday, 23 December

For several years we coveted Miss Taylor's little house, at the gates of Badminton, without ever having seen inside. It had been a sort of bad taste joke that each time we saw David Somerset we asked, 'How is Miss Taylor?' The old lady suddenly died about two months ago, after we had sold Alderley and bought and altered and decorated Lansdown Crescent. To our surprise, about three weeks ago the Badminton agent telephoned to ask if we were still interested in the house, he having been told by David that we were. We have lately been to look round it. The agent added that others had applied to the Duke, and some very rich hunting people, who are his friends, had priority. This morning David telephoned from London to say the hunting people are off and the house is now ours, if we want it.

We are in a great quandary. Alvilde is madly keen on it. I am half-hearted. I have now got to like being here. As for my library, I have never liked a room more. The Badminton house is small, there is no one large room. In other respects it is perfect, and the right size. We now have to make up our minds whether to rent it, treat it as a cottage for the summer, and live here in the winter months, I coming over here by day during the summer and using this library as my office. My fear is that the two places will cost us more than Alderley did. Oh what a huge worry!

Tuesday, 31 December

I delivered the corrected galley proofs of my diaries to Chatto's, and went to Heywood Hill's shop. John Saumarez Smith* said, 'I hear you are publishing some diaries next year.' I asked him how he possibly knew. 'Ah,' he said, 'as a shopkeeper I keep my ear to the ground.' He said he hoped the price would not be too high. Agreed with me that it would be a mistake to include illustrations of country houses. I told him that I had said so to Chatto's in vain, and begged him to tell Norah Smallwood when next he saw her that he thought so too.

Oh God! am I making another dreadful mistake?

---

* Managing director of G. Heywood Hill Ltd, bookshop in Curzon Street.

1975

1975

After their move in November 1974 from Alderley Grange to 19 Lansdown Crescent, Bath, the L.-Ms soon found their maisonette too cramped for their needs. Exactly a year later they moved again, to Essex House, Badminton, Jim retaining Beckford's library at No. 19 for his work.

Tuesday, 7 January

I have received a letter from Martin Gilbert, who is engaged on Vol. 5 of Winston Churchill's Life. Among Sir Winston's archives he has come upon my name as a guest at Chartwell for four nights in January 1928. Can I give him any recollections of the visit? I have replied that I remember it fairly well. I was terrified of W.C., who would come in to dinner late, eat his soup aggressively, growl in expostulation at Randolph's cheek, then melt so as to be gallant with the girls and tolerant of the boys; that one night we remained at the dinner table till midnight while W.C. gave us a demonstration of how the Battle of Jutland was fought, with decanters and wine glasses in place of ships, while puffing cigar smoke to represent gun smoke. He was like an enthusiastic schoolboy on that occasion. The rest of the visit he was in waders in the lake or building a wall, or pacing backwards and forwards in his upstairs room dictating a book to his secretaries. Thump, thump on the floorboards overhead.

John Jolliffe* telephoned. Would I write a book for a small publishing firm he is now interested in, called the Compton Press, about Beckford, 40,000 words to be delivered in May, to coincide with a Beckford exhibition to be held in the autumn? I hate being taken unawares on the telephone and said No, I had not the time, for I have

---

* Hon. John Jolliffe (b. 1935); yr s. of 4th Baron Hilton and Lady Perdita Asquith; writer and publisher.

to do my contribution to the Mitchell Beazley* book, plus an article on Stratfield Saye for *Apollo*. Then I thought, to hell, if someone else can do this book, which cannot be good no matter by whom in so short a time, why not I? Besides, I am interested in Beckford. So the next morning I rang him up to that effect. He said he had not in the meantime approached another author.

Friday, 10 January

A charming man, Michael Russell[†] of Compton Russell Press, telephoned me. It seems that they do want me to do the Beckford book. They are postponing the exhibition until March 1976, which means I shall have more time.

Yesterday I went to Stratfield Saye to glean for my article for *Apollo*. The new duke[‡] is a new broom. Many alterations, several of which Gerry would not have approved. He has certainly improved the outside, planted avenues and greatly tidied up the lawns between river and house; also has cleaned and dredged the river, which is now a feature from the windows. Has made a swimming pool in the Orangery, which is acceptable if people must have these ridiculous heated pools, but I did not like the ignoble blue plastic roof in place of paned glass. Fitted carpets in several rooms, and a certain amount of pastel paint on walls and doors. The present duke has little idea who I am. I did not bother to enlighten him. Why should he wish to know?

Wednesday, 22 January

Last night I had a vivid dream – all my dreams are too vivid – that Rick Stewart-Jones (who died in 1957) came up to me and in the presence of his wife hugged me to his heart, saying, 'Let there never be a misunderstanding between us again. We love one another.' I felt the

---

* Publishing firm specialising in popular illustrated books, founded by brother of J.L.-M's N.T. friend Tony Mitchell.
† Publisher (b. 1933) who established his own imprint the following year, which survived to reprint the original series of J.L.-M's diaries in the early twenty-first century.
‡ Arthur Valerian Wellesley, 8th Duke of Wellington (b. 1915).

warmth of his body, and was surprised by the spontaneous gesture, for Rick was never demonstrative. This may have something to do with Jeremy Fry, who a few evenings ago got locked out and rang me at midnight to let him in. This I did and went up to his flat and talked to him for a quarter of an hour. I was in my pyjamas with a rug round my shoulders. When I left he threw his arms around me and hugged me, with thanks. That was all. Perhaps it was not enough for my subconscious. In which sad case my subconscious will never again have enough.

Friday, 24 January

There can seldom have been such a mild winter, or one so wet. Water and mud along the old London road to Ozleworth such that I had to leave the path and climb into the woods to avoid getting stuck. At Boxwell I met John Huntley* neatly breaking twigs and making a bonfire. I told him we were not very happy in Bath and hoped to return to the country. He said, 'All day and every day of the year I do what you see me doing now, pottering at Boxwell. I often think it is of no use to anybody and an absurd way of life.' 'No, no, no,' I exclaimed. 'You are leading the true life, the only life that matters.' I spoke with so much vehemence that he was startled. His family have lived at Boxwell for 400 years without a break. He is a typical squire, a through-and-through countryman, who is in touch with the earth, and knows every fibre.

A. and I went round Miss Taylor's house with a builder by ourselves in pouring rain. We found the house terribly damp. Most of the walls of most of the rooms saturated, and no windows fitting properly. We wonder how we can face this, unless the estate really means to correct it. I am very uncertain about this Badminton venture.

Saturday, 25 January

I read in *The Times* the debate in the Commons on the Transfer Tax. This is a historic week, for it means the end of the country estate. It

---

* The Huntleys of Boxwell Court had been Gloucestershire landowners since the Dissolution of the Monasteries, the Huntley of the time having been steward of the Abbot of Gloucester.

is the end of the English parkscape scene; the end of a long, tired tradition. We shall be a full Communist state within ten years.

Monday, 3 February

On Saturday Peter Hood* brought and nailed up my bullion fringes for the yellow curtains in the library. Since we came here I had longed for them. And now they are at last set up I am as pleased as punch, and I sit and admire them, and decide that now my library is finished. All I need is a hanging Colza-oil lantern for the hook in the ceiling rosette, and I shall, when we go to Badminton, take away the pair of Marlowes, of Naples, which are wasted, skyed over the bookcases, and substitute the two Puleston and Bailey quarter-length portraits, which are more suitable.

Sunday, 23 March

This morning at the eight o'clock Holy Communion service in Bath Abbey a man beside me blew his nose with the utmost violence, making a truly disgusting noise. I thought how frightful this was, and scarcely less disgusting than if he had relieved himself of some other superfluous bodily waste.

The Tony Powells to luncheon. A. says she never feels entirely at ease with them. I do because one can talk, they both being highly companionable. Yet there is a hardness (or is it an indifference?) about him, and a slight tendency to the tenacious about her. Their false teeth do not fit. In our talking of the grubby girls of today and asking why young men found them attractive, Tony said he had always been attracted by girls who looked as though they had slept under a hedge for a week.

I have received an appeal for money towards Cyril Connolly's fund. Apparently he has left debts amounting to £27,000 and no assets whatever, a widow and two children without a *sou*. A. says this is an appeal which we need not answer for latterly Cyril was very off-hand with us, did not answer letters when invited to stay or acknowledge

---

* Interior decorator.

occasional fagging I did for him over the Pavilions book,* etc. But I am not sure.

Wednesday, 2 April

We went to Scotney [Castle, Kent]† for Easter, the coldest I ever remember. It snowed nearly every day and there was a bitter wind. On the Saturday A. and I visited Penshurst [Place]; paid and went the round. The house well shown, well arranged, notices in good taste. As I was leaving the gatehouse Lord De L'Isle passed me, turned and said I must come in for tea, Peggy would be so pleased to see me. I retrieved A. from the garden and we both had tea with him and Peggy in the new tea room, just opened. They showed us round their part of the house, where they live quite apart from the public sector. She told A. she did not much care for Penshurst, which was for her a duty. She infinitely preferred Wales. I got the impression that neither cared very much for the other. Relations formal and strained. He seemed a very sad man, now superannuated, and apparently much embittered because she prevented his being made Lord Lieutenant through constantly taking him away from Kent. We had a few words in the library about the state of the country. He is appalled by what is happening. Thinks we shall go Marxist within a matter of years. Says he would far sooner be dead. Exhorts me to write and enrol myself in General What's-his-name's register. Bill De L'Isle thinks Heath was the cause of our ills, through sheer feebleness. This conversation arose from my asking him about his Shelley baronetcies, and deploring that no more baronets were created. He said Heath had been determined to stop hereditary honours, that he was the most class-conscious of men. Peggy surprised and embarrassed me by giving me a print in a maplewood frame of my great-grandfather [Sir Joseph Bailey].

In the Scotney library I found two large folio volumes on the landowners of Great Britain in 1873, dukes and the smallest squireens included. My great-grandfather Joseph Lees, to my surprise, owned

---

* *Les Pavillons: French Pavilions of the Eighteenth Century* (Hamish Hamilton, 1962).
† As guests of Betty Hussey.

746 acres at Lees [near Oldham, Lancashire].* Now, my maternal great-grandfather Joseph Bailey owned 600 acres in Radnorshire, 4,800 in Herefordshire and 22,000 in Brecon.

Wednesday, 16 April

Yesterday at Badminton A. was planting things in the garden of Essex House. I have grave doubts about this house. It is dark and depressing inside. And I fear it will be difficult, far worse than here in Lansdown Crescent, to preserve anonymity. I don't want to bid good morning and enquire after every inhabitant's health whenever I walk, not necessarily through the garden gate, but through the front door into the front garden. Today the village was pandemonium with horse boxes and police cars and caravans containing those thousands of people organising the beastly horse trials.

Friday, 18 April

I motored to Fonthill,† and beginning with the 'Inigo Jones' gateway went all round the estate in the car. Called on John Goodall who lives in the Lawn Cottage, where there is a ruinous circular dovecote with the Beckford crest over the doorway. I walked from the road to Bitham Lake and looked up the steep slope, wondering where exactly the Abbey had stood. This I discovered on reaching the great western avenue. At the entrance I left the car, and walked. Was overtaken by a motorist who stopped and politely asked me what I was doing. I explained, hoped I was not trespassing, etc. He was the owner of the Abbey grounds, a man called Rimington. He allowed me to walk round the site of the Abbey and I marvelled that it covered so small an area. To the south is a steep declivity to the American garden, now

---

* J.L.-M's surprise at this great-grandfather owning such a substantial slice of his ancestral estate was probably due to the fact that Joseph was a younger son, his wealth deriving from his marriage to the cotton heiress Sarah Milne.
† Estate in Wiltshire inherited by William Beckford from his father, where he erected the splendid but structurally unsound neo-Gothic Fonthill Abbey, which collapsed soon after he sold the property in 1822.

overgrown, the terrace, and Bitham Lake below. Still a marvellous situation, and unspoilt part of the country.

I am so steeped in Beckford that I identify myself with him – a horrid character, it cannot be denied.

Monday, 28 April

I almost had a breakthrough with Nick, my great-nephew, when he and I went to Stourhead last Sunday, by ourselves. I mean that although I have long loved him dearly and longed to become intimate with him, a shyness on both sides has hindered this. The other day, he driving me there and back, we managed to talk more naturally than hitherto. He is an exceedingly clever boy which should make our companionship easy; yet with someone of two generations' difference it is hard to click in a hurry. When he talks feelingly about the philosophy behind Ezra Pound's poetry I feel totally at sea. When I talk about Bernini, of whom he, a budding art historian, has never heard, he feels at sea. The result is that I get on to bantering terms with him, and this does not always work. Clearly the more we do see of one another, the easier we shall become. He is an enormous youth, over my height, stronger built, and handsome as can be with his dark sleek hair, fine brows and what's called a well-cut profile. If only he would not chain-smoke, and dress like a tramp.

Wednesday, 30 April

I used to think that a man ceased to live when he ceased to be in love. Now I know that he ceases to live when he can no longer look forward. Looking forward is the spice of life – to the article coming out next week, the book next year, the coin cabinet which belonged to Beckford being delivered. The moment when I have nothing to look forward to, then I shall be dead. Oh, the sadness of old age, and me!

Saturday, 3 May

I have bought for fifty new pence a rubber stamp, and having arranged the letters I put on the backs of envelopes, 'Down with the Marxists!'

Curious how one does not mind, on the contrary rather relishes, one's own smells. I am constantly smelling myself; hot vapours arise from me to my nostrils. I only hope others do not notice them. I wonder if they do, and do not like to say so? Yet I believe A. would. We have a pact to tell each other. I would hesitate to tell her, but as yet I never have had cause. I fear the older one becomes, the more and worse one smells. Most of my contemporaries smell, and I back away lest I catch a whiff.

Friday, 9 May

It was a surprise to be approached by Graham Monsell[*] at the theatre the other evening in London, with outstretched hand. He held my hand and said how delighted he was to see me and would so much like us to meet and talk over old times. Old times, my foot! I was terrified of Graham as a boy. At children's tennis tournaments he used to bash his racquet over my head so that I looked like a clown peering through a broken drum, and once at Wickhamford he let out my father's pet parrot so that it flew away, and drove his car out of the motor-house into a ditch. At Oxford he was considered extremely dashing, the 'fastest' man in the university, wore a black polo sweater and allegedly took drugs. Was excessively supercilious, rich and disdainful. Now he is bent, blind, sallow, dusty and diffident. How the late worms change places with the early birds.

Thursday, 15 May

Further Beckford thoughts. Beckford's life was ruined at the age of twenty-four [in 1783] by the vicious persecution of Lord Loughborough, later 1st Earl of Rosslyn, who claimed to be deeply shocked by Beckford's criminal relations with his nephew (in-law), young William Courtenay. I recall at Oxford this Lord Rosslyn's gt-gt-gt-gt-nephew, Hamish Erskine, sleeping with Desmond

---

[*] Graham Eyres-Monsell, 2nd and last Viscount Monsell (1905–93), of Dumbleton Hall, Worcestershire; his father (First Lord of the Admiralty during the 1930s) had been a hunting friend of J.L.-M's parents and their local MP.

Parsons, who was Beckford's gt–gt–gt–gt–grandson. Now, was Lord Rosslyn squirming in his grave during the late 1920s when his collateral descendant was thus indulging in carnal relations with the descendant of his bitter enemy?

Dining at Sally's on Monday, Clare Crossley* was describing the *Great Splash*† film, in which two boys are shown having an affair. She said, 'I have never before seen two men sleeping together. Have you?' I said nothing, but blushed scarlet. George Dix‡ who was sitting opposite me observed this, and said he had never seen me at a loss for words before. I should have replied to Clare that I had not, which is true in that presumably one does not 'see' oneself in such conditions.

Monday, 2 June

Genuinely sad to read in *The Times* this morning of the death of Olive Lloyd-Baker. A. says I must not get kicks out of the deaths of those I know in the obituary columns. But I genuinely liked this spirited, tough, old-fashioned spinster who was a grand landlord with a great sense of responsibility for her estates and tenants at Hardwicke and in London. Hardwicke is in no stretch of the word a great house, but the seat of a good old county family. Olive made a remark which I shall always remember and which John Betjeman relished, 'An ounce of heredity is worth a pound of merit.'

Thursday, 12 June

Often during the day I am visited by, or manufacture, dreams of hate. These are very dreadful. I argue against somebody (it used to be my father in the old days), and work myself into terrible rages while I think of arguments to floor my opponent.

On Tuesday in London Colin McMordie dined with me. It was so hot in Brooks's and the club so full that I took him to Rowley's

---

* Clare (b. 1907); m. 1927 Anthony Crossley (1909–84).
† David Hockney, *A Bigger Splash*.
‡ Wealthy American bachelor; friend of J.L.-M. since 1945, at which time he was a US naval officer.

in Jermyn Street, where a perfectly filthy meal cost £9 without tip. Then we returned to Brooks's. At midnight I told him I must go to bed. So we walked to Knightsbridge where we parted. He is a very nice, intelligent, handsome youth, dressed in a blue striped suit and blue shirt and tie, most dandy. But he is rather precious. Rolls his large eyes and looks one intensely in the face. Talks in a brittle manner about artists I have never heard of. Says he has read all my books and much likes *Heretics*. In spite of all this I was rather bored by him and sensed myself to be a failure in his eyes. I would have preferred less talk about literature and art, and more fun and jokes. Intenseness in the young I find an impediment to intimacy and freedom of speech.

I lunched with Archie Aberdeen[*] in the House of Lords. Years since I was there. It is like being inside Fonthill Abbey, which surely influenced Barry.[†] The 1830s were a suitable decade for that particular place to be burnt down and built again from the ground up, save only St Stephen's Hall which is an inestimable mediaeval treasure. I admired the encaustic tiled floors, the enormous brass Gothic chandeliers, and the stained-glass windows. Must admit the portraits of recent sovereigns are pretty poor, and some of the wall paintings of historic events nauseating. Each peer in alphabetical order, his title and rank on a large card, has a hat peg, now used to hang coat, umbrella and briefcase. I wonder what confusion is caused when a peerage becomes extinct or a new creation is made: from A to Z the whole lot has to be shuffled up or down. Archie was waiting for me beside the equestrian statue of Richard Coeur de Lion. He said he was descended from him, but I said I thought he liked the boys and had no offspring.[‡] Archie was astonished, didn't know about Blondel, and seemed disappointed by my disclosure.

---

[*] Lord Archibald Gordon (1913–84); s. brother 1974 as 5th Marquess of Aberdeen; befriended J.L.-M. in 1930s when he worked for CPRE; on staff of BBC Radio, 1946–72.

[†] Sir Charles Barry (1795–1860); architect, commissioned in 1836 to rebuild Houses of Parliament.

[‡] Historians differ as to whether Richard indulged in homosexual behaviour; but it is generally agreed that he had an illegitimate son, Philip.

Saturday, 28 June

It is satisfactory that some emotions are as strong as formerly. John Cornforth and I motored to Moccas, for I am to write an article on the house for *Country Life*. Although one or two horrors have arisen since my first visit twenty-five years ago, notably a sort of factory by the village cross, and a handful of mean houses too close to the front drive gate, yet once inside the purlieus I still find myself in another world. I have never known a place in the UK seemingly so remote, in a setting so tranquil, so inducive of ecstatic dreams and ancient history. In Moccas I am invaded with the very same sensations which I have encountered in certain Spanish churches where time stands still. There is nothing like a river sluggish since time immemorial to induce a sense of eternity.

Tuesday, 1 July

A. went off this afternoon to the garden party at Montacute [Somerset] at which the Queen Mother is to be received, to mark the eightieth birthday of the National Trust. She can't understand why I don't want to go. My reasons may not be wholly untinged with pique, in that dear Mr Fowler[*] has done the whole place up at great cost from top to toe, whereas Eardley and I spent hours of our life struggling to make a silk purse out of a sow's ear at that house which I love. Moreover, in our simple way, with the minimum of funds allowed us, I believe we made it more sympathetic. Now Montacute is a bit too dolled-up. Although splendid architecture, the house was throughout the Phelips centuries undemonstrative and sparsely furnished. I shall go quietly there on my own one day.

Sunday, 6 July

Found such a good word by chance in the dictionary – opsimath. I am an opsimath, one who develops slowly.

---

[*] Interior decorator (1906–77); partner of Colefax & Fowler, adviser to the N.T. on restoration, and friend of J.L.-M. since 1940s.

Yesterday at six I went to see poor Cecil [Beaton]. He was sitting in an upright chair to the left of the fireplace in his drawing-room. Immaculately dressed in white ducks, white linen coat and blue scarf through a ring round his neck. Looked white, and his eyes very dark. Did not rise when I came in. Was cheerful but is extremely sad. He walks in great awkwardness with a stick, his feet sticking out sideways like a disjointed doll's. Has absolutely no feeling in his right hand which he nurses and rubs. Is longing for life to return to it but I doubt if it will. He says it is hell being unable to work, the one thing he wants to do. 'Shall I ever be better?' he asked. His memory too is poor. Cannot remember anyone's name, not even his secretary's. Says strange things like, 'How is that person who lives near you with a name like Mouse?' I stayed an hour and a quarter, I hope not too long, and as always in such circumstances talked too much. Dreadful to see that man, the sharpest I have ever known with an eye like a lynx's, dulled by a stroke. There were flashes of the old malice, and he laughed, throwing back his head, over gossip.

Thursday, 10 July

Yesterday in London I was waiting for a bus in Tottenham Court Road, in my place in a queue. Behind me a woman under thirty was pushing herself forward. I deliberately elbowed her back to the rear where she belonged and was myself the last person allowed on the bus. I had to stand inside. The conductress politely asked the woman to get off the platform where she had placed herself, saying, 'There is no more room for standing.' The woman, who was foreign, almost coffee-coloured, shouted abusively, 'The English always say no to one.' I said to her tartly, 'Perhaps they only say no to you.' She spat in my face. I wiped my face and spat in hers. She spat back. Quick as lightning I slapped her face as hard as I dared, saying, 'Get off this bus immediately, you odious woman.' And she did. Awkward silence. In that typically English way, no one said a word. At the next stop I got off myself, having I suppose behaved badly.

Monday, 28 July

I seldom get through a night without a disagreeable dream. Dreams are the result of the nightly Mogadon [sleeping tablet], I am sure. In fact I resemble the opium takers of old, Coleridge, Shelley, de Quincey, so many of whom became addicts, and consequently subject to hair-raising nightmares, illusions (Shelley's attack in Wales), miseries. At times I find that sleep exhausts me more than being awake. It would be ghastly to dread falling asleep.

Monday, 4 August

Charlotte Bonham Carter came for luncheon. Brought with her two books which had belonged to Beckford which her grandfather bought at the Hamilton Palace sale in 1882–3; one is Byron's *Vision of Judgment*. Most kind, and I am deeply touched. We had Diana Westmorland lunching too, who is the same age – eighty-two or thereabouts – and Charlotte in spite of her deplorable accident is by far the brisker, walking up and down our steep little staircase without holding the banister rail. Her mind is very active and sharp. Yet she seldom listens and keeps exclaiming, 'My dear, how lovely, how too wonderful!' – which, Freda Berkeley told me, she said to a friend who announced that his wife had recently died, then adding '– and terrible!'

Wednesday, 6 August

At Heywood Hill's shop, John Saumarez Smith showed me a pile of books stacked in the corner. Said, 'Do you know whose book that is?' It was mine [the diaries], to be out on 18 September. I had not seen a copy before. Pleased with the look but much disturbed by the price – £6. Was also shown Harold Acton's *Nancy Mitford*, with photographs, at only £5.25. Hideous jacket of a coloured photograph of Nancy at her pretty writing-table I knew so well, looking like the Duchess of Windsor with high scooped hair. John said he had already taken 75 orders for my book, and that Ali Forbes is reviewing it for the *TLS*. I somehow can't face looking through it.

Monday, 18 August

Today I tore up and threw in the dustbin the original manuscript of my diaries for 1942 and 1943. I had a few misgivings, but decided that what was omitted from the published version was worthless, and worse than that, shaming. Thoroughly illiterate too. I hope in the autumn to go through the ensuing years and edit them, possibly for publication. It will depend on the reception *Ancestral Voices* gets.

Monday, 1 September

Last night we went to the Robinsons for a dinner of twenty-five to celebrate Audrey's seventieth birthday. I can't pretend I enjoyed it in particular, but I was delighted in general. Amazing how my dear little sister has come through, so to speak. She has taken a turn upwards since Tony's* death, and reached a serenity and contentment. There she was, the centre of affection of the marvellous Robinson boys. Henry adorable now (easier than Nick), a jolly boy who has just left Oxford with a second. Nick back from France, where he spent the vacation working as a waiter in Bordeaux, followed home by girlfriend, a beautiful, *racée* Franco-Vietnamese without one word of English. Audrey made to open all her presents in front of a ring of admirers. She seemed very happy. I made a tiny speech towards the end of dinner and we drank her health.

I asked Nick if he found many customers were bloody, as they often are to waiters. He said seldom, but the French employers were. They constantly tried to cheat the waiters of the wages agreed upon. One employer withheld part of his wage on the outrageous pretence that he had taken tips to which he was not entitled. Nick made such a scene that the man gave way, which he would not have done had Nick been guilty.

Friday, 5 September

Ian McCallum has lent me the journals of Roger Hinks.† They are in typescript for no publisher will take them. They are astonishing.

---

* Cecil 'Tony' Stevens; Audrey's second husband and the father of her daughter Dale, whom she married during the war, and who died in 1972.
† Art historian and British Council representative (1903–63).

They scarcely deal with friends unless friends illustrate an argument, or contribute to a discussion. They are about his thoughts, his reading of philosophy and art. An intellectual man, not likeable, prim, prissy, censorious, sitting as I remember stiffly, upright like a ramrod, very ugly indeed, with a supercilious look on his pursed lips, as though he despised the world and its inhabitants. But these journals are unusual. They are very German, might have been Goethe's thoughts. They make heavy reading, though I find them irresistible, if at times boring. Is this because I am not clever enough to understand what he is getting at? The milk of human kindness is absent, yet much moral sensibility and responsibility remain. Idiot publishers including Jock Murray have turned them down. They require drastic editing, and breaking into shorter paragraphs.

Saturday, 6 September

The year of Roger Hinks's journal which I read last night was his thirty-fourth. He was the same age as me when I was writing *Ancestral Voices*. His brightness compares with my dimness at the same age.

Sunday, 7 September

The free-lance journalist Theo Richmond* came from London to interview me for the *Guardian*. He was charming, and sympathetic. His first words were: 'I am afraid I am the wrong Theo.'† Then he said, 'I have interviewed many people, but have never been so alarmed as I am by the prospect of interviewing you.' It was a good beginning. We talked for an hour or more, he having put a dicta-phone on the table between us, which alarmed *me*, although he did promise that he would not take from it every word of inanity I

---

* Writer, film-maker, photographer, and contributor to arts pages of the *Guardian* (b. 1929).
† In his memoir *Another Self*, J.L.-M. describes how, aged nineteen, he fell in love with a youth named 'Theo' whom he met standing in the 'gods' at the opera; Theo reciprocated his feelings, but in the course of valedictory embraces they somehow re-exchanged their names and addresses, so never met again.

uttered. It was to remind him, he said. After he left I thought of many better retorts than the ones I gave. He ended by photographing me from every angle.* Told me he was a Jew from the East End.

Tuesday, 9 September

Eardley and I flew to Copenhagen. The Danes are utterly shameless with their porn shops. Old and young, middle-aged husbands and wives go to them, leaf through magazines of the most indecent photographs in colour, and attend non-stop blue films of indescribable revoltingness. In some shops there are cubicles like telephone kiosks or confessionals, into which they put two kroner, whereupon through an aperture they watch a minute or two of pornography. You see the backs of Danes of both sexes and all ages glued to these apertures – mostly little old ladies with ashen grey buns and string bags. We spent hours in the new Glyptotek. In the National Museum there is a Bernini bust of Urban VII's mother, a Batoni of Peter Beckford in Rome in 1766 and a Pieter de Hooch of *The Concert Players*.

Wednesday, 8 October

Recent National Trust meetings are the most enjoyable of any I have attended over a longish life of committee experience. Relations between staff and committee members are as good as could possibly be. Lunching at Brooks's after the Properties Committee today I met Gerry Coke† in the lavatory, so we sat together at the round table in the window of the coffee room, and were joined by two other old friends, Sam Lloyd‡ and Ran Antrim.§ I told Ran that Terence Morrison-Scott¶ was the best chairman I had sat under (or nearly), and hoped he might succeed Michael Rosse on the Properties. Rather

---

* The best of the photographs has been used for the jacket of this volume.
† Gerald Coke (1907–90); director of companies; Eton contemporary of J.L.-M.
‡ Sampson Llewellyn Lloyd of Bagpath Court, Gloucestershire.
§ Randal McDonnell, 13th Earl of Antrim (1911–77); Chairman of N.T., 1965–77.
¶ Sir Terence Morrison-Scott (1908–91); zoologist; member of N.T. Properties Committee, 1963–83; Chairman of Architectural Panel, 1973–82.

shame-facedly Ran said that Peter Chance* had already been chosen. He is a stuffed dummy with none of Terence's bewitching charm, and exactly the same age as Terence. Terence and Peter were my exact contemporaries at Eton, Michael a year and a half older.

Friday, 31 October

I have been very negligent of my diary lately. The chief reason is our move to Essex House, Badminton. Every evening when I get back there from Bath I hang pictures with A. or arrange something. A year ago precisely we were doing this very thing in Bath and I thought and hoped it would be for the last time.

I attended a Service of Thanksgiving for the life of Dione Murray (*née* Stewart-Jones) whose death in July I knew nothing of until I received a card of invitation from Beanie,† the last survivor of that large family of siblings. Service was in Chelsea Old Church. I sat close to the fine tablet to Rick's memory. The party in Crosby Hall afterwards was like something in the last volume of Proust. Old furrowed, rugged ladies came up and said, 'I am Hester' or 'Janet', and after a palsied look of non-recognition, something dawned and an embrace ensued. I was curious to meet Rick's boy, Barnaby. I had cherished a vision of a young man looking just like his father, which he used to aged four when I last saw him. Instead he looked like his mother, who withheld her presence today. He wore a yellow beard and was covered with yellow hair. Didn't seem interested in his father, barely remembered him. Emma, the mother, will, I was told, have nothing to do with the Stewart-Jones family. Edward [Stewart-Jones]'s widow Hester a nice, sensible woman, I thought. She claimed that all the gushing things which friends habitually say about Rick could be confirmed *and* contradicted. He had every counter-virtue to every virtue. He could be cruel, malevolent and everything that's horrid. I dare say she came up against him. My opinion of Rick is that he was something of a saint, but maddening. He was late for every engagement, which denotes

---

* Ivan Oswald Chance (1910–84); Chairman of Christie's International, 1973–6; Chairman of N.T. Properties Committee, 1976–80.
† Elizabeth Pulford – see entry for 23 June 1972.

utter selfishness. There was much of the prude in his disposition. But he had humour and understanding. And he was virtuous. Curious how today I do not think of him with particular tenderness, regret or love, though I loved him greatly for a time. I know now what I knew at the time but refused to admit to myself, that he was not my 'sort'. He thought me a reactionary, and a person lacking public spirit and philanthropic ideology. For he was a Roundhead, and I am a Cavalier.

Monday, 10 November

I was upset to receive a letter a week ago from Sir Humphry Tollemache* beginning 'Dear Sir'. My heart sank because of the form of address, and the ominous name. Ham House, I thought, and my flippant story of the visit there in 1943. *The Times would* select it. This Sir Humphry is the brother of the man I mistook for the alcoholic family butler. I should have checked that there was no such close relation living. Somehow I imagined the line was extinct. Anyway, he took grave exception to what I wrote. So I sent him a grovelling apology and this morning, thank God, he has written me a very decent letter beginning, 'You could not have written a nicer letter to me and in the circumstances I am grateful for it.' Although I brought this entirely on myself, nevertheless all this past week I have felt upset. On Saturday at the National Trust annual meeting in Bristol Midi [Gascoigne], with whom I had a fleeting word, told me that Helen Dashwood was furious. I have heard this from several quarters. Midi went on, 'People ask why on earth Jim published these diaries.' I said to Midi, 'Have you read them?' She confessed she hadn't, although I sent her a copy weeks ago.

I am feeling very low, as if life were ebbing out of me. Singularly depressed for no apparent reason. I ought to be so happy but, as I tried to explain to A. last night, despondency is based on no reason. It just assails one. She thinks I am taking it out on her, which I certainly don't intend. I merely want to be left alone. I don't want to see people, I don't want to be harassed, asked questions, asked for explanations. When in these moods I am, I know, intolerable to live with and I

---

* Major-General Sir Humphry Tollemache, 6th Bt (1897–1990).

appear ungrateful, inconsiderate, introspective and impossible. I concede all these things. I am sorry. But I want to be ignored, left. And this I never am, or can be. In my youth these moods were worse than they are now. Then I was working and so had to continue consorting with people. Now I no longer work for a living, but am married, and still cannot be left to myself.

Colin McMordie has written to me. I thought our last meeting, when I was a little indiscreet about myself and prying into his emotional life, would have finished him off. It all happened during a fairly cosy talk here one afternoon. But evidently not. He says he derived so much from the visit that he wishes we lived closer and could meet more frequently, etc. I must say that last time he dropped the tiresome affectation and spoke rather appealingly about himself, telling me that he was far from promiscuous, was hurt when people made advances to him on account of his extreme good looks, was desperately lacking in self-confidence. He is clearly looking for a soul-mate. I am not sure how I can help him. But it is flattering when the young wish to see one and confide their troubles. That sweet girl Diana Keith Neal* told me all her tribulations the other evening when she cooked me eggs, about her lover who is a rich playboy living abroad for tax reasons, won't stick at any work, is quickly bored, and desperately attractive. Drop him, I tried to tell her, as kindly as I could. When she left I gave her a kiss. Perhaps she minded. Colin had not minded the one I gave him.

Wednesday, 19 November

Harold Acton lunched with me at Brooks's. I was enchanted with him. We indulged in blissful comparisons of the complaints made by others of our recent books. He has been assailed by Rosamond [Lehmann] and, on R's behalf, her brother John,† for including a passage in a letter from Nance to, I think, Alvilde: 'Rosamond has been trying to get the Wid [Mrs Hammersley] to intercede with the Almighty on behalf of her little girl', or words to that effect, wounding doubtless to Ros who has never got over the death of her daughter Sally. Then Palewski has

---

* Daughter of J.L.-M's friend W. Keith Neal, expert on antique firearms.
† John Lehmann (1907–87); poet, editor and publisher.

been on to him because Ali Forbes disclosed his name in a review of Harold's book in the *TLS*. I said Ali was a friend of mine. He can't still be a friend of yours, H. replied, after what he wrote about you in the last paragraph of his review of *Ancestral Voices*. I maintained that I didn't read reviews of my books and didn't know what the paragraph concerned, knowing full well because A. had told me. Harold says Stuart Preston* is complaining bitterly to all and sundry, just like Helen Dashwood. Also David Horner told him that he thought of suing me for calling him epicene, but refrained because he did not wish to give the book further publicity. I said to Harold that D.H. ought to be flattered, because to be called epicene implied he had the qualities of both sexes, whereas to be truthful I should have stated that only those of the female sex pertained to him.

I closely watched Harold's expressive face across the table. The eyelids are small and semi-circular which contributes to the oriental aspect; the nostrils are tiny and tucked back as though they have been operated upon. Harold's mischievous, extremely courteous, almost dancing voice and gait make him unique among men. We had a good heart-to-heart. He told me that his German companion now lives in Florence. I said I hoped he was nice to Harold. Yes, said H., but he is very expensive, fast cars, elaborate cameras, travel, entertainment without end. 'It is a little sad,' he said, 'having to pay even for affection, on top of everything else. But what can we expect at our age, my dear?'

Friday, 21 November

Was deeply distressed to read this morning a brief notice in *The Times* of dear Monica Baldwin's† death. It was so sudden, and the anouncement so brief and inexplicit, that at once I feared something terribly wrong. And so it proved. This evening I telephoned Bloggs who had just

---

* Anglophile American bibliophile of independent means, then resident in Paris (1915–2005); close friend of J.L.-M. during the Second World War, when he was in London as an intelligence officer with the US Army: the portrait of him in J.L.-M's wartime diary is affectionate but satirical.
† Cousin of Stanley Baldwin and former nun, with whom J.L.-M. had corresponded for many years; author of *I Leap Over the Wall* (1951).

returned from Long Melford where she had moved a few weeks ago. She told me in her last letter of September she was going to a nice Catholic refuge. Bloggs in his slow way began, 'I only returned an hour ago, and have since been reading Monica's letter of farewell, which arrived in my absence.' Then I knew the worst. She wrote to her friend Joan Arbuthnot that she was ill-treated, half starved and spied upon. Can this have been true? She certainly grew increasingly miserable, as I can testify from her letters to me, and could not reconcile herself to the changes within the Church and the condition of world affairs. Yet for her, who had remained staunchly Catholic and devout, albeit latterly refusing to attend Mass, and who (she assured me) went through her Offices daily, and prayed, to have acted so far contrary to express Catholic doctrine by taking her own life is tragic indeed. Bloggs maintains she did the right thing. He said, 'Extreme old age is an extremely melancholy business. I have given a few broad hints to the Almighty. Whether He will heed them is another matter.' I feel sure Monica's life was ruined by the Catholic Church, those thirty lost years of doubt and self-questioning in an enclosed order, to return to a changed and alien world, to which she failed to adapt herself, then to be let down in the end by the Church taking from her all those anchors to which she still clung after her decision to abandon the convent. In ending her life she must have lost her faith, and died without hope, fearing, wretched, despairing.

Monday, 24 November

Am at present engaged in writing long captions for the illustrations to *Beckford*, which I believe is, in spite of its brevity, a rather good little book. I have already begun editing the next series of diaries, *Prophesying Peace*, and am anxious to dispose of them so that I may tear up and destroy the original manuscript, as I have done with *Ancestral Voices*. My embarrassment over those to-be-excised passages is extreme. I am terrified of dying before I have finished.

Tuesday, 25 November

I used to be surprised and shocked because old people accepted the calamities and deaths of their old friends with seeming equanimity.

Now I realise that, had they not done so, they would have gone mad. I have reached the age when I am beset by deaths and calamities. Monica has gone; Miss Long has had a serious fall and is in hospital; John Fowler has had a fit; dear old Florence is dying in a London hospital.*

Monday, 1 December

In the critics' choice of books for 1975 in *The Times* last Thursday, someone spoke of my book in disparaging terms, *i.e.*, faint praise modified by 'Oh, but such ghastly people', or words to that effect. And in the *Sunday Times* yesterday Robert Harling† gave it as his choice, referring to my 'hermaphroditic malice' towards friends, acquaintances, myself, etc. I am greatly distressed that people evidently think the book full of rancour. I don't see myself as bitchy but as an *ingénu*, I mean I see myself as such when I wrote these diaries more than thirty years ago.

Yesterday we lunched with Tony and Violet Powell at The Chantry. Violet has read it twice, she says. She evidently liked it immensely, and talked about little else. Curry cooked by Tony. I always enjoy seeing them. Both so stimulating. I understand how young Hugh Montgomery-Massingberd felt: he longed to talk to Tony about his novels, but Tony would only discuss genealogy. He is hipped on the subject, and his shelves are filled with every sort of reference book, *The Complete Peerage* among them. I of course share this interest to some extent. Some people find him sinister. He is not the least so; but he is inscrutable behind his very affable manner. It is his form of defence. And why not, for he is our most renowned living novelist. He has an enormous behind, and badly fitting teeth. He has reviewed for next Thursday's *Telegraph* Cyril Connolly's letters to Noel Blakiston.‡ Says they are fascinating, for even as a boy Cyril wrote like an angel. 'I am quite sure they tucked up together,' Tony said – in spite of Cyril's disclaimer that the two were never homosexual.

---

* Miss Long and Florence Paterson had been secretaries during J.L.-M's early years at the N.T.

† Novelist and editor of *House & Garden*.

‡ Assistant Keeper of Public Records (1905–84).

Monday, 8 December

On Thursday I motored to Oxford for the day. Drove to Colin McMordie's lodgings in Marlborough Road. He lunched with me in the French bistro off the High Street, and in the afternoon until dark conducted me round the colleges. The purpose was to show me the new buildings and quads which have been built since the war. I would say three-quarters are a success. All have been built with care for their environment. The St John's quad and St Edmund Hall are about the best, being sensitive, original, and yet conformist. Far and away the worst, and by the best-known architect, is St Catherine's Collge. It is an absolute beast, hideous, shoddy, cheap – and unpractical in that the undergraduates' rooms, being bed-sitters, have walls entirely of glass, so that the blinds have to be completely drawn when the inmates want either to work or to change their clothes unseen. With curtains drawn back the rooms reveal underclothes hanging on a rail behind the glass walls. The same raw brick surface is found inside as well as outside the entire building. Flimsy metal struts project from the outside walls; the 'campanile' is contemptible and the whole air is one of meagreness and futility.

Badminton is a village isolated from the present. All the cottages are inhabited by people working on the estate. They are all friendly, contented and respectful. All the men say, 'Good morning, Good night, sir', as of old.

Saturday, 13 December

Last night in bed I finished Christopher Sykes's* *Evelyn Waugh*. What a repulsive fellow! I doubt whether his writings are good enough to justify his abominable character. Yet in a ghastly way I see myself as a pale reflection of the man Evelyn. The same bad temper, grousiness, melancholy, pessimism, disillusion with the Catholic Church, to the extent that I have apostasised, whereas he had the strength and loyalty not to succumb.

---

* Traveller, journalist and writer (1907–86); brother-in-law of Ran Antrim, Chairman of N.T.

Poor Diana [Westmorland] telephoned in tears to tell that her old peke had died. I dared not be too commiserative on the telephone lest she break down. So I wrote her a letter of condolence and walked across the fields to deliver it to Lyegrove. A hard frost, and as I walked through our village, along the disused drive, across the belt of beeches known as The Verge, over a ploughed field, across a grass field, the golden sun waxed bigger and bigger, then dived. On the way home a waxing moon stood stock-still in a sky of powder blue, one bright star twinkling beside it. The rooks flew overhead. Otherwise not a sound but my footfalls on the crackling ice puddles and the rimy tufts of grass. Then a dying horn and the hounds coming home to Badminton after a day of what must have been hard going.

Sunday, 14 December

During my walk yesterday I decided to write a novel. Alderley was to be the setting, and seven inmates, including a whippet, were to record their thoughts about each other and themselves in an absolutely uninhibited manner.* I got extremely worked up and excited, because walking always inspires ideas, and was determined to jot them down on paper the moment I returned. When I got home A. bustled me to change and go off to the beastly carols in the church and supper with the boring Xs in the next village afterwards. All my ideas have evaporated.

Tuesday, 16 December

Now David Crawford† is dead. His obituary in today's *Times* must indicate even to the most prejudiced Leftist that men such as he are unique not just to England but to the world. Such sense of duty, such dedication to the arts and civilised being, such utter selflessness. This race of patricians must disappear through taxation, if through nothing else. I had the greatest veneration for him. He was an extremely

---

* Published by Chatto & Windus in 1978 as *Round the Clock*.
† David Lindsay, 28th Earl of Crawford and 11th Earl of Balcarres (1900–75); Chairman of N.T., 1945–65.

proud man, something of a Puritan, censorious and very fastidious. Yet his charm was irresistible and – as charm usually is – a dangerous quality. You could not discern what he was really thinking. Whenever I saw him I fancied that he liked my company and agreed with all I said. The moment he left me, I realised that he was assessing me at what I am worth. Ran Antrim, to whom I was talking about him, said, 'He was certainly a saint.' I don't think he was that, not at all. Then I asked Ran how he thought Michael Rosse was, as I was alarmed by Michael's sunken eyes. 'He is finished,' said Ran succinctly. We talked of dying. I said I feared the process, lest it was like a nightmare. He didn't think so, because a few years ago he very nearly died of heart failure, and was dragged back to life just in time. He said the sensation was a gentle sinking into nothingness. When Ran smiles, his rugged, creased face becomes smooth for a moment and alight. He is a far more sensitive man than one might think from his cynical manner.

On returning to Badminton this evening I found Tim Mitchell, the agent, having a drink with A. His conversation is fixed on the Beauforts. He venerates them, is fascinated by them, and has a loyalty of the sort which I imagine Cavaliers bestowed on Charles I. When he came he found it very difficult to carry out any reforms of the estate. Whenever he made a new suggestion, everyone said, 'I don't think His Grace would like that.' For that reason incumbents don't stay long in the church here. Unlike the agents, they don't feel the same deep loyalty; after all, they are not strictly speaking the Duke's servants. And mercifully the Duke will not tolerate Series 2 or 3 of the liturgy. The incumbents feel they lack scope for their beastly improvements. Michell thinks this vicar has settled, because he lacks ambition to rise in the clerical hierarchy. When the Queen was here in the spring the vicar and wife, just arrived, were bidden to dinner at 8.30. No one warned them that they should have arrived at 8.15. They were punctual at 8.30, just when the Queen was coming down the stairs. The butler rushed to the front door and beckoned the vicar to run for it. He slipped, poor man, and fell on the wet paving stones, covering his evening suit with mud. Imagine the horror of his situation! The Queen was all affability; the Duchess in presenting him said, 'See the state he's in, Ma'am. He's drunk, of course.' This little joke did not reassure the new vicar.[*] Mitchell said that only dukes may be buried beside Great Badminton church; even duchesses have to be interred in Little Badminton graveyard. The present couple won't have a wood fire in the one dark sitting room they use, but an electric fire. And of course the radiators are not on this winter. The butler spends from May till the following April polishing the silver to be used for the Horse Trials house party and the assembled royals.

---

[*] The Revd Thomas Gibson (b. 1923); Vicar of Badminton, 1974–93.

1976

1976

We lunched with the Beauforts in the large dining room, helping ourselves. The butler, having announced us, disappeared and was not seen
again. I sat next to her. She said, 'Your wife says I may call you Jim.
My name is Mary', as though I did not know it, but it was kindly
meant. A. sat next to him and in spite of her misgivings got on well,
chatting about Westonbirt and the Menzieses. He said to me after that
the reason why he had not called on us was that he was so fond of
Aileen Taylor he could not bring himself to enter our house. I liked
him for this. He said he worried about her death, hoping she had not
been in pain or distress, for she was found dead by Peggy* one
morning in the kitchen. We were shown the Worcester porcelain
she left the Duke. It is in a showcase at the top of the stairs. Just as well
it is, for there it will remain longer than the Somerset family, in all
probability.

   She has a funny little-girl manner of speaking, and is often sharp
and to the point. She took us into the bedroom the Queen has, and
which Queen Mary used during her long stay. It faces south and is
darkened by the great cedar. Q. Mary urged the Duchess to have it
cut down, her objection being the insects which she claimed harboured there and came through the window. The Duchess said, 'Over
my dead body, Ma'am.' The reply was, 'Very well, it must remain, my
dear.' Odd little incidental remarks she drops, like, 'Yes, I have been
to Vienna. I stayed at Schönbrunn, with the old Emperor. He was very
nice to children.' And, 'You know, my grandmother the Duchess of
Teck was rather fat.'

---

* Peggy Bird, the excellent 'daily' whom the L.-Ms had inherited from Miss Taylor.

Monday, 12 January

A. and I dined with John Betjeman and Elizabeth in her [London] house. He holding my book [*Ancestral Voices*] in his hand as I entered and throughout the evening reading extracts. And when he read them, they did seem funny. I accompanied him to his house three doors away to collect a bottle of Australian wine he wanted us to sample. Jolly good it was too. I opened a volume of Lord Alfred Douglas's* poems, with a dedication to J., addressed to 'Moth from A.D.' and dated 1923. I said, How did you know him so early? He said he wrote him a fan letter from Marlborough. They at once became friends, of a totally innocent sort. But Mr Betjeman father, discovering several letters from Bosie, sent for John, then aged about fifteen, to tell him he would not allow the correspondence to continue. He said to John, 'Do you know what a bugger is?' 'No,' said John, knowing perfectly well. 'Well, a bugger is a man who gets hold of another, and by a process of mutual admiration, so works on him that he puts his piss-pipe up the arse of the other. And can anything be more disgusting than that?' 'No, father.' As we were leaving I told John that Bamber Gascoigne's tele series on Christianity was going to be very anti-Christianity. Midi, whom I saw at six, told me so. John said it is no matter how many millions watch a film that is anti, they are not influenced by it. It is pro films that influence people. Then he said something that shook me a little, namely that he didn't mind about religion going, it was the churches going that mattered to him. I said, 'Yes, but John, you and I know that it is the Eucharist that matters to us more than everything else.' And he said, 'Yes, it is.'

Monday, 19 January

This morning there arrived by post from Switzerland a Xerox sent by Ali Forbes of a letter written to him by Stephen Spender, abusing me. In it Stephen says he has always loathed the sight of me, and disliked my very appearance, which is that of a sinister undertaker who with

---

* Lord Alfred 'Bosie' Douglas (1870–1945); yst s. of 9th Marquess of Queensberry; poet and nemesis of Oscar Wilde.

his spade thrusts moribund, not dead corpses into the grave. That he sees my soul as a brown fungus upon a coffin, etc. That he has never spoken more than a dozen sentences to me in his life. Now this is pretty mischievous of Ali Forbes, I consider. None the less I am affected by Stephen's letter. Not gravely, because I do not like him and know that what he writes is pretentious tripe, yet affected by the knowledge that there is someone alive who can write such disagreeable things about me. I have replied to Ali, saying what a pity Nancy [Mitford] is not alive, she would have hooted with laughter; that I have forwarded the letter to the Poet Laureate, and will ask Heywood Hill's shop to frame and exhibit it; that it always interests me that Communists use such extravagant language, and I presume Spender still to be a Communist, although I doubt whether he admits to being a Party member, since most Communists prefer not to disclose this fact. I hope the mischievous Ali may send a Xerox of my letter back to Spender.

Saturday, 24 January

Dined tonight at the House. Rather surprised to be asked so soon after lunching there. We took Eardley [Knollys], who was staying. This time a butler and footman, or their equivalent out of livery, were waiting. That poor, tiresome old Mrs Durant staying again, and Lady Londesborough, looking dreadfully ill, ashen grey and taciturn, like Lady Macbeth, A. said. Duke dressed in the hunt livery, E. and I in dinner jackets. She can be very funny. She said she received a letter from the Bishop of Malmesbury, signed Frankie Malmesbury and a cross after the name. She wrote back asking if the cross signified a kiss. She is always ready to tell stories about Aunt Queen Mary when she was staying here during the war. One day the Queen sat next to another bishop during luncheon. She gave the bishop a large piece of hard, coarse dog biscuit, telling him to give it to the Labrador which was nuzzling the other side of him. The bishop, who was slightly deaf and very old, with new false teeth, proceeded to gnaw it himself, with evident pain. Queen Mary relished the spectacle.

The Duke has limited charm, and his manners are almost the best I have encountered. He told that when he was a boy the family was obliged to leave Badminton every summer for two or three months for Troy House, Monmouthshire, because the water supply dried up. The house was not on the mains, and the wells became exhausted. He told us that the game of Badminton was invented by his great-aunts to amuse themselves on wet days in the great hall. The objective was not to defeat your opponent, but to keep up a rally as long as possible. The old scores give outstanding rallies of 250-odd. I imagine that Victorian lawn tennis, which was pat-ball, had the same objective.

Friday, 26 March

All this week I have been upset by the return by the Compton Russell Press of my Stuart MS, with the curtest note, with no beginning or end, merely the words 'I am afraid we cannnot help you with this', which I consider off-hand and insulting. I had written offering to forego an advance. It is the ultimate rejection of this work, over which I took infinite trouble and spent years of research. Moreover I know it to be among my better books. It is my fault for failing to come to an agreement with a publisher before undertaking it. Now I am beginning my novel, which is moving very stickily. How to make characters emerge is the problem. I suppose one ought to have them in mind before one starts, not let them emerge in the course of writing.

Wednesday, 31 March

I am reading *The Dukes* by a young man, Brian Masters.* It is fair, impartial and amusing. Full of funny stories. One amazing link with the past he gives. Princess Alice,† who is still alive, met someone who was present at the Duchess of Richmond's ball held in Brussels on the eve of Waterloo.

---

* Writer (b. 1939), whose prolific output included biographical works on great women of the past and serial murderers.
† HRH Princess Alice, Countess of Athlone (1883–1981); last surviving grandchild of Queen Victoria.

Wednesday, 7 April

Last night in London I re-experienced a sensation of my youth. I was alone. I was staying with John Kenworthy-Browne, therefore I had no genuine cause of loneliness. But I had tried in vain to get hold of a number of old friends, Patrick [Kinross], Rosamond [Lehmann] and others, for dinner. Telephoned; no answers. Reconciled to dining by myself at Brooks's. Before dinner went for a walk around Westminster, looking at street buildings. Wandered into the Abbey cloisters just as the lights were turned on, in the twilight. Not a soul. There I was smitten with the loneliness of my youth when, friendless and poor, I used to walk the streets and think the passers-by so much happier than I, all so purposeful, so fulfilled, so content. Last night, I did not actually experience this unhappiness again, but I recaptured its flavour of sadness, nostalgia and utter hopelessness.[*]

Sunday, 11 April

The whole Royal Family is staying at the House for the Three-Day Event. What shocks me is that whenever they are here the church is filled to the brim for Sunday morning service. Since I go to the eight o'clock Eucharist and seldom to Matins, which doesn't fulfil me, I did not want to attend today, to be among the gapers. However, A. insisted; and we as villagers were given tickets. We sat in the middle of the nave close to the Royal Family, so I did have a good stare. All the young princes and princesses, and Mark Phillips, sat in one front pew, and a very pretty lot of children they were. Princess Margaret however looks miserable, trussed up like a brooding hen, pigeon-breasted and discontented. I like the Royal Family to exist, but I don't want to know or be known by them. The Prince of Wales sporting a beastly beard, I hope temporary.

---

[*] J.L.-M. is here referring to a solitary six months in 1927–8 when, aged nineteen, he was the only man at a ladies' secretarial college in London. He became more gregarious when he subsequently went up to Oxford, and worked in London during the 1930s.

Thursday, 15 April

We dined with Pam Jackson to meet Debo who is staying. Just the four of us. Debo looking radiant again, and produced lots of samples of the lovely things she now sells in her shop at Chatsworth. I bought a shawl made from her Jacob's sheep and a pair of gloves for A. for Easter.

Much talk about Bobo. The sisters, all the survivors but Decca, are as hostile to David Pryce-Jones as ever. They have a letter ready to send the moment his book is published – it is upon us shortly – dissociating themselves from it, and telling the world that they have all the papers to which he has not had access. Debo said, 'But how can he get her right? He never knew her. She was magnificent, and so clever. Her attachment to Hitler was a mixture of adoration and fun, for she laughed like mad in describing him, and "his sweet old mackintosh".' The truth is that the world today does not find Hitler any funnier than cancer.

Good Friday, 16 April

Ann Fleming asked us to luncheon today, because Roy Jenkins and his wife wished to meet us. We went. The Peter Quennells were staying, and Stuart Hampshire,* Warden of Wadham, a dour, distinguished man with white hair. A. sat next to Roy Jenkins, who was easy and entertaining. He was very polite to me, but I am embarrassed when strangers wish to discuss my books, and I endeavour to ward them off. This does not make me appear sympathetic, I am sure. He said he admired *Ancestral Voices* as an important chronicle of the times. Could not put it down, etc. How often have I heard this said? Whereas Harold Acton's *Nancy* bored him, and he could not finish it. Said she would be totally forgotten in ten years' time, whereas *Ancestral Voices* would be read in years to come. Flattering nonsense. A good talker, expletive, gossipy, indiscreet – overheard him tell Ann how he turned the new Lord Chancellor out of his room at the Ministry. Poor teeth, drinks a lot. Smokes a large cigar. Much addicted to the good life. No harm in this, were he not a Socialist. I was attracted by her much.

---

* Sir Stuart Hampshire (1915–2004); Oxford philosopher.

Unfortunately did not sit next to her and had no opportunity of a talk before or after. I am too shy. She looked at me throughout the meal with a smiling, quizzical eye. Until we left I had no idea she was Chairman of the Historic Buildings Council and that she wanted to talk to me about country houses, so Michael Astor told the Berkeleys. Why had Ann not told me? She supposed that I had known.

Wednesday, 21 April

I am still able to go for quite long walks, even after days, sometimes weeks of no walking. The other day in London I walked from Brooks's to John [K.-B.]'s house in Hollywood Road [Fulham] after dinner and after walking round Westminster for an hour or more before dinner. How much longer shall I be able to do this?

Wednesday, 2 June

Glyn Boyd Harte,* a friend of Colin McMordie, came down from London for the day to draw me. The result was rather startling, in garish coloured pencils; the eyes good and other features, except the mouth – the most difficult feature always, and my mouth has no form and swims like a jellyfish. The whole head a little too narrow. On the other hand, a goodish likeness. A work of art? He is to include it in his exhibition held in York next week. A bubbling young man with whom it was a pleasure to be. We talked ceaselessly, but with one in his twenties the gap is a yawner. He belongs to the new though he is fascinated by our oldie world. I liked him. Very plain.

Friday, 4 June

I rang the Berkeleys this evening to enquire after Patrick [Kinross] who had suddenly gone into hospital two days ago. Babs† answered, and to my horror said that Patrick had died at midday today. Lennox and Freda went to see him in the morning, before they left for Aldeburgh. Babs

---

* Artist, illustrator and dandy (1948–2003).
† Bridget McKeever, the Berkeleys' housekeeper.

very upset, and said Freda would be greatly distressed. I can hardly believe he is gone. He was to have dined with me next Tuesday. He really was one of my oldest and dearest friends. He has given more pleasure to more people than most, on a minimum of money, for he has always been poor. The irony is that at last the money he had inherited from Violet Trefusis had come to him; and his great book on the Ottoman Empire had been accepted by an English (in addition to an American) publisher, and also accepted by the Turks in serialisation form for the largest sum they have ever paid a writer, Turkish or foreign. All this anticipation must have given him great pleasure. He was a tiger for work, and would say he was only happy working. Luckily he was pretty well able to work till the end, and I don't think he once imagined that he would not continue to do so when he came out of hospital. He was always optimistic. The dearest old thing in the world.

Sunday, 6 June

Dining last night at the House I asked Mary Beaufort if I might bring Kenneth Rose,* who is writing a book about King George V and Queen Mary, to see her. She consented, then told me how well she always got on with George V, who terrified most people. He more or less adopted her when Princess Mary† got married. He would bark at her and she barked back. He liked that. Dinners here are sticky, and the food is disgusting. The grey parrot in the Raglan Room is a help after dinner, for he does say the most amusing things. Goodbye and good morning, imitating the rather refined housekeeper Mrs Nettles's voice. He also imitates Master's deep sighs on his return from hunting.

Tuesday, 8 June

Since Patrick was to have dined with me this evening, Feeble and John Betjeman had me to dine with them. J.B. very unhappy over Patrick's

---

* Historian and journalist (b. 1924); writer of 'Albany' column in *Sunday Telegraph*.
† HRH Princess Mary, Princess Royal (1897–1965); only daughter of King George V and Queen Mary; m. 1922 Henry, Viscount Lascelles (1882–1947), who s. 1929 as 6th Earl of Harewood.

death. He recited, in so far as he could remember it, the ode on the Queen's Silver Jubilee which he has completed after much sweat and tears and submitted to the Sovereign. She is delighted with it, and so is the Duke of Edinburgh, even over some complimentary and funny stanzas, not for publication, about HRH discreetly walking behind. The ode is very simple, and will most probably excite ridicule, as John is aware.

Patrick had beautiful, sensitive hands, with long elegant fingers. Why I so greatly lament his death is because he was one of those few to whom I could say anything. Vita was another. There are few such when one starts totting them up. Eardley, J.B. are others. Ros Lehmann too. Jamesey P.-H. was another.

Friday, 11 June

Today went to Bath, and finished typing out another chapter of the novel. Heard my doorbell ring. Then saw a woman looking through the window. Threw up the window and asked her what she wanted. It was Jan Morris. She asked if I would lunch today to meet Elspeth Hoare. Very kind indeed, but I explained I was just off to Patrick's funeral. Asked her to have a drink with me next Wednesday. I hate being dropped in on. The worst of my library is its being on the ground floor.

Train beautifully punctual. Walked to Paddington Green church. Many society people assembling, some in tails and many in deep mourning. J.K.-B. there and sat with me at the back of the church. Lovely church, splendidly restored by the late Erith. A most moving, old-fashioned funeral, done with great style. Masses of country flowers. Large coffin in the sanctuary. I managed to avoid seeing it, only the candles on it. Had to turn away when it came out and managed to control myself. Paddy [Leigh Fermor]* read one lesson with his difficult voice. John Betjeman's address from the pulpit most beautiful. Said Patrick never got angry, yet could be caustic. Worked, worked. All tributes to him something to envy. I waited behind so as

---

* (Sir) Patrick Leigh Fermor (b. 1915); writer, living in Greece; m. 1968 (as her 2nd husband) Hon. Joan Eyres-Monsell, photographer (1912–2003).

to avoid people but Natasha Spender came up to me, and was very sweet. We held hands and both said, forgive, forgive. I was almost in tears by then. J.K.-B. most understanding. Accompanied me into the public park. We sat on a bench and I recovered myself. He then took me to Paddington, gave me tea in the hotel. Oh dear. Dreadful to watch J.B's painful ascent to and descent from the high pulpit. Osbert [Lancaster] there looking a million. Home for dinner.

Thursday, 17 June

Last weekend we stayed at Chatsworth. Andrew [Devonshire] only appeared for breakfast on Saturday, having returned the previous midnight. Other guests were Lady Cholmondeley* and the John Smiths.† I had always been bored stiff by the mention of Lady C's name. But she is delightful, and intelligent, and fascinating. *Très grande dame*, and sharp. Very friendly and pressed A. and me to stay at Houghton in August. Praised *Ancestral Voices*, and told me that Artur Rubinstein‡ said I must publish a second volume. (Have just heard from Norah Smallwood that Chatto's will publish Vol. 2 in September next year. Quite right not to do so before then.) Lady Cholmondeley's voice is so distinctive that I find myself talking like her for three days after leaving Chatsworth. Has that Edwardian preciseness and upper-class assurance. Delivery strangulated. No flush of sentimentality.

Debo says the fate of Chatsworth hangs by a thread. Although their numbers are vastly increasing, the maintenance costs are £100,000 a year, exclusive of their other houses and personal expenses. They have three night watchmen, and three private telephonists, and I should imagine no staff in England is treated more generously.

Billy Henderson§ has been painting [a picture of] the library in number 19 [Lansdown Crescent] all last week, with me sitting on

---

* Sibyl Sassoon (1894–1989); m. 1913 George Cholmondeley, later 5th Marquess.
† (Sir) John Smith 1923–2007; banker; MP for Cities of London & Westminster, 1965–70; Deputy Chairman of N.T., 1980–5; founder of Landmark Trust; m. Christian Carnegie.
‡ Pianist (1888–1982).
§ Painter (1903–93); formerly senior aide to the wartime Viceroys of India.

the sofa. From time to time he calls me from my typewriter and makes me read, cross-legged. Likeness already good, but my long legs won't come right. Room going to be very good, in deep tones. A most sympathetic man whom I already know as well as anyone, so many friends in common. He told me while we walked up the hill after lunching that he was seduced by a master at his private school when he was eight.

Yesterday Jan Morris came for a drink. Billy there when she arrived. She is convincing as a female. Did I not know her story I would certainly take her for a woman. But she is tall, and fairly largely built. Pretty face, rather prominent chin. Good clear teeth. Good legs. Failed to notice hands. Giggly manner, rather coy. First thing I noticed as she stood talking to me in the small lobby of the flat was a slight feminine body smell. Billy left and I talked with her for half an hour. Feeling her way, not absolutely easy. Likeable, and very clever. Wishes Bath wasn't so beautiful because she dislikes its provincial society.

Thursday, 24 June

On Sunday afternoon A. and I motored to stay the night with Mickey Renshaw* at Leeds Castle [Kent]. The owner Lady Baillie† died two years ago and left it in trust to be kept exactly as it was – apart from some extremely valuable furniture which had to be sold to augment the endowment. Castle is to be used for Anglo-American medical conferences. Mickey is not one of the trustees but has been co-opted as a man of taste, having been an intimate friend of Lady Baillie. The chairman Lord Geoffrey-Lloyd‡ was present and acted host. We were received by the family butler and were given tea, Mickey and G.-L. being out for a walk. House redolent of servants and gardeners. We stayed in a suite of magnificent rooms. Whole inside rather 1920s Hollywood style, vastly high bedrooms and tester beds, bathrooms

---

* Journalist, sometime *Times* correspondent (d. 1978), rumoured to be the illegitimate son of Lord Kitchener; friend of A.L.-M.
† Widow of Sir Adrian Baillie, 6th Bt (1898–1947).
‡ Geoffrey Lloyd (1902–84); Conservative politician; cr. life peer 1974 as Baron Geoffrey-Lloyd.

with marbled walls – not my taste, but some marvellous contents, Meissen birds, a Tiepolo picture and one splendid room brought from Thorpe Hall. We were given an excellent dinner, waited on by the butler. The public see the Gloriette which is a detached part of the castle, furnished with rare medieval oak furniture and tapestries, stiff and rather boring. The 1820 wing kept for the occasional conference guests and, it seems, the trustees who go whenever they like, give orders and live in luxury and ease. A kind of All Souls elitist arrangement of which I entirely approve. Endowment apparently £2 million.

From Leeds – which outside is one of the most romantic and lovely castles I have ever seen, with moat on which black swans drift, ragstone walls stretching straight from water, basin of hills, woods, gardens, bird sanctuary – we went to Sissinghurst to stay with Nigel [Nicolson] for two nights. Sissinghurst looking superb. A., who is critical, could find nothing to carp at. She thought the garden as good as when Vita left it. All due to the pair of lady gardeners who remain, having been taught all they know by Vita.* Conditions very different from Leeds; almost spartan and very oaksy, but nice. Nigel's daughter Juliet† staying. Aged twenty-nine, fine countenance, splendid large eyes, largish nose like Nigel's, good teeth, milky skin, whole impression very startling, slim figure like Vita's and the same dignified way of holding herself and walking, almost same articulate manner of speaking. Sweet to us, and very intelligent indeed. A great credit to Nigel.

Object of visit was to read papers and references to Harold for my *DNB* entry on him. Nigel very kindly prepared a paper of notes for me, at the end of which, to my amazement, he wrote, 'Why, dear Jim, do you not write Harold's biography?' The very idea that I could do such a thing! Well, perhaps I could. I am in a state of indecision, perplexity and wonder. Must consult Raymond [Mortimer] and Norah [Smallwood]. But could I possibly? I know nothing about diplomacy and politics. And do I find Harold, whom I loved and revered, quite my sort of subject? I like romantic figures, Beckford, Byron, and H. was never this. Vita was. Oh Lord!

---

* See 26 August 1981.
† Er daughter (b. 1954) of Nigel Nicolson; m. 1977 (diss. 1995) James Macmillan-Scott.

Saturday, 26 June

What an odd man Nigel is. Affectionate, fair, honourable, just, dutiful, extremely hard-working, a first-class writer, an exemplary parent, an aesthete, exceedingly clever yet modest. At the same time is he quite human? He speaks didactically, in a precise, academic manner. He is a cold man who wants to be warm, and cannot be. He has humour, and understanding, being totally without prejudices. Discusses his parents' love lives as though they were strangers. Asked me whether Harold picked up young men of the working classes. No, I was able to tell him. Asked me if I had had an affair with Harold. Yes, I replied, but he did not fall in love with me for longer than three months. Nigel told me that he was in love with James [Pope-Hennessy] at the same time as his father was and had an affair with him. I know more about this incident than he thinks. For Jamesey told me he was in love with Nigel and used to lie with him, though without touching. That has always been Nigel's failing, the inability to make close contact. I expect he regrets it in middle age.

Wednesday, 30 June

Kenneth Rose, having expressed a wish to meet Mary Beaufort to put to her questions about King George V and Queen Mary, on whom he is writing a book, came for the weekend. A grateful, appreciative and kind guest. We dined at the House, always an awkward proceeding. Master, wearing a blue pullover, greeted us with the words, 'I had no idea you were coming.' Present old Mrs Durant with whom I have a semi-historical flirtation, which is trying. Conversation sticky all round, although A. got on well with the Duke. He said he wanted to pay us a visit. So A. said, 'What would you like?' He replied, 'I would like to dine.' So she wrote a letter to Mary Beaufort, quite properly, thinking she would refuse and he would accept, for next Thursday week, whereupon within minutes she telephoned to say she would come, but Master couldn't. We query whether in fact she ever told him. It is possible that he would like to come alone, but we cannot ask him to do so, for we don't know him or her well enough. Kenneth R. who is sensitive to situations remarked that he was short with her, and seemed irritated. We ate out of doors beside the cedar tree.

Brother Dick and Elaine stayed Monday and Tuesday nights. They were good and went out all day Tuesday. Dick as sweet as ever; she older. Dears though they were, we have nothing to talk about except family matters. They had not seen this house before. Yet not one word of praise, or dispraise, nor any notice taken of what we have done, no observations, no questions. I said to Elaine, 'You must see my bedroom.' She walked in, gave a quick look, and walked out without a word. We suppose it is because they are frightened of saying the wrong thing that they say nothing. They do not know. That is the sad thing. Simon came to dinner on their last evening. Same with him. Total non-registers. What communication can there be with such people? Total lack of interest makes for total dullness.

Wednesday, 7 July

Stayed night of 5th with Eardley [Knollys]. Heat wave continuing. Whole country parched, and trees dying. Found E. naked but for a pair of long blue shorts, with white skin, smarmed hair (for he had just had a bath), flabby muscles, pendulous breasts, looking like Picasso aged 90. How can aesthetic persons bear to be seen in this condition at seventy-four even by their intimates? He advised me against the Harold book on the whole. Said I might not understand or be interested enough in the diplomacy periods, for I would have to discover what was the Persian government's attitude to the Soviet encroachments on the district of Izbah in May 1924. Much in this. Had a long talk with Norah, who was most interested and happens to be staying with Nigel next week and will discuss with him. She surprised me by saying that she wondered if the present generation of readers had heard of Harold, and she is going to sound bookshops. I still don't know, and await discussion with Raymond.

Monday, 12 July

Dear Raymond dined with me at Brooks's. The heat appalling. He ate very little, cold galantine and half a melon, I the same, plus one bottle

of Pouilly Fuissé, and the bill just under £10. Upstairs in the subscription room we sat on a sofa under the *Dilettanti* Reynolds. I
cracked my head against the underframe and for a moment thought I
had broken my skull. I then consulted him about Harold. Like most
old people (and as Eardley said, like Raymond always) he hardly listened to what I had to say, and instead talked, most interestingly, about
Harold and Vita, and when I finally interposed, 'But dear R., what I
want is an honest opinion whether you think I am capable of writing
this biography?' the quick reply was 'Yes', and on he went. The truth
is that no person can give one advice. One must make up one's
own mind.

Wednesday, 14 July

Norah telephoned from Chatto's. To my intense joy is enchanted with
my novel, subject to one or two suggestions. Was flattering about
style, felicity of word use. I in seventh heaven. Also she talked to Nigel
about Harold book. Emphasises that Nigel particularly wants diplomatic and parliamentary aspects dealt with fully. I incline towards this
venture now, the challenge. Will depend on talk with Nigel when he
lunches with us next week.

Tuesday, 20 July

Nigel and co-editor Jo Trautman lunched. N. rather engaging in
telling us how he regrets having asked Edna O'Brien* to write Vita's
life, since she does not intend to refer to Vita's writing. We said, 'We
dare say you feel the same about J.L.-M.' N. laughed and said Ben
was delighted at the idea. V. sweet of Ben. Nigel again insistent that
Harold's diplomacy and politics must be dealt with fully. I concur
absolutely. Left it that I would have a go, and if at end of six months
I found the task beyond me, would throw in my hand. In October I
shall visit Sissinghurst and N. will let me take away loads of papers.
The quantity is daunting, as is the whole project. I gave N. my draft

---

* Irish novelist and short story writer (b. 1930).

of the *DNB* contribution on Harold to read and comment upon. Perhaps he will find it so bad that he will want to give me the sack at once.

Saturday, 14 August

David and Caroline [Somerset] dined here, alone. He was dressed in a pair of white linen trousers, narrow towards the ankles, a snow-white shirt with wide collar open at the neck, bronze-browned by the sun, a blue velvet jacket; always so immaculate, simply yet splendidly dressed. Talk of funerals. When the last Badminton agent, by name Rooke, died, he and Master attended the obsequies. The small church was filled with a disagreeable stench. Master, who is a simple man, whispered to David, 'I think there must be a dead rat.' David whispered back, 'No, I think it is a dead rook.' Master gave a guffaw, then suddenly remembered the occasion and frowned at David. David does not seem to know which of Master's titles will not come to him. He said, 'I know the Botetourt one [of 1305] won't.' I said, 'Horatia Durant told me the Herbert of Raglan one [of 1461] won't either.' 'Oh bother!' said David. 'Anyway, I think the Glamorgan one must. I like Glamorgan.' Caroline has a fine sense of what should not be done. The Beauforts have removed two figures of Prudence and Justice from the Grinling Gibbons monument to the 1st Duke, and propose to sell them at Sotheby's. These figures were specially designed to flank the tomb. I begged the Somersets to stop the sale. Caroline realises that it would be an act of philistinism and must be stopped. She does not however relish having to tell Master so. The Beauforts of course are totally without aesthetic sense. I went with Horatia Durant into his room after luncheon on Wednesday. Huge portraits of nineteenth-century Beauforts on horseback with hounds, all chairs and sofas draped with scruffy blankets for the dogs, foxes' brushes mounted, and plastic models of foxes littered around.

In the London Library half-way up the stairs is a large photograph of Harold [Nicolson] which looks me straight in the eyes with a quizzical expression. I interpret it as reproachful and questioning, benevolent as always but expressing doubt as to whether I am capable of writing his Life.

Sunday, 29 August

This evening I rang up Moorwood, and asked after Prue. Nick after some hesitation told me that she had been taken to Cirencester Hospital. Bad news. She was able to walk down the stairs, into the ambulance.

Tuesday, 31 August

Audrey's birthday, and we asked her to dine here, knowing how wretched she would be alone in her mill house. One of the grandsons was to motor her over. They tossed up which one of them it was to be. It was Nick. In order to leaven the family tension we invited Polly Garnett.* She came and chatted non-stop; very decent of her to come under the circumstances. We had warned her about the situation. At 9.10 Ted Robinson telephoned from the hospital to say that Prue had died at five minutes to nine. Discussion what to do with Nick and Audrey and how to break the news. I called Nick to the telephone and let his father tell him. I took Audrey aside and told her. She was stunned, and as it were frozen. No tears, merely anger against fate. Nick drove off and Audrey stayed the night with us.

Saturday, 4 September

Poor Prue's funeral at the dear little church of Bagendon, at which I have attended Prue's children's baptisms and Dale's wedding, and at which my old cousin Matty Leatham (*née* Constable)'s† funeral also took place forty years or more ago. Service of family and close friends only. I bit my underlip and just managed to control myself until, when it was all over, we left the graveside, and Dale‡ broke down and wept. It was moving to watch the three boys and Ted walk into the front pew next to ours. They were wonderfully controlled; also Ted, who

---

* Journalist married to Andrew Garnett, entrepreneur; former neighbours of L.-Ms at Bradley Court near Alderley.

† A great-aunt of J.L.-M's mother had married into the publishing family.

‡ Dale Stevens (b. 1944); dau. of J.L.-M's sister Audrey by her 2nd marriage; m. 1964 James Sutton (b. 1940), yr s. of Sir Robert Sutton, 8th Bt.

organised things throughout, seemingly unconcerned. Afterwards we had to attend a buffet luncheon at Moorwood. The Arthur family had come from Scotland, and I talked to Simon Glenarthur,* a charming young man resembling Matthew but better looking, and handsome Margaret Glenarthur, whose quiet dignity impresses.

Thursday, 9 September

A. and I had a splendid day. Left the house at 8.30, drove to Dartmoor – under two hours to reach Exeter. Reached Castle Drogo before it was open at eleven. Went round and over. Very satisfactory house of clean-cut granite. Inside exposed granite and plaster, rather Florentine Renaissance. Lovely little domed spaces in the corridors. Contents indifferent, but some splendid tapestries. Wonderful setting. Robust, unambiguous, original, and the material most carefully worked out and finished. A new family aspiring to, rather than arriving at, country gentryhood, and now the representative living upstairs in a tiny flat, all within my lifetime.

Picnicked on Dartmoor and at 1.45 arrived Yelverton. Went to interview Lord Carnock,† aged 93, in an old people's home. A midget's head: the back of it, what I could see, reminded me of Harold's. Small, dim blue eyes, very *malin*; downward-drooping mouth. None of Harold's bonhomie; on the contrary. He greeted me with the words, 'Why on earth do you think Harold Nicolson's life worth recording?' I mentioned his having been a public figure. He said his political life was a complete failure. 'His writing,' I went on. 'Everything he wrote was fictitious, and untrue,' he said sternly. I thought I was not going to get on with this old man. Nor did I elicit much from him but disparagement of H. Evidently resentful of H's success. But he told me some things about his childhood which I wanted to know – H's timidity, his sharpness, impishness, quickness

---

* Simon Arthur, 4th Baron Glenarthur (b. 1944); son of Audrey's 1st husband Matthew Arthur, later 3rd Baron Glenarthur, by his 2nd marriage to Margaret Howie.
† Erskine Arthur Nicolson, 3rd Baron Carnock (1884–1982); elder brother of Harold Nicolson.

and wit as a child. Lord C. kept harping on the unreliability of H's historical books. Didn't do justice to their father, nor to King George V. Herbert Samuel* told him that Harold was a joke in the House. Said that in the Thirties H. wanted to go back to the Diplomatic Service, but they wouldn't have him. Sorry as I was for this old, not undistinguished man languishing in a hideous little bedroom, with a few coloured photographs of horses and hounds framed and dotted on the walls, his pathetic little bottle which a nurse ran in to empty, his three pipes, his fingering nervously with the wire of his deaf aid, I could not like him.

No man is a hero to his valet, or to his family, it seems, yet he might have attributed some virtue to his distinguished, marvellous brother. Told me he only once saw Vita. Clearly had no love for her either. Kept saying, 'But of course I am quite uneducated and stupid' – stupid he is not. I felt constrained to say, 'I think you are too diffident.' This provoked a spark of assertiveness. 'After all,' he said, and puffed himself, 'I did my duty in the first war, which is more than Harold did. He ought to have fought but didn't. I got the DSO, the Legion of Honour, St Anne with Swords.'

After this strange encounter we motored to Powderham Castle. An open day. Wish I had gone while I was writing my *Beckford*. I went twenty years ago, and had forgotten much. The Rococo and neo-Classical additions extraordinarily interesting and good. Staircase a *tour de force* built by Kitty's† grandfather, elaborate plaster panels on ceiling and walls. But the present Earl of Devon a man of little taste. He has painted the walls of staircase a peacock blue and given the plaster relief a fawn hue instead of white. The Music Room done for Kitty by Wyatt extremely beautiful, with niches filled with urns on pedestals. I am sure this is how the niches at Claydon should be treated. A gorgeous full-length of Kitty in masquerade dress over the fireplace,

---

* Herbert, 1st Viscount Samuel (1870–1963); Liberal statesman.
† Sobriquet of William Courtenay (1768–1835), only son of 2nd Viscount Courtenay, with whom Beckford fell in love during a visit to Powderham Castle in 1779 (when Beckford was eighteen and Courtenay eleven); the ensuing scandal, to quote from J.L.-M's biography of Beckford, led to 'social ostracism, persecution, loneliness and permanent discontent'.

which we could not get close enough to see properly. Also another likeness of him with father and mother, I think by Downman, likewise invisible.

Thursday, 7 October

John Pope-Hennessy has lent me Harold's letters to Jamesey. I have been nervous of reading in them something disparaging about myself. But no. Jim has a heart of gold, H. wrote before the war. Yet these letters to Jamesey put me in my place, in that James meant so much more to Harold on account of his lively little mind. Harold clearly loved James until his dying day. He wrote to him when abroad that he missed him; that when in the evenings the door opened and someone else entered the room, he was disappointed. Almost an infatuation. Very touching. But naughty Jamesey traded on this.

Sunday, 17 October

On Wednesday I motored 150 miles to Sissinghurst for the night. Nigel had collected piles of files, boxes (wooden and tin), letters, diaries and papers relating to Harold's life up to 1929. He also prepared a careful list of each item, descriptive of contents; also a pile of books relating to Balliol, Wellington, etc. He is the most thorough person imaginable, and so helpful that I am overcome by his kindness. He is alone, without the children, and without any help in the house. So he took me to dine at Biddenden. On our return we talked about Harold and Vita till 1.45 a.m., very late for me. Then I had to read one hour in bed before I could get to sleep. Up betimes in the morning, looked through the papers to see that I needed them all. In pouring rain we stacked the things in the back of my car. By eleven I knew that N. was longing to get to his work, so I said goodbye and wandered round the garden in the rain under my umbrella. Even in mid October, in drenching rain, garden looking splendid. On leaving, I said to Nigel that it was a great responsibility having the loan of all his mother's and father's letters. He gaily said, 'It wouldn't matter much if they were lost. I have read through them all; and you will do the same. And I don't suppose anyone else will ever do so.'

1976

Saturday, 30 October

Zita James, whom we met (after many years) lunching with Eliza Wansbrough, told me that the young come from far and wide to sit at her feet and the feet of her sister, Teresa Jungman,* with whom she lives, just to hear them talk, and listen to their voices, and look at their hair-styles. Reason – that they belong to the Twenties, and figure so prominently in the diaries of Evelyn Waugh and other Twentyish persons. Yet to me Zita does not evoke the Twenties. The once dashing, sophisticated, fashionable Eton-cropped friend of the Sitwells and Elizabeth Ponsonby is now a withered, soberly-dressed-in-tweeds Cotswold lady of over seventy, without a trace of affectation or withitry. Very sympathetic and sensible. Both sisters are desperately hard up. Zita told me that Teresa has masses of Evelyn's letters which she will not allow anyone to read, in spite of constant approaches from thesis writers, nor sell, although they must be quite valuable.

Tuesday, 16 November

I am deep in Harold. Reading through all his letters, and Vita's to him. There are blanks in his life which I see no means of penetrating. One was the year in Madrid, 1911. Precious little about the first war years. His letters to Vita are all love letters, not long, and less interesting than his letters to, say, Sligger Urquhart,† or even to his parents during his Oxford and German cramming days. Love letters are not on the whole rewarding. The great test of my endeavours will be searching through Foreign Office papers in the Public Record Office. That tiresome man Sir Alan Lascelles refuses to see me. A pity because he is about the only survivor of Harold's Oxford friends. I have always found Sir Alan disagreeable, grumpy and disapproving. Why does he dislike me? Is it *Another Self* or *Ancestral Voices* which has made him take against me? Or merely that he considers me a poor

---

* Zita James (1903–2006) and Teresa ('Baby') Cuthbertson; 'the Jungman sisters', daughters of Mrs Richard Guinness by her first marriage to Dutch-born artist Nico Jungman; as girls in the 1920s, they had been prominent 'Bright Young Things'.
† Francis Fortescue Urquhart (1868–1934); Dean of Balliol College, Oxford, 1916–33.

fish? Or is it disapproval of Nigel's *Portrait*, and a distaste for being involved in further stuff of that sort?

Thursday, 25 November

To London on Tuesday, staying the night with Eardley. Quite an enjoyable and profitable visit. London Library all afternoon. As I walked into Brooks's at 4.30, a familiar voice sounded out of the gloom, 'Oh Jim, I guess I've been hoping to run into you.' It was Stuart Preston. Very friendly, not the least apparently cross with me. I made no mention of *Ancestral Voices*, but was effusively affectionate. We had tea upstairs together, and talked about friends and books (except mine). Eardley took me to the circus on Clapham Common. Didn't like the animals, though proud lions made at the crack of a whip to stand on little pedestals and the noble elephants made to dance; but the acrobats took the breath away, swinging and turning somersaults and landing in nets. The next day, St John Stevas,* a nice, rather queenly MP with a rather queenly house in Montpelier Square, showed me his newly acquired portrait of the Cardinal Duke of York. It is nice, and I would like to have it, but it is not by Batoni as he thought but a version of Hamilton's portrait in the National Portrait Gallery. Ran into Bruce Chatwin in St James's Square, overjoyed that he had handed in his book on Patagonia. At Wildenstein's in Bond Street I saw the ubiquitous Stuart again, wearing a funny little brim-less cap and a striped scarf as of house colours. Then the Keats–Shelley Committee. Dear Sheila Birkenhead† in the chair, Baba Metcalfe‡ and Mary Roxburghe.§ I don't like society ladies' committees: their forced bonhomie and business-like attempts to be non-society are unconvincing.

---

* Conservative politician (b. 1929); cr. life peer as Baron St John of Fawsley, 1987.
† Hon. Sheila Berry (1913–92), dau. of 1st Viscount Camrose; m. 1935 Frederick Smith, 2nd Earl of Birkenhead (1907–75); Chairman of Keats–Shelley Association, 1977–92.
‡ Lady Alexandra Curzon (1904–95); yst dau. of Marquess Curzon of Kedleston; m. 1925 Major E. D. ('Fruity') Metcalfe (d. 1957).
§ Lady Mary Crewe-Milnes (b. 1913); dau. of 1st and last Marquess of Crewe; m. 1935 (diss. 1953) 9th Duke of Roxburghe (d. 1974).

Saturday, 27 November

Mary Beaufort came to dinner with us at her invitation. The Territorials were dining at Badminton and she was turned out of her own house so that the men could tell each other 'coarse stories', as she put it. Her interests are confined to Badminton and the Royal Family. She asked what our Duncan Grant* picture was. She had heard neither of him nor of Bloomsbury. Anyway she thought the picture perfectly hideous. Told us she was at the Opening of Parliament this week in a dress worn by her grandmother the Duchess of Teck. During the Queen's Speech Michael Foot,† dressed in a shabby blue serge suit and red tie, was looking around and not attending respectfully. Master, standing beside the Queen with drawn sword, longed to cut him down to size. I wish he had. Mary told us that the Emperor Franz Joseph she remembered was a benign old man with white whiskers, immensely distinguished in a white uniform with red tunic and gold epaulettes. She and her brothers used to drive from Schönbrunn to the Gloriette where they ate ices and rich cakes and were sick in the wagonette on the return journey. Said even Princess Mary was terrified of King George V. When the King swore Queen Mary used to laugh if someone else was present, but when alone was not amused.

Having read Vol. 6 of his letters, I think I have fallen out of love with Byron. The Venice period of his life shows him in a very unattractive light – unscrupulous, vain, cruel and vulgar. But then, one should overlook the shortcomings of genius.

Sunday, 5 December

When I went to A's room to say goodnight she said that Benjamin Britten‡ had died. The news announcer referred to Peter Pears as 'his close companion', to whom the Queen had sent a telegram. Quite

---

* Bloomsbury artist (1885–1978).
† Labour politician (b. 1913), then Lord President of the Council; Leader of the Labour Party, 1980–1.
‡ Composer (1913–76; cr. life peer, 1975); professional and domestic partner of (Sir) Peter Pears (1910–86), with whom he lived at Aldeburgh and ran the Aldeburgh Festival.

right, but I thought what an advance this was, that the Queen should tacitly but publicly recognise a homosexual relationship. I hardly knew Britten, though knew Pears a little better. Britten didn't need people, I gather. Led an inner life. My first memory of the two is in Ursula Nettleship's house, next to 104 Cheyne Walk where I moved during the war.* I thought what a plain, abstracted, dim-looking man B. was. He once came to Alderley and we walked round the garden together, murmuring politenesses. Yet I felt an affinity unexpressed. Lennox [Berkeley] said that before Britten had published a composition he recognised genius in him, so that when his first piece (Michelangelo's sonnets?) was performed he was not the least surprised by its reception. Britten was of course suborned by the Soviets in Russia and foolishly claimed that Russia was a paradise for artists – because he and Pears were treated as VIPs in that hellish country.

Sunday, 19 December

Philip Magnus lunched at Brooks's. His strong advice was not to do the book in two volumes. One was quite enough, because, he stressed, Harold was a 'lightweight'. I hate that expression. For who are the heavyweights? – Churchill, Lenin, Hitler, I suppose, men of no one perfected distinction to their credit, whereas Harold was a writer of rare quality. How I hate politicians, great and small. Magnus did not much like Vita. Disapproved of her for her sloppy dress, trousers, chain-smoking throughout meals at embassies when they visited them during their cruises. Then, Magnus is a highly conventional man. He counselled me to tell all about H's sex life. Strange, from him. Then tea with Miss Niggeman† and maiden sister at Temple Fortune Court, North-something, miles beyond Golders Green. Took me more than an hour and a half to get there by a series of buses. Dear sweet people in a 'how' sort of flat, not small, but decaying Twenties, parquet floors lifting and old-fashioned bath tub with enamel off. Yet spotlessly clean; coloured photographs, framed, of flower pieces. Miss N. gave me some further papers relating to Harold, her book of lists of his

---

* As described in J.L.-M's diary for 16 November 1942.
† Harold Nicolson's devoted secretary.

friends telephoned over the years, obituaries, etc., quite useful. I don't think Miss N. liked Vita much either. She disliked Sissinghurst, for its cockroaches, mice, moths and corruption, and said whenever she left the place she felt a weight off her soul.

Friday, 24 December

Off for Christmas to Englefield Green. Have not been there, or seen the Droghedas, since Christmas 1974. Joan much smaller, frailer; Garrett with a stoop; Rhoda Birley almost senile, forgetful and unable to converse at all.

Saturday, 25 December

Motor in two cars to St George's Chapel, Windsor. The Ds and Derry sit under the stalls – Garrett under his own yellow banner with red mullets and moor's head and mantling crest – we three others on the knife board opposite them. Each time I notice something new. This time, the splendid closed gallery at the north-east corner of the chapel with portcullis emblem and rose emblem and fairy lattice coving. Was it constructed for Catherine of Aragon? The stall banner two away from Garrett's bore a pair of shoes, very modern in design and common, like Dolcis shoes. Are they Mr Wilson's?* Had a splendid view of the entire Royal Family, headed by the Queen, passing by the opening on the way down the north aisle to the choir opening. Queen Mother's hat like an apricot cockerel, enormous and unbecoming. After the service to the Dean's House where all the Royal Family assemble, they having walked through the Castle grounds from the west door. Found myself, having divested myself of G's borrowed overcoat, standing beside the drawing-room door. Couldn't back away. The Dean approached leading the Queen, followed by all the others, some of whom shook hands and said Happy Christmas in a jolly way. I was perpetually bobbing my head. A. the other side of me never stopped curtseying for five minutes.

---

* He had been appointed a Knight of the Garter after his retirement from the premiership in April.

Sunday, 26 December

Derry and I and Folly* walked in the morning across the Park to the Copper Horse and the Castle, about four miles. On the way Folly put up a hare and dashing after it caught herself in a barbed-wire fence, spun round and yelped with pain. Arrived rather hot at the Charterises'† house, the Winchester Tower, to find the Prince of Wales, Princess Alexandra and A. Ogilvy there. Was presented to the Prince and had a few words with him. He began, 'Did you start the National Trust?' Told him it was founded in 1895, even before my day. Thought the N.T. such a splendid organisation and asked if I had read Roy Strong's‡ excellent book on the Destruction of the Country House. I had contributed the opening chapter, but did not tell him this. He has the best complexion of a young man I have ever seen, the picture of freshness and health. Examined his gold signet ring, which has a crown and Royal coat-of-arms, somewhat worn. I longed to know to whom it had previously belonged. He asked how we liked living at Badminton, and said, 'Master is my hero.' When we were beginning to have a rather earnest talk about preservation our host interrupted by showing the P. a lump of carved marble, asking him what he thought it was. Couldn't guess. Charteris said, 'I think it is two people copulating.' The Prince in his rather sweet, intense way, said, 'And how do you make that out?' He examined it with close scrutiny, but could not satisfy himself. When he left he shouted to me, 'Give my regards to Master.'

---

* The L.-Ms had recently acquired two whippets, Folly and Honey, to take the place of Fop and Chuff who had died in 1973.
† Martin Charteris (1913–99); Principal Private Secretary to HM The Queen, 1972–7; Provost of Eton, 1978–91; cr. life peer as Baron Charteris of Amisfield, 1978; m. 1944 Hon. Gay Margesson.
‡ (Sir) Roy Strong (b. 1935); art historian; Director, Victoria & Albert Museum, 1974–87.

1977

1977

At dinner last Sunday at the House, A. sitting next to Master repeated what the Prince of Wales had said to me, namely that Master was his hero. He was touchingly diffident, surprised and delighted. 'But he can't have said that. It's not possible. You're pulling my leg.' How extraordinary these Beauforts are. Meals are dreadfully boring, and the food horrid, in spite of chefs and cooks. There is no waiting at the table and he does all the handing round and collecting of dirty plates, and the stacking. Poor old Horatia Durant and Miss Betty Harford* staying. Conversation out of the question, and platitudes and *politesses* without end.

I have had unfeigned tributes from the two partners in David Higham's agency to *Prophesying Peace*, David H. comparing me with Pepys. Whereas I know it lacks the spontaneity and sparkle of the first volume. Last night in Bath I tore up the original manuscript of the two years 1944 and 1945.

A. and I were asked by George Weidenfeld to his party given for Nigel Nicolson's sixtieth birthday. I didn't want to go, but on pressure from A., agreed. Truth is she will go to any party, I will go to any lengths to avoid one. It was awful. Crowds of strangers, hardly a soul I knew. Drank Dubonnet, seized a dry chicken leg and some carrots. No table to sit at; balanced glass in left hand, plate in other. Finally Baba Metcalfe, with the pertinacity of a woman, forced her way to an armchair, pushed me onto the stool beside her, and we ate from our laps and talked. She told me how she had had to take

---

* A cousin of the L.-Ms' former neighbours at Ashcroft near Alderley.

her father's* papers away from Philip Magnus because it was apparent he would never start the book. Instead she gave the them to Nigel, who suggested that as so many books on Curzon had been published, a book on the first Lady Curzon, Baba's mother, would be more suitable. Already Nigel has written half the book. Talked to Ben [Nicolson] who will lend me all the letters his father ever wrote to him. Said never did two brothers have a more perfect, understanding, adoring father. Talked to Anne Lancaster who says Osbert had another 'turn' in the Opera House five days ago. He sent her to the party to collect gossip and regale him.

Wednesday, 26 January

Last week Nick Robinson brought Nick Crawley, his Cambridge friend, to lunch with me in Bath. Afterwards we walked round the city, and I showed them the Holburne of Menstrie Museum† and Pump Room. I broke through the barrier. It was a help having the other nice boy with him. Then on Saturday Richard [Robinson] lunched with us alone, and we walked with his and our dog in the rain. He is nineteen and delightful, possibly the easiest of the three great-nephews. Told me he had a girl; met her at a New Year's ball, and is very excited about her. Said he had not imparted this information to the brethren, which flattered me. Also he talked freely about his father. This is a great worry, for Ted simply soaks, cannot attend to business and is a responsibility for the boys, who do not know what to do with him.

On Sunday we were taken by Billy Henderson to lunch with Michael Pitt-Rivers‡ at Tollard Royal [Dorset]. Michael must have

---

* George Nathaniel Curzon, 1st and last Marquess Curzon of Kedleston (1859–1925); Conservative statesman (Viceroy of India, 1898–1905; Foreign Secretary, 1919–24); m. 1st 1895 Mary Leiter, 2nd 1917 Grace Duggan.
† Museum in Great Pulteney Street housing art collection of Sir William Holburne (1793–1874).
‡ Michael Augustus Fox-Pitt-Rivers (1917–99); m. 1958–65 Sonia *née* Brownell (widow of George Orwell); owner of 7,500-acre Rushmore Estate, Dorset; after a sensational trial at Winchester in 1954 he had been sent to prison for eighteen months, together with his cousin Edward Montagu (3rd Baron Montagu of Beaulieu) and the journalist Peter Wildeblood, on charges of gross indecency.

been handsome, now about sixty and a bit heavy. He has a friend, William Davies, who has lived with him for about fifteen years and been dangerously ill with anorexia, owing to slimming. Is very affable, but frail and thin, with gold hair cascading over girlish face, but longish teeth which give away the age, wearing Mediterranean clothes, gold rings, bangles and medals round the throat galore. Michael P.-R. also singularly dapper, wearing country tweed suit with blue velvet collar to the jacket. Immensely rich, large landowner, breeder of Arab horses, planter of millions of trees. Explained that his name came from his paternal grandmother, daughter of the first Lord Rivers, who married a Lane-Fox. M's full name is therefore Lane-Fox-Pitt-Rivers. What could be more territorial? House half-timbered, strange for Dorset, and painted pink. No family portraits or outstanding treasures. A Japanese garden and pavilion just below the house, amusing but unsuitable in this context. Nice, civilised set-up. A's friends, not mine.

Wednesday, 9 February

I believe I ought to record my reasons for having left the R.C. church and returned to the C. of E. First, this Pope [Paul VI]'s encyclical *Vitae Humanae* [1968], condemning birth control out of hand. I regard overpopulation as the fundamental evil of our time. Secondly, the effect of the Second Vatican Council [1962–5] on the Liturgy – the scrapping of the Vulgate, and the vulgarity of the new rituals. Thirdly, the hideous Irish situation. The Irish Church is something so loathly that I cannot bear to belong to the larger body which contains it. Furthermore, I no longer believe in the dogmas which I used to take for granted, such as the Assumption, and Consubstantiation. Now I regard Holy Communion as commemorative, a sort of pledge of betterment, a swearing-in of allegiance to God, an act of amendment, an act of supreme worship. Holy Communion means more to me than anything in the world, but I no longer believe that Christ is in that wafer.

Monday, 21 February

Lunching with Joanie Altrincham on Sunday, I talked to John [Grigg] about my biography of Harold. I said how strange it was that when

Lloyd George was premier he could be living in sin with Miss Stevenson and nobody knew, or rather the public didn't know.* John said that everyone in high places knew well enough; that in those days living in sin was no impediment to a politician's career, whereas today it is, and he instanced the sad case of Lord Jellicoe having had a tart. We agreed the reason lay in the media today rootling out scandal and exhibiting it to the masses, whereas sixty years ago a public figure could be indiscreet discreetly. Today such behaviour is impossible. The unknowing public is far more censorious than a man's colleagues and friends.

Wednesday, 23 February

To London for the day to give Nigel and Ben [Nicolson] luncheon at Brooks's. We discussed the book. Nigel not in favour of two volumes: people would say, who *is* this man deserving of so much record? I asked them both many questions. Who was Aunt Frederica? Aunt Frederica? they repeated, and could throw no light. They are funny the way they talk about their parents dispassionately as if they were persons of ancient history, nothing to do with them. 'I don't think Vita actually had an affair with her.' 'No, Niggs, she may have slept with X.' 'My father was certainly much in love with so-and-so.' 'You know he wanted to go to bed with Patrick Buchan-Hepburn,† who wouldn't let him.'

Tuesday, 1 March

This evening, the Vicar commented to A. on the autocracy which governs this village and his church. When the Queen stayed last year Master invited the Bishop of Gloucester to preach, without consulting him, the Vicar, whose sole right it is to approach bishops for such a purpose. Master just shrugged off his remonstrance. Then the Vicar said

---

* Frances Stevenson (1888–1972) became Lloyd George's personal secretary in 1911, his mistress in 1913, and his second wife (the first having died two years earlier) in 1943.
† Diplomatist and Conservative politician (1901–74), with whom H.N. became infatuated in Tehran in 1926; cr. Baron Hailes, 1957.

that both David Verey* and the Archdeacon had got on to him, having heard a rumour that the Duke wanted to sell the Grinling Gibbons figures from the tomb in the church. The Vicar mentioned the matter to Master, who was furious, and said he would do what he wanted with the figures. They were his property, because Queen Victoria had given the monument to his grandfather. The Vicar retorted that, on the contrary, any object given to the church automatically became church property. So the figures have been packed up again and put in the stables.

Wednesday, 9 March

Went up to London to give Raymond [Mortimer] luncheon at Brooks's. I asked him how much he would mind references to his love for Harold. Answer was that he would mind any direct reference to the love affair, because at his age he could not stand an onslaught from critics like Auberon Waugh. So I promised to be discreet. Raymond deplored Nigel's publication of *Portrait of a Marriage*, and said it astonished him how deeply both boys disliked their mother. Anyway, we had an enjoyable luncheon and talk for about two hours, at the end of which I got little. Philip Magnus is right – one gets little by word of mouth. Only the written word is of use. Yesterday I met Lady St Levan† at the Francis Hotel in Bath. She was very nice indeed, and has a twinkle like Harold. She told me Harold was the kindest of men but insensitive in one respect – that because he was always laughing at himself, he imagined others would not mind his laughing at them. Many of them did.

Thursday, 10 March

Claud Phillimore, passing through Bath, came to see my library. A highly civilised, gentle man. He, like everyone else I meet now, talked

---

* Architectural historian (1913–84); m. 1939 Rosemary Sandilands (1918–2001), garden designer, who later edited *The Englishwoman's Garden* with A.L.-M.; they lived at Barnsley House near Circencester.
† Hon. Gwendolen Nicolson (1896–1995); sister of Harold Nicolson (and sometime lover of Vita Sackville-West); m. 1916 Sir Francis ('Sam') St Aubyn, 2nd Bt (1895–1978), who s. uncle 1940 as 3rd Baron St Levan.

about 'the book'. Begged me not to analyse H's relations with men, and merely leave them to the imagination or interpretation of the reader. I said I intended to do this, yet was faced with the difficulty of withholding truth. After all, if the subject of one's biography loved women one would be bound to say so. Yes, he said, but don't elaborate on whether they went to bed together. I said I would never do that unless I had proof positive, and unless the action had a distinct influence upon the story.

Saturday, 19 March

Today A. and I attended a ceremony at Tewkesbury commemorating the hundredth birthday of the Foundation of the SPAB [Society for the Protection of Ancient Buildings]. We lunched with a select few in the town. Hugh and Fortune [Grafton] were our hosts. I sat on Fortune's left, A. on Hugh's left, K. Clark on Fortune's right, Lady Pilcher on Hugh's right. So we were greatly honoured, seeing that I have not been on the committee for twenty years or more. Then we went to the west door of the Abbey, which to my surprise was packed with SPAB members. We, the illustrious few, processed to the front of the nave. A. and I sat in the choir stalls. The bishop and other dignitaries in the presbytery. Good service, Hugh G. reading parts of [William] Morris's original manifesto addressed to the Nation on learning of the threat to Tewkesbury Abbey in 1877, and K. Clark delivering a splendid talk about past and present threats to the heritage.

Monday, 21 March

A. and I had just got into the house from walking Folly in the park when the telephone rang. John Fowler in a husky voice announced that Robin Fedden died this morning in hospital, of cancer. And we had not even known he was ill. Robin was a brilliant man. I always felt he was wasted at the National Trust, because he was not a mere expert. He was a very good writer, in which capacity he never fulfilled himself. I had hoped he might on retirement write his masterpiece, but he was always diverted by pot-boiling. He did not lack industry or facility. If anything, his prose was too highly polished, but his style was impeccable. He was distracted, like Alan Pryce-Jones, by the plaudits of rich and beautiful people – in his case, women. A cold man, yet he was very affectionate, and loyal. Drink was his undoing, and I suppose undermined his extremely tough constitution. I mourn him.

Friday, 25 March

In London I went to dear Robin's memorial service in Victoria Road. The church was packed with his friends. I was not moved to tears, as I was at Patrick [Kinross]'s funeral. Does this mean that I was made of sterner stuff today? No, I think in the end it is a question of affection. Only when one's friends die and one accompanies them to the grave's edge does one realise precisely what they have meant to one.

Tuesday, 5 April

A. and I motored in the Mini all the way to North Wales, to stay Friday to Monday at Vaynol with Michael Duff. A very long way, and a terrible bite out of working days. The party consisted of Michael and three young men, all charming – Gervase Jackson-Stops, nicknamed 'Jerks-and-Stops' on account of his speech impediment; his friend Simon Blow,* handsome but for a duckbilled-platypus nose, also highly intelligent and sympathetic, albeit neurotic; and Tatton Sykes,† son of that archaic stick Richard Sykes, he too intelligent and gentle, wearing a moustache which makes him look just what he isn't – common. The three youths all aesthetes and good old no-nonsense Tories. Michael much aged, and clearly not at all well; stiff neck corroded by radium treatment, but still straight as a poker and handsome. Very funny his stories of Queen Mary and her ladies-in-waiting‡ are, though after three days one is surfeited. Besides, one cannot believe a

---

* Writer, former racing jockey (b. 1943).

† Eldest son and heir (b. 1943) of Sir Richard Sykes, 7th Bt (1905–78) of Sledmere, East Yorkshire, whom he succeeded as 8th Bt the following year.

‡ Michael Duff's mother Lady Juliet (1881–1965), o.c. of 4th Earl of Lonsdale, had been one of them.

single word he says. Very snobbish these upper-class people are. However, we quite enjoyed ourselves. Vaynol is a not-nice house which has been poorly truncated by Michael lately so as to be lopsided. The fake plasterwork on the staircase walls of poor quality. Went to Plâs-Newydd, not at all a worthy house for the N.T. to hold, apart from the Rex Whistler room which by any age would be considered an artistic *tour de force*. Situation of course splendid, although they have spoilt the lines of the tubular bridge, so much in the forefront of the landscape, since I was last there. Lord Anglesey* a hearty, bluff, casual man who reminded me of the late Charles Cobham† without his endearing manner. Very polite he was to us. Michael doesn't like him, but then they are polarities, these brothers-in-law. Their estates march. Vaynol gives an impression of doom; already has that given-up look, for there is no heir, or rather a nephew-heir whom Michael does not care for and who presumably will not live there. Bangor, horrid town, is creeping up.

Tuesday, 12 April

Eardley [Knollys], with whom I stayed the night, asked Richard Shone‡ to dine. Richard is very bright. He knows Bloomsbury backwards. Knows what Clive Bell thought of Lytton Strachey's review in the *TLS* of E. M. Forster's book in 1921. Will be helpful if I want to know what 'they' really thought of Harold and his writing. His book on Duncan Grant and Vanessa Bell§ has already sold 3,000 copies. He is going to stay with Duncan and suggested my coming down while he is with him, for he can make Duncan talk, knows how to stimulate the old man. R. told me that Duncan did tuck up with Harold; hence Vanessa's caustic remarks about both the Nicolsons when they

---

* Henry Paget, 7th Marquess of Anglesey (b. 1922); military historian.
† Charles Lyttelton, 10th Viscount Cobham (1909–77), of Hagley Hall, Worcestershire.
‡ Art historian (b. 1949); on staff of *Burlington Magazine* which he later edited.
§ Though she was married to Clive Bell, Vanessa's great love and professional collaborator was the basically homosexual Duncan Grant, who fathered her daughter Angelica, and with whom she lived at Charleston on the Firle estate in Sussex.

were together in Berlin in 1929, she, Vanessa, also being jealous of Vita's intimacy with [her sister] Virginia Woolf. These Bloomsbury incestualities!

Sunday, 17 April

Stayed this Friday to Sunday at Chatsworth. Andrew there, an unusual occurrence. Very charming he was with his superb manners, which can raise frontiers between him and those less sophisticated, but not between him and *hoi polloi*. He speaks fast in a rattle, and is inclined to laugh in anticipation of a subtle *dénouement* towards the close of his esoteric stories. Being deaf and dense I can't always catch the point of these stories, and so laugh in a wry, unconvincing manner. Much talk of Diana [Mosley]'s book [*A Life of Contrasts*] which was out on Thursday. All papers full of it. I have now read. It is courageous for it makes no apologies for her pro-Nazi bias, although she does not condone all the horrors perpetrated. She is right however in stressing that the enormities of Hitler do not equate with the enormities of Stalin and other Communist leaders, which are glossed over by our left-sympathising countrymen. Yet, as a reviewer has said, one black is not rendered white by another black. Today too sees the first extract in the *Sunday Times* of Decca's forthcoming autobiography [*A Fine Old Conflict*], which is going to be beastly. I spoke to Diana on the telephone. She asked if I had noticed the graceful tribute she paid me at the beginning of her book. I said, Yes, thank you, but it was you all who taught me about the delights of Keats and Shelley when we were children, and not I you. Diana's prose style is better than Nancy's; it lacks N's debutante touch, and is confident and adult.

Sunday, 24 April

A. and I went to Holy Communion this morning at eight. In spite of the fact that Badminton is crowded up to the eaves with visitors for the beastly Three-Day Event, there were only four of us in the congregation. When we passed through the garden there was no flag flying from the flagstaff. When we came out of the church at 8.30 the

Royal Standard was up. Queen evidently sleeps with her window shut, not to be wondered at in that huge ice-box of a bedroom. Vicar upset because Princess Margaret had signified her wish to attend Communion at Acton Turville at 9.15. He also had to preach to the Royal Family at 11.30. I did not go to Morning Service, but A. accompanied Fortune [Grafton]. They were put in the pew in front of the Queen. She gave a nod to Fortune which apparently meant, 'Come in afterwards, whatever happens.' So after church she and A. went to the House for drinks. Alvilde talked to the Q. who was totally relaxed. A. began by saying she always got lost in the House in spite of the fact that she showed visitors around on opening days occasionally. This led the Q. to say that she was opening Sandringham to the public this summer and had to go there tomorrow to arrange the house for this purpose. 'Mummy is simply furious with me for opening it,' she said. I agree with Mummy. I see no need, and it will be an awful imposition. A. advised her to cover with polythene any fabrics within reach of fingers, for visitors touch everything.

Friday, 3 June

On Tuesday I motored to London for the National Trust's Architectural Committee meeting. I am going to resign from this committee because it bores me looking at drawings of tea rooms and lavatories, and besides I am bad at forming and giving opinions on contemporary designs. Then motored to Sissinghurst, ghastly drive out of London, no better than it used to be twenty-five years ago. Nigel took me to dine at a scampi inn at Benenden; food horrid, pretentious and expensive, over £12 for the two of us. The next morning filled the car with a second batch of Harold papers. Then motored to Charleston to lunch. There were staying Eardley, Richard Shone and Paul Roche,* and a boy of 23 who had returned from Canada in order to cook for Duncan. Air of decay about the house, of faded artistry. Duncan is a splendid patriarchal figure. Is wheeled in a chair; has a long benign Father Christmassy white beard, and wears a wide-brimmed

---

* Friend of Duncan Grant.

straw hat with long pheasant's feather swept back from the crown. Paul Roche ties his beard under a bib when he eats. He is apt to clean his paint brushes on his beard. Is naturally distressed by the barn beside the house having been bulldozed last week to the ground by the Firle estate's orders, without a word of explanation, let alone a word of regret to Duncan. After all, Duncan has lived with this barn for over forty years, and it features in many of his paintings. It is a bit hard at his age, 92.

Stayed the night at Wadhurst with Terence Davis,[*] not seen for many years. He has a charming young Belgian baron living with him. Terence told me that, having sold his London house to Ruby Holland-Martin,[†] he went to see Ruby one Christmas at Overbury. Took his parents, Birmingham business people. Terence was terrified lest his father should say 'cheers' when offered a drink. Was offered a drink; and did say 'cheers'. Immediately Terence tried to cover up the deadly word by saying, 'Chairs? Yes, I suppose they are by Chippendale.' 'No, Hepplewhite,' Ruby said.

Wednesday, 15 June

Ben Nicolson and Norah Smallwood stayed for the weekend. A good combination, for they are both indoor persons, given to much chatter. The weather was atrocious. No sitting out, but cowering over a fire while the rain poured down. Ben looks just like Harold's caricatures of him when he was a boy. Stooping, rabbity mouth open, long, drawn face, extremely thin, but now lame owing, he told me, to smoking too much, which has caused a blockage of an artery. Very uncouth, unshaven and grubby. Nasty old clothes, and trousers too short, showing a length of sickly white legs. But sweet and benevolent, and intellectual. Very pleased with the issue of the *Burlington* celebrating his thirty years as editor. Norah brought me the jacket of my book [*Prophesying Peace*], an apricot ground with Reynolds [Stone]'s most Rococo squiggles round the letters. Also brought me a page of *Round*

---

[*] Architectural historian (1924–83).
[†] Edward 'Ruby' Holland-Martin (1900–81) of Overbury Court, Worcestershire; Director of Bank of England and sometime Hon. Treasurer of N.T.

the Clock, which is in good large print. Reading the one page taken at random, I thought what drivel it was. Had much talk with Norah and Ben about the [H.N.] book. They advised not to fear repeating what is known already from Harold's *Diaries* and Nigel's *Portrait*.

Wednesday, 22 June

Last weekend we had to stay two boys A. has lately taken to – Sebastian Walker* and Donald Richards, or the beast and beauty, for the first is very plain with turned-up nose and dreadful little toothbrush moustache and bad complexion, while the second, though short, is extremely pretty, aged 27. They live together in a nice house in Islington in blatant sin, making no bones about their relations – in fact, a bit too much the other way. They say things like, 'Unfortunately, being gay, we got no wedding presents two years ago.' I like their frankness but not their flamboyance. Sebastian is a cheeky monkey. He calls everyone by his or her Christian name, whether he knows them or not. Called Sally Westminster Sally, and referred to Mary Beaufort as Mary. They both make a lot of money, Sebby as a publisher's agent, selling textbooks overseas, the other (who is Australian) as a stockbroker. They say they are so rich they don't know how to get rid of their money. Sebastian used to work for Chatto's and is about to return as a director. He told me he intended to succeed Norah as Chairman. They shocked us rather by disclosing that they used to shoplift, for fun.

Yesterday I went to London for two little ceremonies. The first was the presentation of a red rose to the Lord Mayor in the Mansion House at 11.30 a.m. on behalf of Lady Knollys, in permanent rent, or rather contrition, for having built in 1381 a bridge across Seething Lane connecting her house to a garden without first obtaining the Mayor's permission. We (Eardley, Lord K.,† and I) were lined up on either side of the Egyptian Hall. The Lord Mayor walked in, wearing a badge (no chain) of office and a tail-coat. Followed by a Master of the Watermen in long sable and ermine gown. On either side stood a row of Doggett's

---

* Later a successful publisher of children's books (1942–91).
† David, 3rd Viscount Knollys (b. 1931); grandson of 1st Viscount, Private Secretary to King Edward VII; cousin of Eardley Knollys.

Watermen, wearing scarlet uniforms and caps, holding an oar each. The Master read aloud an explanation of the purpose of the ceremony. A clerk presented to the Lord Mayor a freshly picked red rose on a golden embroidered cushion. During the address the Lord Mayor stood with dignity and aplomb, only his eyes smiling. The ceremony over, we moved to the next room and were given sherry, and a red rose each.

Then at 6.30 to 24 Chester Square to attend the unveiling of a plaque to Mary Shelley* who lived in this house towards the end of her life. A Mrs Hass organised the whole thing, and put up and paid for the plaque. She made a speech just like Joyce Grenfell[†] and called upon an earnest young lady with scooped-back hair, pince-nez and a green cloak to read a poem of Shelley's to Mary. This she did on the pavement in the most affected, genteel and emotional manner, so that I could hardly contain myself. Refrained from catching Sheila Birkenhead's eye for fear I should explode. Traffic roaring past and passers-by were amazed at the spectacle.

Sunday, 3 July

We motored to Weston for luncheon, having heard bad accounts of Georgia's health. A divine day, the first this summer. Sachie, eighty this November, very well, though bent about the knees. But poor Georgia not in good shape. Had a heart attack and on recovery tripped in a torn hole in Charlie Brocklehurst's[‡] Aubusson carpet and fell on her face. But as full of fun and chat as ever. Their recent burglary much upset them. They lost many small treasures – family miniatures, the canteen of Sachie's forebear which he used on service in the Peninsular War. Sachie bubbling with stories. I talked to him about Harold. He admitted that they (the brethren) did not like Harold. Why, I asked? Sachie did not seem to know, but said Harold was too Foreign Officey for them. Agreed that Edith[§] did not care

---

* Novelist (1797–1851); m. 1816 Percy Bysshe Shelley (1792–1822).
† British actress and comedienne (1910–79), famous for her satirical renderings of upper class Englishwomen.
‡ Charles Phillips Brocklehurst, of Hare Hill, Macclesfield, Cheshire.
§ Poet (1887–1964); sister of Osbert and Sacheverell.

for Vita. 'But then, women writers are always rivals.' I said the
Nicolsons were rather shocked by the Sitwell play taking off Sibyl
Colefax. 'Yes,' said Sachie, 'I can see now it was a cruel thing to have
done. When young one did foolish and regrettable things.' We lay on
garden *chaises-longues* in the shade at the back of the house. I am
becoming deafer; it was a strain to hear both Sitwells. S. has just read
Tom Driberg's* book, and is nauseated.

Friday, 15 July

This morning *The Times* had a longish obituary of poor old Joan Evans.
I had no inkling that she was on the point of death when I took Ben
to see her a month ago. She told him before he left that he must go to
the bookshelf in the passage and choose himself a volume. She was full
of sense and talk. I say 'poor old', yet I cannot pretend that I loved her.
She was so feminist, the successful girl from St Hugh's, so pedantic, academic, censorious of others not so educated as herself, so conceited.
Yet she was a scholar of some renown, a writer of good English, a
clever, well-informed woman. She was also generous, and I enjoyed her
company, although she did all the talking, never wished to know what
I was doing, and never once referred to the fact that I wrote at all.

If a single individual could report his experience of death, the
conduct of every human inhabitant of the globe would be influenced
by it; would be different.

Wednesday, 20 July

To Cambridge by 8.30 train from Liverpool Street. Took a taxi to
King's College, sought out the library, presented my letter from
Quentin Bell, was handed the thirty letters from Harold to Clive Bell,
when a youngish man introduced himself to me. It was Robert
Skidelsky. Full of praise for *Another Self*, which his great friend

---

* Flamboyantly homosexual journalist, Labour politician, Anglo-Catholic layman
and spy (1905–76); cr. life peer 1975 as Baron Bradwell; his posthumous memoirs
Ruling Passions, much expurgated by libel lawyers, had recently appeared.

Michael Holroyd* recommended so warmly. Interesting about Mosley, whom he has grown to like and respect. Diana is more politically passionate than he is. Says Mosley never hated the Jews; merely thought that international Jewry was a bad thing, and that East End Jews ought to be removed. 'Where to?' I asked. He said I ought to write a book about the Mitfords *en bloc*. I couldn't, greatly though I love them. At eleven Dadie [Rylands]† appeared beside me. Very affectionate and begged to show me his rooms and have a talk, which I did at three. Dadie's rooms lead straight off the College library, to which he has a key and access at all hours. We sat in his bay window overlooking the broad sward, the Chapel, the river and the punt poles. All so tranquil and civilised. Dadie said he rather disliked it now. Knew none of the dons, felt out of things, was not interested in the young. The room we sat in was the scene of Virginia Woolf's description in *A Room of One's Own*. Doors and fireplace surrounds painted by Carrington.‡ Curiously old-fashioned in that the shelves are jammed with china and the sideboards groaning with silver, brightly polished. 'My bedmaker does that,' he said. Showed me portrait of Lytton [Strachey] which he is leaving to the College. Dadie much older; little round pebble of a head, somewhat skull-like, thin skin stretched. Those piercing bluest of blue eyes. Somewhat protuberant in the stomach to which he pressed my hand on greeting.

Thursday, 21 July

In the train this morning a child banged the table next to me, ceaselessly, from when we left Paddington until we reached Swindon. The grown-ups in attendance never remonstrated, never showed signs of irritation. On the contrary, their eyes met in doting adoration. I could have wrung its neck. How idiotic people are about their own children.

---

* Writer (b.1935), who had achieved fame with his biography of Lytton Strachey.
† George Rylands (1902–99); Shakespearean scholar and Fellow of King's College Cambridge; old friend of Eardley Knollys.
‡ Dora Carrington (1893–1932); Bloomsbury Group artist who was in love with Lytton Strachey and committed suicide after his death.

Monday, 25 July

Derry [Moore] motored Diana Cooper to us for the weekend on Saturday. To my amazement, when A. warned Diana that we were to go to the Llewellyn–Barlow wedding that afternoon and would be away an hour or two, she volunteered to accompany us. Now, imagine another old woman of 85 wanting to do such a thing, a country wedding of people of whom she had never heard before! Such is her curiosity, love of the unexpected, the novel, and her enjoyment of every event. If asked to describe Diana as she is today, how would I do it? Physically, she is tottery on those tiny feet (how tiny they are, almost like Chinese). Her face is still miraculously beautiful. That flawless profile, nose and chin. Less good full-face. Yet the cold blue eyes are absolutely clear and fresh, those eyes which I once thought insolent, and which frightened me. Again she told us how shy she is; she has to fortify herself with a stiff drink before she goes to any party. I must say this weekend she drank little, was never tipsy, and behaved admirably. When she doesn't behave admirably, she becomes slightly tiresome. For the same reason, shyness, she wears her wide-brimmed hat, to hide under, she said, while clawing the brim over her face. She never has been able to speak one word in public; when she was an MP's wife, and an ambassadress, it had its drawbacks. Yet she could never do it.

What puts her shoulder-high above her contemporaries is her interest in everything; her love of discussion; her voracious reading of new books; study of new theories; wanting to know the meaning of words from the dictionary, a date from a dictionary of dates. She is ready to do anything, go anywhere. She is the perfect guest, being undemanding, taking the rough with the smooth. After lunching at the Barlows',* and going to the church, where she put herself in the best seat while I parked the car (when asked by an usher whether she was the bride's or bridegroom's friend, she said she knew neither), on return to Badminton she went straight to bed. Slept till dinner, which was with the Somersets. On return home sat up talking till midnight. Enjoys food, she says, though she eats nothing to speak of, like a bird. Doesn't

---

* Basil and Gerda Barlow of Stancombe Court, Gloucestershire.

mind what time she has breakfast, or what breakfast is. She is exceedingly quick on the uptake, is naturally clever, and also well-educated. In spite of deafness, and use of deaf-aid, she hears everything. Her memory is phenomenal, and she can and does quote reams of poetry read fifty years ago, and what she was told by, say, Mr Balfour before 1914. She is a miracle of a woman. A phenomenon.

Oh, and the most distinctive, indefinable magic about her – her voice. It is one of those now extremely rare Edwardian patrician voices. Vita had it; Diana Westmorland has it. The words are thrown out from the back of the throat, so that each falls clear like a pebble onto water. The articulation is perfectly rounded and smooth. No syllable is slurred. It is a proud voice, having nothing to conceal, everything to declare about the personality of the owner. For it denotes lack of self-consciousness and self-importance, humility, yet also self-confidence and assurance without swank. It denotes that devil-may-care, dismissive manner of the well-bred, who know they are as good as anyone, who take nothing too seriously, themselves least of all. What is the tone of this voice? Deep, a trifle raucous, commanding. Very intriguing, very splendid. Diana is constantly laughing, because everything, however serious in life, is a mild joke, yet she never laughs in a full-blooded way like, for example, Loelia and Midi. Her eyes glimmer; the corners of her lips lower with mild cynicism, and a short, silvery shout emerges when she is much amused, followed by a few trills. Never a guffaw like, say, Penelope [Betjeman]'s.

Thursday, 11 August

Dined with John [Betjeman] and Feeble. John looking better, but very shuffly. Is suffering from Parkinson's, which he discusses merrily. Takes an infinity of pills. A lovely joyous evening, John quoting from a newly discovered queer vicar, the Revd Bradford,* who wrote sentimental poems to boys in the 1920s. Very funny about his two new loves, one a girl secretary, the other an announcer on TV, a young man whom Feeble and I both find repulsive. He is the sort of youth, John said, whom he would have fallen for at school and been turned down by. When the said

---

* The Revd Edwin Emmanuel Bradford (1860–1944); Scots Presbyterian minister.

announcer appeared on the screen John addressed him in heart-rending terms of endearment and howls of laughter. John says the two most inspiring pieces of architecture he has seen this year are the rooms newly decorated and opened at Somerset House, which transcend anything of the kind seen in Italy (he hates abroad), and Scott's cathedral in Liverpool, far more exquisite than he had been led to believe.

Friday, 12 August

Lunched with K. Clark at Albany, just the two of us. He was charming. Said how much he had enjoyed *Prophesying Peace*. I thought him much older. He totters, but does not shuffle. His eyes are watery, and somewhat dead. His mind as sharp as ever. He has not a grain of humour, which makes him seem stiff. While we were eating downstairs we heard a crash upstairs. I rushed up to see whether anyone had broken in because when I arrived the front door was open. In fact he had shut it behind me. I went into all the rooms but could see nothing untoward. After luncheon we went to the sitting room and K. smoked a cigar. Suddenly he said, 'Oh dear, my little Renoir drawing has gone.' There was a blank space on the wall facing him. I looked. The drawing had fallen off the hook without even receiving a scratch on the frame, and lay on the floor. I admired a small Constable coloured sketch of clouds. K. said he had bought sixty such sketches just after the war for £100 each. He has recovered nearly all the treasures stolen after Jane's death, because he has photographs of every single thing he possesses, every medal, every ring.

Saturday, 13 August

In a London self-photographic box by the Passport Office I had two snaps taken. They were so gruesome, I looking like a sinister undertaker, that A. insisted I have others taken in Bath. I went to Woolworths and tried again. Result just as bad, although am rendered snarling like a sinister footpad, instead of smirking like a confidence trickster. My God, how absolutely hideous I have become. Sad really, when you think. As long as I keep clean. I suppose all I *can* do is to maintain that one standard.

Saturday, 27 August

Reading Harold's letters and diaries written during the last war I am struck by his intense patriotism, and Vita's too, the very polarity of Bloomsbury's contempt for such an attitude. Does anyone under fifty have these feelings today? How can they? For England is just not the same country, physically or ethnologically. Having been in London this past week I have seen that half the inhabitants are coloured. How can these people cherish the old affections and traditions which we were brought up to accept? They are aliens with alien beliefs, and no understanding of our ways and past greatness. England to them is merely a convenience, a habitation, rather hostile, where wages are high and the State provides. Then, physically, the decimation of trees is reducing the country to a barren waste. All the elms have gone; the beech trees are on the way out; so are the sycamores. And the ash trees. The traditional landscape will by the end of the century be extinct. And surely when a man feels patriotic, he is thinking of the hedgerows, the wild flowers, the woods, the green fields of the England of his youth.

Friday, 7 October

John Betjeman quotes the following couplet composed by the Widow Lloyd[*] about Hedley Hope-Nicholson,[†] that painted (but delightful) old queen:

H is for Hedley, the pride of Old Place,
What he earned from his bottom he spent on his face.

Sunday, 16 October

Walking down Broad Street, Bath the day before yesterday, I was stopped by a short but sturdily built man saying, 'Excuse me, sir, do

---

[*] J. D. K. Lloyd (1900–78); conservationist and historian, known as 'the Widow Lloyd' from the peak of hair on his forehead.
[†] Art collector of Tite Street, Chelsea (where his collection was preserved by his son Felix).

you speak English?' – a foolish remark which set me on my guard. Then he began to ask me the way to somewhere, and I knew what was coming. He was a sailor, going from Portsmouth to London, and could I help him? He was so sorry to trouble me. So I gave him fifty pence, but with reluctance, making a wry face. He stared at me with would-be honest steel-blue eyes; thanked me with a 'God bless you, sir.' What is one to think? Was he genuine? Should I have given him nothing and directed him to the town hall for advice how to get help? In any case I should have been more generous and less grudging. But the truth is that these days one is the victim of fraud and deceit, if not violence and theft, which makes one wary, suspicious and reluctant to get into conversation with strangers.

Saturday, 29 October

Left at 8.30 for Knole [Kent]. Was greeted by Lionel Sackville in the Green Court. We sat on a bench, talking. He never was a handsome man but with age and tribulation he has acquired a distinction which reminded me of his cousin Eddy and his Uncle Charlie. Did not go into details about his marriage, but merely said that his wife, whom he had left, refused to quit Knole. He had moved into rooms which Eddy once inhabited, over the Wicket, and eats with his brother and sister-in-law.* His condition is sad. Took me into the garden and then the chapel and, having asked one of his daughters if it were safe for him to enter his own apartments, tiptoed, finger on lips, through the colonnade room into the library. Then accompanied me round the state rooms, all looking very spruce and polished. I was rather shocked to see that some of the fabrics which we had mended twenty-five years ago were badly in need of attention again. Approved of the way they have regilded the furniture in

---

* Lionel Sackville-West, 6th Baron Sackville (1913–2004), m. 2nd 1974–83 Arlie, Lady de Guingand; his cousin (and J.L.-M's friend) Edward ('Eddy') Sackville-West, 5th Baron Sackville (1901–65), writer and musician; his 'Uncle Charlie', 4th Baron (1870–1962), Major-General; his brother Hugh Sackville-West, MC, m. 1957 Bridget Cunliffe.

the Venetian Ambassador's room. Lionel did not seem to know which were Vita's rooms. He is rather ignorant, for Nigel told me later that she never had rooms in the north wing, as Lionel suggested. We lunched with his brother Huffo and nice wife. I sat next to her and the eldest boy, aged 20, handsome but for spots – the future Lord Sackville, intelligent, alert and sympathetic; also sympathetic to my mission. They had kindly invited a couple called Martin who own Long Barn.* Funny little military man with grey moustache and Jewish-Greek wife. I took to her immensely. I followed them to Long Barn. They love it. It is not a covetable house, much bogus half-timbering, low doorway and sloping floors. Curious taste Harold and Vita had for 'ye olde', like my parents.

Tuesday, 8 November

I have been thinking how the older one's friends get, the less beloved. One must remember them in their heyday. But the heyday vanishes slowly, so that one gets accustomed to the declension into querulousness, self-pity and lack of laughter. When they die these last are the years and moods one remembers. One has forgotten the years of splendour, beauty and hilarity.

On Friday morning last week BBC2 telephoned in the way they do, without warning. Will I consent to be interviewed by Robert Robinson† in his books programme? They will send a girl from London to see me on Wednesday. They will 'shoot' on Monday and Tuesday next. Before I have time to reflect, I say 'Yes'. Then the horrors of the whole affair dawn: the nuisance, the complications, the upset of my library.

Wednesday, 16 November

Monday and Tuesday were devoted to filming with BBC2. I was a little nervous, and not good. I lacked sparkle and self-assurance. Robert

---

* H.N's and V.S-W's house before they found Sissinghurst.
† Writer and broadcaster (b. 1927).

Robinson, who interviewed me, was extremely kind and sensitive. He told me beforehand what sort of questions he would put to me, and when I objected to one he did not press. The team were charming. Consisted of young producer, David Speaght; Sue Anstruther, a sweet girl, secretary to Robinson and general dogsbody; four cameramen. Started off early Monday afternoon in Lansdown Crescent in the library, after which I was made to do a preliminary walk along the railings of the crescent. Then was seated with my back to the drinks cupboard door, tied to my chair by wires attached to a tiny buttonhole like a dandelion flower when the fluff has been blown off. The process is extraordinary. When I had run through my piece Robinson was filmed putting to thin air, so to speak, the questions he had already put to me. But I noticed that the second time he put a question it did not always correspond to the original one. I asked if the original wording he had put to me or this new wording would be recorded. Answer was of course the latter. At the end of every ten minutes the spool ran out. A pause ensued and we proceeded with the interrupted talk. This system does not make for continuity, and is off-putting. But the whole programme, I learn, is done in snippets, and will be pieced together in the studio. Not only will much of what I said be omitted altogether, but sentences will be joined up in a remorseless way, so that the sequence will be higgledy-piggledy. For example, on the second day we went to Lacock [Abbey, Wiltshire] and Dyrham [Park, Gloucestershire]. I was filmed walking with Robinson outside these two houses. The cold was penetrating. I was so frozen that once I could not release the words from my mouth and had to get into the car with the engine running and the heater on in order to thaw before resuming. When we got to Dyrham Robinson said, 'Oh, you never told me the story of the heiress of Lacock jumping from the battlements to elope. Let's have it now.' He told the cameraman to turn the machine upon me, so I added this anecdote, very lamely – sadly, for it was a good one – there and then, in between what I was saying about the architecture of Dyrham.

I enjoyed the experience, but did not excel. I might improve with further tuition. I am sure I look glum. When all is over and it is too late I think of a better answer than the one I haltingly gave. *L'esprit de l'escalier.*

Wednesday, 23 November

A dinner party for Woman's seventieth birthday in Elizabeth Longman's flat in Rutland Gate. Lots of old friends, but oh so depressing! Difficult to hear owing to the low ceilings. But I sat next to Diana [Mosley]. She retains for me the same ineffable magic. The same Mitford jokes – which require tuning in to. We talked about writing and being interviewed on television. Talking of Harold [Nicolson] she told me the story, which was already familiar to me, of Sir O. refusing to see Harold who, on an official delegation of MPs to Holloway Prison where the Mosleys were incarcerated during the war, asked if he might visit him in his cell. Diana's argument was that Harold had delivered such untruthful propaganda stories about Germany over the wireless that Sir O. was infuriated. But, I protested, Harold was not an out-and-out hater of Germany. On the contrary his views were balanced and sober and fair. We kissed; we parted with unaffected protestations of deepest devotion. But it was no go really. I wonder if we shall meet again. Diana told me she was now a great-grandmother. I think of her, as it seems yesterday, that radiantly lovely Botticelli Venus aged 17, sitting on a Cotswold wall near Asthall [Manor, Oxfordshire], whom I, her elder by two years, worshipped.

Friday, 25 November

My broadcast tonight at 11.35. A. could not keep awake. I went to bed, and at 11.30 crept downstairs, wrapped in a brown sheep's plaid given me by Sally. I waited in trepidation, and with some reason. I am *furious*. Strong emphasis given to the social side; no mention at all of the National Trust's work and my part in it. All questions and answers of any seriousness cut out; only the silly and frivolous left in. Worst of all, a ghastly, vulgar man seen reading extracts from my diaries, not even paragraphs. Merely random sentences of the most banal kind, strung together and read in a voice meant to be superior, disdainful, snobbish. A loathsome man. The whole performance geared to yesterday's upper-class bashing. I am amazed at my own apprearance. A drooling dotard, a mixture of Eddie Marsh and Paul Hyslop,* speaking in a

---

* Architect (1900–88); friend of Raymond Mortimer.

quiet, subdued, professorial voice. Embarrassing questions put to me about class. Damn, *damn* class! Oh how bloody the BBC can be! And what power they have to give a performance a strong slant by cutting, inserting, omitting, magnifying, and all by a sleight-of-hand which they cannot be arraigned for. Damn their eyes! I shall never do another, if invited.*

Sunday, 27 November

Saw myself again on repeat performance. Really, it is not I who am so bad as the others. The ghastly man reciting those shaming extracts, and Robinson with his casual, slightly off-hand manner. I am modest, in view of the questions put to me, rather distinguished and distinct.

Saturday, 10 December

A. has been cross with me and hurt all day because when she told me after breakfast that we were going to a luncheon party at Petty France, for which she had bought two tickets, I said I wouldn't go. What I cannot explain, and what she naturally cannot understand, is that I just could not. For the past few days I have been feeling awful, overcome with a loathing of my kind. Yesterday we had a luncheon party, and it was an agony for me to speak to my neighbours, silly Sally [Westminster] and that idiotic Clare Crossley. So today I could not face a repetition of this sort of thing.

Saturday, 17 December

A. went to London for the day yesterday, so I, much to my inconvenience, came back from Bath earlier than I wished, at 3.45, to take the dogs for a walk. Twice they bolted, and finally in the Slait field they bolted again. By now dusk was falling. It was bitterly cold. I whistled, and whistled. Nothing happened. I got crosser and crosser, and turned and walked home the way I had come. When I reached the house they were not standing by the gate, as I hoped. So I got into the car and

---

* He did several – notably appearing in the BBC series *The Aristocracy* in the 1990s.

motored to the gate of the Slait field. There was Folly. I slapped her until she whimpered and drove her home. Still no sign of Honey. So back I drove to the Slait field. It was dark now; a sickle moon above the beech belt on the horizon. I hooted. Presently a guilty Honey sloped towards me. By now I was crosser. I lashed at her with the lead, she screaming as she always does whether one hits her or doesn't, squirming as I held her by the collar. I was angry, but I don't think I even touched her.

Nevertheless, I have been saddened ever since. Did I derive any satisfaction from thus belabouring them? Certainly not much, but possibly just a little. A satisfaction in letting off steam. I didn't want to hurt them, but I did want to make them understand they had misbehaved. How honest am I being? Am I a bully? For I love them so tenderly that I feel I have been a brute, taking advantage of my superior status in the hierarchy of living things. My remorse later in the evening took the form of almost passionate embraces and out-pourings of love. Why do I love them better than any human being – save A. – in the world? I have only known them one year. It is absurd.

Sunday, Christmas Day

We are staying with Rory Cameron at Les Quatre Sources, two miles north of Ménèrbes. His house is only a little advanced since we stayed here in September last year. Rory invited the Stephen Spenders to Christmas luncheon. When I told him they disliked me he asked Hiram Winterbotham and his [servant] Ball to come too – as things turned out a mistake, for Hiram monopolised the conversation. The Spenders could not have behaved more kindly to us. She embraced me, and he brought a present from his library, a book on Byron's sex life, with a *dédicace* from both of them written on the flyleaf. There is little or nothing, beyond the large bright blue eyes, of the young Stephen I remember [from Oxford]. He is a collapsed pudding. I was disconcerted by Stephen's camera. He snapped away throughout luncheon. I remembered his remark to Ali Forbes that I resembled a sadistic undertaker.

I have not enjoyed this visit much. Rory is duller than he used to be. His friend Gilbert is duller than anything imaginable. Ugly to boot, and a figure of fun, a market gardener masquerading as a lounge lizard. Dressed in chi-chi clothes and highly scented. He has a good figure but an undistinguished, weak face. Horrid black moustache which conceals to some extent the weakness of his mouth. Has no back to his head. Has been in London learning English for months and can barely speak a word. His French conversation is limited to '*Plaît-il?*' and '*Oui, les montagnes sont très jolies.*' Rory told us he still worshipped him. Our last night we dined with Ken Villiers, nice, bumbly and old. There were two women, one a decorator, chirrupy and spouting endearments, the other a widow of some prominent surgeon, dressed in green evening 'gown' – and some six queers and their boy-friends. The horror of these sorts of people. Nothing to communicate; camp as can be.

I read this week, at Rory's, volume 3 of Virginia Woolf's *Letters*, also Nigel's excellent *Mary Curzon* (a spoilt social climber), Dostoevsky's *The Gambler* and two other short stories – and Bruce Chatwin's *In Patagonia*, which has had undeserved rave reviews. No form to the book, a random selection of unpleasant incidents. What a ghastly country it must be. I think that the quality of a book depends very much upon the mood in which one reads it. I am in a bad mood; very depressed at present. Also physically tired, and stiff in the joints.

1978

1978

Have received a number of letters from strangers about my television. One man simply demanded to see me and said he would get in touch after Christmas. Claimed he had met me thirty years ago. Yesterday morning he telephoned. Politely I said I was very busy and could not see him for several weeks. I took his telephone number (which I destroyed), and rang off. This morning the doorbell rang. I thought it might be Ernie come to mend the window catches. Went to the inter-com and a voice said, 'I am Mr Giles. I want to see Mr L.-M.' I pretended to be his secretary, and said Mr L.-M. was out. What message could I give him when he returned? The answer was, none. I returned to the library and since I did not hear the front door shutting I pulled down the blind by the window behind me. Ten minutes later I cautiously opened the door leading to the front hall and saw through the glass door that a man was still standing by the inter-com bell. Shortly after I watched him leave the building and sit on the bench on the pavement in the bitter cold. I went to the kitchen, cooked myself something to eat, returned to the library and still saw him seated outside. Not till three o'clock did he leave.

Today I received a letter from my old friend Archie Aberdeen telling me he waited up to watch my broadcast in apprehension, because Robert Robinson is a formidable interviewer. He thought I would be diffident and ill at ease. Archie says: 'Did you know how good you are on TV?' Now this is flattering because Archie was Director of Talks for years. Yet I know how nervous I was. I was not as good as I could have been, or would be, given another opportunity.

Thursday, 12 January

Paul Wallraf* lunched with me at Brooks's. I could hardly hear a word
he said, for he speaks English badly, softly and seldom finishes a sentence. He was very sweet, and helped me with the correct spelling of
a few German names. But he could give me no description of Harold's
flat in Berlin. Talked about his horrid war experiences in the Isle of
Man. His release was deferred because he got into trouble. He used
to work in a quarry for the sake of exercise and his health. Close by
was a small cottage. He became friendly with the couple who lived in
it. The wife was sorry for Paul and used to give him extra food and
cigarettes. This was found out. I asked him what became of the
couple. He said the wife was his secretary now, and she and her
husband both lived in the Wallraf Building, Grosvenor Place. He told
me he was going to be 80 this year; Muriel is 81. He has two German
boy-friends, neither of whom consents to go to bed with any man
under the age of seventy. The mind boggles beastlily.

Tuesday, 17 January

Now that I have reached the years 1956 and 1957 in my reading of
H.N. and V.S.-W.'s correspondence I am getting depressed. Knowing
as I do the actual dates of their deaths and the sad *dégringolade* in store
for Harold, the ailments and minor illnesses I am reading about bring
home to me the little of the life, which they loved, to be left to them.
And, it follows – how little is left to A. and me. I have read this morning
of Harold's seventieth birthday celebrations, which he pretended to
enjoy and which he really hated. I shall not get the same recognition –
indeed I pray that no one will know beyond my family – but I already
feel what dear Harold felt. Another thing which upsets me is to read
how much he disliked A. Vita took him to task once. This morning A.
asked me to get her car out of the motor-house. Then we could not
find the key. So she said, Oh never mind, I'll do it when I find the key;
and I, without waiting or helping her to look for it, left. All day I have

---

* German-born bisexual London art dealer; friend of Harold Nicolson and James
Pope-Hennessy.

felt a penitent beast. I have grown to love her so deeply for her goodness to me. As Vita wrote to H.N., Alvilde fusses over Jim like an old
hen. What is this but true, deep love? The darling.

Friday, 3 February

On Sunday, a terrible day of bitter wind, horizontal sleet, and deep
mud, I had elected to walk from Badminton to Ozleworth with Bruce
Chatwin. Did not like to put it off when the morning arrived because
a streak of wan sun appeared just as I was telephoning him. After my
(not his) Holy Communion and breakfast, he was driven over by
Elizabeth his wife. Bruce had a dog and I took Folly. We strode across
the park, via Worcester Lodge, Oldbury, across the main Stroud road,
and half-way through Tresham where we decided to give up. We were
very wet and the path from Tresham to Holwell was very bad.
Elizabeth met us in the car. When we reached Holwell she plied us
with hot lemon and whisky, and then a delicious lunch of pheasant
stew and red wine. I gorged. Felt all the better. My acute depression
lifted momentarily. I had an 'Up' on the Chatwins, she for being so
well-organised and welcoming, he for being so clever and interesting.
Bruce had told me of hair-raising experiences he went through in
South America. In one country, I forget which, he was arrested for
some misdemeanour, passport not visaed, and beaten up. He was
hit about the face, stripped of all his clothing – a pretty sight, to be
sure – and humiliated in public. 'How awful!' I said. 'Well,' he
replied, 'I must confess to having rather enjoyed it.' 'Then you are a
masochist,' I surmised. 'Just a bit,' he answered.

I am delighted. For once I have done something for someone.
Denys Sutton telephoned to say he has engaged my gt-nephew Nick
on the staff of *Apollo* at £3,000 p.a. So there is a possible future for
him, so long as that magazine can keep going.

Wednesday, 15 February

Today I went to Magdalen, Oxford. Drove there, since the oil tanker
drivers' strike seems about to end and no shortage of petrol threatened
after all. The anxieties we live through, on a perpetual knife-edge of

some deprivation. I was given a special pass to park in the College precincts off the Longwell entrance. It was odd to ring the bell of the President's Lodgings boldly, and equally fearlessly to enter when a nice housekeeper lady, with whom I shook hands, opened it. I told the President that it was the first time I had set foot within these august portals since my interview with Sir Herbert Warren* quite fifty years ago; for when I was resident in College I never once was invited inside by Sir Herbert's successor, I being an undergraduate of no distinction or promise. I lunched alone with the President, James Griffiths,† at the end of a long table in a large dining-room. Building dates from 1880s. Gothic but decent. Walls hung with portraits of bewigged presidents. No one served at table. Sparsest fare of cold spam and mixed salad without dressing. Beer from a pewter tankard to drink. Followed by biscuits and mousetrap cheese. No coffee. I rather took to the President. A sensible, easygoing, un-pompous man. He described the problems confronting him concerning the reparations of the College buildings. And indeed, after being shown around for two and a half hours by the enthusiastic sub-bursar, Latham, I understood them. They are these: in the past and within recent times the buildings have been so poorly restored that hardly a stone of the original early Tudor survives. I should say only the early eighteenth-century New Buildings are unchanged, and even so the middle of the south front was refaced just before my sojourn in the late 1920s. There are moreover no photographic records of the gargoyles, heraldic emblems and carved work from which to judge whether the present substitutes, made of synthetic stone in the 1930s, are faithful copies. All the 1930s work both sculptured and façadal has deteriorated and must now be totally renovated. They are at least using a special stone brought over from Lorraine, at great cost. I went away in a haze, uncertain what to recommend.

I liked the President, though he is not my sort of man. Not a Classical scholar but a professor of physics. But his love of Magdalen where he has spent the greater part of his life – fifty years, no less – is

---

* President of Magdalen College Oxford from 1885 to 1928 (1853–1930), an admirer of J.L.-M's uncle Robert Bailey, who 'fixed' J.L.-M's admission to the college in 1928, though he had retired by the time J.L.-M. had come up.
† J. H. E. Griffiths (1908–81); President of Magdalen, 1968–79.

touching. He is a tall, ungainly, ill-dressed man with a smiling, pleasant face. There was a curious faint smell of scent about him.

Wednesday, 22 February

At four I had my interview with Harold Macmillan.[*] I arrived punctually at Messrs Macmillans' offices in Little Essex Street, a hideous building in this nice old area next to the Temple. Taken up in a lift, down a long passage, ushered into a dark, ugly and very hot board room. Mr Macmillan was sitting, back to the window, alone at one end of a long table. He is very old, was slumped in his chair, sucking at a pipe which was not alight. Voice rather hoarse. Kept running his hands through his long silken white hair, or patting his dark grey pullover on his rather protuberant belly. Gave impression of being lonely, sad and a little disillusioned. Said in the course of talk, 'Nobody wants to see me now.' In spite of this initial gloom, and the unattractive setting, he exercised his spell upon me. When he smiles he is very charming, and those leonine eyebrows are the most expressive features. He dearly loves and admires Debo.[†]

Object of the interview was Harold N. He said he knew him very well, but not intimately. Liked him very much. He was a dear fellow, a decent character; easy to get on with; very kind to his colleagues, and particularly to Ramsay MacDonald[‡] when he was ill and gaga. But he lacked push and virility. Was too soft and sentimental for politics. Compared him with John Buchan[§] who was hopeless at

---

[*] Conservative statesman (1894–1986); Prime Minister, 1957–63; cr. Earl of Stockton, 1984. During the late 1930s, he and Harold Nicolson both belonged to a group of MPs who were liberally inclined in domestic politics while supporting Churchill in his opposition to appeasement.

[†] Macmillan's wife, Lady Dorothy Cavendish (1900–66), was Andrew Devonshire's aunt.

[‡] J. Ramsay MacDonald (1866–1937); Labour Prime Minister, 1924 and 1929–31; Prime Minister of National Government coalition, 1931–5, leading small National Labour Party of which Harold Nicolson became an MP in 1935.

[§] John Buchan (1875–1940); novelist; elected to Parliament as Scottish Unionist MP for Scottish Universities, 1927; Governor-General of Canada, 1935–40; cr. Baron Tweedsmuir, 1935.

organisation. Admitted that at the time of Munich H.N. showed distinct courage, but it was courage of the passive sort. I asked if the House listened to his speeches. He said Yes, but the Chamber would not fill the moment it was known he was to speak. I asked if he remembered H's maiden speech at the time of the Hoare–Laval crisis. He did, but he said the speech Lloyd George made on that occasion was tremendous. Exhorted me to read it; it made Members sit up, and turn white. He could move mountains because he had the spirit of leadership. H.N. did not possess that quality. Thought that H.N. made progressively better speeches, but once the Phoney War was over and the war in earnest began, there was no place for Harold – Macmillan spread wide his arms – he was no longer needed.

He, Macmillan, in those days saw Winston constantly. His little group of Pug [Ismay],* Eden, Bracken,† Cherwell,‡ Macmillan himself could say what they liked to him. Winston relished argument and passionate disagreement, if need be. The inner group would say 'Winston, you are talking balls. The way you must act is like this.' W. would listen, complain they were all against him, even cry, and then do what he thought best as a result of the discussion. Now, Harold was not on those terms. He would look at Winston with adoring eyes like a faithful spaniel. This is not what Winston liked, or admired. He did not care for deference, although he would not brook disagreement from those outside the favoured circle.

Duff Cooper was also hopeless at organising. No good at all as a Minister. Yet, unlike Harold, he was pugnacious, passionate; a fighter. Macmillan said the person in politics today who most reminded him of Harold was President Carter.§ The same shilly-shallying, the same

---

* General Sir Hastings Ismay (1887–1965); military adviser to Prime Minister, 1940–6; cr. Baron, 1947.
† Brendan Bracken (1901–58); Irish adventurer and newspaper publisher; Conservative MP, 1929–51; close to Churchill, whom he served as PPS, 1939–41; Minister of Information, 1941–5; cr. Baron, 1952.
‡ Frederick Alexander Lindemann (1886–1957); German-born Oxford physics professor who advised Churchill during 1930s, particularly on air defence; Government Scientific Adviser from 1940, serving as Paymaster General 1942–5 and 1951–3; cr. Baron Cherwell 1942, Viscount Cherwell 1956.
§ Jimmy Carter (b. 1924); President of United States, 1977–81.

sentimentality. I asked if his colleagues knew about his curious married life and his propensities. Macmillan said, almost aghast, 'No, in no sense whatever. In fact I don't think I knew then. I don't think anyone did. Besides, it was not a subject we would discuss. You must remember that thirty-five years ago we were all – well, if not quite all, nearly all in the House were gentlemen.'

He said he hadn't been in the House of Commons for fifteen years, and nothing would induce him to enter it again. Told me that for seventeen years he was a backbencher and did not get office of the humblest sort during that time. 'That was unusual.' He repeated that I must not think he considered Harold's political career a failure. There were plenty of men who went into Parliament with far less success than Harold, but they were not men of ambition. Harold *was* ambitious, and he himself considered his political career had been a failure. Of course he ought to have had a peerage. Pity Winston did not make him a peer. I asked if Attlee disliked him [H.N.]. All Macmillan said was, 'Attlee was a strange man, a cynical man. One did not know whom he liked and disliked.'

He thought Vita a great drawback. If H. had been an ordinary man he would have got rid of her. I dissented, and told him how devoted they were. Nevertheless he thought Harold enjoyed being a martyr, was slightly masochistic.

Finally he said: rhetoric and writing are two different arts. The greater of the two is writing. Harold was a great writer. Balfour's name came up and I suggested that he was as a person languid and soft. 'He was far from soft. He was lethargic, but he was ruthless. Unlike Harold, his spine was made of steel. He would sacrifice a friend of forty years without a murmur, without a moment's hesitation, if he decided it was necessary to get rid of him. That was the difference. Besides, Balfour did not care a damn what people said or thought about him. Harold did. He worried if he were criticised. He wanted to be liked. A fatal propensity.' He then made a curious comparison of Balfour and Lord Burghley.* Surmised that Burghley, with his quiet, confident, astute manner, maintained Queen Elizabeth's confidence through not being flashy, passionate or volatile, but by

* William Cecil, 1st Baron Burghley (1520–98); chief adviser to Queen Elizabeth I.

remaining calm, apparently unambitious for glory. Balfour was this sort of man.

Macmillan gave me a lift in his car as far as Charing Cross. On parting he repeated that he had been taking the part of devil's advocate, in order to help.

Saturday, 25 February

Having brought from London six copies of my novel [*Round the Clock*] I proceeded to read it, putting myself in the position of a stranger. I was so horrified by the jejuneness, the feeble dialogue, that I could not get beyond Chapter 3. Now, how is this? When I finished writing this novel I was pleased with it. Until this moment I have been pretty confident that it was all right. Now I don't believe it is at all all right and am sure it will get a bad reception. I am plunged into a trough of anguish and dread its launching on 16 March.

Friday, 3 March

Having picked up *Round the Clock* again and read it through, I reverse my opinion just expressed. I think it is rather good, and well written.

Nothing has brought home to me more strikingly the mortality of human beings than the discovery among the folded leaves of Harold's letters of cigarette ash dropped from his holder, and still powdery fresh today so long after his death. Even cigarette ash can be preserved longer than the flesh and blood of a genius. No, the ash I found was between the leaves of a pamphlet by Harold, *Swinburne and Baudelaire*, given by him to Vita in 1930. So it is her cigarette ash, of 1930.

Tuesday, 28 March

My biennial tour with Alex Moulton took place today. He called for me at ten o'clock precisely in his latest Rolls-Royce, last year's model, for which he paid £22,000, no less. We drove to Derbyshire and looked at the dismal little bull-ring pavilion at Swarkestone where we picnicked. Purpose of this tour was to visit houses built by Smythson,[*] who according to Mark Girouard[†] was the builder of Alex's Hall at Bradford [-on-Avon, Wiltshire]. Then proceeded to Wollaton [Hall, Nottinghamshire], where I have not been these forty years or more. It was crammed with sightseers, but we walked round the interior which is exactly as I remembered, full of stuffed giraffes. Nothing inside to wonder at except the great hall, which is *tour de force* Elizabethan, with its very high clerestory windows and vulgarly carved roof figures. Also, what I had forgotten, the staircase walls and ceilings painted by Thornhill,[‡] which make a fine composition. Formerly attributed to Verrio,[§] how I can't conceive because the superior hand of Thornhill seems clearly apparent. Next looked at the outside of Wootton Lodge, Staffordshire, where I stayed with Diana Mosley in December 1936 and listened to Edward VIII make his abdication speech, while the tears poured down our cheeks. Then it was one of the most romantic houses conceivable. Today, having been bought by a rich businessman, it is totally ruined. The window quarrels have been replaced by plate glass, unsightly additions have been made to one side, a preposterous and hideous fence of high iron spikes, such as might have confined the inmates of a prison, erected and behind it a belt of churchyard Lawsonias planted. From Wootton we drove to Baslow, on the edge of Chatsworth Park, and stayed at The Cavendish. Debo made and decorated this hotel which she took me round before it was opened. Extremely comfortable and *bien*, but fearfully expensive. Bill over £27 each.

Wednesday, 29 March

This morning we walked in the park. Alex went right up to the house but I turned back because I didn't want to be seen, as it were, prying by Debo, if she were about. Then we drove to Barlborough [Hall, Derbyshire] which though a school is beautifully kept. Can't be faulted. No unsightly school extensions. Gardens well looked after.

---

[*] Robert Smythson (1535–1614); architect.
[†] Architectural historian (b. 1931).
[‡] Sir James Thornhill (1675–1734); artist.
[§] Antonio Verrio (1639–1707); artist.

Might be a private house. We rang the doorbell and the housekeeper said she was sure the headmaster would not mind us walking round the outside. He did not appear, and we did not see inside. I have often been here before. Roaring noise of the motorway about half a mile away. Then to Bolsover. The little castle still undergoing repairs and so not open. But what has been done to the riding-school and long open gallery was very good indeed. Picnicked again and drove to Hardwick [Hall]. Alex had not seen any of these houses and was amazed by Hardwick. Kept photographing frenziedly and with evident enthusiasm. Now would I, if taken by him to a museum of bicycle wheels and gearboxes, have acted similarly? I asked to meet the new curator, a retired Air Commodore, nice man. He found us in the tea room. Said how much he enjoyed my books. Alex said brightly, 'I didn't see any of them on display in your shop', to which the Air Commodore remarked, 'No, I'm afraid not.' Does this mean the Trust considers my diaries unsuitable? It gave me in its magazine a most grudging little notice of four lines on *Prophesying Peace*.

On to Marston, near Grantham, to stay with Henry Thorold. This was a grim experience. Weather exceedingly cold. There is no central heating of any kind; bath water tepid and so no bath. We were shown to our bedrooms, which were large, and no electric fires even. I was so perished I could not even change my polo sweater for dinner, and put two extra jerseys over it. Special dinner party laid on for us – Myles [Hildyard]* and his ambassador brother Toby, the Babington-Smiths (she was Penelope Packe, an absurd lady), and Henry's dear old senile aunt, aged 86. Party did not go with a swing, owing to the cold. We sat in the hall, an apartment with three or four open doorways, and one green log emitting a thin trickle of dun smoke. Henry is inexhaustible on his subjects, which are architecture and genealogy, particularly his ancestors. Good, clever, endearing man notwithstanding. O God, I am a cad!

Tuesday, 4 April

Motored this morning to Caversham Park outside Reading, the Written Archives Centre of the BBC. Has a small cosy reference

---

* Squire of Flintham Hall, Nottinghamshire (1914–2006); war hero and local historian.

library with a few seats. I had to book mine a month ago. I spent all day from 10.30, when I arrived, looking through H.N's correspondence with the BBC, mostly about his own programmes, only a few letters about BBC policy when he was a Governor during the war. All his letters were courteous and affable, and only a few caustic. He made friends with all those with whom he had dealings, and clearly they became fond of him. I enjoy researching in libraries. The other researchers are people after my own heart, nearly all young and earnest. During the short breaks for coffee and tea we talk about each other's work. There is a readiness to share and help which is *gemütlich*. One young man came upon a reference to the Germans during the last war making propaganda out of a talk given by H.N. on the wireless. I went to the canteen in the big house, which once belonged to a relation, one of the Crawshays,* in the last century. Much messed about, this house still preserves its south façade with extended colonnades, its giant order of Corinthian pilasters. In the grounds I noticed a charming Doric temple falling into ruin, one vast urn on a plinth, a group of a well-known rape, and a canal and terraces. A fine site now overlooking gasworks and the railway conglomeration of Reading.

Saturday, 8 April

Today the Hunt was pursued by a gang of antis. When finally they killed somewhere in the Vale near Hillesley the crowd of hooligans attacked the Duke, pulled him off his horse, kicked him, spat on him, and pulled a huntsman off his horse, gravely injuring him. He was only saved from death by Kershaw the MP† rushing to his assistance. The Duke who is 78 and has suffered two strokes was badly shaken, but more distressed by the hostility than by his physical hurt. I met Caroline walking to the House to enquire how he was. She dined with us and said that Master refused to discuss the matter, brushed all reference to it aside. The Hunt has to be very careful not to apprear provocative or revengeful. But I

---

* Richard Crawshay (1739–1810), the founder of this family and of the great Cyfarthfa Ironworks at Merthyr Tydfil, was the uncle of J.L.-M's great-grandfather Sir Joseph Bailey.
† (Sir) Anthony Kershaw (b. 1915); MP (C) for Stroud, 1955–87.

am sure if I had been present I should have lashed out when I saw them assaulting. Yet I don't like witnessing a kill, and I think the Hunt would have been wise to go home sooner than kill.

Tuesday, 25 April

I dined with that funny old Philip Magnus, at Pratt's. He looks a million; is bent, and gaunt. One quarter of his left face is blotched, as with eczema. I enjoyed the evening. Pratt's is congenial and cosy. There is a cold billiard room on the ground floor, through which one passes to the staircase, and descends to the basement. Here is a kitchen room, with large open fireplace and glowing coal fire. A large dresser with blue and white kitchen plates on shelves. Red walls. Two stuffed fish in glass cases, caught by HRH The Duke of Edinburgh at Eastwell Park in 1880 and presented to the club. Coloured engraving of Captain Toosie Somebody (odd name) standing beside his horse at the Battle of Inkerman. Drawings of D'Orsay gentlemen and prints and 'Spy' cartoons cover the walls. Next door the dining-room, pitch dark but for candlesticks alight. A large circular table. There was Peter Rawlinson,* newly ennobled. I don't know if he remembered me. We talked. On one side I had Philip, on the other a nice member of the House of Lords but I did not hear his name. Kenneth Rose came in after dinner. Very sensitive he is, very knowing. Philip said to him, 'The first thing I read on Sunday mornings is your funny little paragraph in the *Telegraph*.' 'Funny little?' echoed Kenneth. He laughed it off. But Philip said later, 'I suppose I made a gaffe.' 'I suppose you did,' I answered. If I lived in London, and were a bachelor, I would like to be a member of Pratt's. Actually, Tom Mitford proposed me during the war, but when he was killed I withdrew my candidature.

Wednesday, 26 April

After working in the London Library in the morning, went to Shaldon Mansions in Charing Cross Road where Robin Maugham

---

* Barrister and Conservative politician (1919–2006); Attorney-General, 1970–4; cr. life peer, 1978; he had served with J.L.-M. in the Irish Guards in 1940.

has a sleazy flat overlooking the noisy bus-filled street – or rather, his boy-friend, a tall American, has. Rang the bell and was greeted by tall boy-friend and a smaller, younger boy, a sculptor, who immediately departed, giving Robin a smacking kiss as he went. I haven't seen Robin for many years. He is rather handsomer than I remember; has lost that footman-y appearance. Must be about sixty. Looks delicate. Has just had a minor operation and must undergo a major one, he tells me. His voice trails off, and I being deaf found it hard to hear what he said. He has very kindly lent me a large packet of letters written to him by Harold, who was certainly very devoted to him. He said Harold was in love with him, and his father knew it and strongly disapproved. Told me also that his Uncle Willie was likewise in love with him, and this was the cause of Willie's ambivalent attitude towards him. Robin's book [*Conversations with Willie*] has just come out and I suppose it will sell like hot cakes. Stupidly I went and bought it from Heywood Hill and read it. It is very second-rate. He is a nice man, generous and friendly and natural, but, as Harold remarked, a vulgar man with no literary style or sense. I suppose I derive some useful thoughts about H.N. from these meetings with his friends, but I am seldom told anything interesting which I didn't know already.

Thursday, 27 April

David Somerset told me that Master, when engaging servants today, asks them what their religion and politics are. If they are foolish enough to disclose that they vote Labour they are of course not engaged. If they admit to being Roman Catholics, this is worse. I said that I came across a letter written to my grandmother by some châtelaine presenting her compliments in the third person and giving a good character to Alice Spinks, adding that she only left her service because she had become obliged to wear spectacles. Master's attitude was on a par with this woman's before 1914.

Wednesday, 3 May

A. and I motored to London in pouring rain for Mickey Renshaw's Memorial Service in the Guards' Chapel – not a totally bad building but the material horribly artificial and lifeless. That is the main difference between old buildings and the contemporary made of pre-fabricated stone and brick – the old live whereas the new are born dead. The service was well-chosen, beautiful psalms, hymns and Bach anthem. No address. Indeed, how could one eulogise poor Mickey? We took Philip Dimmick and Mrs Radcliffe, M's old housekeeper, to lunch at Alfredo's restaurant. They both told us how impersonal Mickey was. There was little warmth in him. Philip, who was his lover presumably, said Mickey never once asked him whether his parents were alive or where his home was. Mrs Radcliffe, who had worked for him for thirty years, said the same – Mickey never once asked if she had any relations. Strange man.

Thursday, 11 May

I having written to Eardley that I was in the depths of depression, he telephoned yesterday evening suggesting that we go for a long walk today. We agreed to meet at Hungerford at ten, which took me less than one hour down the motorway. I took both dogs. They were the cause of *Angst*. Whenever let off the lead they bolted. We walked down the Kennet Canal to Pewsey, so inevitably there was barbed wire along the towpath, and the dogs kept escaping into the fields and woods beyond. A lovely day, a hazy sun through mist. Cool wind, and perfect for walking. Some long stretches of the canal beautiful, with tall trees and steep banks covered with primroses and a few as yet unblown bluebells. Watched snipe dipping and darting over the water. Some lengths of the canal recently restored, locks mended, which is nice to see. Unfortunately the mud and stones and bricks dredged from the bottom have been chucked on the banks, thus rendered ugly and untidy. We passed one long tunnel with entry of brick on the curve. A large stone tablet, also on the curve, with beautiful lettering, recorded that through the consent and enterprise of Lord Ailesbury and his son Lord Bruce, Rennie made this waterway in 1810. E. very angry that the beautiful tablet, so carefully carved, so carefully cut so as to be on the curve of the tunnel entrance, should be allowed to dis-integrate. He reminded me that we had admired it thirty years ago, and said that in another thirty we would no longer be able to read the inscription at all. We sighed and said no more. In thirty years he would be one hundred and five, I, one hundred.

Friday, 19 May

A. and I went to a ghastly party at the House, for which we paid £5 each, to hear Mr Heath speak. This he did very well for twenty minutes at most, after we had spent one hour (and should have spent two, had we arrived when invited) fighting for a glass of champagne (which I dislike) and sandwiches. Heath told us that Callaghan* cannot be trusted as a moderate man, since he gives way on all critical occasions to the extreme Left. Standing on a small platform in the large green drawing-room, he looked like a figure cut from a turnip, as it were for All Hallows' E'en, quite square and pointed, his profile, nose and mouth sharp gashes. Yet I admire the way he marshals his sentences, and he speaks with the authority of an elder statesman. Our local MP very second-rate, with an ugly voice and cataract of clichés.

Wednesday, 24 May

Stayed the night with Eardley. Richard Shone joined us and I took them both to dinner in Soho at an Italian bistro. Richard, in the course of telling me that he and J.K.-B. both have articles in this month's *Burlington Mazagine*, announced that Ben Nicolson died last Monday. While changing trains in Leicester Square tube station he fell down. By the time he was taken to hospital he was dead. It took two whole days to identify who he was. Although I was never a close intimate and disapproved of some sides of Ben, I have been upset by his death, probably because I have read so much about him in Harold and Vita's correspondence over the past year. They loved him, and cared and worried deeply about him. What I disliked in him was his near-Communist inclinations, his flouting of the ordinary social graces – for he was dirty and ill-mannered. He despised all Vita stood for, was never nice to her, was an inverted snob, anti-Establishment. But he was a true eccentric, honest as the day, a

---

* James Callaghan (1912–2005) had succeeded Harold Wilson as Labour Prime Minister in 1976.

considerable scholar, and both innocent child and wily expert. Poor Ben! I shall miss him at Brooks's – he will become just one more ghost – where I would often see him slope into the coffee-room at 1.45 or even 2, clutching a book or a paper, bending forward with the weight of his own thoughts, dishevelled, his jacket collar sprinkled with scurf, his mouth half open, and not wanting to be talked to or disturbed.

Tuesday, 6 June

Hugh Montgomery-Massingberd came for a midday snack at Lansdown Crescent today. A. provided the said snack. She was enchanted with this young man's exquisite manners, which seem not to belong to this age. I let him look through the Red Books, with reluctance, because I am shy at strangers seeing the idiocies, the embarrassing comments I have jotted down all these years about country houses. But if the new Committee on which I have agreed to sit to guide the compiler of the Country House Index wants my notes, I suppose I ought not to withhold them.

Monday, 12 June

At 6.30 I called on Duncan Sandys* in his nice Georgian house in Vincent Square. We talked of old times with George Lloyd.† He told me how as a very young man he was looking for a leader and thought he found one in G.L. But it didn't come to anything, though he always admired and liked him. I watched this man who used to alarm me, with his fiery red hair, his show of intense virility and heroism, his unscrupulous, mocking, rather diabolic manner. I could only see a broad smile, a twinkle in blue eyes, a kindliness which were never there in old, or rather young, days. What hell the young can be to

---

* Right-wing Conservative politician (1908–87); Eton contemporary of J.L.-M.; m. (1st) 1935 (diss. 1960) Winston Churchill's eldest daughter Diana; cr. life peer 1974 as Baron Duncan-Sandys.
† George, 1st Baron Lloyd (1879–1941); proconsul and Conservative politician, whom J.L.-M. served as private secretary, 1932–5; Chairman of British Council, 1937–41; Secretary of State for the Colonies, 1940–1.

each other, to be sure. He was extremely friendly and said we must meet more often, in fact received me as though I had been one of his oldest friends. But that comes with age, and the death of so many others who meant so much to us.

Saturday, 17 June

We lunched today with dear Billy [Henderson] and Frank [Tait]* at Tisbury. Delicious food as always. Only Cecil Beaton there. He greatly improved healthwise; can talk consecutively now, and make jokes. Said H.N. had his eyes permanently glued to men's private parts, which he found very unattractive. Now surely this is a deliberate fabrication. I must have noticed it, were it so. I find people who were not Harold's friends do say very disobliging things about him. Cecil also said that physically he found H.N. repulsive. Well, every man his taste.

Frank told a story about Nancy Mitford which typifies her sense of humour. He was a very shy young man of 22, fresh from Australia, of middle-class upbringing and learning to be a doctor. He was sitting next to Nancy at a smart, cosmopolitan luncheon party in Venice. He took a large mouthful of lobster which he knew at once to be bad. So, tucking the lobster into one cheek, he turned to Nancy and asked, 'What am I to do? I know what is in my mouth is bad.' Nancy's immediate reply was not 'Spit it out' but 'Swallow it, if it kills you.'

Friday, 23 June

We drove to Firle for the weekend, arriving at six. The Beits staying. A happy weekend party. I got through to Rainald [Gage].† He is nigh impossible to hear and talks half to himself, half to you. He took me to Charleston one evening because he wished me to see for myself the condition of the house. Took no notice of my telling him I was there last year when Duncan was still alive.‡ I was slightly

---

* Australian child psychiatrist (b. 1923); friend of Billy Henderson.
† Henry Rainald Gage, 6th Viscount Gage (1895–1982), of Firle Place, Sussex (whose estate included Charleston); m. (2nd) Diana Cavendish, Hon. Mrs Campbell-Gray.
‡ Duncan Grant had died on 9 May.

embarrassed, for we drove up to the house and Angelica Garnett[*]
arrived in her car behind us. Rainald merely asked if we might see
inside. This shy, on-her-guard woman had to say yes. She brought
us a delicious bottle of white wine, as though such a gesture was the
droit de seigneurie expected of her. I must say that without Duncan
and his court, and his pictures which lent colour to the background
muddle, the house looks infinitely drear, dirty and dilapidated.
Rooms adrift with old saucepans with unspeakable things sticking to
their bottoms; empty toothpaste tubes on chairs, dust, dirt, peeling
wallpapers, and the structure apparently needs £40,000 spending on
it. Rainald to his credit does not wish to be accused of destroying a
Bloomsbury shrine, yet has to do something by way of repairs. I suggested his selling the house outright to Angelica G. who says she
wants to go on living there, where she was born in 1918. But R. says
the house is in the middle of the estate, is the core of a farm, and
understandably does not want to part with it to someone who might
die or re-sell to a rich tycoon who would probably spoil it altogether.
He left us to go and look at his cows; and we talked. I found her very
sympathetic to talk to, and we got on. When we left she shook me
with both hands, always a sign of cordiality, and asked me to call
again at any time.

Thursday, 29 June

Upset this afternoon by Denys Sutton telephoning to complain of my
dear Nick. He *will* call him Robinson, which I find offensive.
Apparently he comes into the office late, at 10.30. Well, I said, you
must tell him to come in at whatever time your office opens. But, I
added, I thought he worked after hours and took proofs home to read
over the weekends. Followed by a long dissertation by Denys
about the young today from Nick's sort of background having no
conception that the old life of hunting and shooting was as archaic as
the dodo.

---

[*] Writer and artist (b. 1918); officially the daughter of Clive and Vanessa Bell, though
her real father was Duncan Grant, who brought her up at Charleston; m. 1942 the
writer David Garnett (1892–1981), Duncan Grant's sometime lover.

Monday, 10 July

Went to see Lord Boothby* at 5.30 in his flat in Eaton Square. He was in his pyjamas and dressing-gown. Looks much changed. The sofa and armchairs all covered with towels, I suppose because Lord Boothby is incontinent, but it was not attractive. Lady Boothby came in after me and stayed throughout the conversation. Then his publisher came and talked about his forthcoming book of memoirs. Boothby showed me several letters he had received from Harold, very sympathetic, generous, helpful ones they were, written at a time when Boothby was in some trouble. They disclosed that H.N. was homosexual, Lord Boothby remarked to me. I thought they disclosed that Boothby was too, or H.N. would not have written to him recommending a harbour in Greece where pretty sailors were to be seen drinking and smoking.

Poor Boothby is a warning example of how the old become painfully vain. He kept reading extracts from the books of famous contemporaries in which they praised him. He praised himself, spoke of his power of rhetoric. Said he would speak on any occasion about any subject, knowing he was swaying his audience. It is love of power, I suggested. Yes, he said, smiling. An engaging fellow. Not a great man, as Eardley observed.

Friday, 14 July

Tonight Julian Berkeley† and his friend Tony Scotland‡ came to dinner with us. Two such handsome young men, Julian a real pin-up like his mother, and improved beyond words. Now adult and intelligent. A very earnest, serious youth, a deep thinker I should say. So is the other, whom I liked immensely. In the middle of dinner we listened to a broadcast on Edmund Gosse,§ recorded speaking about Hardy's death in 1928, a few months before his own. Most interesting listening to the voices and

---

* Robert ('Bob') Boothby (1900–86); charismatic bisexual Conservative politician, whose friends included Harold Nicolson and the Kray brothers; cr. life peer, 1958.
† Second son (b. 1950) of Sir Lennox Berkeley and Freda *née* Bernstein; musician and founder of Berkeleyguard Automatic Security Systems.
‡ Writer, broadcaster and journalist (b. 1945); on staff of BBC Radio, 1970–91.
§ Sir Edmund Gosse (1849–1928); writer, critic and civil servant.

pronunciation, absolutely different from anything heard today. Choice of words and phrases archaic, precision of diction, 'litera-cher', 'pick-cher', which surprised the commentator and the two boys, but not us who were accustomed to this form of pronunciation. I think Gosse was typical of the professorial class of his day rather than the landed gentry.

I can't get out of my head those two boys, so beautiful both with their long, dark, curly, glossy hair, and both so nicely dressed and spruce. I thought how lucky they were to belong to the generation they do belong to. There is no concealment of their relationship. They live together, share a London flat and country cottage, do everything together, are devoted, monogamous I should guess, and not the least chi-chi. It is wonderful that today these situations are just accepted. There is no disguisement. I respect them, and rejoice in their content and happiness.

Friday, 4 August

I firmly believe that the most beautiful lines of English prose come in the Benedictus – 'And thou, Child, shall be called the Prophet of the Highest, for thou shalt go before the face of the Lord to prepare his ways . . . Through the tender mercy of our God, whereby the dayspring from on high hath visited us, To give light to them that sit in darkness . . . and to guide our feet into the way of Peace.' What does it matter if these truly divine words mean little? They are magical, numinous and enough to turn the most sensitive atheist into a member of the Church of England. And then the ancient chants that accompany these words, the canticles, do not detract from the poetry but somehow strengthen and add to it. Usually I disapprove of fine poetry being put to music, for the one destroys the other. But not so with the Psalms. Yet our vandal bishops can scrap these divine poems and substitute words of infinite banality. They make me sick.

Sunday, 6 August

My seventieth birthday. Dear God, how could you do this to me? The obscenity, the ugliness, the squalor of old age. Well, I feel well, though doubtless I look mangy and a million. We had our party today. I was dreading it. I need not have, for I enjoyed it very much indeed. Everyone has been so kind. The whole thing was organised and run by Alvilde, who is a genius at this sort of thing. We had Clarissa* staying, and Billa [Harrod]. Billa is the best value, just the same in spite of her recent widowhood and so sensible about Roy's death, seeing it as a sort of triumph, or transfiguration. She and I began the day going to Holy Communion at eight.

We had about fifty to luncheon. We hired a tent from Cheltenham, thank goodness, because the weather was, is still, lousy, cold and grey and rainy, off and on. The tent just outside the kitchen door held twenty-five; the rest of us in the two little front rooms. The Droghedas chucked, the Rosses couldn't come, and Debo couldn't come. She and John Betj. sweetly telephoned. But Diana Cooper motored down with Jack Rathbone and Philip Dimmick from London. Eardley came; the Somersets; Osbert Lancasters, he looking very frail and shaking. I gave him a copy of my novel. He left his present for me behind in London. I rather hope it may be one of his drawings. The Lancasters stayed with the Somersets, as did Derry [Moore] and Archie Aberdeen. I was given masses of presents, all things I wanted, mostly books. How lucky I am. How kind people are to septua-genarians. My dear little great-nephew Henry came and helped wait and hand drinks and was generally useful and adorable.

Saturday, 12 August

Nick rang me up from London and is much distressed and hurt that Denys Sutton has sacked him from *Apollo*, the only reason given that Nick's heart was not in the work. Of course Sutton is a beast and no one can work under him for long, but Nick is so calm and industrious that I hoped he would stick it out for a year or two, and gain valuable experience under this clever, informed taskmaster. Norah Smallwood lunched with me in London on Thursday. I told her about Nick. She remembered meeting him and liked him, and said she could give him a job, of a publicity sort, at Chatto's. I

---

* Hon. Clarissa Chaplin (b. 1934); J.L.-M's stepddaughter, o.c. of A.L.-M. by her 1st husband, Anthony, 3rd Viscount Chaplin; m. 1957 Michael Luke.

don't know if this is the sort of work he wants, but it is at least something.

Saturday, 26 August

The depression from which I suffered so grievously during the spring and early summer has quite gone, and I am content again. On analysing this return to 'normality' – if it is normality – I can find no explanations for it. Because I am not in better health; if anything, in weaker health: I get more tired and I suffer from eczema and tingling on my face, and palpitations. Nor have I particular reason to be more self-confident than I was in the spring. I still do not know whether my biography is going to be any good. When I was depressed, I had not even begun [writing] it. Now that I have begun it I have reason to suppose it is not a success. And the verdict of Chatto's, to whom I am sending the first few chapters, is a cloud before my eyes. No, it is altogether strange. I believe that I suffer from depression when my mind is clear of fog and I can and do look into life with penetrating eyes, and see life for what it really is, a hollow sham. Now that I am out of depression I am living in a happy sort of daydream, avoiding the realities and delusions of existence. I know this is not the customary way of looking at this matter. When one is depressed one is supposed to be ill, mentally if not physically. I find the very opposite to be the case. When one is happy and contented one is living in illusion, a fool's paradise in glorious fact.

Saturday, 2 September

Golden autumn days, the very air washed like brightly polished guinea pieces of my youth; the cubbing mornings crisp with sharp tingles and the hedgerows that remain – most are burnt to cinders by the bloody stubble-burners – netted with silver spiders' webs. The beauty of England at this time! – and we are going abroad in a week. Now is the moment to stay in England. It is the only reliable time of the year, weatherwise, and seldom lets one down. All other seasons do, the summer worst of all. No summer this summer, so to speak, at all, at all.

The 18th to 23rd [September] A. and I spent in Constantinople.*
First two days fine, warm and beautiful; the two remaining days horrid,
overcast and raining. Went up the Bosphorus the first day. Shores over-
built, old wooden houses mostly gone, the rest going. Hideous substitutes. The waters swarming with jellyfish, a revoting spectacle, like
drifts of spermatozoa. The Golden Horn even more disillusioning, a
stinking sewer. Dead, black water. We held our noses until the ferry
got back. Town pullulating with people. Population has trebled within
one generation. Conditions of people bad. Trouble brewing, and I
guess there will be a Marxist revolution within five years. Santa Sophia
does not disappoint. Even more wonderful than when last seen, the
scale and proportions reducing men to insects. Stone ramp upstairs for
the horses which carried the Empress of Byzantium and her suite to
the galleries. Blue Mosque disappointing. Being repaired and redecorated, not well. St Saviour in Chora a true gem of a church, with
double narthex, and the finest frescoes of the time of Giotto to be seen
anywhere. But oh! the walking difficulties, up hills, narrow pavements
with holes in them so that each step has to be watched. I visited the
old British Embassy, built by Barry. Rather like Bridgewater House or
the Reform Club. A very good building, one of the few secular buildings left of any merit. Fine grand staircase with double flight, marble
walls, portraits of King Edward VII and Queen Alexandra. Ballroom
huge with high coved ceilings through two floors. Very splendid, and
a good walled garden. How much longer will the Government keep
this building before finding its maintenance too expensive? What a
power in Turkey Great Britain was in the nineteenth century!
Harold and Vita's house has gone. I saw the street in which it was, but
no trace of house, or garden, where Vita began her horticultural career
on steep terraces overlooking the Bosphorus and Santa Sophia.

Monday, 23 October

We motored to Newburgh [Priory, Yorkshire] on Friday to stay for
two nights with A's first cousin Malcolm Wombwell, recently

---

* Where Harold Nicolson had been Third Secretary to the British Embassy at the
time of his marriage to Vita Sackville-West in 1913.

widowed aged 85. He lives in what he calls the flat, on the first floor of the new wing, comprising the drawing-room with three inner domes and plasterwork on ceilings and walls. The visitors' book, still in use, is the earliest I know. It begins in 1858. Victorian signatures splendidly Baroque, with flourishes; today's like housemaids', unreadable and inelegant.

What has given me immense pleasure is a visit to my dear old friend Rupert Hart-Davis,* who lives in a rambling rectory at Marske near Richmond, in Swaledale, the river rushing below, the moors behind. A. was not feeling well so I went alone, and lunched. I had misgivings about seeing him after so many years, but A. insisted. It was a great success. He was so affectionate. His wife is sweet and lovely, clever I should say, retiring and adoring. I liked her immensely. We talked non-stop for hours. Since my return I have had a letter from Rupert offering to read through my Harold book. His house is more crammed with books than any I have ever seen. From floor to ceiling there are books in every room, and all so neatly shelved. He can lay a hand on any one he needs. He lent me several letters to him from Harold. He fetched them from Harold's books. Took a book from the shelves and out tumbled letters. What an orderly man. He has an orderly mind. I do love him. I think he is a great man in his way, which is scholarly without being pedantic. He is a practical man, yet poetic. He looks like a retired major, with his long, thin face, a little heavy about the jowl, and the absurd little grey moustache. A little of *embonpoint*. He said I was sadly bald. What an honour to be asked to let him read my manuscript. He is the successor of Eddie Marsh as England's proof-reader-in-chief.

Sunday, 5 November

Chloe† is staying. Has come over from France to stay in her father's flat [in London] for the winter. Thinks she is going to paint. A. took her to Chatto's where Norah received her kindly and ordered a painting

---

* Sir Rupert Hart-Davis (1907–99); publisher, editor, writer, and friend of J.L.-M. since Eton; m. (4th) 1968 June Clifford.
† J.L.-M's step-granddaughter Chloe Luke (b. 1959); eldest dau. of Hon. Clarissa Chaplin and Michael Luke.

from her. So did Maclehose, her partner, so they must think she has talent. But this child will never thrive in my opinion because she is wholly undisciplined, and not dedicated. Is a hard little nut, a proper little madam, and not very easy to communicate with. She might well join the Baader-Meinhof group* if she fell in love with a member of that gang.

Sally W. brought to dinner on Saturday one of her royal Siamese boys whom she befriends in the holidays from Malvern College. Not an attractive boy, a bit of a podge with large round horn-rimmed spectacles, *décolleté* to the navel, wearing bejewelled bracelets and chains with charms round his neck. Now, this makes him sound more exotic than he is. Said he disliked his housemaster and does what he can to disoblige him. Proudly told us that the whole house went on strike the other day, and refused to speak at meals. Who on earth would be a schoolmaster unless driven to it by extremes of penury? A. said to him at dinner, 'Won't you have some salad?' He replied, 'Oi don't loike greens.'

Thursday, 9 November

To London for the day to attend Oliver Messel's† Memorial at St Martin-in-the-Fields. Went first to London Library; looked up names of foreign embassy officials mentioned by Harold in 1924. Called at Chatto's to leave a letter. Asked to see Nick, who appeared looking more handsome than words can express, but pale. His long, dark, glossy hair like a Bronzino portrait. Don't think he is very happy but assures me he will stick it out. Church full of old people. Peter Coats‡ with snow-white hair, but hair; Diana Cooper in trousers which upset Michael Rosse. Princess Margaret. Went on by tube to 18 Stafford Terrace§ for buffet luncheon. Anne very upset

---

* German secret society of Trotskyite terrorists.
† Theatrical producer, designer and artist (1904–78); brother of Anne, Countess of Rosse.
‡ Garden designer and horticultural writer (1910–90); distant family connection of J.L.-M.
§ Anne Rosse had inherited this house, filled with wonderful Victoriana, from her grandfather, the *Punch* cartoonist Linley Sambourne. It became a National Trust museum.

indeed because she must leave this house she loves above all others. I understood it was to be turned into a museum. Met Tony Snowdon by front door. We grasped each other's hands. He said he had not been invited to luncheon and was leaving. We swore eternal friendship, in that way friends do who meet once in ten years for ten seconds after obsequies. I congratulated him on the way he read the second lesson. He said he was terrified, and when I told Anne after, she said crossly it was high time he snapped out of this rot, and made a speech somewhere. With him was Linley Messel's boy, Thomas, who read the first lesson. He said, 'Are you the author of *Heretics in Love?*' For a time I could not think whether I was. Harold Acton there. He said the new book on the Sitwells* is shameful: readable, very, but journalese and containing the love letters which Osbert wrote to David Horner. Harold said he would never speak to David again, for Osbert was an extremely circumspect man and made no reference to his queerness. Sachie is dreadfully upset thereby.

Sunday, 26 November

Leaving church this morning Mary Beaufort asked us to dine tonight; old Horatia Durant staying. We were told to arrive at 7.45 because they wanted to look at a film about Lily Langtry.† After a rushed drink of sherry we were bustled into the dining-room. I sat next to Horatia with no one the other side of the huge table. Mary was opposite me behind a pot plant. Dinner eaten with great rapidity. No waiting. We choked over soup, fish, fruit salad; hardly time to toss down a glass of white wine. Master stacked the plates. Hustled back to the panelled room. Master turned on the telly and for a quarter of an hour we watched a film about naval privateers in Regency times in which a whore was being tossed from hammock to hammock. 'Unlike Lily,' Master growled. Then I ventured to suggest that it was not the Lily film, but another, as it proved to be – viz., *Mutiny on the Bounty*. Hurriedly we switched on to the right film. Therein Lily made to go to bed with a young man for a diamond necklace. Raped another

---

* *Façades*, by John Pearson.
† Actress and courtesan (1853–1929).

called Sir George Arthur. Mary did not see for she was asleep. Neither Master nor Horatia made a comment. At nine the News came on. When it was over, we rose, and left. A purposeless occasion, surely.

Wednesday, 29 November

At six to St James's Palace, Georgian Group party attended by the Queen Mother. We were lined up in the Throne Room to be presented. Next to the Fleetwood-Heskeths,[*] Mo shrunk to half size. Queen Mother reached us. Peter Chance who was piloting her murmured about me being an art historian and A. a garden expert. Queen Mother thereupon said to me, 'Is it very dry with you?' That was all that passed. But the poor, sweet woman spent an hour and a half on her feet talking, non-stop, no repose, with some 150 people. I suppose she could do it in her sleep, just exuding sweetness and charm, and talking inanities.

Sunday, 3 December

Have thought of a new book to be called *An Old Man Walks*. I go for a long tramp, describing the scenery through which I pass and every single object my eye lights upon, whether tree, bird, blade of grass, church, barn, pylon, beautiful or revolting, and each object makes me go off at a tangent upon some theme which perplexes or worries or saddens or enrages me. Also the memories they induce, the hopes they engender, the philosophy they arouse – life and death, God and the Devil, belief, disbelief.

---

[*] Peter Fleetwood-Hesketh (1905–85); architect, illlustrator, Lancashire landowner, and sometime honorary representative of N.T.; m. 1940 Mary Monica Assheton (d. 1979).

1979

1979

A[lvilde] went to Holy Communion at Big Badminton this morning at eight. The congregation consisted of herself and Mary Beaufort only. I walked across the park to Little Badminton at ten. Besides myself, there were three old women. If I were to live another twenty years there would, I dare say, be no church services functioning in England at all. Now I keep asking myself, are we churchgoers better than those who don't go? I don't think we are, if one takes a cross-section of both parties. Women like Peggy [the daily] who don't go are generous, cheerful, hard-working, honest, honourable. I am rather mean, gloomy, hard-working yes at my own work and lazy if it comes to doing things for others, honest in my way but generally dishonourable. In balance I come out lower on the scale than Peggy. Yet I worry inordinately about spiritual problems, traditional manners and the Faith. I may not be as good as Peggy, but I think, and she doesn't. I measure the depreciation of standards since my youth. She does not. Does this make her inferior to me? I think not.

Today the thaw has come after ten days of bitter cold and frosty roads and snow. All is grey and slush. On Thursday, as I was returning from Bath, just past the Lansdown Tower in the darkness, a blizzard started. I was almost blinded. I saw ahead a stationary car, abandoned, half on the verge, half on the road. I skidded into it, going possibly 25 mph, and badly buckled my front mudguard and the passenger door. The total estimate for repair is £100.

At this particular moment the political situation in this country is about as menacing as it has ever been.* The lorry drivers are on

---

* It was the so-called 'winter of discontent', the chaotic period of severe weather and unofficial strikes marking the last months in office of the Labour Government.

unofficial strike for higher wages. Already petrol is scarce, and by the end of the week there will be none on sale at all. The food shops' stock is exhausted. I suppose the Government will give way. If they stand firm there will be a general strike. All communication, all industry will cease. People will not be able to get to work. We shall be stuck here.

John [Kenworthy-Browne] has presumably not returned from America yet: at least he has not telephoned. I have felt uneasy and unhappy. It is absurd that after twenty years and more I should mind as much as I do. I miss him when we are out of touch. Yet when I am with him I am frequently irritated. I just long for him to telephone and say he is glad to be back, and did not enjoy his visit much; and above all that John Pope-Hennessy* was hell to him.

Monday, 8 January

Having written these uncharitable words I go to Bath this morning, and there I find a letter from John written in New York. It must have been waiting for me over the weekend. All my anxieties are allayed. I feel relieved and happy. I have made a plan to see him next week. Already I am in no haste to see him. The assurance of his affection is enough. It is all very stupid, but strange.

Sunday, 28 January

Yesterday we lunched with Ann Fleming at Sevenhampton. John Sparrow, John Gere, nice clever man from the British Museum, and the Roy Jenkinses. I sat next to Ann and Mrs Jenkins, whom I liked immensely. Very intelligent, a little 'blue', dressed in subfusc, no nonsense, and no trailing of coat, sympathetic. A sort of Girton girl. We talked about the Historic Buildings Council and the National Trust. She said that the HBC Secretary, clever young man of thirty and no Socialist, is shocked by the aristocratic, paternalistic constitution of the Trust. I said I used to be worried by this before the war when every chairman of committee had to be an Earl.

---

* Then based in New York as Chairman of Department of European Paintings, Metropolitan Museum of Art.

After luncheon, A., Mrs J. and Ann went for a walk with the dogs. We four men stayed indoors and had a long and rather fascinating talk about politicians and great statesmen. Macmillan modelled himself on A. J. Balfour to the extent of folding his bow tie under the points of his collar when a younger man. Jenkins has a great admiration of Baldwin, on whom he has written a monograph. He said Baldwin was a very tragic figure in the end. Retired aged seventy in a blaze of glory, KG and Earldom. Then his last ten years a purgatory: reviled and harassed very unfairly. Told story of Baldwin in first-class carriage from Worcester to London when Prime Minister. A man got in and sat opposite. Kept on looking at Baldwin. At last tapped him on the knee and said: 'Baldwin?' B. said yes. Man said: 'Harrow 1885?' Baldwin said yes. 'And what, pray,' asked the man, 'are you doing now?'

Jenkins spoke about interpreters at important meetings with heads of state. Whenever he is talking to Giscard* he insists on speaking in English through an interpreter the moment questions of intricacy arise. G. speaks fluent English but won't, because he believes every foreigner ought to speak French. Does not like Giscard; finds him proud and icy cold. I asked if a good interpreter imitated the intonation of the speaker, put on a voice of anger, impatience, cynicism etc. He said the good ones do not do this. Jenkins knows that when a colleague says I understand French though I don't speak it well, he cannot understand at all. Just as when a foreigner speaking English does not occasionally ask what exactly some expression means, he really does not know our language well.

Annie says Roy Jenkins is shy. This may account for his behaviour when they were announced. He shook hands with a perfunctory smile and flew to the drinks table and mixed himself a stiff Martini. Sat down and read the newspaper, while we were left talking to Mrs.

For some odd reason he thinks highly of my two books of diary. 'They give the best impression of life in London at that period I have ever read.' Thinks *Prophesying Peace* a bad title, and asked what it

---

* Valéry Giscard d'Estaing (b. 1926); President of France, 1974–81.

meant. I said 'Peace' should be read as meant caustically. He said Ann lent him her copy of *Ancestral Voices*. He left it behind in the train, then had to buy two more copies, one for her and the other for himself to keep. Flattering.

I asked if he was sensitive to criticism in the press. He said it depended. If it was a leader in *The Times* he minded. If it impugned his integrity he minded. If it merely disagreed with his policy he didn't mind at all. It also depended who the critic was.

Friday, 2 February

In a sense I have today finished the first volume of my Harold [Nicolson] book. By which I mean that I have typed down the last chapter and corrected it. Now I have to go through the whole thing, trying to reduce it drastically, correct again, and re-type from beginning to end, before I can send it to Chatto's. I know it to be far too long and I have the utmost misgivings. A. has read each chapter and says she enjoyed them all. She was only bored by the political sections, some of which I may be able to reduce. I see that I began the actual writing on 20 June last year, so it has taken me a little over six months. This means that had I not had interruptions, like going abroad, going to London etc., I could have written it in four months.

Saturday, 17 February

On Friday the 8th, A., Caroline Somerset and I went to Berlin for a long weekend on package terms, amounting to £154 inclusive of flight and hotel, the Savigny in Brandenburgerstrasse, modest and clean. We came back on the Monday afternoon. It was bitterly cold, and when the wind blew straight from the Steppes the very marrow of the back was pierced as with knives. But the hotel, the museums, cafés, shops, buses were very hot, so I never once wore the fur lining I had dragged all the way to Berlin. It is the most hideous city I have ever seen, worse than Constantinople, even Athens, though more agreeable than either. I refer to the West sector, which is a hotchpotch of the worst-taste modernistic buildings, evidently put up in a hurry after the war by speculative builders. Our last morning we went to the East sector, and I regret to say that the Communists have done far better. Their new buildings are commonplace enough, but they conform in height and scale to the fine wide boulevards. Many of the houses of faience, which instead of giving a public lavatory look are almost pleasing. They also had better old buildings in their sector and gradually they are reproducing them exactly as they were. Berlin, which I had always supposed to be ugly before 1939, must have been a fine city. Many of the early nineteenth-century palaces, the Schinkel School ones, very impressive indeed.

In the West, Tiergarten scruffy, barbed wire and no statues that I could see. Stunted trees all new since the war, old ones cut down for firewood. Walked to look at Brücken-allee where Harold's apartment was.* Gone completely, even the street, and site occupied by tower blocks. Reichstag impressive, though of William II date, and melancholy next to the Wall. Wall not quite so terrifying as I had expected, because white cement, with rounded capping. A sad, moving little group of crosses marking the site where fugitives from the East were shot down by the stinking Communists. The area by the Wall very desolate, a sort of no-man's-land, blighted. In fact the scruffiness is beyond all belief.

Stayed Monday night with Eardley, and on Tuesday to the Properties Committee. Michael Bloch,† the young man who had written to me about Philip Guedalla,‡ whose biography he is writing, lunched at Brooks's. Suave and dark, with large luminous eyes like Brian Howard's,§ but not chi-chi like Brian. Quiet, soft-spoken so that I strained to hear, and very intelligent. Unfortunately Alvilde called punctually at 2.30 to motor me home and I had to dismiss him, not without arranging to take him to see Rosamond [Lehmann] whom he pines to know.

---

* He had served in Berlin as Counsellor at the British Embassy from 1927 to 1929.
† Writer (b. 1953); student (undergraduate and postgraduate) at St John's College, Cambridge, 1971–9; called to the Bar by Inner Temple, 1978; editor of this volume.
‡ Historian and essayist (1889–1944).
§ Oxford aesthete (1905–58).

Sunday, 25 February

Went to Toty de Navarro's[*] funeral on Thursday, Requiem Mass at Broadway. Not a soul I knew except Alice Fairfax-Lucy and she not a local. It was strange being in the church which I used to frequent when I lived at Wickhamford, during weekends with my parents, after they forgave me. What a dreary, thin, tasteless, unspiritual building. Its flat roof ceiled with cheap wood, its Stations of the Cross made of plasticine and painted mustard. Hideous Romanesque altar. Toty's coffin standing below the altar steps on the Gospel side. A poor organ, a limited choir in the loft. Dreariness, dismalness, death and shoddiness. A ghastly service which lasted an hour and a half. And when we left poor Dorothy and her son stood at the gate after the committal and she said to me: 'What a beautiful service it was. We were so lucky: we got special permission from the Bishop to have it in Latin.' Now why the hell should they have to get the Bishop's consent for the Mass to be sung in the language it always was sung in since the first century AD? In that Broadway church I did not experience one second of spiritual devotion, not one flicker. Just irritation and revulsion. I wonder did I ever like the cheap mumbo-jumbo in the days when I got used to it? I am really quite anti-Catholic now. How my great-aunt Katie would smirk.

Saturday, 10 March

Now on the 7th I motored up to London to meet by appointment at Brooks's Michael Bloch. I got there at 6 and he had already arrived. I had forgotten what he looked like. He is slim and willowy. His Brian Howard eyes are large and luminous and fine. He has an oval face, alabaster skin. Don't know how handsome. Full, dark hair cut like nephew Nick's. We

---

[*] José Maria de Navarro (1896–1979), only surviving son of the actress Mary ('Mamie') Anderson (1859–1940) who retired from the stage in 1880s to marry Antonio de Navarro (1860–1932), a wealthy Spanish-American, and settle at Court Farm, Broadway, Worcestershire. J.L.-M. received hospitality and support from Mamie after he became a Catholic in 1934, when he was for a time unwelcome at nearby Wickhamford. 'Toty', archaeologist and Fellow of Trinity College, Cambridge, m. 1940 Dolores MacKenzie ('Dorothy') Hoare (1901–87), Fellow of Newnham College, Cambridge.

talked in the upstairs Subscription Room, he drinking Bloody Marys, until we drove at 8 to pick up Rosamond for dinner. I lost the way: he who cannot drive was no help, not knowing where any street was. We took Rosamond to dinner round the corner. Over £16 it cost. They sat together and I opposite. I could barely hear for the noise. The meeting was a success. She liked his intelligence and positive views.

Last week we had one lovely day, sun and calm, without a breath of wind. Honey and I went for a walk this evening just before sunset, in Vicarage Fields. Coming back, facing the sky, which was a gash of crimson and orange, the darkness was creeping up from the grass, and I had the sensation of walking in space. I moved very fast, without the least effort, racing across the fields, Honey beside me, like wind through wheat, feet barely touching the ground, without effort, without breathlessness. It was almost a mystical experience. March has always been a queer month for me, full of emotional events and portents. What is this one to bring?

Monday, 12 March

I have that ache in the abdomen, but I will not allow myself to go over the brink. Unfortunately I sense that damned spring approaching and that awful wanderlust feeling, that misery which I never seem to grow out of. How I hate the unsettling, beastly reminder of lost opportunities, the reminder that there can be no further opportunities, that bloody spring.

Tuesday, 13 March

A letter this morning. I could not bring myself to open it until after luncheon. Took a strong drink. Was ever a man of seventy more blessed? It is going to be a platonic relationship, and possibly the deepest of my whole life.

Saturday, 17 March

Telephoned J[ohn Kenworthy-Browne] and talked to him about a bust of John Francis's which I have found in a junk shop in Bath and asked his advice. He gave it at length. Then I said I supposed he was busy packing for his jaunt to Sicily tomorrow. He said: 'No, I fear it is off. My father died half an hour ago. The person I was going with is dreadfully put out.' He thought his father's funeral would not be for ten days (which is unusual) and supposed he could go to Sicily just for the week. I said I really did not think he could. He agreed, but it is sad for him.

Sunday, 18 March

When we last parted M. said, 'Do let's write.' Well, my trouble is that I find it easier to write every day than to write once in a while. Moreover, trite observations and sentiments seem less trite in a daily missive than in an occasional missive from which more is expected.

Saturday, 24 March

Tony Powell said to me that his 'book', as he calls the twelve volumes, was being filmed for television in 1982.* He said he would like to live to see it, but were it not for that, he would be content to die now. He does not the least wish to see more of this disagreeable world. Told me this in greatest good humour, with a cocktail in the hand; and I knew he was speaking the truth and not for effect. I said, 'I expect you get letters from strangers saying what a snob you are.' 'I do,' he said, 'but this morning I received a letter from a black man in New York saying how much he appreciated the sort of people I wrote about, and ending "Your brother".'

Monday, 9 April

The weekend is over. I drove in pouring rain, without once stopping, to Cambridge. Arrived at 7.15, put car in a multi-storeyed carpark, and walked to 9 King's Parade. An opening opposite the gate of King's led

---

* Having bought an option on the television rights to Anthony Powell's twelve-volume novel *A Dance to the Music of Time*, the BBC decided that their proposed serial would be too expensive to produce. A four-part serialisation by Alvin Rakoff appeared on Channel Four in 1997.

down a passage. No. 9 painted over a door. I rang. Presently M. appeared smiling. Led me to his charming room with two Georgian windows facing the Parade. Typical undergraduate's room, cheap but not unattractive, flowered wall-paper *à la* Zuleika Dobson, dresser of Art Nouveau, hideous modern chandelier from supermarket, comfortable stuffed chairs, one very large table covered with typewriter and papers. Books everywhere, on shelves and on floor. We drank whisky. We talked. He is easy to talk to. At 9.30 we went to dine at a disgusting place down the street where we ate lamb goulash and drank red plonk. Afterwards we visited a Russian lady he knows, Vera Traill,[*] living in penury and surrounded by empty bottles of *vin rosé*. She intelligent and sharp. Much badinage. She is a friend of John Lehmann,[†] that sinister figure which looms, and of Moura Budberg,[‡] who was a kleptomaniac ever since her menopause. When after her death friends went to her flat they found their choicest possessions lying around.

Then M. and I went back to No. 9. One dim lamp, the gas fire and Bach played softly on the gramophone. The whole occasion like that of any undergraduate, though he a graduate. He told me about his life. We talked till 2 a.m. by the fire. He read me from the beginning of a play he is writing, and from books, including my own. Then he accompanied me to St John's College, to the guest room where I spent the night. The moon was scurrying through the clouds as we strolled through the deserted quadrangles, lit by the single passageway lamp. He fetched me in the morning and took me back to his rooms to have breakfast, the landlady, who clearly adores him, talking beside the table. He says she does not mind how many male friends he has in his rooms, but hates girls, and whenever they telephone him says he is out.

Good Friday, 13 April

Eardley and I spent two days this week motoring in Somerset. Like old times. How often have we two not done this in the old days,

---

[*] Film critic (1906–87); daughter of the Tsarist politician A. I. Guchkov.

[†] Michael Bloch had briefly been his secretary.

[‡] Baroness Budberg, *neé* Maria (Moura) Zakrevskaya (1892–1974); Russian émigrée active in London literary circles; sometime mistress of H.G. Wells.

35 years ago. We spent Tuesday night with the [Reynolds] Stones. Were shocked to discover that Reynolds is inexplicably senile. At breakfast on Wednesday he insisted on reading a passage from K. Clark's book on Beardsley, and could not get the words out. It was like a child suffering from the inability to coordinate. The words just meant nothing to him. Janet seized the book in her bossy way, but he would not let her take it, and persisted. Eardley and I did not dare look at each other. However Reynolds was able to tell me a charming story while showing me a nice panel of early Renaissance tapestry they have hanging over their staircase. It belonged to Dr Luxmoore, who cultivated the garden at Eton in which I used to sit for dreamy evening hours with dear friends like Tom [Mitford] and Desmond [Parsons]. He was very fond of it, but during the First World War decided he ought to sell it in aid of the Red Cross. His friends, led by Reynolds's mother, knew what its loss would mean to him. They clubbed together and bought it. One afternoon while Luxmoore was out they re-hung it in its old place on the staircase. Nothing was said. No thanks, no reference to what they had done came from Luxmoore. One day three months later Mrs Stone happened to accompany Luxmoore upstairs. She noticed that as he climbed the stairs he shielded the left side of his face with his hand. The top of the stairs reached, Mrs Stone wheeled him round and took his hand away from his face. Luxmoore was amazed. In gratitude he left the tapestry to the Stone family in his will.

I received a letter from Ros which slightly upset me – that Misha* had been to see her again, as indeed he told me. She can't make him out: he is like a character in a novel who is not fully formed. Her brother John says he is mad. Now mad is the last adjective I would apply. Emotionally unstable possibly. He reminds me more and more of Jamesey [Pope-Hennessy], without the bitchiness.

Tuesday, 17 April

Yesterday a Bank Holiday. Motored up to London alone. Stayed the night with John, at his nicest and best. Following afternoon the

---

* Michael Bloch.

N.T. Properties Committee. Virginia Woolf's house at Rodmell under discussion. I have never been inside but from knowledge of outside am dubious. However, she must be the greatest literary genius of the century in English. Just re-reading *Mrs Dalloway*. No writer has thrown such vibrant, impressionistic light on everyday things as she. I marvel over every sentence. Not that I am not at times bewildered and bored by the narrative.

Met M. for tea at his club and had dinner cooked by him at his flat, excellent dish with caraway. Not entirely satisfactory evening. A handsome young friend of his, Charles Orwin,* who works at Fabers and is a fan, joined us. Somehow I felt out of my element. At 10.45 said I must go home. We talked of promiscuity, whether it blunts the sensibilities. I said I was not sure, but I am. It must. It does.

Saturday, 21 April

We have Jimmie Smith† staying for the Badminton Three-Day Event. Although the weather is warm, Jimmie seldom goes out of doors. He has become fearfully old, or rather death-wishy. He walks with a stick even indoors, though can do perfectly well without it. Otherwise full of chat and his friendship with the Queen Mother. We were thereby invited to take him to the Beauforts' after-dinner party which they gave for the Queen's birthday. Mary Beaufort had hired a 'funny man', as she called him, from Bristol. It was rather painful. All one-person performances have to be extremely good or they are embarrassing. This little man was no Ruth Draper, and signally unfunny. Only the Royals in the front row were holding their sides, whether out of pity, good manners or enjoyment, who can tell. Twice the performer called for assistance from the audience. Each time Prince Andrew and Prince Charles volunteered to go forward. Both very good, unshy, and the Prince of Wales was frankly funnier than the 'funny man' in his clowning. A ghastly party, and we had drinks afterwards in the dining room. What was nice was that the Beauforts had asked people from the estate, Leslie the

---

* Publisher (b. 1951).
† Hon. James Smith (1906-??); yr s. of 2nd Viscount Hambleden; Governor of Sadler's Wells Theatre and member of Royal Opera House Trust.

butler's wife and two sons, farmers, estate servants, their wives dressed to kill and talking away with the Royals at their ease. I did not speak to one Royal: had my eye on one or two, female, but was not presented.

Monday, 30 April

Now that I have divested myself, temporarily I suppose, of Harold, I am at a loss. Feel bereft, with no purpose in life, in spite of my reviews for *Apollo* and articles for *Country Life*. I understand how Virginia Woolf had a breakdown when she finished a book. Only she didn't have hers returned, underscored, or larded with requests to rewrite parts. Non-writers don't understand how writers feel like emigrants in an alien new world, having left forever the shores of yesteryear.

Sunday, 6 May

We played a small part in the General Election, acting in turn as tellers at the village hall, used as the polling station. Bywater, the Duke's secretary, knows which way every single inhabitant of the village voted. He said that several of them subscribe to Tory funds yet vote Labour – out of fear of the Duke, I suppose. Wonderfully cheered by the victory.*

Monday, 21 May

A disagreeable incident. I took the dogs round the village. Crossing the recreation ground they bolted towards Vicarage Wood. I heard furious yells. Stalked cautiously round the entrance gates and saw the Duke with a pair of binoculars. I retreated, coward that I am. Alvilde very boldly decided she must look for the dogs; ran into the Duke who was beside himself with passion. He had been watching his cherished vixen and cubs. He was almost apoplectic. Said he would not have our bloody dogs on his land. Bloody this and bloody that. He would get his gun and shoot them. A. kept her head and temper, apologised and said what a good idea. Then he called at the house. I went to the door.

---

* At the general election on 3 May, the Conservatives under Margaret Thatcher were returned to power with a parliamentary majority of forty-three.

Again he ranted. He sent the keeper after the dogs; keeper called and also said he would shoot them if ever again they were seen loose. Duke then telephoned, abused A., and slammed down the receiver. All for a trivial cause, in concern about some cubs which his hounds will tear to pieces before the autumn is through. Ghastly values, ghastly people. How I hate them. I shall never set foot in the big house again, in the unlikely event of being asked, and shall never speak to the hell-hound again beyond a curt good-morning if I pass him on the road.

Friday, 25 May

A. and I flew to Bulgaria[*] for three days and nights, staying at Hotel Sofia, Sofia. Terence Mullaly[†] our guide. Intelligent, agreeable man. Sofia an attractive town in centre with many decent, early nineteenth–century, neo-Classical buildings. Periphery horrid, tower blocks rising in ever-increasing numbers and heights. Extremely clean cobbled streets which are hosed at night and even during the day by stalwart women wielding heavy hose-pipes. First thing one sees in early morning is these women sweeping up ends. Heavy fines for throwing litter. The buildings are colour-washed tawny yellows and orange. We watched the *jeunesse dorée* strolling arm in arm in front of the hotel, facing the statue of Alexander II which has been allowed to survive. Bulgarians just as well-dressed as the English plebeian young. City full of parks and gardens, densely tree'd and freshly green. Archaic Roman fragments in the underpasses, Roman bas-reliefs. Imagine how they would be vandalised in London. Mosque Jami-demi by architect of Blue Mosque. But disappointing. We could not enter. Portico of three bays, with ablution niches honeycombed. The Church of Santa Sophia dates, we are told, from Constantine the Great; but the interior walls are plastered over and painted a dreary brown.

On Saturday we dined at a Folk Music restaurant just outside Sofia. Frightfully hot and airless. Bulgarian band and professional dancers in national dress laid on. The native guests, full of vodka, joined in and

---

[*] Where Harold Nicolson had lived in childhood when his father was British Minister to Sofia.
[†] Art correspondent of *Daily Telegraph*, 1956–1986 (b. 1927).

danced and sang with abandon. The English party sat looking on with selfconsciousness and embarrassment.

This trip has put me in a bit of a quandary. Made me ask myself whether these apparently happy people are not right to be Communists. They have no one to whom they feel inferior. Of course they are regimented. But it does possibly mean the greatest happiness of the greatest number. Mullaly told me that his opposite number in the Communist equivalent of the *Daily Telegraph* is paid what amounts to £20,000 p.a., far more than he earned. The privileged here lead luxurious lives, and are allowed to leave their earnings to their children. Thus a meritocracy, not to say a new aristocracy, is being established.

At Plovdiv, the old town is preserved. We walked through it, between ancient houses with overhangs. Entered one, decorated in Turkish style about 1840. An old woman spoke to me in French. She said she admired our Queen. I said we did too. She keeps a photograph in her bedroom where it cannot be seen by strangers. A man selling cherries in the market to Kate Vestey said, when told she was English, 'Maggie Thatcher, she great, she great.'

Tuesday, 29 May

Feel fearfully depressed, because I unwisely telephone Norah at Chatto's to ask if Ian had finished with my typescript. She was short and curt. Said it was too detailed and much too long.

Thursday, 7 June

Joined National Trust Arts Panel party for Plymouth, spending the day at Saltram, beautifully kept, then Penheale to visit Mrs Colville who surprisingly remembered me visiting the house years ago. Looked at her Italian drawings, Leonardo, Raphael, and Donatello model of the Gatemalata equestrian statue. We stayed the the night at the Bedford Arms where Eardley and I so often stayed. In the morning to Cotehele. Strange to be there after so many years, for I originally arranged this house, having done all negotiations with the dear old Mount Edgcumbes. I suggested that the N.T. put up a memorial tablet to them in the chapel at Cotehele, which was accepted.

These all-male parties depress me somewhat. And I have been feeling deeply depressed about my book and Ian Parsons' comments. But have decided to wait till I pick up the MS with his suggestions for cutting on Friday, and devote all next week and most of the following to deciding whether or not to chuck the whole thing. I think with no work I would be too unhappy to continue living, and so must make every effort to resume. Am depressed too about M. and how little I see him.

Saturday, 9 June

The Downers are staying the weekend. Alec has been extremely ill but now appears quite cured. Went for a long walk with me in the park in the morning. Said his illness had clarified his spiritual condition and sharpened his mind which is now working better than he ever remembers. Has a great admiration for Mrs Thatcher. Thinks she has the qualities of Queen Elizabeth I. Wants to tell her that a large section of the Australian people still hold this country in high regard, and her government must not let this affection evaporate.

Tuesday, 19 June

To London last evening and met the Rosses at Brooks's. Had I not been pre-warned I would never have recognised Michael. His declension is pitiable and terrible. I do not suppose he can live more than a few months. He is more like a corpse than a living being, tiny drawn face with tight slit of a mouth, unsmiling. When he stands up he is a bag of bones. Anne incredibly brave, but told me she had been knocked endways first by Oliver's death last year, then by parting with Stafford Terrace, and now by Michael's condition. It was difficult to know what to say. Yet Michael is lucid and compos, and talks perfectly well and sanely.

I had John K.-B. and Nick Robinson to dine with me. Introduced them to the Rosses. Nick very smart for the first time ever in a nice blue suit and looking extremely handsome. I felt proud of him. Yet I don't think John cared for him; thought him arrogant, which is of course nonsense.

Thursday, 21 June

Listened while shaving this morning to Handel's *Lascia ch'ia pianga* from *Rinaldo*. Was moved to tears by the beauty. Handel so often repetitive and dog-trotting; but this somehow inspired with desperate love and sadness. O the hell of love, hoping for the letter. Will there be one this morning? No. Will there be one tomorrow? There is – which may be worse than if there hadn't been one. And so the agony goes on.

Received a sweet letter from Janet Stone about Reynolds's stroke. My first, horrid thought was this. Supposing Reynolds dies, supposing Michael Rosse dies and the funeral means putting off my visit to Cambridge next week, I shall make every excuse and endeavour to go to Cambridge. Just like the duc de Guermantes' behaviour [in Proust's novel] when his cousin Amanien d'Osmond was dying and he dismissed all remonstrances in a determination to attend a costume ball. So here is inconstancy, disloyalty: putting someone I have known for a few months before old friends of a lifetime. But the truth is that friends of a lifetime become a duty, not a pleasure. (Eardley is the exception.) My old friends are becoming gaga when they don't die. Joan Drogheda cannot take down a telephone number and has to call Lady Poole to do it for her. Anne Rosse mumbles about my coming to Nymans [Sussex] and does not explain whether she wants me to stay or merely lunch, not taking it in that luncheon would mean a drive of 300 miles in one day from Badminton.

Tuesday, 26 June

Poor Reynolds has died, and will be buried next Friday. Alvilde said to me rather tartly, 'Lucky for you the funeral is not to be when you are going to Cambridge. Would you chuck your new friend, etc.?' Indeed just what I had been debating with myself. She divines my thoughts if she does not read my diary.

Thursday, 28 June

I am now back from Cambridge, and feeling so-so. Spent two nights there, one in a room in M's lodgings, the second in his college. We breakfasted together each morning in his college cafeteria. Our first evening we walked through the fields to Grantchester where we dined expensively at the pub for £15. We walked back across the fields in the dark, arm in arm, the lights of Cambridge guiding our footsteps. Yesterday I went to Wimpole* for the day. He all day read the first half of my H.N. book, and absolutely contrary to Ian Parsons deplores the excisions. What am I to do? He says all the cut-out bits are the most interesting bits. He has found several mistakes of mine concerning the Balkan Wars. What a clever youth he is. But I gave him a talking-to about his life of restlessness and procrastination.

Saturday, 30 June

Went to Oxford for the Magdalen Gaudy, the first time I ever attended such a thing. It was both boring and interesting. Arriving at 5, I parked the car the far side of Magdalen Bridge and introduced myself at the Porter's Lodge. Was directed to the President's Garden where tea in progress on the lawn. Sunny but a cold wind. Shook hands and chatted, then slunk off. Took my luggage to the room allotted me. Large sitting room and bedroom, panelled. Could be so nice, but is horrid. Broken down furniture, dirty carpets, sofa legs propped up by telephone books. In the bedroom, no back to the bed, no bedside lamp, naked bulb hanging from ceiling. No washbasin. No amenities. No scout of course. To wash and pee was obliged to descend three flights of stairs, walk along open colonnade, plunge downstairs to a basement and lavatories. Here two cracked wash-basins, a leaking urinal and baths too squalid even to be considered. Almost as comfortless as Mount Athos, and without the spirit.

Luckily Alan Pryce-Jones was present. At dinner he sat at High Table. But first there was Evensong in the Chapel, candles in hurricane globes, all lit. Singing by choir first rate. By now I had changed into a dinner jacket. Alan opposite me in tweed jacket, no porter having been found to direct him to his room. Then sherry drunk in the Cloister garth. Met and knew a mere handful of friends – Oliver

---

* Wimpole Hall, Cambridgeshire, formerly the seat of the Earls of Oxford, bequeathed to the N.T. by Mrs Bambridge (Rudyard Kipling's daughter Elsie) in 1976.

van Oss,* George Coulson, Lawrence Radice.† Dinner in Hall went on for three hours. This was the worst part because I had boring neighbours, one a parson, the other a don, botanist, both nice but dull. They undoubtedly thought the same of me. Loving cup sent round after toasts. Then two of the worst speeches, Alan agreed, we had ever listened to, one by Greenham, RA,‡ the other by the President. I could have done far better.

At 11.15 this was over. With luck among the 150 guests, all ancient, I re-found Alan and sat in his room in St Swithin and gossiped for an hour. He was off next day with Mollie Buccleuch.§ Showed me a scurrilous reference to her in *Private Eye*, stating that she was the randiest duchess since Lady Castlemaine,¶ or words to that effect. I asked if she had seen it. He thought not, for no one would show it to her. Alan amused because he noticed among the guests an ancient man bent and walking on two sticks. When he was taking his College Exam in Hall this man came to his room at night and slipped, without a word of by-your-leave, into A.P.-J.'s bed. Told me that Lord X. was charming and might be 'a friend of Mrs King', as he expressed it.

Sunday morning after Holy Communion in Chapel I motored home.

Monday, 2 July

A. walked into my bedroom at 8 to say Anne Rosse had telephoned. I said, 'Then Michael has died?' 'Yes,' she said. 'Anne wanted you to know.' Wept while I shaved. For no man was better than Michael, unless it was Reynolds, or is Lennox. I rang up Tony Snowdon to find out where Anne was. He said Michael died walking up the steep steps of Stafford Terrace. I then spoke to Anne who was very brave as I

---

* Headmaster of Charterhouse, 1965–73.
† International civil servant.
‡ Keeper of Royal Academy Schools, 1965–84 (1909–92).
§ Vreda Esther Mary ('Mollie') Lascelles (1900–93); m. 1921 Walter Montagu-Douglas-Scott (1894–1973) who s. 1935 as 8th Duke of Buccleuch and Queensberry; cousin of Alan Pryce-Jones.
¶ Barbara Villiers (1640–1709); mistress of Charles II, who created her Countess of Castlemaine and Duchess of Cleveland; ancestress of J.L.-M's friend Hugh, Duke of Grafton.

would expect, and said how happy she was that he did not have to return to hospital. Funeral to be at Womersley* by Michael's choice, because apparently the family mausoleum at Birr [Castle, Co. Offaly] has been vandalised, that dreadful cave full of coffins where we buried Desmond in 1937 which I remember too well, having travelled to Birr with Robert Byron.† I suppose no woman ever loved her husband more than Anne. Find myself thinking of the Rosses all day, and their consistent goodness to me throughout the long years.

Friday, 6 July

I left home at 7.30 in my little Renault for Womersley. Arrived about noon. Waited in the road outside the village so as not to get there too early. It was boiling hot and I was in a muck sweat. House full of black-dressed people; mostly family, Susan de Vesci‡ and children of all sorts. All very sweet to me, except old Lady de Vesci,§ very formal and stiff, well over ninety but I fancied not pleased to see me. Tony Snowdon came up and kissed me on both cheeks. Then Anne entered in black, wearing her pearls and diamonds, a little veil over her face, but looking so pretty. Her courage stupendous. I heard her say, 'Where is Jim?' so I presented myself. She dragged me into her little sitting room, that little room where she and I used to dine and gossip during the war, under Oliver [Messel]'s portrait of her, so white and fluffy. Told me how, when poor Michael collapsed climbing the steps to Stafford Terrace, she had to hail a young man passing by to help her carry him upstairs, where he died in her arms. She feels relief now the strain is over. The service a beautiful one. When the coffin was taken out I waited behind, disliking the committal at the graveside. But evidently the coffin was taken away in the hearse for cremation because I saw Anne standing inside the west door

---

* Womersley Park, Yorkshire, the Rosses' English seat.
† Travel writer (1905–41), who like J.L.-M. had been in love with Desmond Parsons.
‡ Susan Armstrong-Jones (d. 1986); dau. of Anne Rosse by her 1st marriage; m. 1950 6th Viscount de Vesci (whose uncle the 5th Viscount had married Susan's step-grandmother – see note below).
§ Lois Lister-Kaye (1882–1984); m. 1st 1905 5th Earl of Rosse (d. 1918), 2nd 1920 5th Viscount de Vesci (d. 1958); Michael Rosse's mother.

shaking hands with the congregation as they passed out. When the last person left I had to go too. Then the fatal thing. Anne clasped me in an embrace and wouldn't let go, and said, 'Do come and see me in London next week,' and sobbed; and I broke down too. Felt ashamed, couldn't reply but just nodded my head affirmatively.

I drove on to Flintham to stay the night. Myles [Hildyard] had staying his niece and Andrew Murray-Thriepland whom Myles has long loved in vain. He has lost his looks which must have been considerable. We began dinner late, and sat over the dinner table till one o'clock. It is years since I have done such a thing.

Sunday, 8 July

Derry and Alexandra Moore staying the weekend. Derry very restless like his father and dashing from place to place. Not such fun as when he stayed with us as a bachelor. We all went to the Hollands' evening concert.* Pianist, Howard Shelley, like a young handsome Beethoven, playing Chopin. Joan Holland telephoned begging us to come early as she had reserved us to talk to Prince and Princess Michael of Kent,† guests of honour. Needless to say they came just before the concert began, so our presence was of no account. But during the interval I was sent for. We were presented to the Prince, a nice-looking, vacant young man. A. talked with him while *she* collared me. She was very effusive about my books, said she had read them all (they all say this) and had always wished to meet me, etc. Said she had a mind to send me *Ancestral Voices* for my autograph. She is larger than I thought from photographs, but profile very good. Wore a sort of Druid's robe, with her long fair hair down her back. Certainly agreeable to meet but very un-royal. Too much enthusiasm, too little dignity. But I liked her. Eardley tells me she is tough and acquisitive. She did tell me that the moment she married

---

* Sir Guy Holland, 3rd Bt (1918–97); m.1945 Joan Street (who m. 2nd 1999 26th Baron Mowbray); they gave an annual concert in aid of the National Art Collections Fund.
† HRH Prince Michael of Kent (b. 1942); m. 1978 (as her 2nd husband) Marie-Christine von Reibnitz (renouncing his rights to the throne as she was a Roman Catholic).

she went straight to the V&A, where she had worked in her humble days, and requested the return of those pictures and works of art given to the museum [by her husband's family] on semi-permanent loan, making herself unpopular in consequence with John Pope-Hennessy.

Monday, 9 July

A delicious day with Eardley. Met him at Swindon at 10.30. While I went to telephone I told him to sit in the car, forgetting Folly in back seat. She bit him through the upper lip which bled profusely. Obliged to stop at chemist to buy and apply TCP. We walked along the Ridgeway for 12 miles. Ate picnic which E. carried in his knapsack. Beautiful day, not too hot, sun out and clouds in distance. Distant views of Downs. Wild flowers in profusion – eglantines, blue vetch, yellow bedstraw, wild mignonette. We gossiped ceaselessly. No one in the world with whom I am happier than with E. For his seventy-seven years he walked like a stripling. Neither of us a bit tired. Folly the tiredest.

Tuesday, 10 July

Tiresome day at re-opening of Bath Assembly Rooms. Decorated by young Mlinaric.* Not good work. Posh luncheon. Hanging about for Princess Margaret. I felt sorry for her. She looked extremely nervous. On the platform her hand was shaking. Making strange grimaces with her mouth. I suppose she is frightened of insults, and somebody told me that when she visited Bristol lately, a person in the crowd shouted, 'Whore!' I am sorry for underdogs. She is her own worst enemy of course, and if you are royal you must be immaculate or expect the consequences. But she consorts with the raffish, and this the public do not like.

Wednesday, 11 July

Motored to Oxford. Met M. by appointment in the art section of Blackwells. We strolled down Ship Street and ate a strange dish of salad

---

* David Mlinaric (b. 1939); interior decorator.

and cream. Chatted away about our various doings since we last wrote
and met. Each time I see him I feel wound up like an old grandfather
clock. He accompanied me as far as OUP where I had interview with
Jeremy Lewis,* nice, extrovert young publisher, and Richard Brain,†
whom I liked for his handsome face and merry, mischievous eyes.
They explained the Country House Anthology I am to do – 30,000
words only.

Sunday, 15 July

How long am I to suffer? The last spell endured 15 years at least, and
is not entirely over today. Does this mean that I shall be 85 before I
have recovered from this one? In other words, are all my remaining
years to be spent aching, waiting for the post, the telephone call, the
fleeting meeting, the mild jealousies, the angst? Pray to God No.
I remember in 1958, when I was last smitten, Richard Rumbold‡
advised me to record every sensation in my diary. I don't think I did
so then. And now that I do so, it makes a catalogue of moans – not
attractive or an inducement to sympathy.

Last night we dined with the Somersets. The Beits staying.
Clementine told me that she read Proust over and over again. He was
the greatest novelist in the world, and George Painter's biog. the greatest biog. ever written of a novelist. I sat between Daphne§ and
Caroline. With Daphne, I refrained from mentioning the death a week
ago of her son Valentine Thynne¶ and talked about the Rosses. Then
I turned to Caroline, who immediately wanted to talk about her
brother's death, which she has dreadfully on her mind. She said
candidly that she had not loved him. But she was filled with guilt; feels
she ought to have bothered more about him; is appalled by the manner
of his death by hanging. Explained that when found his face was

---

* Writer and publisher (b. 1942).
† Publisher's editor (b. 1928); J. L.-M. had possibly forgotten that they had met
during the 1950s, with Harold Nicolson.
‡ Writer and journalist, protégé of Harold Nicolson; committed suicide, 1961.
§ Hon. Daphne Vivian (1904–97); novelist, mother of Caroline Somerset; m. 1st
1926 6th Marquess of Bath, 2nd 1953 Xan Fielding, war hero and writer.
¶ Lord Valentine Thynne (1937–79).

1979

peaceful. No tongue hanging out, protruding eyes or look of agony. Is therefore satisfied that he did not suffer. They do not know why he did it. He was drunk at a charity ball, and rather a nuisance following his brother Christopher and Princess Margaret. So Christopher turned on him and said, 'For God's sake behave yourself and fuck off.' Valentine walked home and killed himself. Christopher is distraught, feels responsible. He wrote a touching letter of regret and love which he put in the coffin. Caroline was irritated by the widow's theatrical behaviour at the funeral. She prayed by the graveside with her hands clasped above her head, heavily veiled. When she unveiled herself her face was the studied Madonna Dolorosa. Whereas the seventeen-year-old boy's face was contorted by the sobs he vainly tried to control.

Tuesday, 24 July

Last night, while walking the dogs in the lower woods, I thought dispassionately that I would commit suicide if only I knew how, and if by so doing I might not cause distress to A. Talked to Diana W[estmorland] at tea yesterday about June [Hutchinson]'s terrible depressions. Junie admits that she has every reason to be blissfully happy – she has a husband and a son whom she adores, a house she loves and enough money – yet she undergoes depressions in fits. I suppose I am the same and have always been so, only my depressions are presumably less dire, and cannot be strictly measured by fits or seasons.

To my immense surprise while I was reading after dinner last night the telephone rang and I was read a telegram from Nigel Nicolson. 'Half way through. Marvellous. Nigel.' Now what a reassuring message to get. How charming of him to bother. He knew I was in a state of anxiety. But he would not have sent it if he did not mean it. Of course, there is still the second half to be read. Still, I *am* pleased.

Wednesday, 25 July

Motored with A. to London this evening. Occasion was *the* meeting with M[ichael] B[loch]. We had John B[etjeman] and Elizabeth C[avendish] to dine with us at Brooks's. I think A. liked M. though she finds him looking, as she says, unhealthy. After dinner, M. and John had a long talk about Uranian verse, and liked one another. I worry about John, who is worse. Finds walking a great effort. E. leads him by the arm, making encouraging noises as one would to a recalcitrant horse. He has both sleeves of his shirt, without links, hanging over his hands. This, and his staggering gait, make him seem drunk after dinner. I felt sad. A. and I drove away, having put John in his car, and leaving M. on the pavement.

Friday, 27 July

Terrible drive to Nymans [Sussex], boiling hot day, London for 40 miles without a break it seemed. Harold Acton staying with Anne [Rosse]. As an old friend he feels for her. Anne very brave during lunch, but oh dear her sorrow wrings the heart. She took us round the garden. Not a sympathetic garden; still the stockbroker's, with too much colour, great clumps of herbaceous pink, and those metallic blue hydrangeas in the woods. In memory of Michael, Anne gave me a pottery vase, early Georgian. Very sweet of her.

After a glass of lemonade at 4.30 I proceeded to Sissinghurst. Only Nigel and his charming Adam,* aged 21, sympathetic, sensitive. Nigel hospitable and kind. Took us to dine at a pub, excellently. Made me read long letter he has written me about the book; full of undeserved praise, which I am sure is sincere. Criticism that there are not enough judgements, assessments of H.N. Does not think it much too long and agrees that Ian Parsons' cutting far too drastic. Is prepared to accompany me to Chatto's and face them. Will be my ally. And says that, if Chatto's demur, there is always Weidenfeld & Nicolson, who, he indicated, would surely take it on his recommendation. Greatly cheered.

Saturday, 28 July

Awoke early at Sissinghurst. Walked in the garden in the cool of the morning, like God. And surely God never walked in a more beautiful garden. Once again I was overcome by its perfection, above all the layout which is the work of a genius, H.N.

---

* Writer (b. 1957); o.s. of Nigel Nicolson.

Sunday, 5 August

On Friday Tony Scotland and Julian Berkeley called on me in Bath after luncheon. I gave them coffee and peaches, and we talked. Object of the visit to discuss Tony's predicament at Radio Three. He tells me that the new supervisor McIntyre* is a fiend, who is upsetting the whole staff of announcers. Tells Tony that he dislikes his voice which gives the impression of a man too pleased with himself, who is admiring his face in the glass. Also threatens to stop the programme which he, Tony, has invented, *The Arts Worldwide*, which has proved such a success. It seems that the man McIntyre is a sort of Reith, who loathes homosexuals and dislikes gents. Tony's voice, which is soft, persuasive and totally without camp or show-off, is in fact one of the best of the announcers. I said there was little I could do beyond writing to a BBC Governor, if I knew one. Then found in *Whitaker* that George Howard is a Governor, and have written to him. Tony is handsome and charming.

Saturday, 11 August

I can honestly say that one of the chief distresses of my long life has been my baldness. Old men can look perfectly respectable provided they have all their hair, and snow-white hair, if abundant, palliates the ravages of age. But my late youth, when I managed otherwise to keep my looks, and my middle age, when I managed to keep my figure, were marred by baldness. And the efforts I have been put to in endeavouring first to disguise the incipient patches, then to train the hair over the developed patches, the combing, the avoidance of wind, have amounted to a constant irritation and nag.

Friday, 31 August

On Tuesday afternoon to London. Was met at Paddington by M. whose train from Plymouth arrived before mine. Together we

---

* Ian McIntyre (b. 1931); Controller, Radio Three, 1978–87; author of *The Expense of Glory: A Life of John Reith* (1993).

went to Chatto's where I delivered MS for second time, accompanied by letter to Norah. Then to Buck's, Brooks's being shut, for cup of tea. London mysteriously empty. We went on to Liverpool Street and caught train for Cambridge. M. has a new room in corner of a court at top of tower above the Library of St John's. Charming, romantic, isolated little room. We dined at Chinese restaurant.

The following day – my Mama's birthday – too beautiful for words. M. worked till tea time while I wandered, and sat in St John's garden, and visited Fitzwilliam Museum, where ate in canteen. Joined M. in his rooms for tea. He took me to a drink in the college bar with a don and a fellow postgraduate. Then took me to see *Lady Windermere's Fan*. Both evenings we sat in his rooms talking to 2 a.m. He is touchingly candid. After the play he took me for a walk in the gardens in the dark, and along the roof of the new block. He has an engaging air of innocence, a questioning look in the large brown eyes. Greets one with a deadpan expression, observing everything, followed by that disconcerting silence. I left Thursday morning by train. He insisted on accompanying me to the station in bus, put me on train, gave me a look of goodbye, turned on heel and sauntered off. *Abschiedsstimmung*.

In London J. lunched with me at Buck's. Again in a sadly melancholic state. He is over-sensitive. Doesn't seem in the least cheered by the success his book is having, and the excellent sales.[*] A. not particularly agreeable to me on my return. She says things like, 'It is hurting for me, and makes me feel that I am inadequate and can't give you everything you want in your life.' Well, the truth is that no one person can give anyone all he needs. Why do we look for extraneous interest in books, the arts, music, poetry or the company and conversation of others?

Thursday, 6 September

On 4th A. and I motored to Boughton [Northamptonshire], 240 miles there and back. First time either of us had been there since Mollie [Buccleuch] was reigning in full fig. Now house open to the public. Being a weekday there were few people. Not that people matter, but

---

[*] Robin Fedden and John Kenworthy-Browne, *The Country House Guide*, Jonathan Cape, 1979.

the sad thing is that the magic of this highly romantic, lost-in-the-wood palace has vanished. Every small, homely object has been removed. Ropes everywere, and bareness. Mollie living in the south-east corner. Nice apartment, but inconvenient: one has to enter it through her bedroom. Not, we gathered, treated well by present Duchess,* who clearly has ghastly taste; has put a small pool in the grass court outside the great hall, with raised cement curb. Mollie waited on by her sole person, the 'lady' chauffeur. So strange to see Mollie, nearly eighty, the grandest of the grand, stack between courses and wheel a trolley into the kitchenette. How are the mighty fallen! She sweet and affectionate, with that drawly, exaggerated Twentyish voice. Walked in the garden afterwards, and visited the David Scotts.† He 92, a great charmer in fullest possession. Showed us his collection of pictures, all bought by him for a song. Includes Edward Lears, Rembrandt etchings. She a well-known garden lady with whom A. at once clicked.

Yesterday Eardley and I walked about 17 miles along the Ridgeway, me carrying a full knapsack in practice for Mount Athos. Wonderful September day, golden sun and not too hot. A. asked me what E. and I talk about. I said what do oldest friends talk about on walks? Everything. Non-stop. Politics, the world, friends, his painting, my writing, our loves, sex, God.

Friday, 7 September

I took A. to Heathrow and saw her off. Terrible queues, crowds, muddle at Terminal 3. A hell on earth. I kissed her fondly and left for home and the dogs.

Sunday, 9 September

Am terribly lonely here without A. The house is empty of life, and thick with coffee cups. The dogs wander around like lost souls as though they had slipped their leash from their God, the all-provider,

---

* Jane McNeill; m. 1953 Earl of Dalkeith who s. 1973 as 9th Duke of Buccleuch.
† Sir David Scott (1887–1986); diplomatist, cousin of Duke of Buccleuch; m. (2nd) Valerie Finnis (1925–2006).

in a miasma of bewilderment. The telephone never rings. It is her house, not mine; I am a lodger here. I do not share her life. She said sadly at Boughton about the Scotts, 'I can think of nothing lovelier than a husband and wife sharing the same interest', *i.e.* the garden. I have not been nice to her lately. I am in deepest depression. I have a conviction that my life will end shortly, and just as well too. I would rather be dead.

Is it not miraculous that tears are given only to humans? Surely there is something divine in them, expressing as they do compassion, sorrow, love, anxiety and all feelings that associate us with the angels. I am not sure whether dogs shed tears. I rather hope they do for they have as much of the divine in their souls as humans.

Yesterday I lunched with my great-nephews at Moor Wood. I have sacked Derry Moore from being my executor, putting Nick in his place. And I have made M. my literary executor.

Wednesday, 12 September

Motored to London in afternoon, arriving at Chatto's at 4.30 where met Nigel, already there discussing his next Virginia Woolf volume with Norah. 'Well,' Norah began, 'you asked for this interview. What is it you wish to say?' I said, 'You will have received my letter, which explains that I cannot reduce the book further than I have now done.' Nigel absolutely splendid and backed me up, praising the book as he had done in his letter to me and assuming that I had now met his suggestions. Result that Norah reluctantly agreed to take the first vol. on Nigel's recommendation, but warned that they would print few copies and sell them at a high price. I said I would rather the book had a *succès d'estime* and was a valuable work than a popular but indifferent best-seller.

Monday, 1 October

Came into Chesterfield Hospital* at 5 last night, brought by A. At 7.15 a.m. given injection in right thigh. Felt dizzy, but conscious.

---

* For minor surgery the precise nature of which J.L.-M. does not specify.

Was determined to concentrate on M. to see if I could carry him into unconsciousness. Was wheeled downstairs into anteroom to operating theatre. Looked around, observed things, said a word to nice anaesthetist I had met previous evening; thereafter remember absolutely nothing. Do not remember being given another jab. Was it the first one, administered three-quarters of an hour previously, that worked magically at the prescribed moment? Was plunged into total darkness and oblivion. *Nox est perpetua una dormienda.* M. did not accompany me. Woke up feeling well in bed upstairs and dozed all morning. By afternoon was reading *War and Peace*, and Rupert [Hart-Davis]'s new book about his mother.

Next day came out and taken back to Badminton. Received an urgent telegram from M. in Paris begging to see me when he gets back, anywhere, any time.

Friday, 5 October

This morning, while resuming Vol. II of Harold, *i.e.* preparing the notes for the actual writing, I await call from M. Punctually at 11 he telephones. The matter he wishes to discuss is most exciting. He has been invited to write the authorised life of the Duke of Windsor. He cannot believe it is true. Must discuss it with me instantly, and whether he should chuck his career as a barrister at the Temple, due to begin on Monday. I must say it does call for immediate and serious discussion. Is coming down tomorrow for the day, but is anxious to know if I am really well. I say I am, and seem to be. But are you really, he repeats?

Saturday, 6 October

M. comes down to Bath, arriving 10.30. Met by me at station. With burning zeal he tells me of the offer received from Maître Blum* to write the Duke of Windsor's life from the Abdication onwards, based on his papers, dealing with his ill-treatment and griev-ances. I hope it arouses the interest he is confident it will. We discuss

---

* Maître Suzanne Blum (1898–1994), the formidable Paris lawyer of the Duchess of Windsor, whom Michael Bloch had befriended in 1978.

how he must not chuck his Bar apprenticeship, which is to start on Monday, for that would upset his father. He taps away in his shirt sleeves at typewriter on my desk extracts of letters from H.N. to Tommy Lascelles – highly indiscreet of me to let him, for Maître Blum believes Lascelles was the villain who engineered the Abdication. M. full of his Paris visit, relating some things which disturbed me, but I do not want him to refrain from telling me everything.

Thursday, 11 October

At Heywood Hill this morning, John Saumarez Smith spoke of Helen Dashwood. She came into the shop with the book I had sent her, David Cecil's *Jane Austen*, saying she was returning it and asking if John would credit it to her account. John said flatly he would do no such thing. Either she exchanged it for another book or he took back the one I gave her. No letter of thanks from her.

At 12.30 I went to the Temple to lunch with M. in Inner Temple Hall. Totally rebuilt since destruction of Victorian Gothick one during War. Good plain luncheon, potted shrimps and mutton. Surrounded by correctly dressed young men of the Establishment. M. finds it quite fun, but is convinced that in a few months he will be released and committed to work on Duke of Windsor book. Maître Blum telephones him every morning. She and he are convinced it is the book for which the world is waiting. I pray it will be so, but query whether there are not too many books on the subject coming out. M. said that under a new scheme he can apprentice himself to a lawyer of any Common Market country, and thinks he might do so to Maître Blum. This would mean living in Paris, which idea delights him. I am of course depressed by this information. We walked into No. 4, King's Bench Walk,* my first entry since Harold left it in 1945. Unchanged except that it is being redecorated, and an opening has been made into No. 3 next door. We sat on a bench in the sun in the garden. These short meetings, in public, so to speak, are not the most satisfactory.

---

* Harold Nicolson kept a first-floor set of residential chambers on this staircase from 1931 to 1945, where J.L.-M. was his paying guest in the mid 1930s.

Saturday, 13 October

Nan Bernays* took a party of us after lunching with the Somersets to see the eighteenth-century grotto at Goldney House, Clifton. Perhaps the best English grotto I have ever seen, and in splendid order. Done about 1730–60, of felspar, like amethysts, and huge shells brought from the east by the Bristol merchantmen. A stream of water pours down a rill from a figure of Neptune holding an urn. A really splendid and little known treasure this.

Monday, 15 October

I was writing a poem to M. at Brooks's when he appeared at 6. Delicious talk for an hour until we parted, for I was to receive J.K.-B. J. very sweet. We ate at Brooks's and went back to his house where I stayed the night. He is not a cheerful companion whereas M. bubbles with enthusiasms. The latter so taken up with Maître Blum and the Duke of Windsor that he can hardly concentrate on anything else.

Tuesday, 16 October

Mark Norman† last night at Brooks's asked whether I would rather the Trust accepted houses which it could not afford to maintain and went bust or declined them and kept its independence of Government interference. I replied that I would rather we risked acceptance of an important building which might be demolished if we refused it; and that even if the Trust were taken over by the Goverment, it would not be interfered with any more than the National Gallery was, for the Government realised that such bodies had to be run by experts. Mark said that had the Trust been a government body during my time I would not have been kept longer than a week for I was far too independent.

---

* Nancy Britton (d. 1987); m. 1942 Robert Bernays MP (killed in action, 1945).
† Banker (b. 1910); Eton contemporary of J.L.-M.; Deputy Chairman of N.T., 1977–80.

Thursday, 25 October

Motored A. to Heathrow as she is going to stay with the Beits for the Wexford Festival. We had an uneasy drive, for she would interrogate me as to where I was staying tonight, making repeated innuendos. Went on to J.K.-B. where I left him Vol. I of my Red Book since he is doing Essex for Burke's *Country Houses*. Motored on to 1, Hyde Park Gardens.* Joined by M. to hear lecture by Kathleen Nott.† As M. and I agreed, it would have been far more profitable to read this lecture than listen to it, a state of affairs which I find with the vast majority of lecturers who are not Kenneth Clarks or Harold Nicolsons. We left in pouring rain, bought snacks at a delicatessen and ate them in M's flat. Then motored to Curzon Cinema to see *The Europeans*. Pretty scenes of puritanical American life in clapboard houses, but too obvious, too American, and not to be compared with the subtlety of a Visconti or a Zeffirelli. M. came to breakfast at Brooks's next morning whence he left for his Chambers. I begged to be told if I had become a bore.

Saturday, 27 October

I motored, with dogs kindly invited, to stay with my dear Eardley at The Slade [Hampshire]. Mattei‡ and Dadie Rylands staying. Enjoyed visit enormously. Mattei I find extremely cosy and sympathetic. He is a gentle character, radiates charm, is singularly detached from cares of the world yet wise in his judgements. Dadie much aged since last seen. Also very deaf. In other respects unchanged. Alert as ever, and delightful; stimulating and fun. We all talked for hours, ate excellent food cooked by Bach [Eardley] and Mattei. Dogs good too, and we walked down footpaths happily.

---

* Headquarters of Royal Society of Literature; formerly residence of General Sir Ian and Lady (Jean) Hamilton, distant family connections of J.L.-M. who frequently entertained him there in the 1930s.

† Poet, novelist, and author of works on philosophy; FRSL.

‡ Mattei Radev (b. 1927); Bulgarian-born picture framer and gilder; friend of Eardley Knollys.

Thursday, 1 November

Took train for Headcorn, walking from station through the dear little town to Sutton Chart where Mrs Lamont lives. She eighty-three, clearly once handsome, now very lame with bad hip and swollen ankles. She was Vita's last love, who looked after her during her final illness and was with her when she died. I was not sure how much I liked her. She cordially disliked Harold and both boys. Thought H. dishonest. Why, I asked? Because his political views were not genuine. That is all. Thinks Nigel a cold fish.

She told me that the moment Vita died she climbed up to her tower room. Harold was pacing the lawn in anguish. She rifled Vita's files and extracted all her own letters to V. I asked if she still had them. No, destroyed them, and destroyed all V's to her save the few poems enclosed. Saw no reason why others should ever read them. She said that V. loved her very much and that my A[lvilde] was jealous of her because she, Mrs Lamont, received everything from V. that she could desire. I was extremely guarded about A. and said I knew nothing of her true relations with V., never thinking it my business to enquire. All I knew – this a backhander perhaps – was that letters from V. to A. arrived almost daily for several years.

Saturday, 10 November

A. has invited M. for the weekend of the 24th. Eardley says I am mad to allow it.

Thursday, 15 November

I am reading Vol. 5 of Virginia Woolf's letters. It is entitled *The Sickle Side of the Moon*. I think these titles a silliness. Why not simply Vol. 5? It is interesting to compare the letters to the diaries. The letters are far freer, which is at first surprising. But the truth is that one is never freer than when addressing the perfect recipient with whom one feels totally in accord; whereas in a diary one is addressing onself, not an inspiring or reciprocating individual. It is a masturbatory exercise. Different recipients provoke one to adopt different styles of writing – facetious, self-pitying, too clever by half, guarded – depending on one's relations with him or her.

Saturday, 17 November

Never has a scandal caused more stir than the Anthony Blunt revelations.[*] No one seems sure what really happened. Why, if he was exonerated 15 years ago, should he now be stripped of his knighthood, an unprecedented thing to happen since the Middle Ages, and disgraced? Did he spy after receiving the knighthood? What did the spying since the War amount to? And if it happened during the War when he was working at MI5, why was it spying, seeing the beastly Russians were our allies? I cannot get out of my head that shy, courteous, withdrawn figure. Although I deprecate more than most people anyone giving information to those bloody Russians, yet I cannot help feeling sorry for Anthony being hunted, persecuted all these years later, at his age too, and in his indifferent state of health. I last saw him when I went to Wimpole in July. It was then that in talking to him I mentioned that I had come across many letters to H.N. from Guy [Burgess][†] in Moscow. He drew himself in, but I persisted in talking about Guy, unaware of the terrible secret and fear he must be bearing. I told him the letters showed Guy's intense home-sickness and longing to see his mother again. Then Anthony waxed angry. Said what a terrible man the stepfather was. He loathed Guy and said pestilential things about him trying to turn the mother against him. I could not help saying, 'But Anthony, one must remember that he was a simple colonel, in whose eyes Guy had brought disgrace to family and friends. After all he was a spy.' No response to this. Yet I hate the idea of his being persecuted. Irrational? Am I not a little unsound about patriotism, loyalties, the last refuge of the scoundrel, and so forth?

---

[*] Blunt (1907–83), art historian and Surveyor of the Royal Pictures 1945–72, had just been officially disgraced and stripped of his knighthood following the exposure of his former career as a Soviet agent (known for some years to British intelligence) in Andrew Boyle's book *The Climate of Treason*.
[†] Diplomatist and Soviet agent (1911–63); defected to USSR with Donald Maclean, 1951; a contemporary of J.L.-M. at Lockers Park preparatory school, 1919–21.

Ghastly dinner party at Berkeley Castle on Friday. Some twenty relations* present, all dreadfully boring and conventional. A hired chef for the occasion providing six courses of pretentious, messy *cordon bleu* food. This definitely not the environment to suit me. I thought of The Slade, Eardley, Mattei and Dadie, our free talk, outrageous statements and ceaseless mirth. That is my sort of society.

Saturday, 24 November

Fanny Partridge and M. came to stay last night for the weekend. Agony for me. There is a tense suspicion, and a shyness on M's part which does not make hostmanship easy. I wonder if sensitive and highly intelligent Fanny is aware. And I hear him saying casually, 'I shall be working under Maître Blum soon.' 'How interesting,' the others reply. I sit mum, nursing my own feelings.

Monday, 26 November

Weekend been and gone. Fanny's presence a great help. Also other guests well chosen – Elspeth Huxley† to luncheon on Saturday; tea with Diana Westmorland; Tony and Violet Powell to luncheon Sunday. M. pleased to meet all these celebrities. Delighted with everything. Takes out his notebook and jots down what people tell him. He was sweet to A. and I have yet to hear what she really thinks. There was a good deal of, 'Don't tell me you want to sit up late.' The second night, when Fanny went up to bed and I said to A. that I was going to have a drink with M., she stayed up too, in defiance. I was determined to out-sit, and did by twenty minutes. During which epilogue I talked severely to M. about the pressure of demands from friends, books, uncompleted doctoral thesis and reviews, and his absolute need to straighten these demands out. I did not enjoy this weekend and do not want him and A. to meet often because I have a nasty suspicion that she wishes to break up the relationship by any means.

---

* Of the owner John Berkeley, a distant cousin of the L.-Ms' friend Lennox Berkeley.
† Writer, especially about British Africa (1907–97).

Sunday, 9 December

Derek [Hill] who is staying the weekend at The Cottage to paint Anne Somerset,* lunched to meet, look at and assess nephew Nick [Robinson]. Also Mary Beaufort came. She is vaguer than ever and takes little in. It is better to have her alone, or just with Caroline whom she knows and loves. Derek was tired and would not do a sketch of Nick there and then which I had rather hoped, but is going to get in touch with him. Told me he admired his appearance which reminded him of Rosamond Lehmann's. I can understand but only just. Derek full of complaints of the Somersets. Caroline makes no sense and is in bed most of the day, David out hunting, and the children listening to television full blast while sprawling all over the room like oafs. Derek likes attention, is sulky when deprived.

Monday, 10 December

A letter this morning from M. I droop when I am out of contact like a lily yellowing at the edges. No wonder A. who misses nothing resents these moods which are beyond my control. I wish I could snap out of them for it is ridiculous. At my age they may signify that I am still alive, while before he came on the scene I considered myself pretty well dead. And better dead than moribund.

Wednesday, 12 December

In the morning took the dogs for a walk in The Slates and was overcome by angst. What was the cause? I was about to see M. which I was looking forward to. My angst is so constant, so fearful that I can hardly bear it. Did it originate in fear of my father, which led me to become deceitful, timorous and dishonest as a child? I am all these things now in different degrees. In a funny way my fear of him has transmitted to fear of A. It is mixed up with appalling guilt – that I treat her badly, inconsiderately, selfishly. How I envy those friends who are unaffected by this disease (for it is nothing less), friends like David Herbert who never repine, never feel guilty, always see the best side of life.

---

* Only dau. (b. 1955) of David and Lady Caroline Somerset; m.1988 Matthew Carr.

1979

Sunday, 16 December

Such a Trollopean scene today. Sally Westminster asked us to luncheon to meet the Beauforts and the Weinstocks.* The first idea that we should make it up with the Duke and be friends again. Second idea that it would be an uplift for the Weinstocks to meet the Duke and Duchess and learn what real aristocrats were like. Sir Arnold W. sat on the Duchess of Westminster's right, the Duke of Beaufort on her left. In the middle of luncheon, Master said to Sir Arnold, 'Nice coverts you have got in the place you've just bought', *i.e.* the large house near Lacock which belonged to Sir Geoffrey Parsons. Sir Arnold replied, 'I refuse to let the hunt come near me. They make such a mess. And they are so rude. You as doyenne [*sic*] of the hunting world ought to teach them manners is all I can say.' Master went scarlet in the face and didn't say a word more. The peccadillo of our dogs chasing his vixen last May paled beside this enormity. Lady Weinstock who was sitting between me and Master then turned to me and said, 'And what is your view of hunting?' I whispered in her ear that I preferred not to discuss the subject in present company. 'But I don't see that it matters who knows what we think about hunting,' she expostulated. Dexterously I shut her up.

Sir A. is a very brash, quick-witted, well-informed, pushing little man; also very ugly. The occasion was like Sir Leicester Dedlock meeting the manufacturer son of his housekeeper who had bought an estate next to Chesney Wold in *Bleak House*; or the Duke of Omnium keeping his temper in the company of an insolent *arriviste* at Gatherum Castle. Well-meaning Sally behaved with commendable calm and changed the conversation.

Saturday, 29 December

Christmas with the Droghedas at Parkside again. Three nights. The Joseph Coopers† staying. He a jovial, entertaining extrovert. Christmas Day we went to St George's Chapel. We sat in the Garter Stalls; mine

---

* Sir Arnold Weinstock (1924–2002); Managing Director of GEC, 1963–96; m. 1949 Netta, dau. of Sir Michael Sobell; cr. life peer, 1980.
† Pianist and broadcaster (1912–2001); m. (2nd) Carol Borg, 1975.

319

had been Winston Churchill's which I found unendearing. Lovely service. All the Royals present, including new Princess Michael, too much dolled-up with that large hat and larger feather. Patricia Hambleden told me 'they' all hate her like rat poison. We lunched with Patricia on way home. David Herbert and Michael Duff staying. Michael incredibly thin and beautiful like a ghost. David confided in A. that he is dying. This little party which should have been such fun – when the same five of us last lunched here we laughed immoderately – was *morne*. On leaving I embraced Michael on both cheeks.

I find that septuagenarians all speak with horror about the fatal ailments of their contemporaries as though each case is a tragedy which somehow ought to be avoided. But it's just death, let's face it. We are dying all of us over seventy, and some of us are not yet in the terminal stage. That's all there is to it. Bad news of Raymond [Mortimer] again; he is bedridden, and said to be sinking.

At Parkside watched [again] film of Leslie Hartley's *The Go-Between*, one of the most beautiful films I have seen. Lovely setting at Melton Constable [Norfolk]. Takes place at height of summer, cloudless skies, burning sun high in heavens. The boy most poignant. Of *Death in Venice* standard. I remember Leslie telling me that the story was autobiographical. The experience had a devastating effect upon him, and turned him away from women.

This film has given me the idea for a novel.* Its setting the First World War. Unsympathetic father away at the front. Young, pretty mother and beautiful young son, same age as Go-Between boy, left at home. German prisoners of war working on the estate, kept at arm's length by guards. One, an educated Count, with English mother and speaking perfect English, is befriended by boy. Sex-starved Count starts affair with boy. Mother somehow finds out. She takes Count away from her son. Father returns on leave, discovers the affair, or affairs. Then what?

---

* Eventually published by Robinson Books as *The Fool of Love*, 1990.

1980

1980

On Wednesday went to London for the night. Telephoned J.K.-B. who said I might stay with him. Did some shopping, visited London Library; went to Post-Impressionist Exhibition, but such crowds it was like being on a conveyor belt and I could not study a single picture with ease. After one hour left, walking in the rain, to visit Freda [Berkeley] in King Edward VII Hospital. She told me how unhappy A. was being made by me. I told Freda how unhappy this was making me, but asked her next time A. consulted her to impress on A. what little cause she had for unhappiness on my account. I could not help being in love, but my love was platonic and surely no harm to anyone but myself.

Walked on to Hyde Park Square and joined M. in his flat. We had sandwiches and cake and tea before going to Sadler's Wells to see *The Pirates of Penzance*. Great fun. M. told me he is leaving for Paris on 12 February. This makes me mournful. But he says he will frequently be over, and asks me to stay in Paris. He said his father dissatisfied that he had not finished his thesis, and I said I did not wonder, for he had paid for his education. He sent me some of it, which reads brilliantly. Silly ass he is.

Yesterday motored Audrey to lunch with Harry Ashwin at Bretforton. Harry very inaudible; had to strain to hear him. Is extremely thin, walks painfully with a stick, is irritable and wretched. Said, 'I have nothing to look forward to, nothing.' After lunching we retired to the library and talked. At once the church bell tolled three times. His gaze lit up. 'That will mean £30,000 for me,' he said. I enquired what he meant. He replied that every time one of the villagers dies and a cottage is vacated, he sells it. He gets only a few shillings a week rent. Immediately the bells broke into a loud, prolonged carillon. 'Damn!' said Harry. 'It's not a death, just the bell-ringers practising.' The din continued for the rest of our visit, and Harry relapsed into intense gloom. We could hardly hear ourselves speak for the din. It reminded Audrey and me of the tennis tournaments at Bretforton on Saturdays when we were children. The Bretforton church bells – the church is at the end of the garden – always did this for hours on end. But oh the mournfulness of this funny old Victorian house, with its musty smell of black treacly oak panelling, and stuffy bewhiskered ancestors!

Saturday, 12 January

Dear old Raymond [Mortimer] died this week. Expected and not to be mourned for he was eighty-five and exceedingly unhappy. The last day he did not speak at all, and the following morning he was found dead in his bed. I grew very attached to him. There was something paternal about him, and sweet. At first I was scared of him for he was censorious and picked one up, demanding explanations of one's idiotic remarks. He was solely a critic and not creative, with a lynx eye for the syntactical faults of other writers better than himself, as I have discovered from H.N's papers. He quite properly held my writing in contempt and latterly would not even review my books. This made A. cross, and hurt me a bit. But I bear no resentment whatever. There is to be no memorial service at his request. In a way this makes me sad, for he seems to disappear in a puff of wind. Will he be remembered by posterity? Only by specialising scholars. Yet for fifty years and more he was a famous and feared reviewer. He knew every literary person of his own and the ensuing generation. He was received at every party of note, and was revered and respected by everyone with aspirations, either social or literary.

Knowing that he was going to die, I inserted [into the Harold Nicolson biography] last week a few things about him which I would not have included had he lived. I felt a cad doing this, but when I last spoke to him about his relationship with H.N. he said he did not the least mind what I published provided he was dead.

Saturday, 19 January

The price of gold has risen to unprecedented heights, and the result is that queues of people take their old trinkets to Hatton Gardens to be sold and melted down. Watched on TV Victorian and even Georgian salt cellars being hammered into pulp and thrown into furnaces. Had to turn my head away. It is the old world disintegrating before one's eyes.

A. telephoned me yesterday in Bath to say that Cecil [Beaton] died early that morning. Billy [Henderson] was with him the previous afternoon reading to him and he said he did not feel well. I never knew Cecil intimately, and used to be frightened of his tongue, which used to be vitriolic. He was the most observant man I have ever met. Nothing escaped his beady or quizzical eye. The smallest blemish of face or hand was noticed. Consequently he was extremely sensitive of people's appearance. He could not stand people, like Harold [Nicolson] and Derek Hill, who would say waspish things about him. He was an exceedingly amusing talker, the King of Sophistication. He was more sophisticated than intellectual. There was a meretricious side to him, all that stagey scenery side. Chi-chi rather than real. But in old age he became very distinguished looking, almost beautiful. Always splendidly dressed. His voice almost as affected as Raymond's, very Twentyish and not euphonious, cracked. With his intimates he lost all his spikiness and was almost simple. No, he was never simple. Since he was nice to me I liked him very much. And occasionally I could make him laugh. Surprising the columns of obituary given him by all the papers. He was a personality right enough, and with him passes an age, and the Twenties have gone for good. And a good thing too.

Tuesday, 22 January

I telephoned Dr King to say that the new sleeping pills he has given me don't agree with me at all and asking if I might go back to the old ones.* He explained that the old ones leave traces in the system which

---

* In *Another Self*, J. L.-M. writes that he had been addicted to sleeping pills since being cured of a neurological illness during the war.

take a long time to work out and counsels me to persevere with the new ones until the end of the week. I explained that they only allowed me to sleep until about 3.30, then I woke up and did not just lie awake but had headaches and nightmares. He said it was the symptom which all drug addicts suffered from when cut off from their mixture at first. So I am faced with some nasty nights ahead. Nearest analogy to these waking nightmares I can find is being on the Wembley Giant Racer in 1926, which terrified me, or looping-the-loop, which I also did as a child, in Captain Burgess's Moth over Broadway Hill in 1925, tumbling over and over with giddiness and headache.

Sunday, 3 February

Bad nights persist – headaches and throbbing in the ear, and during the day I feel giddy. Dr King asks A. whether it is not due to her going to India. A. replied, 'Don't you believe it. He doesn't mind my going in the least,' which in fact is not the case, for I do mind. Lately I have wondered if I am not seriously ill.

Strange goings-on with the Guinnesses in the village. She in taking to the bottle has attacked her husband with a knife and slashed him about the face. Rushes wildly about the village street, swearing and making dreadful scenes. The Vicar and his wife are Samaritans, even sleeping in her house. They got her to a home in Bristol but she absented herself. Why has this nice, dull woman turned into a sot? I suppose because she has nothing whatever to do.

Thursday, 7 February

I went to London for the day just to see M. who leaves for Paris on Wednesday. Felt rotten. When I got to Piccadilly Circus I could not remember where the London Library was and had to enter a shop, lean against the counter and reflect. At Brooks's was again so over-whelmed with giddiness that I had a neat whisky, a drink I seldom touch. When M. came and we went into the Coffee Room I could barely concentrate and at one moment wondered if I would not have to ask him to leave. Then recovered. He accompanied me to the Privy Council Office where I retrieved my MS from Norman St John

Stevas.* No word of thanks in the parcel. Then talked at M's flat. He will not be away more than four weeks before returning here, so the gulf will not be too long. Feel very happy indeed about this relationship, free of passion and deep-seated on both sides. He saw me off at the station.

Next morning I telephoned the doctor and said I could not continue like this. Did I have a tumour of the brain? Or diabetes? He said No. I don't understand how he knows without my undergoing examination. He told me to go back to my old pills – Dalmane – for a week and report to him next Tuesday. Since I returned to the old pills, which has been for two nights now, I have been quite well again. All dizziness, all illness gone. Furthermore, I am now able to write with renewed vigour.

Today Stuart Preston came down to Bath for luncheon. Alvilde came over and the three of us ate at La Vendange. He and I talked in the library afterwards. He told me Guy Burgess was endowed with an asset which had to be seen to be believed. It was the secret weapon of his charm. Anyone so endowed could get away with murder, and he did. Yes, I said, but surely not with every sort of man. 'Every sort of man,' S. said. He was surely very grubby, I said. 'Very,' he said.

Friday, 15 February

Have felt so much better over the past week that I have at last been able to write fairly well. Have received two letters from Paris and on Wednesday M. rang to remind me (I needed no reminding) that it was a year since we first met. A short conversation, but how heavenly it was.

Have just returned from taking A. to Heathrow. She flies to India tonight and will be away a month. She has left a myriad of notes and instructions, and has bought me piles of food with directions how to cook it. At the airport she found a porter in a flash, and after a prolonged embrace, we parted. When I lost sight of her dear, grey head and upright little figure, I wept.

---

* St John Stevas – Lord President of the Council and Minister for the Arts, 1979–81 – had asked to see the MS of J.L.-M's book on the Stuarts.

Mary Beaufort asked herself to luncheon with A. yesterday. It was at eleven o'clock, which meant that A., who was busy packing, had to make an effort to entertain one elderly Duchess. Mary said to her, 'I only like the Royal Family. No one else interests me in the least.' A. asked her why the Queen looked so sad these days. Mary said she *was* sad; it was the times.

Sunday, 17 February

Today I lunched with Billy Henderson and Frank Tait at Tisbury. Enjoyable day. Frank who is a great friend of the Sutherlands* says poor Graham is dying of cancer of the kidneys. Ten days ago he went for a check-up. They told him something seemed to be the matter. Now he hasn't got more than a few days to live, Frank says. Then, on the midnight news, announcer said that Graham had died.

Monday, 18 February

Papers all publish hideous photographs of Graham in old age, face collapsed, whereas he was a singularly handsome man until he was sixty. Why does one have to be recorded for posterity in one's hideous decline if in one's heyday one has been good looking? There was a time when A. and I saw a lot of the Sutherlands at Roquebrune. In fact she found their house above Mentone for them. Then came a coolness. Cathy, a very mischievous little woman, made trouble between us and the Kenneth Clarks by repeating something we had allegedly said about one of the Clark children. I was made by A. to tackle them about this one day when we went to San Remo together. I said to Cathy that she must have known that what she repeated was not true. Graham flew to her defence and got extremely red and huffy. Our relations were never the same after that. My impression of Graham is that he was a clever but not an intellectual man. He talked a good deal of hot air. Had theories which he propounded as though he were a sage. But intellect and artistic genius do not always go together; and I believe G. did have

---

* Graham Sutherland (1903–80); artist; m. 1927 Kathleen Barry.

genius. He is certainly one of the best British artists of the mid twentieth century. Socially he was very unsure of himself – small blame.

Tuesday, 19 February

Went to London for night. Peter Quennell lunched at Brooks's. Talked about Jamesey Pope-Hennessy and the letters he is editing. Says his visits to royalties when he was writing *Queen Mary* are brilliant and funny. Is publishing visit to the Windsors, but not to Balmoral to see present Queen, or to Gloucesters (uproarious) because the Duchess is still alive.

Went to see Diana Mosley. We talked about Maître Blum whom she thought rather mad. She wants to meet Misha and warn him. She spoke of the films they are making about the Mitfords, three of them coming. One features me in the incident where Lord Redesdale turned me out of the house.* Diana very beautiful, tall and straight.

Then I dined with John Betjeman and Elizabeth Cavendish and their new doctor, a charming woman whose husband is Chairman of British Rail.† Much hilarity and laughter. John read us part of a poem which he is composing about Magdalen, his contribution to the Fabric Fund. Elizabeth and he had stayed last weekend at Royal Lodge – surely a change in the tradition of royalty never to countenance domestic irregularities. John was given a bedroom next to the Queen Mother's and not next to E's. Nevertheless she went to say goodnight to him and tuck him up. She told the policeman on duty, who apparently sits all night on a chair outside the QM's bedroom, to see if John needed anything during the night, which this kind man did.

Tuesday, 4 March

I motored to London this morning. Freda [Berkeley] received me with the news that Michael Duff's death was in *The Times* today. Not

---

* The alleged incident, described in *Another Self*, took place in about 1926 when J.L.-M. was eighteen. The war veteran Lord Redesdale had taken exception to a remark of J.L.-M. at dinner that, eight years after the war, Britain should 'make friends with the Germans'.
† Gillian ('Jill') Rowe-Dutton; m. 1951 (Sir) Peter Parker.

unexpected because at Christmas he looked so ill and ghost-like. Dear
Michael, an affectionate, funny man, an anachronism, one of the last
bright young people of the Twenties. David Herbert will be miserable, except that he is never miserable about anything. I embraced
Michael warmly when we parted because I knew I should not see him
again.

Motored to Islington to lunch with Paul Hyslop. He lent me two
packets of Raymond's letters from Harold. I have never read any of
Harold's letters so uninhibited. As much lust letters as love letters, and
curiously not as quotable as Harold's to Vita. In fine, I wonder, could
H. love anyone?

Wednesday, 5 March

Handsome David Ford* came to tea and talked about his photography
of the Bath prints. A nice young man indeed. Norah telephoned that
galley proofs of H.N. Vol. I are ready. I told her that Paul H. had lent
me a vast batch of H.N's letters to Raymond and I hoped that, if I
needed to, I could add some quotations to the proofs. She asked what
they amounted to. I said they were love letters. She gave a contemptuous laugh which annoyed me. Struck me as retrograde that she of
all people, chairman of a great publishing firm, should find a relationship of this sort between two eminent and intelligent men a joke.

Sunday, 30 March

This morning A. said to me while we were at the sink, 'Would it be
a nice idea if I joined you for a night or two in Paris on your return
from Viviers?' Quite calmly I said no, because M. would be there then,
as she knew, and I had arranged to spend a day or two with him. This
caused hurtness of feeling. Silence, followed by caustic remarks. I hate
being made to feel guilty when I have so little to feel guilty about.
Nearly all my life I have been pursued by this guilt complex induced

---

* American publisher's assistant (b. 1946); commissioned by Bamber Gascoigne to
prepare a book of illustrations of Bath for which J.L.-M. had been invited to write
the text: see 16 May 1980.

first by my father, then by A. It was only for the years between 1945 and my marriage in 1951 that I was wholly free from guilt, and happy.

Tuesday, 1 April

A. went to London, and left with my luncheon packet a note to be read and digested. Such a sad note and so accusatory that I can hardly bear to refer to it. Even suggesting that it might be better if we separated. But oh dear, what cause? Not my purely socratic friendship with M. Not the charge that I, aged seventy-one, am not attentive enough. In the evening we discussed the matter calmly and affectionately, and embraced, and agreed to let it pass. I am still riddled with guilt, and yet I am guiltless – surely?

Sunday, 13 April

Yesterday in Cirencester a huge reception given by Paul Weller the bookseller to over one hundred and fifty people to celebrate Alvilde's and Rosemary Verey's garden book.* It was a best-seller in last Sunday's list. A. had to sign over 100 copies, and is enjoying a swim-gloat which I delight in.

Tuesday, 15 April

Stayed last night with J.K.-B. who took me to an Italian film, *La Luna*. Beautiful photography of Rome. Strange story of beautiful boy of fifteen who takes to drugs. His mother, operatic singer, very pretty and young, is in love with him. There are scenes in which they go to bed together, which rather shocked me. J. says idiotic to be shocked. What is there to be shocked by? Yet I am by shots of son putting hand on mother's cunt and mother committing fellatio with son.

    Lunched with dear Midi [Gascoigne]. She talks much and asks questions to which I doubt whether she wants an answer. But a darling nevertheless. Happy in her soulless flat in Cranmer Court, a sort of St Andrew's Hospital for the wealthy senile. Left her to join

---

* *The Englishwoman's Garden* (Chatto & Windus).

M. who took me to meet Hugo Vickers[*] who is writing Cecil Beaton's life. A handsome youth possessing that rare ability to smile with the eyes. He met his subject only twice, but Cecil took to him and engaged him to do his biography. He says Cecil only published one-eighteenth of his diaries, assiduously kept in his own handwriting until the day of his death. After his bad, penultimate stroke, his lady friends Clarissa Avon[†] and Anne Tree thought it would be safe to regale him with outrageous gossip which he would be in no condition to record. They were mistaken; he learnt to write with his left hand. Now they are trembling, because Cecil was scrupulous in attributing what he learned to its source.

Saturday, 3 May [Paris]

Walked with M. across the Tuileries, over the Pont Royal to 53 rue de Varenne. He took me upstairs to the *grenier* under the eaves where he works, where I shall be able to picture him in the weeks ahead. While I telephoned A. he discreetly withdrew, and on return said his Master would receive me. Didn't want to be received, but could see that M. considered reception by her the highest honour. We waited till she was ready. Then ushered into her library where previous day she had been photographed and knocked sideways by the charm of Lord Snowdon. Very distinguished old lady, very correct, but thinner than I imagined, sharp features, strong eye. Talked of Duke of Windsor's '*droiture*'. Asked us to translate. Sense of duty? No. Sense of honour? Not quite. Honourableness? More like it. He was a gentleman with a strong sense of what was fitting. This formidable interview over, I slipped away.

I lunched with the Margeries[‡] in rue St-Guillaume. She unchanged since 1932 or 1933 when I met her with Georges

---

[*] Writer (b. 1951).

[†] Clarissa Churchill (b. 1920); niece of Sir Winston and yr sister of J.L.-M's old friend 'Johnnie' Churchill; m. 1953 Sir Anthony Eden, Prime Minister 1955–7, cr. Earl of Avon 1961.

[‡] Roland de Margerie; French diplomatist, First Secretary to London Embassy, 1933–9; m. 1921 Jenny Fabre-Luce.

Cattaui.* A blue-stocking, whom Harold found maddening. He a distinguished old man, tiny and owl-like. A granddaughter lunched. Could see she was embarrassed by her grandmother who never stopped talking. Husband said little, but always to the point. Produced large packet of letters to him (not her) from H.N. down the years. She said that I must now read these, and whichever ones I liked they would copy for me. But before I had got through the first letter she interrupted, and continued to do so. He sat quietly, merely answering the questions I put to him. At one moment, irritated, he said to her, '*Tais-toi! Il veut lire.*' Madame de M. took exception to a remark in H.N's published diary that when the Margeries were coming to London she need not suppose she would succeed in establishing a salon.† It has rankled all these years. After all, she said, salons do not happen just like that, they happen if a woman has friends among intellectuals, poets, artists, writers, composers. He reminded me that he was responsible for H's successful retrieval of the Duchess of Windsor's papers left in the hotel at Evreux. At H's request, he sent letters to those in authority asking them to help H. 'She of course left the papers on purpose, in self-advertisement', interjected Madame de M.‡

M. and I dined with the Mosleys at the Temple de la Gloire [Orsay]. Met at station by Irish manservant and driven to Temple. I enjoyed the evening enormously. Besides us four, Alexander Mosley§ and pretty young wife whom I discovered to be a daughter of Mary Anna

---

* Egyptian diplomatist and writer on contemporary English and French literature (1896–1974); was in love with J.L.-M. in London in 1930s, at which time he was First Secretary at Egyptian Legation; a convert from Judaism to Roman Catholicism, he acted as witness at J.L.-M's conversion in 1934, and became a priest in Switzerland.

† What in fact H.N. wrote (on 8 November 1933) implied no criticism of Madame de Margerie: he thought she would find it difficult to establish a 'literary salon' as 'our decent literary people are all Bohemians, and our social literary people aren't decent'.

‡ While in flight from Fort Belvedere to Cannes in December 1936, Mrs Simpson had left at a hotel at Evreux some handwritten notes relating to her telephone conversations with the King, which the hotel owner subsequently showed a friend of H.N. Harold wrote to the Duchess of Windsor (as she had become) gallantly offering to retrieve them, which he did on 10 July 1937.

§ Paris publisher (b. 1938); e.s. of Sir Oswald Mosley and Diana *née* Mitford; m. 1975 Charlotte Marten.

Marten.* Sat next to Diana who exuded charm. She said I had been a help in persuading the film director not to turn Lord Redesdale into a monster. And that I was the last friend who had stayed at Swinbrook to be alive. Tom greatly changed. Now a very old man. Shapeless, bent, blotched cheeks, crooked nose, no moustache, and tiny eyes in place of those luminous, dilating orbs. I sat with him after dinner on a sofa and talked for an hour. 'Let us talk of Harold, and then of Uncles and Aunts,'† he said. But we never got to the Uncles and Aunts, and he had not much to say about Harold. 'He was a dear man. The most loyal of my supporters.' Sir O. has mellowed to the extent of never saying anything pejorative of anybody. I asked him what Hitler was really like. Tom replied that he was gentle and gentlemanly. He slipped shyly into a room. His bombast was reserved for the platform. Unlike Musso, who was all bombast and impossible to talk to. Not so Hitler. Had only he, Mosley, spoken German in those days he believed he could have influenced Hitler. As it was he only learnt German in prison from a fellow prisoner, a black band-leader, charming. Hitler never wanted to fight England or the British Empire, he wanted unity with us in the fight against Bolshevism. But, I said, he wanted war with other, smaller countries which he could overwhelm. Tacit agreement. I asked boldly if he thought he had made a mistake in founding New Party. He admitted it was the worst mistake of his life. The British do not like new parties. Said that if he had led the Labour Party he would have kept Edward VIII on the throne. He [the King] was eminently suited to be an intermediary between his country and the dictators. Said that the critics of both him and the Duke of Windsor never made allowances for the fact that they detested war, having experienced the horrors of the trenches. They wanted to avoid it happening again at all costs.

We discussed Britain's present situation. He thought hopeless, so long as we did not produce and sell as much as the French and the Germans. Not all the fault of the Unions. He always got on well with

---

* Hon. Mary Anna Sturt (b. 1929); o.c. of 3rd and last Baron Allington; m. 1949 Commander George Marten.
† Sir Oswald's maternal aunt, Dorothy Edwards-Heathcote (1884–1965), had married J. L.-M's paternal uncle, Alec Lees-Milne (1878–1931).

them. Cook the Communist* was a great friend, who made outrageous statements in public but was reasonable in private conversation. What was now needed was a great figure from the West who would go to Moscow, breakfast every day for six months with Brezhnev,† and talk heart-to-heart with him about the common threats to civilisation.

On and on we went until Diana joined us from the small sitting room to say the Alexander Mosleys were going and would motor M. and me back to Paris. Tom said, but we haven't discussed the Aunts and Uncles yet, what charming people they were (when they were alive he never bothered with them at all). I helped pull him to his feet. He stands unsteadily, but assured me his head was all right. Held me by both hands and said I must come again. Why not come tomorrow? Come and stay. Charming he was. Diana seems to like M.

Friday, 16 May

Incensed by the Pope's telling black Kenyans last week that contraception a sin not to be practised, I wrote a good letter to *The Times*. They have not published it, which does not surprise me. Rees-Mogg would never tolerate any criticism of Pope or Church. Yet this is the most critical subject facing mankind. The population of Kenya has doubled within twenty-one years.

Oxford University Press have written again to me. They definitely want me to do the Country House Anthology. Then there is Bamber [Gascoigne]'s Bath book which I am being bamboozled into. When Vol. I of Harold comes out, will I be invited to write something which really appeals to me, which these two do not?

Wednesday, 21 May

A delicious day. Alex Moulton called for me at 8.30 and we went off in his heaven-borne Rolls for Wales. Weather broken after three

---

* Arthur James Cook (1885–1931); miners' leader and notable orator (of Communist sympathies but only briefly a party member) who supported Mosley's 'New Party' in 1931.
† Soviet leader (1907–82); effective ruler of USSR from 1964 until his death.

weeks sheer sunshine, but beautiful with purple storm-clouds over the Black Mountains and golden sun thrown as a backcloth. I think the country, my maternal country around Glanusk, the most beautiful probably in Wales. At Picton Castle we stopped on the creek, ate picnic brought by Alex, and had a kip in the car. We talked of sex, death and despondency. I speak pretty freely. We both agreed that we had been failures, I more so than he, for he has invented some important things which will endure – the Moulton bicycle, his motor car suspensions. But he has not got to the top in his profession, and I suspect thinks that not being made a knight but only a CBE is a seal of his failure. I honestly seek no worldly honours, only some recognition from the public and approval from those writers who matter. But I have not achieved this. Moreover my National Trust work has received no recognition. Told him I did not attribute my failings to anyone but myself, my character.

We visited the Graham Sutherland museum at Picton Castle. What was he striving to do? These symbolisms of what? Figments of a disordered imagination? He was not a deep or clever man, rather pretentious – but he could paint. His colours blend and never jar. His drawing superb. Imagination, when not totally abstract, fine.

Tuesday, 3 June

Have been thinking of J.K.-B. since I stayed with him last week. He leads a quiet and virtuous life. I wish though that he could be happier. He has few enthusiasms. So unlike M., who is back in England and telephones me excitedly to say that Edward St George,* the new husband of Henrietta Fitzroy, is one of the most interesting men he has ever met. It is always like this. Why, I ask? Because he is so clever and amusing, a big-shot in the Bahamas, and has offered to help M. in his research into the Duke of Windsor's governorship there.

---

* Lawyer and Chairman of Grand Bahama Port Authority (d. 2005); m. 1979 Lady Henrietta Fitzroy, daughter of 11th Duke of Grafton KG.

Saturday, 7 June

Desmond [Shawe-Taylor] was shocked at breakfast when I told him I was no longer the least interested in the National Trust, or in architecture. Why, he asked? Well, I think it may be because I have given up the battle of conservation. The world is ruined, and that's that. Besides, having looked after the N.T.'s buildings for so many years, my interest has just evaporated, and that's all there is to it. But it shouldn't be, he said. Are you no longer interested in the buildings of Venice or Rome? You were never in charge of buildings in those two cities. I am not interested in them from a scientific point of view, I said, only from a general aesthetic one, or for associative reasons. The intricacies of architecture bore me now.

Adam Nicolson stayed a night with us. On a walk, pack on back, along Cotswold Way. Is writing a book on walks for the National Trust. Arrived at door having come from Bath by byeways and visited Dyrham [Park, Gloucestershire] en route. Looks so young, fresh, fair and clean. A charming boy, intelligent, sensitive. I have absolutely no shyness with him. He has a nervous laugh, rather engaging. His looks more Vita's than Harold's; long oval face, not chubby like H's; but fair, unlike Vita. Fairness inherited from mother, all peaches and cream. Adam wants to go into Parliament, but would only stand as a Labour candidate, and fears his Eton and Castle background may make this impossible.

Wednesday, 11 June

A letter from M. this morning expressing deep affection. He has met Betty Hanley,* who has some Windsor letters, and who asks him to lunch at her cottage in Essex next weekend to meet Ian McCallum. Here the green-eyed monster enters, for Ian is a tremendous pouncer and quite unscrupulous and lecherous. I couldn't bear it if he had an

---

* Miss E. D. Hanley, American-born owner of a business in Westminster which had the Royal Warrant for the supply of lamps and lampshades. Her aunt having married the French time-and-motion tycoon Charles Bedaux, she spent much of her early life at Candé, the Bedaux property in Touraine where the Duke and Duchess of Windsor celebrated their wedding in June 1937.

affair with M. And there is A. quizzing me about M. on every possible occasion, making snide little remarks about young men who write books about society people in order to oil their way into society. And suggesting that M. come to stay with us again. My dependence on M. is such that I can honestly say I wish I had never met him. In some dreadful way I almost wish he would die so that I could thereby possess him totally. At times I feel I am going mad.

Thursday, 12 June

M. came down by train for the day. My heart bounds to see him emerge from Bath station, smiling softly. Spent day in flat discussing his predicament – has three books to be completed by the end of this year, plus doctoral thesis. Impossible I should say, but he works quickly when he does work. A. came over to lunch with us in Bath. Was sweet to him. Whether from shyness or not he does not speak at first. Have noticed this on other occasions.

Strange how he is not much interested in art or artefacts. I showed him a ravishing pair of ormolu candlesticks in a shop and he did not register. Said possessions meant little to him. When I asked if there was any object in my library he would like to have, he said he did not think he would have anywhere to put it. I take it for granted that my friends are interested in the arts, but I suppose such people are a minority.

Caroline Somerset told John Wilton[*] that, at dinner last week, she had a terrible bore on her right, Lord Cowdray, and an even worse bore on her left whose identity she had forgotten. 'That was me,' said J.W. sourly. She is the vaguest girl in the world.

I forgot to record that last month A. became a great-grandmother. Chloe, Clarissa's eldest child, has produced an infant. I am appalled.

Tuesday, 17 June

Alvilde and I lunched at Coutts Bank in the Strand. Extravagant luncheon with cocktails, white wine, red wine, port and brandy for those who wanted. Those who seemed to want were our hosts, the manager

[*] John Egerton, 7th Earl of Wilton (1921–99).

of our branch and his associates. Painfully suburban lot, so unlike our hosts of last visit, John Smith and Tim Egerton. Conversation kept going by A. I dried up, absolutely no lien of sympathy or interest. They want to get hold of our, or rather A's money for investment. We agreed merely to let them do our taxes for us.

The Manager told us that one day Baroness Burdett-Coutts was shocked to see crumbs on the beard of one of the staff. On making enquiries she discovered that the man had been eating sandwiches prepared by his wife. She at once gave orders that henceforth no member of staff might wear a beard or moustache; and further, that the Bank must supply every member of staff with a proper midday meal. Ever since, the male staff have had to be beardless and moustacheless, and have been given free luncheon. They still of course wear frock coats.

Wednesday, 18 June

I went to Hampstead to see Derek [Hill] and the portrait he has done of Nick. Awful visit. D. in dreadful mood, saying everything had gone wrong that morning and he had just returned to find a flood in the bathroom. Showed the picture with pride and expectancy of approval. I looked at it long and carefully. Could not say a word, for the portrait was not of Nick. Hardly recognisable. D. dreadfully hurt and upset. I took away the sketch to look at it with A. who quickly found several things wrong. He is asking Nick to sit again. Meanwhile I felt so guilty that I agreed to buy for £250 a little picture of a monk on the quay of Karakolou Monastery, Mount Athos. It turned out when fetched not to be the one I had seen and liked. Took it anyway and must give D. the money in cash. Admired a glazed, painted plate he had. He said it was by Ann Stokes, widow of Adrian who lives in Church Row. Went to her house and bought one fresh from the kiln, warm still like a hot-cross bun. Took it to Mulberry Walk as a seventieth birthday present for Diana Mosley.

Wednesday, 25 June

Dined with the Garnetts at Bradley Court. Tony Snowdon staying. He and his troupe spent day trying to photograph Keith Steadman's garden [at Wickwar]. What with pouring rain and this garden having no shape, no architectural features, and being a tangled muddle, he failed utterly. He greeted me with warm hugs. Very sweet and charming as usual. How small he is, almost a dwarf, but large hands I noticed which suggest potency. After dinner he sat at my feet by the sofa and talked about [his mother] Anne [Rosse] and the family. Complains that she doesn't 'play straight' and is alienating the children who are ready to be as kind to her as they can. She has already driven off young Tom Messel who was her slave. She refuses to meet or speak to Tony's new wife Lucy. He invites his mother to luncheon, asks others to meet her, cooks delicious meal (has no servant), and Anne chucks at last moment on spurious grounds that she does not feel well, though he later finds she entertained sixty to drinks that evening.

He spoke lovingly of Michael [Rosse] who never in all the years he knew him treated him as other than a beloved son. Tony said the only two happy marriages he knew of were those of his mother and Michael, and of Oliver [Messel] and Van the Great Dane.* Talked of his photography. Said he could modestly claim to have revolutionised photography in the late Fifties and Sixties by getting away from the Cecil Beaton technique, which was to make women's faces look like masks with gashes for lips. Whereas he emphasises lines and crows' feet, without being unkind like some photographers. A sweet little man to meet, but I suppose, being a Messel, he is a bundle of insincerity.

Sunday, 6 July

A. and I stayed at Deene Park with the Brudenells† for one night. I met them with Derek Hill. Liked them immensely. The house is splendid, large and grand, but with no outstanding feature. No, I am wrong – the early sixteenth-century great hall with hammerbeam roof. Cardigan of Balaclava fame dominates the house, and his widow, the nymphomaniac beauty. Beautiful she certainly was, her portraits reminding me of Anne Rosse, but more regular features. Those of her

---

* Van Ries-Hansen; Danish theatrical producer and friend of Oliver Messel.
† Edmund Brudenell (b. 1924) of Deene Park, Northants; head of junior branch of family of Marquess of Ailesbury; m. 1955 Hon. Cynthia Manningham-Buller.

as a young woman show her with raven black hair; in middle age with red tresses. On Saturday afternoon a horticultural symposium held in great hall, on which A. served and acquitted herself very well. [Robin] Lane Fox* held forth too much and was too pleased with himself. Anne Lancaster and Fred Whitsey the others. Edmund Brudenell, Levantine, quick, with perfect manners. She very capable and quite handsome, suggesting to me what Harriet Baring or Caroline Norton must have looked like. Two dark sons, twins, address their father as Squire. I went to Communion Sunday morning in ugly church in park, about to be declared redundant. One twin read the lesson, the other took round the alms bag. Was impressed by the earnestness of both; the taciturnity, expressing hidden turmoil beneath. Splendid family. Enormous dining table covered with great white linen cloth and bedecked with silver.

On Sunday we called on the Sitwells at Weston. Georgia reclining on a chair from which she did not move. Her legs like matchsticks, shoulders like those of a starving Vietnamese, grey face, large luminous eyes. Clearly doomed. Sachie blooming but very bent. Both pleased to see us.

Friday, 11 July

While we were dining, telephone rang. It was Gerda Barlow asking us both to dine on Friday week. I said I was going to London that day and did not think I would be back in time. This provoked a storm of nagging from A. Why was I going? Michael, she supposed. But he was coming here to stay next weekend. I didn't say that I wanted to see him alone. I just said, 'Yes, it is Michael, and I don't yet know whether I shall be seeing him in the evening or afternoon.' Hurt feelings. Then she said, 'I was upset when you said last week that you did not mind when I and Vita corresponded.' 'No,' I said, 'I was not jealous.' 'No, you are never jealous, you don't know the meaning of the word.' God in heaven, thought I, I am wracked with jealousy, but I said, 'It is always the greatest mistake to show it, however much you

---

* Ancient historian, fellow of New College, Oxford, and gardening correspondent of the *Financial Times* (b. 1946).

feel it.' And so it went on. There are times when I wish I lived alone, and was free.

Thursday, 17 July

They all came on Saturday morning at midday, Burnet [Pavitt] motoring Diana Cooper and M. I told M. that I felt an invisible string attached to him, which might grow taut, might grow lax, but was there when others were about. It is also there when we are apart, wherever we may be. It tugs at my heart. The weekend was successful in that he was delighted to meet Diana. He thought her ravishing, and was fascinated. We dined at Sally [Westminster]'s, where he stayed the night, being brought over by Sally on Sunday morning when she joins the procession round Badminton estate with David and Master. I can't pretend I enjoyed his being here.

Sunday, 20 July

Motored to London, though feeling tired and irritable. Full of traffic, summer sales. In despair where I should park car. Thought of Burlington House. Went straight there and got permit from Society of Antiquaries. The only use I ever make of this ridiculous Society. Walked to Air Street to deliver A's gold watch to little shop kept by two old, nice Jews. They in a dreadful state because two nights ago burglars broke into the manager's house in the suburbs at dead of night, forced him to give them the keys of shop and safe, and went straight to Air Street where they cleared the shop of their goods and clients' clocks and watches. The hell of it. Then to dentist. Walked down Bond Street. Called at D'Offay's Gallery where Bloomsbury pictures on display. Those by Carrington far the best in my opinion. To London Library. I congratulated [Douglas] Matthews, the Librarian Designate, on the splendid index to my H.N. which he has done. Eardley lunched with me at Brooks's which was about to shut for summer vacation. We had a filthy luncheon and were unable to eat the treacle tart which I refused to pay for. Bill came to £11 as it was. At 2.30 to Chatto's. Audience with Norah handing over Index and Corrections. Norah sat there huddled and aged, going off at tangents about irrelevant subjects.

This again irritated me. At 4.30 to Oxford and Cambridge Club to tea with M. who had invited Caroline Blackwood* who had asked to meet me to talk about her father.† Chain-smoking, churchyard cough, beautiful blue staring eyes, raddled complexion. Attractive. I spoke of her father when I knew him best at our prep school and Eton. A difficult girl. No come-back, no return of the ball.

Got out car from Burlington House and drove to Radnor Walk for drink with Betj. and Eliz. The darlings. She left us to go to a meeting across the street. I told John I had just seen Caroline B. for the first time. He told me he once saw her twenty years ago and was so moved by her resemblance to Ava, and so attracted to her, that he decided he could never meet her again. Then told me that he was more in love with Ava than with any human being he had ever met in the world. His Oxford career was ruined by this unrequited love for 'Little Bloody'. He loved his gutter-snipe looks, his big, brown, sensual eyes, sensual lips, dirtiness generally. Never received so much as a touch of a hand on the shoulder. He then said that in after life no loves ever reached the heights of schoolboy loves. I told him about Tom Mitford and myself at Eton, and how on Sunday eves before Chapel at 5, when the toll of the bell betokened that all boys must be in their pews, he and I would, standing on the last landing of the entrance steps, out of sight of the masters in the ante-chapel and all the boys inside, passionately embrace, lips to lips, body pressed to body, each feeling the opposite fibre of the other. John's eyes stood out with excitement. And then? he asked. And then, I said, when Tom left Eton it was all over. He never again had any truck with me, and turned exclusively to women. J's eyes filled with tears.

At last Vol. I is really finished. I have nothing further to do. Very disappointed that Chatto's have had refusals from America. Nevertheless, I showed with pride to Norah a letter I received this morning from Anne Hill, who writes that John Saumarez Smith raves about the book which he has read in page proofs. J.S.S. is very censorious, so this is gratifying.

---

* Lady Caroline Blackwood (1931–96); novelist.
† Basil Blackwood, 4th Marquess of Dufferin and Ava (1909–45); contemporary of J.L.-M. at prep school, Eton and Oxford; Undersecretary for the Colonies, 1937–40; killed in action in Burma.

Extraordinary to think on J.B's last words to me today; that he, aged seventy-four, suffering from Parkinson's Disease, crippled so that he can barely move without help, still has the desires of a youth of twenty. That is little satisfaction to him, poor old boy.

Friday, 1 August

Droghedas to stay last weekend. Not relaxing. Like the full operatic orchestra, with temperament. Garrett looking pale, drawn and much aged. Is very restless; has to be on the go. Has to visit gardens. Joan fusses. Is hurt if left alone for more than five minutes. Their last evening, very sweet. But what with his insistence on being entertained and her refusal to sit and read, we found them a tiring couple.

Met the Beits, again staying with Lowensteins. A protracted argument with Clementine about the Mosleys. I told her I found Diana adorable and Tom 'sweet'. Absurdly wrong adjective, of course, for he is not sweet: I meant charming. Clem insists that if Hitler had invaded Tom Mosley would have been a Gauleiter. I said next time I met him I would ask him outright what action he would have taken. Can't believe that a man who fought throughout the First War as he did would have actively collaborated with the Germans.

On Tuesday, Colin McMordie came down for the day from London to Bath. I was touched that he thought it worth while making the long expedition. Much improved. Less affected. Still extremely handsome. About the most handsome young man I know. Now about thirty. Has matured. Shares an exclusive gallery with a 'friend'. Specialises in early nineteenth-century French romantic landscapes. Sensible choice. Says he adores Paris and would not live anywhere else. Has achieved his ambitions. Wants nothing more. Looks radiantly content, which is nice to see. Made him walk in the Park with the dogs. Nice boy.

On Wednesday was driven by Bruce Chatwin in an old rattletrap to Nymans. On way there and back we talked very freely. He asked if he might come with Derek [Hill] and me to Mount Athos. No, I said, you can't. Was I fear rather bossy. Would not let him open roof of car. Bruce asked if I had known Robert Byron. Able to say yes. Told him of R's love for Desmond [Parsons], transferred after D's death to me, to my discomfiture. He admires Robert's writing but says the strained jokiness of that generation embarrasses him. Also finds Waugh's facetiousness embarrassing. Found myself lecturing him about treatment of his wife, but good-naturedly. He asked me frankly if I was glad I had married. Was able to say Yes. I don't think he is at all. Is going off for three months writing and will not tell wife where he is going. I said that was cruel. He agreed. Is convinced that he has made the grade and is now a literary man. Has two more books coming out. He has yet to grow up; laughs far too much when telling his own stories.

Stayed Wednesday night with M., he having taken me to theatre, *Dr Faustus*, strange and haunting play. We talked for hours into the night, and night became morning.

Sunday, 17 August

Last week spent visiting three lots of friends in East Anglia. First Nicholas Guppy* and young wife of twenty-five, he being fifty-four, handsome still but with greying hair and a stomach. Then Heywood Hills† at Snape where I used to stay throughout my engagement to Anne when her mother was living at the Priory. Then two nights with Billa Harrod, who is bent but otherwise little changed. Horrible experience at the Hills'. In the field next door was a bird-scaring gun which started at 6 a.m. and went on to sunset. Honey is gun-shy and behaved with hysteria, poor thing. When I put her out of doors to pee in the morning she took fright and bolted. We notified police and neighbouring farmers and searched in vain. Finally police telephoned that an errand boy of fifteen saw her nearing the main road, took compassion, induced her to follow him and allow herself to be shut up. Retrieved Honey with much rejoicing. Oh the misery of those hours!

We also lunched with the Gladwyns at Bramfield, nice old Georgian house on the edge of the village of that name. Most hospitable. They

---

* Underwriting member of Lloyd's.
† George Heywood Hill (d. 1986); founder of bookshop in Curzon Street, 1936; m. 1938 Lady Anne Gathorne-Hardy (1911–2006), o. dau. of 4th Earl of Cranbrook, to whom J.L.-M. had been engaged in 1935.

hired a cook specially for us and gave us champagne and Mouton Rothschild 1976. It was A's birthday, so she was pleased. Gladwyn quiet, morose and yet humorous. Cynthia a great gossip about friends' *moeurs*. Heywood Hills say she has a passion for vulgar sea-side post-cards, the broader the better. She showed me a portrait of herself by Jacques-Emile Blanche, dated 1911 and giving the sitter's age as 13. She must therefore be 82. Incredible.

Unfortunate thing happened on last morning at Billa's. Letter arrived from M. which I was expecting. A. came down before me and saw it at my place. She was cross, said it was insensitive of me to have M. write to me there. All the way home in the car she would hardly speak, except to say that she thought she would not do another gardening book because she had so much on her mind which made her unhappy. Now this does not seem to me to be reasonable behaviour.

Wednesday, 27 August

The Times has agreed to publish an extract of H.N. in September. I looked to see yesterday what extract they had chosen. Discovered that it was the bit about Harold's affair with Raymond. Telephoned Norah to say I would not agree. She urged me to reconsider. Said it would be good publicity. I replied that I would have to consult both Paul Hyslop who had lent me the letters and Eardley with whom I was going to stay last night. Paul said he didn't mind in the least. E. read the offending pages and thought they would pass. So I told Norah I would agree after all.

Saturday, 13 September

The remainder of this week has been spent in Bath typing out Chapter 5 of H.N. Vol. II. Much distracted by builders from No. 20 sawing stones on pavement, young men of radiant beauty. Then distracted by the filming of house on the other side, No. 18, a film called *Nanny*. Film people very jolly and friendly. Much walking up and down pavement, and I'm sure I shall be detected peeping from behind my window curtains.

Sunday, 14 September

A. who is undecided whether to write another gardening book, which I am encouraging her to do, suddenly thought she would like to see George Clive's garden at Whitfield, Herefordshire. So I accompanied her on a sudden whim. Whitfield is a delightful, 'dim' later Georgian house, unpretentious with nice rounded window bays extending from ground floor to roof line, and little about it of architectural importance. A family house set in unspoiled, remote country. Full of family portraits, a large cosy library, whole house crammed with books, old morocco and modern. George Clive, a charming boy (whom I discovered on returning home and looking up to be forty), fair, very youthful face, huge hands, a bit of a podge. Knows a great deal about trees and shrubs. A. impressed by his knowledge. He is carrying out many landscape schemes, fountains, follies, bassins etc. His mother Mary Clive* lives with him. Delightful, intelligent, well-read and unpretentious like all Pakenhams. Her voice reminded me of her sister Violet Powell. While A. went round the garden, she and I had long talk. She reminded me that we once met at dinner with Patrick Kinross, and Angela† to whom he was then married; Evelyn and Laura Waugh‡ and Nancy Mitford were the other guests. Also Eleanor Smith§ who, she remembered, bored us all with talk of circuses. I had totally forgotten the occasion. It must have been before George was born, before the war in fact.

Sunday, 5 October

Past week spent typing out Vol. II. But why do I bother? On Friday when about to leave Bath for home telephone rang. Hoped it might

---

* Lady Mary Pakenham (b. 1907); 2nd dau. of 5th Earl of Longford; m. 1939 Major M.G.D. Clive, Grenadier Guards (killed in action, 1943); writer.
† Angela Culme-Seymour (b. 1912); m. 1st 1934–8 Johnnie Churchill, 2nd 1938–42 Patrick Balfour (who s. 1939 as 3rd Baron Kinross).
‡ Evelyn Waugh (1903–66); novelist; m. (2nd) 1937 Laura Herbert (with whose sister Gabriel J.L.-M. had once been in love).
§ Lady Eleanor Smith (1902–45); dau. of 1st Earl of Birkenhead; enthusiast for circuses and gypsies.

be M. It was Hugo Brunner from Chatto's to announce that the print-ers were in a state of anarchy and the release date of book, 28th, had to be put off. Doesn't know when book will now come out, perhaps 15th Nov. I am sickened by all this. It is the second postponement because of bloody printers. Also I fear that because of anarchical state, book, when or if it ever does appear, will be full of mistakes. Very depressed by this, and not hearing from M., who went to Paris a few days before I got back [from visiting Mount Athos with Derek Hill].

A. went to London during the week for one night. On her return she telephoned me in Bath. In moment of euphoria I said that at breakfast that morning the sun was shining, the day was lovely, I felt a twinge of Wanderlust. 'Why should I not come with you to Australia?' I said unguardedly. She had been thinking of going alone in November. When I got back she said, 'It will be very unkind of you if you change your mind now. You know it is what I have wanted to do for years and years.' So I have not changed my mind. We at once sent a telegram to the Downers in Australia to ask if we would be welcome. By that time I should have finished typing out Vol. II and got it off to Nigel. I shall have a break before getting down to my Anthology and Bamber's Bath book in the winter months. This morning received reply from Margaret Downer, 'All Downers will be delighted. Love. Writing.'

It is astonishing how snobbish the English gentry are. Wherever we go to lunch or dine we are placed at table according to rank. Sally Westminster will always be seated on the host's right and Caroline Somerset on his left, regardless of how many other women may be present with far greater pretensions to intellect and distinction, such as Elspeth Huxley, or even older women, or women strangers who have never been there before and therefore, according to the rules of hospitality, ought to be treated with special deference and politeness.

Sunday, 12 October

The son of old Mrs Rich, wife of one of the gardeners to the House here, came to ask A. if he might work one day a week in the garden. Naturally she was delighted. We have known this boy for his regular attendance at Communion in Church, and lately for the rather surprising spectacle of him dressed in a becoming white stole, tied round the waist with a cord, and following the Vicar to the altar, where he stands and kneels like a server but without actually serving. When we told Peggy she pursed her lips and said she must tell us something about him. He was not like other boys. His contemporaries in the village called him Queenie or some such name. He had been known to pinch cigarettes, and could not be trusted alone in the house. Now he looks to us a very nice, quiet, sensitive young man, quite handsome, very neat and intelligent. But in a small village community the likes of him are shunned. They drift to the towns, where they feel persecuted and prostitute themselves.

On Friday we motored to Devon. Stayed the night with Anthony and Rosemary Chaplin.* Rosemary is enchanting, sensitive, very intelligent, sane, a bit of a poet. Anthony has declined greatly. He has lost all looks, has a strange, sinister line about the mouth, is grey in the face, and is argumentative and gushing by turns. In fact he is an alcoholic. Pours down brandy, three and four glasses after dinner. Starts off with elevenses of rum, continues at luncheon, ending with four liqueurs. He makes me feel sad. He has achieved nothing much in life, thrown his talent away; composed a few cadenzas perhaps for the piano, what else? Has produced no son. The title will die out. He affects not to care. Thinks only of himself and his ailments, brought on by drink. One of his daughters by Rosemary has married a Liverpool Geordie who lives on his wife and the dole. An argumentative youth who talks the hind legs off a donkey on subjects of which he knows nothing. Sounds hell to me. The other daughter lives with a married man who can't marry her, also of no breeding. And then there are his and poor Alvilde's grandchildren who only like French boys from neighbouring villages. Oenone† told A. the other day that her sister, the youngest granddaughter, has a French boyfriend who is over here in London with a job at Boot's Cash Chemists and taking

---

* Alvilde L.-M's first husband Anthony, 3rd and last Viscount Chaplin (1906–81), father of her daughter Clarissa; m. (2nd) 1950 Rosemary Lyttelton (1922–2003), dau. of 1st Viscount Chandos.
† J.L.-M's step-granddaughter Oenone Luke (b. 1960); 2nd dau. of Hon. Clarissa Chaplin and Michael Luke.

the dole money as well. A. was furious and told Oenone she would report him if she could. Oenone merely expressed surprise at A's attitude and thinks the boy is behaving perfectly sensibly. Now if this does not come from lack of education on the part of the Luke family I don't know what does.

Betty Watkins the postmistress is Secretary of the Badminton Village Club. They had a disagreeable meeting the other day at which the Club Steward was sacked, quite rightly, because in a drunken brawl he had assaulted one member and then turned on the octogenarian father-in-law of another and knocked out his false teeth. As President, the Duke of Beaufort was present at the Court of Enquiry. The peccant Steward's wife, whom everyone hates, turned on the Duke and called him a 'bloody bastard'. Rather near the knuckle, with John of Gaunt and all. Don't suppose he has ever been so addressed in his life. Apparently he stared straight ahead in ducal dignity without moving a muscle in his face.

Saturday, 25 October

Yesterday I went to London for the day to meet M. for first time in five weeks. We together collected from Chatto's the first five copies of my Vol. I. Gave him the first copy. Norah spoke to me warmly about the book which has already sold 2,000 copies. About all that will be sold, I gather, for the price of £15 is exorbitant. Even Vol. I which looks nice enough is very thick and the print small. M. has got rid of his moustache, thank the Lord. Maître Blum made him go out and have it removed instantly. We spent the afternoon together happily, and had tea in Jermyn Street in a tiny tea room. He accompanied me to Paddington.

Said to A. last night how odd it has been that many of the people whom I have liked, admired and felt closest rapport with have been people I met but from time to time and hardly knew, such as William Plomer, Bloggs Baldwin, Alick Downer and Sheila Birkenhead.

Finished last night Isabel Colegate's *The Shooting Party*. Her best novel yet, firm, balanced, well-written. Yet makes me hate Edwardians. I firmly believe I have turned against the aristocratic tradition. Their arrogance was unpardonable.

Wednesday, 29 October

Last Saturday the Johnstons[*] motored us to Llanstephan to see the new house Nicky has built for Hugo Philipps.[†] Mollie is divine, very pretty, sweet expression, intelligent as one would expect from daughter of Lord Sherfield. Hugo is not handsome and unlike Ros to look at. Large nose, harassed face, seeming over sixty whereas he must be in fifties. Not easy to communicate with but a nice man. The house they live in is hideous. Of a machine-made brick, uniform, rather dark earthy brown but not pretty. No variety in texture or shade. Building in lovely position in old park overlooking River Wye and Black Mountains, yet looks like an institute or a large lavatory. No proportions. Lacks verticality. Really a horror. Will it ever be admired? I bet not, for it is ignoble. Such a dear man, poor, crippled Nicky Johnston. Our bathroom had no window and air conditioning operates when light turned on, inexcusable in the country I think. Moreover the air conditioning produces a howling draught from under the bath while one is drying oneself on the mat.

Am in a stew about Australia. Feel I ought to prepare and have done nothing, read nothing about the continent. Yet am rather excited and pleased to go, happy that I shall be seeing M. the night before we leave at dawn on Sunday the 2nd.

The L.-Ms spent three weeks in Australia, staying first in South Australia, where A.L.-M's father had served as Governor in the 1920s, then in New South Wales. J.L.-M appreciated the kindness they received everywhere, and admired the flora, fauna and landscape, but was bored by the many parties given in their honour.

Wednesday, 26 November

A. and I went to Australia on the 2nd November and returned on the 23rd. For several days after arrival and return we both suffered from

---

[*] Nicholas Johnston (b. 1929); architect; m. 1958 Susanna Chancellor.
[†] Hon. H. J. L. Philipps (1929–99); son of Rosamond Lehmann and Wogan Philipps, 2nd Baron Milford (and father of Roland Philipps [b. 1962], Managing Director of John Murray from 2003 and publisher of this volume); s. father as 3rd Baron, 1993; m. 1959–84 Hon. Mary ('Mollie') Makins, dau. of 1st Baron Sherfield (she later m. 2nd Viscount Norwich).

jet lag, feeling very tired but unable to sleep when one should. During our absence my book came out. To my intense joy M. telephoned me from London while I was in my room at the Adelaide Club, to say there were two very favourable reviews in the *Times* and *Daily Telegraph*. On the whole I am told the reviews are good and the book has been taken notice of. Came back to a pile of letters but only one was from a comparative stranger to whom I had not given a copy, Sir David Scott. I always maintain that thank you letters containing praise of a book don't mean much.

Thursday, 4 December

Tom Mosley has died. Talked about this to Philip Magnus at Brooks's. He told me that Mosley was a knave. I asked why. He said that in the Thirties Tom asked P.M's cousin Lionel Cohen how much he would give his party to call off the persecution of the Jews. Hard to believe. Then in the evening they put out a film on the British Movement, the most disgusting exhibition of sheer ignorance and bestiality I have seen for a long while. Inarticulate thugs and skin-heads, lusting for violence and blood, crooning anti-Jewish and anti-black slogans. I cannot believe that Tom would have approved, or that these ghastly toughs from the overcrowded cities are his disciples. But I am ignorant of his recent activities over here. Did he have an office, and was he still the head of a 'movement'?

Saturday, 6 December

Below Tom Mosley's obituary in *The Times* was one of Romain Gary,[*] who has killed himself. I remember him in Roquebrune days [1950s] when he was married to Lesley Blanch. He used to wander down to our little house at midday. Would protest that he could not stay to luncheon. Often A. had just enough for her and my slender midday needs. Then he would stay. Having protested that he ate nothing but

---

[*] Romain Gary Kacew (1914–80); Russian-born French novelist; m. (1st) 1945–62 (as her 2nd husband) Lesley Blanch (1904–2007), English travel writer and historian.

special biscuits which he would produce from his pocket and munch, would invariably accept our food and eat it. Very gloomy, morose, eccentric, tied-up little man. He would wander in the hills behind the village apparently aimlessly, apparently in despair, and thinking about his book. I was doing the same, I suppose, but I walked purposefully for miles. Was also unhappy for I hated Roquebrune, the isolation, the pent-upness of our doll-like house and the claustrophobia of the village on a steep precipice betwixt mountain and deep blue sea. Never felt any affinity with Romain, who was too abstracted, and distracted.

Saturday, 13 December

Last weekend Dick and Elaine [Lees-Milne] stayed with us. Had not seen them for nearly two years. Was much shocked and saddened by their appearance. Dick has developed a large paunch for he can't take exercise or walk more than a yard or two, owing to asthma. Puffs after leaving the car and walking into the house and has to squirt stuff into his nose. Elaine is worse. Very haggard, has continuous pains in stomach and eats nothing. Goes to bed at 9.30, stays in bed in morning and rests after tea. My heart yearned for them. Went to see Diana Westmorland on Thursday evening. She has had a *coup de vieux*. Does not seem to take in much unless one speaks slowly. One must not change subjects too swiftly with the old. She said to me, 'I ought of course to die. In a way I want to for I hate being alive. And yet, I don't want to.' She said sweet old age was a damnable lie. There was nothing whatsoever to be said in its favour. Every day she noticed some deterioration.

Tuesday, 16 December

Last week I stayed the night with John [Kenworthy-Browne]. We dined at Brooks's and went at my request to the cinema, *Caligula*. Roman orgies. So boring that we left in the interval. Then Stuart [Preston] came down from Paris. Somehow I cannot recapture with the Sarge the easy intimacy of yore. It is a bit of a strain. Talk does not flow. Then yesterday M. came down for the day to Bath. We lunched and chatted with oh what ease and affection. He presented me with the copy of *King George V* which Harold presented to the Duke of Windsor and the Duke had bound in red calf, together with a letter from Maître Blum which exculpates me if anyone questions how I came by this book. My first sight of M. for six weeks.

1981

1981

No New Year celebrations. I went to bed early on the eve and read. A. went to a New Year's drinks party at the Loewensteins'. I motored to London for the night and stayed with J.K.-B. London strangely deserted. I met M. at the Paddington Hotel at 7.15. We went to his flat to listen to a repeat of Vita's 1950s broadcast on Walter de la Mare. Vita's mellow, fruity, southern, Keatsian voice has a shrillness in the top notes which I do not remember, possibly the fault of M's wireless set. Next morning went to Colindale* and read several broadcast talks in old *Listeners* given by Henry Green about whom I have to write something for the American *Twentieth Century Writing* mag.

Last Saturday Pam [Jackson] brought Diana Mosley over to lunch with us. Diana very gaunt, thin and sad. Pam told me that the hour and a quarter wait in the extreme cold in the chapel of the crematorium in Paris, waiting for the ashes to cool, was a mournful proceeding. The sons read Tom's favourite passages from Swinburne between the music. Diana said that she and the sons would have to close down Tom's office which he had kept all these years in Victoria Street. Could no longer afford the rent, £4,000 p.a. for two rooms. I should have asked her what the office was for. Still don't know whether he supported the National Front, or what. Greatly enjoyed seeing Diana. Always so much to talk about. Said she had been asked to edit Nancy's correspondence, but couldn't possibly undertake it because of the terrible things N. wrote about her loved ones.†

---

* The British Newspaper Library in North London.
† A volume of Nancy's letters edited by Diana's daughter-in-law Charlotte Mosley was published by Hodder & Stoughton in 1993.

Tuesday, 13 January

Have finished titivating Vol. II of Harold and am taking typescript to London this afternoon. M. has been the greatest help, reading through the whole thing and making suggestions. I know it is an indifferent volume. And Vol. I has not caused the repercussions I in my self-magnifying way thought it would.

We watched a programme about Willie Maugham. Were glad he was not shown as the cad which recent books about him have made him out to be. Robin Maugham asserted that Willie was not an unhappy man at the end of his life, that he enjoyed his riches and travels. Then the other night saw the end of a programme about Fothergill,* the proprietor of the Spread Eagle at Thame, which I frequented when at Oxford. Wish I had seen the beginning. Went there, I remember, with John Gielgud† during that short-lived affair. Fothergill was a left-over from the 1890s, being a friend of Bosie, Oscar Wilde, etc., and a disagreeable fellow too, very rude to customers whom he disliked. Would send them packing before they had finished eating and not bother to ask for payment. Just hoofed them out if he got into arguments with them, for he was always roaming around the tables. Excellent food of course. I thought him a million in those days when he was probably in his fifties, the 1890s being closer to me then than the 1930s are now.

Wednesday, 14 January

Coming out of Brooks's, ran into Alan Clark.‡ He stopped to say how much he enjoyed my diaries, which he kept beside his bed and read and re-read. Now how can people like them to this extent? I asked Alan how his father was. Said that he was well physically, except that he was inclined to shuffle. Mentally not so alert. Was forgetful, but when concentrating on a subject and able to give undivided attention

---

* John Fothergill (1876–1957); hotelier and writer; author of *An Innkeeper's Diary* (1931).
† Sir John Gielgud (1904–2000); actor.
‡ Hon. Alan Clark (1931–99); e.s. of Kenneth Clark; writer, politician and diarist, at this time a backbench Conservative MP.

his mind was as clear as ever. I am getting like that. Interruptions disturb one's concentration so that one cannot quickly return to the subject one is working on.

Thursday, 22 January

Rupert Loewenstein tells me that the Trees have a collection of drawings by Cecil Beaton of Vita [Sackville-West] and Violet [Trefusis]. Says I really ought to see them. They are far more vicious that those of Anne Rosse which the Trees now own and I have seen. But I don't think I could bear to see Vita made fun of – fun hardly being the word, for they are appalling and brutal. Cecil was a bitch really.

Saturday, 31 January

I have begun work on Bamber Gascoigne's *Images of Bath*. Have now sorted out all the photographs of prints which I intend to illustrate in the text. David Ford is my collaborator and in the process I have got to know this charming, handsome, rather pathetic young man. He has told me his story. He is thirty-four. Grew up with anti-Vietnam generation of students. Says I have no idea how that war divided America down the middle. He had begun a lucrative job on Wall Street but found colleagues so unsympathetic that he left, much to his conventional parents' chagrin. Crossed the Atlantic, determined to work in England. Has remained ever since. Yet has no proper job. Prospects bleak. Started doing social work, meals on wheels, helping the aged and stricken in London. Liked it. Then got bored. Wanted something more cerebral. Attached himself to Bamber and Christina who are his protectors, I think. Something vulnerable about him. He told me he hated being young. When I expressed amazement, assuring him he was at the peak of life, he solemnly avowed that he wanted to be old. I have not pressed him to tell me about his love life, although I already know he had a serious affair which broke down and upset him deeply. He is, I think, very serious, probably romantic, and not promiscuous. I carefully refrained from plying him with indiscreet questions or appearing to be inquisitive. But when he packed up his files yesterday and said goodbye, I said, 'Let me give you a chaste embrace', and did so. Far from there being any resistance he warmly reciprocated, and made as if to kiss me on the mouth. Perhaps all the young kiss on the mouth these days without implying emotion. When I was their age it meant only one thing, that both were in love and intended to go to bed together there and then. Alas for those halcyon days. I have grown fond of David and shall miss him.

Saturday, 7 February

At breakfast [in London] I told Eardley that Norah wanted me to cut out a reference to Vita's amusing remark when she learnt of Angelica Bell's engagement to David Garnett, 'It's a case of adding incest to sodomy.'* He said 'Ring up Fanny Partridge immediately', she living in the flat below. Did so, and she said certainly don't cut out. Garnett was her brother-in-law and also the father of her daughter-in-law. I was delighted to tell Norah this.

Tuesday, 10 February

Motored to London for Sheila Birkenhead's party in Wilton Crescent for the Queen Mother. Invited at 6 for 6.15. Walked into house at 6.05. Ushered into room upstairs. Before I could embrace Sheila I was seized, no other word for it, by that predator Rosalie Mander,† wearing a horrible pink knitted dress and grey felt hat covered with stains and dust. She transfixes one like a butterfly on a board. Did however say that my books got better and better. Bill De L'Isle likewise rather a bore, dribbles while he talks and keeps wiping the wet off his chin, drove me relentlessly into the fireplace until I had to say I was burning the seat of my trousers. He said that Shelley from whom

---

* David, who married Angelica Bell in 1942 as his second wife, had been the homosexual lover of Angelica's biological father Duncan Grant. His first wife was Frances Partridge's sister Rachel ('Ray'); and his and Angelica's daughter Henrietta married Frances's son Burgo.

† Rosalie Glynn Grylls (1905–88); writer on nineteenth-century literary figures; m. 1930 Sir Geoffrey Mander (1882–1961), sometime MP for Wolverhampton; during 1930s they donated Wightwick Manor, Staffordshire, to N.T.

he is descended, he now being the Shelley baronet, was a silly man.[*]
I agreed. But would you have liked him, I asked? To my surprise he
said he would because he liked aristocrats to be radicals, no matter
how silly they were. Talked to Quentin Crewe[†] in his chair. He unable
to shake my hand. But said he was about to write a book about the
Sahara, necessitating his going there, camping in tents. Courageous
for a man so crippled and immobile as he.

Dear Sheila has dreadful teeth but I love the woman. She took
groups of people up to Queen Elizabeth. Then watched to see if the
encounters were successful, and when it was time to remove them.
She edged her way towards me. Out of the corner of my eye I saw
her coming. Tried to hide behind the Leigh Hunt family. But she
caught me. Made me stand expectant while Q.E. talked to a group of
three. Sheila kept saying, 'Push your way in.' 'I can't,' I said, 'it's not
in my nature.' Then the Q. turned from the others towards me, and
they took the hint and dissolved themselves. We confronted one
another. Was I to speak first? She smiled awkwardly. Then Sheila said,
'He wrote a book about Rome.' 'Oh, how interesting,' she said. 'Yes,'
I said, 'but a long time ago. It is full of mistakes and luckily now out
of print.' Q.E.: 'Do you like your books when you have done with
them?' J: 'No, I rather hate them. I used to hate them only when they
were finished. Now I hate them before they are finished. I would', I
continued, 'make a bad parent if I treated my children like my books,
which are said to be the brain's children. I would dislike them before
they were grown up.' 'You certainly would make a bad parent,' she
answered. That was a pretty silly introductory exchange. A glazed look
came across her eyes. She said desperately, 'Where do you live?' I told
her Badminton. Eyes lit up for there was a subject for conversation.
How much she liked the place and village. Asked which house ours
was. I explained, by the lodge to the gates. She asked after Master and
Mary Beaufort. Said how sad that Mary was becoming so vague. I said
she often did not know who we were. 'She can be quite funny,' she

---

[*] The ostensible purpose of the gathering was to present the Queen Mother with a
copy of Shelley's poems, obtained by J. L.-M., which had belonged to the poet's
daughter Ianthe.
[†] Author and gastronome (1926–99); *In Search of the Sahara* was published in 1983.

said. 'And sharp,' I added. Where did we live before? Explained Alderley, which we loved; which became too big; had to move. 'Do you go back there?' 'Not unless I have to,' I said, 'although the new owners are charming friends of ours and love the place.' I said one ought never to return to places one loved. She agreed. Became wistful. Said she adored her two old homes. I said feebly, 'But one must preserve the magic of beloved houses in one's head, and not allow the images to get misted. If one refrains from re-visiting, which merely causes confusion in the memory, they remain as one knew them.' She liked this, and said, 'You have said something which I shall think over.' Then turned to the next guest. I can't pretend it was very satisfactory, but then I always find these royal encounters unnatural, artificial and profitless. I had the opportunity of looking at her close to. Her teeth, which are her own, are bad. She has little finger nails upturned at the ends – not pretty. Her hair straight, wispy, stringy. Nevertheless she has dignity and charm – how often has that been said? – however evanescent; and stamina. For an hour and a half she stood – never once sat – talking to total strangers and making herself agreeable.

Saturday, 7 March

On Thursday lunched at Hole-in-the-Wall with Julian Mitchell,* Tony's playwright brother. He wanted to talk about a play or novel he is writing – not yet sure which – on the theme that the Cambridge traitors, Burgess, Blunt, etc., were chiefly actuated by the inhibitions imposed on them regarding their homosexuality. Wants to know from those who lived through the Thirties how circumspect they were obliged to be. I assured him that they had to act covertly and could never let their tastes be known. Only the most bold and rash did so. Julian believes their pro-Sovietism was a getting their own back on England. Interesting. Yesterday he spent day with John Gielgud who sent me affectionate messages. I told him how intimately I knew John in 1931 when I was an undergraduate at Oxford. For six weeks I was

---

* Playwright (b. 1937); the play he had come to discuss with J.L.-M. was *Another Country*.

infatuated with him. Then it passed like a cloud. I like Julian Mitchell. He is unattractive, with the sort of beard which continues down his open neck, but sensitive. I talked to him about my *Heretics in Love* which I knew was a poor novel but thought might make a good film. Gave him a copy which he took away, and he will let me know his opinion.

Saturday, 14 March

Malcom Muggeridge* has become a good old trouper; after years of travels by deviant ways he has come to the straight and narrow. I have pondered much on the wise things he has been saying on the telly lately. When asked about the outcome of the last war he said he knew all along that only Communism or Nazism could be the victor. Now I always felt this way, though believed that Nazism would be defeated in the long run. That the war would be a blow for democracy I always foresaw, just as I saw Communism as the greater evil because most lasting and insidious. Nazism, terrible though it was, was ephemeral by nature. It could only flourish with trumpets, while the other works slowly, underground, in silence. I shall never forget learning, in hospital in Birmingham, that Russia had become our ally. To me it meant the end of all things, our compromise with evil.

Thursday, 19 March

To London to meet M., who returned yesterday after several weeks in New York and the Bahamas. He came to Brooks's from Trumpers where he had all his long hair cut off and looked like a skinned guinea pig. Was in good form until the end of dinner when I noticed his large eyes turning into slits and said he was dog-tired and ought to go home to bed. He admitted it. He is like a child, falling from one mood into another. I drove him back to Hyde Park Square and told him he must work like a demon at his book and finish it as soon as he can.

The Peter Hayman case revolts me. The appalling hypocrisy of the British. Bloody Tory MP called Dickens insisted on publicising in

---

* Writer, journalist and broadcaster (1903–90).

Commons name of ex-diplomat Hayman for indulging in admittedly rather sordid fantasies, but not culpable in law. Today tells press that he is leaving his own wife, after which, not before, he goes to telephone wife to this effect. If that isn't double shittiness, what is?

Saturday, 28 March

Terrible spring depression during past week. Bloody spring. Depression is not relieved by left eye having blown up. Don't know what is the matter but woke up on Tuesday with sharp pain seemingly behind eyeball. After two days went to Dr King who looked through a telescope and said I should apply some grease four times a day and I would be all right. But I am not all right and discomfort persists. Last night I discovered I could hardly see with this eye, certainly not to read even with spectacles.

Have been ruminating upon possibility of becoming totally blind. What would I do? For I write or read most of the sixteen hours of the day. And use eyes ceaselessly. Would I go into monastery and pray? Would I commit suicide? What would poor A. do? I would be the heaviest burden upon her, heavier than I am already.

Sunday, 29 March

It is Sunday. For once we have no engagement of any kind. It rains all day relentlessly. In the evening, for the days are longer now the clock has changed, I walked with Honey on her lead down the Luckington Road. The landscape is grey, dank and dripping. A sour mist of damp hovers over the fields. The horses look shaggy and saturated. The ducks in the farmyard I pass shake their wings as though they have emerged from a pond, whereas there is merely ubiquitous wetness. I think about Jamesey Pope-Hennessy, the book about whom by Peter Quennell I am reading with sorrow. I find a chord of sadness throughout. There was something wrong with the way of life which caught up with him. The fascination of *la boue* became a fixation, and surely he wasted too much time with empty-heads like Len. Or am I being snobbish and limited? He would have said so. I know I irritated him increasingly. Few letters to me have been included by Peter, whereas

I thought there were some very entertaining ones he omitted. It is so long since I read them, and it required a little courage to read the few in this book.

Monday, 20 April

It is Easter Monday. We have had Heywood and Anne Hill staying since Friday. The perfect guests whom we treat as we do each other. No effort required, no making of conversation. One can wash up the breakfast things while they are finishing eating at the table and talking. Whereas last weekend we had two strangers, a couple A. had met in India. Oh the strain! Heywood is as round as a tub and brick red in the face. When I think how pretty – the just word – he was in youth, and desired by all. He is like a dormouse which uncurls itself in order to make a sly remark and giggle, immediately curling up again. Very sweet, still very perceptive and intelligent. But very quiet and slow in movement.

Sunday, 26 April

On Friday to Sissinghurst. Nigel me met and daughter Juliet who was also on train. The cold at Sissinghurst intense although no snow yet. Enjoyable visit to meet Victoria Glendinning.* Not what I expected, which was a blonde divinity *à la* Diana Mitford for some reason. She is in fact slight, with dark hair and clever but plain face. I think she will make a good and fair biography of Vita. Anyway we got on and I gave her my address and telephone number in case she may want to communicate when she starts writing. Nigel handed me a very laudatory review he wrote of my Harold I for *Book Choice*. Strange of him to review a life of his father but he did it, as he does everything, well. Juliet enchanting and husband James Macmillan-Scott even more so. After dinner I sat up till 2, talking with him on sofa. Extremely handsome man of about 28, now a banker. He told me he has to have many women, business acquaintances, to dine when he travels. They all

---

* Hon. Victoria Seebohm (b. 1937); dau. of Baron Seebohm; writer and journalist; m. 1st 1958 (diss. 1981) Professor Nigel Glendinning, 2nd 1982 Terence de Vere White (1912–94), writer.

expect him to go to bed with them unless they make it clear during the meal that they don't. He says you have to keep your wits about you to catch the projected hint. Says it is such a bore. Says he has no prejudices or disapproval regarding sex and was surprised that I of this mind too. But he got bored with sex. Was just as content with platonic love. I said Yes, that is all very fine for you who can get the other without raising a finger. He, James, said that age was no bar to him if he loved. Well, well.

Monday, 18 May

Listened on Thursday to the programme *Books* on Radio 4 about my published diaries. Commentator and a man called Christopher Matthew. I did not like it. Spoke of them as gossipy, which they are not entirely. Spoke about the exclusive circle in which I moved during the war, as though composed of an extinct species like pterodactyls. Both men agreed that such people as Bridget Parsons, the Dashwoods and of course Emerald were confirmed good-timers, the most despicable of beings. Whereas my real friends were Harold, the Pope-Hennessys and other writers and intellectuals. Matthew took as a general theme for the diaries a remark I made when I broke down on the road and was told my car had run out of water, 'I am humiliated. I am always humiliated.' Have the modern bedint reviewers no sense of humour?

On Thursday evening, when we had the clock man from Hawkesbury Upton over to collect my gold clock and Joan Lindsay and Cynthia Llewellyn-Palmer were here for a drink, the bell rang. It was Mary Beaufort, looking so changed, so strained and sad that I barely recognised her. She said A. had told her she might come to luncheon. It was then 6.15. Her wig slipped over her forehead, just above her nose. However she stayed for a quarter of an hour and made some sense. Walked home by herself. Daphne appalled when she learnt this. She had escaped her nurses.

Caroline told A. that when Mary's brother* died the other day, Mary told David who was with her that she must telephone the

---

* George, 2nd Marquess of Cambridge (1895–1981); e.s. of Adolphus ('Dolly'), Duke of Teck (1861–1927), brother of Queen Mary, who gave up German titles in 1917 to assume marquessate; m. 1923 Dorothy Hastings.

Queen. This he did, and got the Queen on the line. Handed receiver to Mary, who had already forgotten and said to the Queen, 'And who are you? What do you want?' After that conversation she said she wished to speak to her brother. David said that would be difficult and had she not better speak to her sister-in-law? 'No,' she replied, 'she is an absolutely horrid woman.' Next day Caroline took a party of distinguished American ladies to the House by appointment. Mary greeted them with kindness, mistook them for a choir, and said, 'Now tell me, what you are going to sing?'

Monday, 1 June

Had hoped to find letter from M. in Bath, but no letter and no telephone call. Haven't heard from him since I telephoned him last Tuesday. Thought I did not mind any more. Find I still do. Damn!

Folly killed a squirrel. Caught it in a flash. I saw a slight tussle in the grass. It was dead in an instant. So curious how dogs do not kill in anger, unlike wild beasts which look angry. Our dogs do not know what hatred is. It is the chase. When I called her she left the corpse, and on our return from the walk she did not nose it out. Do all creatures die with their eyes open? I wish they didn't.

Tuesday, 2 June

We attended garden party at Montacute to mark fiftieth anniversary of presentation of the house and village to the National Trust. I remember Oliver Esher describing to me how he stood on a very small wooden pedestal with the Princess Royal in pouring rain and a howling gale so that neither could hear what the other said. I think my second-hand recollections which I gave the Wessex Office today were passed on to the Duke of Gloucester,* because he mentioned

---

* HRH Prince Richard of Gloucester (b. 1944); yr son of HRH Prince Henry, Duke of Gloucester (3rd son of King George V) and Lady Alice Scott; architect and photographer; m. 1972, Brigitte van Deurs; following death of elder brother in plane crash, 1972, succeeded to dukedom, 1974.

these facts which he could not have known otherwise. He is an undistinguished youth, badly dressed in a sloppy City suit and yellow shirt, hair falling over his face which he brushed back with his hand. He made quite a good speech read from typewritten sheet. Was followed by Hugh Grafton whose speaking has much improved. Saw a number of grisly old faces there from the distant past. I shun them because after initial words of greeting there is nothing further to say. Was accosted by Yates the old custodian's son, bent like a crochet–hook, toothless and purple of visage, but wearing very smart spongebag suit and old-fashioned square bowler like the Yellow Earl of Lonsdale.* Presented himself to Duke of Gloucester as son of the late squire who came to Montacute after Lord Curzon. This must have surprised Baba Metcalfe for she was present. Warmly embraced me, and asked us to meet her when the ceremonies over to accompany her round the house and be shown her old bedroom as a child here in the 1920s – for Lord Curzon died in 1925.

Like all talks with royal personages on these occasions, and indeed my few audiences with popes, my conversation with the Duke of Gloucester was clipped, awkward and pointless. A. and I were stood in a line of folk. He was brought up to us by Miss Brotherton, Chairman of the Wessex Committee, whom we had never met before. She got our names right. The young Duke shook hands and stood silent. Then he said, 'I think I have read several of your books?' I said he might have done. 'Do you still write them?' (I suppose I looked old and gaga.) 'I don't write books about architecture any longer, Sir.' 'Why is that?' 'Oh, because the young architectural historians are so clever that I daren't.' 'That seems a pity. Do you really think they are?' 'Yes, they are so highly trained by the Courtauld Institute and universities that they become immensely erudite on a specialised subject.' 'What do you write, then?' I murmured something about H.N. which he was evidently unaware of. It must be agony for 'them'. I fancy one should be tremendously jolly and crack jokes. That is what 'they' like.

---

* Hugh Cecil Lowther, 5th Earl of Lonsdale (1857–1944); landowner and sportsman.

Wednesday, 10 June

Went up for Pat Trevor-Roper's dinner party at the Beefsteak Club, in that absurd baronial hall. At least thirty guests, all at one enormously long table. Like a Waterloo Banquet,* without the groaning silver plate. I sat next to Diana Cooper on my right and Pat's left. On my left a nice man called Michael Howard,† distinguished Oxford don. Howard said H.N's fault was a desire to be liked. I said it was softness. He told me that when he was twenty-two he went to a psychologist and said he feared he was homosexual. 'If that's all, don't waste my time,' the psychologist said.

Diana talked to me practically throughout, for Pat much occupied by neighbour on his right, Lady Dufferin, whom he kept pawing and kissing. Diana wearing a short black veil which just covered top of her nose. I was very close to her and was amazed by the beauty of her profile and clarity of her blue eyes. But she talked of her extreme unhappiness. Began on drugs and ways of ending things. Thought her friend Randolph Churchill's wife‡ had been so sensible and brave doing herself in. Said during First War she administered drugs. They were laudanum then. She only quite likes her biography by Ziegler,§ but wants him to think she is very pleased for she likes *him* so much. Says some revelations in it about her and Duff which astonish her. Things she never knew about. Her marriage was a blissful success because they agreed from the start never to be faithful. They always loved one another. She was never jealous. Never had been. All children should be brought up to eschew jealousy.

There is something pitiable about Diana who for decades had the world at her feet, and still has really; but the world means nothing to her. She is deaf, wears concealed hearing-aid which causes her pain when noises made like the fire brigade passing (it did while we were talking) and can taste nothing. Cannot tell the difference between garlic and *eau de cologne*. Smell too completely gone. She ate one

---

* The Duke of Wellington's annual banquet at Apsley House for veterans of the battle, who crammed around a long table bearing a huge silver centrepiece.
† Sir Michael Eliot Howard (b. 1922); Regius Professor of Modern History, Oxford.
‡ June Osborne; m. 1948 (diss. 1961) as his 2nd wife Randolph Churchill.
§ Philip Ziegler (b. 1929); writer and publisher.

course only, namely avocado pear covered with banana and shrimps, not nice, and drank moderately. I found it tiring talking to her with so much conversation on all sides. A strain bending down to catch her words. Such a banquet can only be satisfying to the host for his generosity. There is nowhere for guests to mingle and talk. No changing of seats. At midnight there was a move to go. I had a word with Gladwyn and asked him why no government would reform the House of Lords. Surely, I said, it would be sensible to do so before Benn* has authority to abolish it. Gladwyn did not agree. He said reform would give the House of Lords power which it now has not got. As it is, the House does no harm and in fact much good. Any tampering with it would be a mistake. It must either be left alone or abolished. He thought Benn would not get power unless unemployment reached the 4 million mark. Then anything might happen. Walked back to Eardley through empty streets.

Thursday, 11 June

Selina Hastings† motored down from London to lunch with me in Bath and talk about Nancy [Mitford] and Rosamond [Lehmann] whose lives she is writing. She turned on a tape recorder after luncheon which cramped my style. Although I did not hear it whirling I was conscious that it was on, and felt constrained. Anyway a dangerous thing to have permitted. I begged her not to let anyone hear what I said for the last thing I wished was to offend the Mitfords or Rosamond. She promised. Indeed I was delighted with her. She is near perfection. Is gentle, moderate, pretty, intelligent and sympathetic. I have not been so attracted by a girl her age for years.

---

* Rt Hon. Anthony Wedgwood Benn (b. 1926); charismatic Labour politician; succeeded as 2nd Viscount Stansgate, 1960, and secured a change in the law which enabled him to renounce peerage, 1963, and return to House of Commons; Secretary of State for Energy, 1975–9, subsequently the leading radical in Parliamentary Labour Party.

† Lady Selina Hastings (b. 1945); dau. of 16th Earl of Huntingdon; writer and journalist.

Monday, 29 June

I went to London for the day to take my page proofs to Chatto, having first had a long interview with Douglas Matthews, Librarian of the London Library, who is making an index of Vol. II as he did of Vol. I. A clever, well-informed man of great modesty. Amazing the number of small mistakes he found – such as 'awarded the Legion of Honour' whereas it should be 'made a member of'. Main purpose of visit to see M. who goes to Paris again on Thursday. He lunched and I went to his flat for a cup of tea. I said that at times I told myself that I could bear it if he disappeared from my life, but that after three days I had a longing for him, and would be wretchedly unhappy without him. His retort was, 'You will get tired of me first.'

I am saddened that when with Eardley, our old-established delight in each other's company, our perpetual laughter and giggles, seem to have abated. He seems staider, a trifle disapproving, unresponsive. Yet he writes me such affectionate letters. I have so often seen old friends estranged purely through old age. I hope this does not happen with us.

Wednesday, 8 July

The Duke of Beaufort admitted to David that not only had he not written his recently published Memoirs, he had not read them. They were written by his *maîtresse en titre*, Lady Cottesloe, and he has not so much as glanced at them, though published under his name. Vicar says it is embarrassing reading.

Friday, 17 July

A. and I motored to Firle for weekend. Dreadful motoring, down twisted, narrow roads, always at end of a queue with slow caravan at its head. Arrived exhausted. The Beits staying. An enjoyable weekend in this lovely, Frenchified house. Clementine has become a bore, poor thing. She buttonholes one and relentlessly makes one listen to long, unpointful stories. My affection for her sorely strained. Alf I like much, for he is on the ball, interested in everything, and amused if not amusing. Rainald Gage older than ever, fat, round, crumpled, inarticulate. Gasps like a stranded fish and talks to himself, or rather murmurs. Impossible to hear what he says, and Diana hardly easier, for she gabbles.

Saturday, 18 July

Gages and Beits went to Glyndebourne on Sat. so A. and I dined with Jack and Frankie Donaldson. Frankie told me she was writing a history of British Council and had many questions to ask me about George Lloyd. Then said she had been approached by Sidgwick & Jackson through Lord Longford, the recent chairman, to write life of 2nd Lord Esher.* Thought him a fascinating subject and suggested my doing it. I thought it over during the night.

Sunday, 19 July

Donaldsons come to luncheon. I sit next to Frankie and tell her I am interested in Lord Esher project. She will telephone Frank Longford.

Go to church at 11. George Gage† reads both lessons, quite inaudible. Am handed a Prayer Book bound in red morocco of 1790 with Gage coat of arms embossed. In prayers for Royal Family, George and Charlotte are neatly pencilled out and William and Adelaide substituted. Service in Series I of course. Something most feudal about our filing in last, and ushered into two pews isolated for the family. After service we inspect the Gage tombs in Gage chapel. Gages have been here since 1440s.

Before luncheon, A. and I go to Professor [Quentin] Bell's and buy five of his pottery bowls and plates. Very beautiful they are. Charges us £100, quite cheap. Are given a glass of wine. He charming and belies the impression conveyed over television of pedantic

---

* Reginald Brett, 2nd Viscount Esher (1852–1930); shadowy figure who advised monarchs and prime ministers while refusing high office and leading a clandestine homosexual life; father of Oliver, 3rd Viscount, who had been J.L.-M's first boss at the N.T.
† George John St Clere Gage (1932–93); e.s. of 6th Viscount Gage, whom he s. 1982 as 7th Viscount.

Father Christmas. True, wears long beard, but underneath a sweet and gentle face. Speaks softly, diffidently. She tall, badly dressed, clever, direct. Liked them both. We also went over Charleston again. It is bought now by National Trust and work is about to begin. The condition is terribly down-at-heel. I don't fancy it because the Vanessa–Duncan decoration is of ephemeral sort, which they dabbed over from time to time. Was never intended to be permanent. A waste of money.

A. and I to Glyndebourne Opera. *Ariadne*. Much Wagnerian screaming. But lovely music, similar to other Strauss operas. We motor home, through suburbs from Gatwick to Heathrow, arriving home at one in the morning. Very tired.

Tuesday, 21 July

A. and I to London for Buckingham Palace Garden Party. In great discomfort for foolishly put on my best pair of black shoes which pinch fiendishly. We went with the Berkeleys, driven by dotty George in their car. A fine day, but coolish. Claps of thunder, but did not rain. Thousands of guests. We had to walk beyond the entrance to Queen's Gallery in Buck. Pal. Road to join queue to Palace. Shuffled painfully. A. dressed in pretty striped black and white dress and white bowler hat with veil, most becoming. Ushered through the main courtyard facing entrance. Fine protective canopy carried by metal struts of Nash date, and great globe lanterns with crowns thereon. Up staircase to transverse gallery; pretty Regency staircase at one end. Royal portraits. Through large central room giving on to gardens. Homely yet majestic. In four corners of this room most splendid Chelsea dinner service, the Mecklenburg-Strelitz service in blue and white and gold. On to terrace of garden. This side of the palace is Nash in beautiful Bath stone. The Edwardian block we see by Blomfield is a brute and grotesquely disproportionate to the old palace. It is a crying shame that the Hilton Hotel was allowed, also beastly skyscraper to south. Both overlook and ruin privacy of gardens. Huge but pretty pavilions erected on either side to accommodate staff and teas, which we ate on tables on the lawn. Walked down to the lake but both so suffering from foot trouble that we could not walk round the lake. Looked at herbaceous borders however. The best sort of municipal style, a galaxy of colours.

After waiting for apparently endless stream of visitors descending the steps, at four o'clock the Queen and Duke of Edinburgh appeared, followed by the Kents. 'God Save the Queen' played by a band which was inaudible. The Queen descended steps and mingled with guests. We did not see her again. In fact saw no one we knew, save George Howard, Sir Harold and Lady Wilson, Enoch Powells and Ted Heath. Freda [re-]introduced me to last. I liked his firm handshake and cordial expression of blue eyes.

Wednesday, 22 July

Had an interview at Sidgwick & Jackson with Frank Longford who was chairman until lately and is now a director, the new chairman Armstrong, who did not impress me, and a bright girl called Margaret who spoke of Diana Mosley as Diana. There is always a bright girl with credentials in every publishing house today. They are keen that I should undertake biography of 2nd Lord Esher. Discussed matter for an hour. First thing is for them to find out whether Lionel Esher* will approve of me, which I doubt and told them so. Don't think he likes me much since the brush I had with him over Bath. How much do I want to tackle this man's life? He is not romantic. He is an Establishment figure with a skeleton in the cupboard. Longford kept on emphasising this as the most interesting and important aspect. For Lord E. was the *éminence grise* of his time, a sort of Lord Goodman, with immense influence. Lord L. very flattering and friendly. Frankie Donaldson says he is a monster, with a mind set on self- and family advertisement. But if he advertises my book it will be a nice change. He says it is the sort of book which will be serialised.

---

* Lionel Brett, 4th Viscount Esher (1913–2004); grandson of Reginald, 2nd Viscount, and son of Oliver, 3rd Viscount; architect (who had supported Sir Hugh Casson's proposals for Bath, opposed by J.L.-M. and Bath Preservation Trust); m. 1935 Christian Pike, artist.

Monday, 27 July

Lunched alone with Rosamond who is inundated by biographers of people she knew. Says there are ten besieging her at this moment, including her own, Selina Hastings, and she hasn't a moment to herself. Yet I think she is delighted to be the grand old lady of letters, to whom the young come and sit at her dear feet. She is having a swimgloat over the republication of her novels and much public recognition. She complained that her brother John was discontented with his lot whereas he has received several honours and she has none. I wish she could be made a Dame. There is no doubt that everyone likes recognition however much they may protest that honours mean nothing to them. We ate smoked salmon and cheese and drank Malvern water with lemon. I talked to Ros about her letters to me. She says I should lend them to Selina who will be discreet. Somehow I don't like the idea. It may put a constraint on our future correspondence. Like speaking to Selina with the tape recorder whizzing round.

Wednesday, 29 July

Stayed at home all morning watching and listening to the Wedding [of the Prince of Wales and Diana Spencer]. A. and I greatly moved. It was the best form of pageantry – the fairy-like beauty of the carriages, the coachmen's liveries, their cocked hats with tassels hanging from the corners, the grey horses' manes plaited with silver thread, and the ravishing beauty of Lady Diana's dress, train of 25 feet, gossamer veil, her sidelong glances from those large round blue eyes. She is adorable.

Thursday, 6 August

My seventy-third birthday. A. went to France on Monday to stay with Rory Cameron to get some sun and warmth. In her absence I realise the amount of hard work she has to do – buying food, gardening and cooking. The hatefulness of having a birthday alone only made endurable by the sweetness and attention of M. Sally [Westminster] asked me to dinner; gave me delicious four courses and claret, and a present of a small malachite dove bought in Moscow. Deeply touched by her kindness, yet I would have preferred to remain at home.

She told me that the Prince of Wales is a weak character. At the Buckingham Palace ball on eve of wedding, he left his bride for several hours to spend the time of night with the Goons in another room. The pathetic little Lady D. was left alone, without an escort, to make conversation to people she did not know. This confirms what I have heard from other sources, that he is not in love with her.

Friday, 14 August

Frank Longford telephoned today to say that their project of a biography of 2nd Lord Esher is off. Lionel [Esher] has apparently given it to Michael Howard to do, he being a scholar of military history and in all respects well qualified to deal with it. Far better than I. I thanked Frank and thought that would be the end of Sidgwick's flirtation with me. But no. He said, 'Don't think I have done with you. We are determined to get you to write a biog. for us.' Insisted on my lunching with them in London week after next. Meanwhile they are going to think out subjects for my choice. Asked if I would prefer a man or a woman. Said I didn't mind. Did I want a literary character? Rather foolishly I replied that being no literary critic, perhaps not. What I would like is a romantic personality. I can truthfully say that I am more interested in and excited by M's projects than my own.

Saturday, 15 August

We dined with Ian McCallum at Claverton. After dinner Ian said the most monstrous things – that there was no more freedom in this country than behind the Iron Curtain; that he strongly advocated unilateral disarmament on our part; that the police incited the blacks; that we tortured people in Ireland; that Mrs Thatcher was responsible for the anti-conservation movement; that all politicians were rogues – and expressed the sort of sentiments one associates with Guy Burgess and A. Blunt. I was furious. Argued vehemently. The Briggses who were present agreed with me. Isabel, sitting next to me on the sofa, said Ian's was a policy of despair, and most reprehensible. That

England still maintained the decencies of life and was the happiest country to live in. I told Ian he was talking rubbish when he affirmed that one could no more express one's beliefs in this country than in Russia. I have never liked this man and always suspected he might be a traitor. Now I am certain he would be for twopence, to his personal advantage.

Wednesday, 19 August

Brian Masters motored from London to lunch with me in Bath. Talked of his new book on English hostesses of this century. Talked of Sibyl [Colefax], the Londonderrys. I said what a nice man I found Robin Castlereagh.* He said, 'But you have not read the letters he wrote his father. They are the unkindest, most unfilial letters I have ever read.' Brian M. is a nice young man. Extraordinary how he has adopted the manners of the aristocracy whom he has made his great study. Even so, one can see his origins are proletarian. I say this without any disparagement. His new book on Georgiana Duchess of Devonshire,† which is excellent, well written and witty, has had no reviews and sold a mere hundred or so copies. How is it that good books like this one receive no acknowledgement whereas trash sells? Or rather, had this book been written by Antonia Pakenham,‡ who can't write for nuts, it would have had huge sales.§ I have written the Lit. Ed. of *Sunday Telegraph* begging him to review.

Have received a charming letter from Lionel Esher. Says I would surely not like his grandfather who was a detestable character. He thinks an American biographer will write it, but is not sure and will

---

* Robin Vane-Tempest-Stewart, Viscount Castlereagh (1902–55); son of 7th Marquess of Londonderry (whom he succeeded, 1949) and Edith, Marchioness, *née* Chaplin (aunt of A.L.-M's first husband Anthony Chaplin, 3rd Viscount).
† Lady Georgiana Spencer (1757–1806); m. 1774 5th Duke of Devonshire; famous for her complex romantic life, her love of gambling, and her political campaigning on behalf of Charles James Fox.
‡ Better known as Lady Antonia Fraser (b. 1932); dau. of 7th Earl of Longford; m. 1st 1956 Sir Hugh Fraser, 2nd 1980 Harold Pinter.
§ A later biography of Georgiana by Amanda Foreman (1998), drawing on Brian Masters' earlier work, became a bestseller.

let me know. Decent of him to write. Norah writes that she would like a third volume of my diaries.

Wednesday, 26 August

The two lady gardeners from Sissinghurst* lunched at Badminton on Sunday. Delightful they were too. Sibille Kreutzberger told us of her life experiences. Her father was a Lutheran pastor in Hanover, her mother a Catholic. In 1938 the parents brought Sibille and her sister over to England where after a desperate search they found a kind family to look after them. They had foreseen war coming. When it broke out the father felt his duty was with his parishioners, and returned, accompanied by his wife. On the journey home the wife gave birth to a son, who remained in Germany and lives there now. The father was sent to Auschwitz camp where he somehow survived the war, only to be killed by an army truck the moment he was released. He had not known that his wife had been killed in an air raid during the war. Sibille was loved and cherished by the English foster parents. She went to Waterperry Horticultural School where she met Pamela Schwerdt, from whom she has not parted. The foster parents died last year and left Sibille a tidy fortune.

Thursday, 27 August

I lunched with Frank Longford, Armstrong and Margaret Willes at Gay Hussar in Greek Street. Delicious and expensive luncheon. I eagerly awaited suggestions for book they are determined I shall write for them, if it is not to be Esher. Their suggestions however quite preposterous. A Memoir of Vita; a History of the Mitford Family; a Biography of Cyril Connolly. Since I have written two enormous vols about Harold and Vita the first is out of the question, especially in view of Victoria Glendinning's forthcoming biog of V. I pointed out what they already knew, that Jonathan Guinness is writing history of Mitfords, and another would neither be welcomed by the family nor was called for.

---

* Pamela Schwerdt and Sibille Kreutzberger, who went to Sissinghurst as head gardeners in 1959.

As for Connolly, I never much liked him and was not qualified to write about an essentially literary figure. A wasted meeting. Nevertheless I liked them all. They explained that the publishers of today could only afford to produce books on subjects widely disseminated on television, such as Royal Wedding, the Mitfords, or Bloomsbury or Nicolson scandals. Deeply depressing.

Friday, 28 August

Rosemary Chaplin, with whom I condoled on the death of Sir Alan Lascelles,[*] said she was sad, but since he had lent her two books which she could not for the life of her find, he being extremely fussy and listing names of borrowers and even asking for return of books after a fortnight, she felt extreme relief. Nevertheless she was reproaching herself for these callous thoughts.

Saturday, 26 September

Chatto's have received a favourable report on my old, knocked-about *Countess and Cardinal* from a great Stuart expert, Professor Kenyon of St Andrews University. To my surprise, they offer to take the book provided I correct, add, amplify and do all the things the learned professor recommends.

Saturday, 3 October

Visited Diana Mosley in London Hospital, Whitechapel.[†] As I entered the ward, she espied me through her open door, and I heard screams of laughter and cries of 'Jim'. D. lay in bed with Pam and Margaret Willes in attendance, looking extremely well, with good colour. Others left and we talked alone for twenty minutes. Her left side, which a fortnight ago was paralysed, is improving. She can

---

[*] Lady Chaplin's late brother, 2nd Viscount Chandos (1920–80), had m. 1949 Caroline, dau. of Sir Alan Lascelles.
[†] She had suffered a stroke (though made an extraordinary recovery and lived for another twenty-two years).

already feel it, and even use the left hand. I gave her a clip-board for letter-writing, with which she seemed pleased.

Tuesday, 6 October

Clarissa [Luke, J.L.-M's stepdaughter] came for the night, looking huge and wizened about the eyes. She is leaving London and her husband Michael for France where she has a twenty-five-year-old lover. A's attitude is too extraordinary. She encourages it. I of course do not criticise, and merely say to myself that the affair will end in tears. Such affairs always do unless they are platonic which I gather this one is not. I told A. that Susanna Johnston was having an affair with a youngish journalist whom we met when lunching with the Johnstons on Sunday. Apparently the Johnston children took against this man and put messages under his pillow saying, 'Please leave our Mummy alone.' Nicky had them up and told them they must allow their mother some romance in her life. A. approved of this story and asked why Michael Luke could not show the same enlightened attitude towards Clarissa. I merely remarked, 'Because he is wildly jealous.' I refrained from pointing out that she had behaved in a similar way towards me in the past, and the not-so-distant past either.

Friday, 9 October

This evening I motored A. to Heathrow whence she embarks for Australia. We dined at the airport and I left to stay with Loelia Lindsay for the weekend. An emotional farewell, both of us almost in tears.

Monday, 12 October

Dined with Sally to see the first instalment of *Brideshead Revisited* on television. It could not have been better. The principal characters – Sebastian Flyte, Charles Ryder and Anthony Blanche – were true to life as I remember their prototypes. Sebastian reminded me of Desmond [Parsons]. Blanche the living spit of Brian Howard.

Wednesday, 21 October

Set off punctually at 8. Folly very miserable; always knows when one is off for the night. Wouldn't eat her breakfast, and lay with her head on my foot, gazing reproachfully at me, while I ate mine. I need not have fussed about distance. Arrived at midday. Stopped on an old bridge within sight of the Old Rectory, Lower Tatham [Lancashire], where the Holts live. The most beautiful country, this. River Wenning rushing below me as only moorland rivers rush. On my left, Hornby Castle, of red sandstone. Landscape like Claude. At 12.30 a car drove up, stopped, and a middle-aged, ex-good looking man said, 'Are you J.L.-M.? I am John Holt. Please come along, and don't wait here.' So I went on. Holts live in a nice rambling old rectory. He very bedint, nice farmer, she rather bedint which surprised me a little, being the daughter of a very well-off squarson and heir of the Thurland estates. She is my third cousin. Also present her first cousin (and again my third) Olive Wilson of Rigmaden, over from Windermere and not the least bedint. All very friendly. Phyllis has no Lees portraits, and what she has in silver, furniture, etc. comes from the Browns, no relations of mine. However she has a miniature of James Lees, our great-great-grandfather, with hair neatly plaited on the back. A duplicate (and rather better) version of Frida Lees's one. They were both very interested in my old Lees album and produced albums of their own. What emerged of interest was that Dora Livesey, who married their grandfather Eric Brown Lees, was one of the little girls beloved of Ruskin. Cousin Olive possesses 150 unpublished letters to her grandmother from Ruskin, also drawings and sketches by Ruskin and by Dora, who was an art student. This discovery would interest some Ruskin scholar, did I but know one.

Phyllis confirmed what my father always told me, that John, her great-grandfather, brother to mine, Joseph,[*] was very eccentric. Had to arrive in the drawing room on, say, his right foot. If he arrived on his left, would go upstairs and start all over again. The process was repeated if he did not succeed the second or third time. The three

---

[*] Joseph Lees (1819–1890); m. 1843 Sarah Anne Milne (their son, the diarist's grandfather James Henry Lees-Milne, being the first bearer of that surname).

Lees brothers, John (hers), the eldest, James (of Alkrington) and Joseph (of Lower Clarksfield, mine) were known as Nimrod, Ramrod and Fishing Rod, after their attributes. They thought of nothing but sport, and my father told me that, left orphans, they defied their tutors, never went to school, and were completely uneducated and philistine. Phyllis let me take away an account in *Oldham Chronicle* of 1864 of her grandfather's coming of age at Upper Clarksfield, filling a whole page of closely printed words. Evidently they were well off for the time, employing 2,000 workmen in the coal mines discovered beneath the Clarksfield estate.

At four I left them and motored across the Pennines to Swaledale, arriving at Marske Old Rectory at twilight. Warmly greeted by Rupert and sweet wife June. She is a darling, simple, good, kind and adoring, a sort of secretary-housekeeper-companion. His fourth wife. He is a lucky man. Rupert little changed in appearance. Still very hale. Wanted to give me his edition of Sassoon's* diaries, but I had brought my own review copy which he wrote an affectionate *dédicace* in. For hours we talked and talked about books and writing. He told me that the 'P.' in the diaries, the second lover of Siegfried, was Prince Philipp of Hesse,† Harold's friend, with whom they were all in Rome in 1921 when the affair started. Since the Prince is still alive – must be ancient – Rupert did not spell out his name. Rupert told me he is about to sell his library complete, subject to a life interest, to an American university. They have offered him £250,000 which he does not think enough. His condition is that the books are kept together, representing a unique collection published within half a century or more.

Sunday, 25 October

M. rang last night that he was going to buy the Sunday papers at midnight to read reviews of H.N. Vol. II. I told him not to bother as there

---

* Siegfried Sassoon (1886–1967); poet and writer.
† Philipp, Prince and Landgrave of Hesse (1896–1980); art-loving great-grandson of Queen Victoria who became a prominent Nazi but spent the last two years of the Second World War in captivity after the defection of the King of Italy, his father-in-law, to the Allies.

would be none. Today I went to church at 9.15 and just before I left to take Diana W. to lunch with Nan Bernays, Freda Berkeley rang to say there was a rave review in *Sunday Times*, another in *Observer*. *Sunday Times* review by Michael Howard ends, 'If there has been a better biography in the past fifty years, I would like to know which it is.' This evening I heard from Victoria Glendinning, Frankie Donaldson, Bamber, Rachel and Nan Bernays (to whom I sent copy because of frequent mentions of her Rob), all telephoning to congratulate. Very cheering. M. as thrilled as I am.

Wednesday, 28 October

The picture of Rupert at Marske is ever before me, in his armchair, semi-recumbent, right foot on a gout stool *à la* Lord Holland, June crouching beside him as though eager to do his slightest bidding, I in the visitors' chair opposite him, in his long library, the only library I know which is literally lined with books on all four walls from floor to ceiling. Not an inch of space for a picture. He told me that last year he published four books, this year three. Amongst other things he told me that he was considering destroying the diaries of Duff Cooper (his uncle) which were left to him. He said they contain nothing that redounds to his reputation. Mostly snippets of his affairs with women, going into unnecessary detail. Little about politics or literature. Of no value. Thought John Julius, who stood to inherit them with other papers of his father, might be distressed and shocked. What should he do? I said that as a rule I was strongly against the destruction of papers. Not having seen the diaries, my opinion could not be of much use. But my answer would be no, don't destroy.*

Tuesday, 3 November

Dined with Alex Moulton at Bradford. Made him watch *Brideshead Revisited* on TV. He kept interrupting with questions. Are those young

---

* John Julius Norwich persuaded his uncle not to destroy the diaries but to hand them over to him, and edited them for publication by Weidenfeld & Nicolson in 2005.

men meant to be in love? Why does Sebastian dislike his mother? I was very bored by Alex this evening. Throughout dinner he told me that he was about to administer chastisement in his role as President of the Bradford-on-Avon Preservation Society to the members at their AGM, some of them having criticised his work on re-roofing the Hall. He said he would tell them they were ignorant people with no taste. I told him he could not possibly behave like this. Besides he has absolutely no taste himself.

Wednesday, 4 November

Motored to Oxford this afternoon. Met M. and Charles Orwin at station. They took me to tea with some young men in Holywell. All very polite and charming to me, but I find such encounters awkward. We went on to the Bodleian, to a party given by Granada Television for an exhibition (costumes and photographs) of the *Brideshead Revisited* serial. I was asked because I suggested Castle Howard to them. Greeted by the producer, Derek Grainger. Talked to the young director, and a few of the cast who were present – not unfortunately including Charles Ryder and Sebastian Flyte. Talked to Count Nikolai Tolstoy* about his *Stalin's Secret War*. Liked him. He is prim and Edwardian, wearing high-cut waistcoat and watch-chain. Said his father had escaped from Russia in 1922 at age of nine. I told him that this very morning I had selected his book as one of my three choices for the year. Dropped M. in Hyde Park Square and C. in Exhibition Road. Latter parted rather emotionally because he was returning to an empty flat, having had a break with his lover.

Thursday, 5 November

Victoria Glendinning lunched with me at Como Lario. Much enjoyed our talk. She wanted to know whether Harold was aware of

---

* Count Nikolai Tolstoy (b. 1935); English-born writer of Russian *émigré* origin, who in 1989 lost a famous libel action after alleging that the British politician Lord Aldington had knowingly repatriated Russian prisoners-of-war to their deaths in 1945.

the true cause of Vita's muzziness. I told her I was sure he knew about the sherry addiction but that he would not admit it even to his diary. She told me that Vita did not by any means always tell Harold the truth about her affairs. Had more than he ever knew of. Victoria herself has never experienced the twinges of lesbianism or written about a lesbian before. I said I hoped she liked V. She assured me that she did, and hotly defended her against her critics. She is not going to mention the word 'snob'. We embraced warmly on parting. She wants to see A. alone. Quite right.

Saturday, 7 November

John K.-B. came at midday and stayed until 5.30. We walked around the park, the dogs on leads, for hounds in the distance were drawing Apsley Wood. John had never been to Essex House before. He went around looking carefully at everything. Said that if ever by mischance I should be widowed, he would look after me. We have now known each other twenty-three years. He is fifty, the age (as he reminded me) I was when we first met.

Sunday, 22 November

A week ago I collected A. from Heathrow at 8 a.m. I was late because her plane from Sydney arrived one hour in advance of scheduled time. Having parked the car I went into a seething mass of brown, black and yellow arrivals. Just heard tail-end of a message to me. Then saw a figure waving. My first sight of A. a great shock. I saw a white-faced, drawn old lady. This separation of five weeks is the longest we have had in our thirty years. I was very upset, and still am by her appearance. True, she was full of spirit, having enjoyed the tour immensely, and on the way home chatted like one possessed. And this I think explains what happened to her so soon afterwards. Before evening she had collapsed with exhaustion and developed a high temperature. Bronchitis, her dreaded ailment, had developed.

On Thursday, although she was by no means fit, she had reduced her temperature, and insisted on coming to London in order to see the Denis Thatcher play* for which I had got tickets – this day (19th) being the thirtieth anniversary of our marriage. We meant to go and come back in the day. I had Selina Hastings to lunch with me. Delicious luncheon, delicious girl. Not beautiful, but a sparkling face, lovely skin and huge, liquid, enquiring eyes. Much talk about the Mitfords. She says that Nancy's letters to Palewski make very pathetic reading, letters of pleading, ungovernable love on her part. I'm glad I don't have to read them.

A. picked me up and took me to Brooks's where we had a rather nasty and expensive dinner. On to Whitehall Theatre. Then arose the awful business of parking. Having dropped A. at the theatre I desperately drove round and round blocks of ministerial buildings. Finally I found an empty place at end of a dreary street and rushed back to theatre. When the play was over – a rather unfunny farce – it was pouring with rain. I had no umbrella. Went in search of car. Could not find it. Gone. Returned to now emptied theatre where poor A. was hugging herself and coughing her heart out on pavement. Told her car either impounded or stolen. We went to West Central Police Station where a nice, efficient sergeant policewoman, to whom I gave number of car from my pocket diary, pressed buttons, rang bells, and declared that no such car had been impounded and it must therefore be stolen. By now A. was shivering with cold and misery. We telephoned the Berkeleys, mercifully just returned from dining out, and they said we might both stay night with them. All our belongings were in the car. Then I said, perhaps I was mistaken in the street, so at enormous cost we got taxi to take us back to Whitehall. There was the car all the time in a street parallel to the one I had gone to earlier, intact. By now it was after midnight and we went to the Berkeleys. A. has been very good about this lamentable evidence of my senility.

Last night I felt so tired, dispirited and drained that I wondered if death was near at hand. When people say with astonishment of someone that he died suddenly without warning, having been talking and laughing three hours earlier, that signifies nothing. He may well have felt drained, worn out, exhausted, but was able, as we

---

* *Anyone for Denis?*, written by and starring John Wells.

all are, to rouse himself to make a final social effort before giving up the ghost.

Sunday, 29 November

Had a lovely visit to London this past week, staying with Eardley whom I had not seen for seven weeks, since slight coldness on my part over his refusal to have me and dogs to stay at The Slade. M. lunched on return from Paris, looking gummy-eyed because he will stay up at night and rise at midday. But a joy to see him, and we talked in Brooks's library till 3.30. I went on to exhibition of Julian Barrow* in St James's. He there standing in a corner. Every single painting sold. A highly competent and intelligible painter, like Graham Rust, and consequently popular. Wish I had bought agreeable picture of Beckford's House, Lansdown Crescent.

Walked to tea with Diana Mosley in Debo's house, 4 Chesterfield Street. Amazed how well she seems to be. She was wearing a snood over head, just a touch of hair growing over the forehead, as she had to be shaved for operation. We talked about Tom [Mosley] whose papers she is sorting through before selling to Warwick University. Before I left Nicky Ravensdale† came. Nice middle-aged greying man. Is writing memoir of his father of whom he is palpably fond though not liking his politics. There ensued an interesting conversation about Fascism which I had never before had with Diana. I told her I could not stomach those dreadful pre-war Albert Hall meetings, with Tom in black uniform, lights trained on him, him declaiming like Mussolini. Her explanation was that the sort of people to whom he was trying to get his message across liked uniforms, were sentimental, enjoyed the drama and could only be reached by ranting oratory. The accompanying thugs were a necessary bodyguard for without them

---

* Artist (b. 1939), who was to paint several excellent portraits of J.L.-M.
† Nicholas Mosley, 3rd Baron Ravensdale (b. 1923); e.s. of Sir Oswald Mosley by his 1st marriage to Lady Cynthia Curzon (through whom, in 1966, he inherited the Ravensdale peerage created for his grandfather, Marquess Curzon of Kedleston); novelist, whose two volumes on his father, *Rules of the Game* and *Beyond the Pale*, were published in 1982 and 1983.

he would never have been heard. They were there to eject the Communist rowdies sent to break up every meeting. I suppose some truth in this. She said that those of his contemporaries still alive agree he was right in all his prognostications. He was a great thinker. He would walk alone round the Temple, working out projects in his mind. He thought more than he read. Moreover he bore no resentment against his critics. He was in that sense a big man. Ravensdale occasionally took out a notebook and jotted down. She says the office is still in being. Doing what? I asked. Issuing literature, including a regular magazine, *Action*.

Delicious evening at Eardley's with Richard [Shone]. I went and bought odd assortment of cold food in Sloane Street and E. provided wine and did the work. Always hilarity with Richard and amusing and edifying conversation. The following day, Friday, spent the morning at Hayward Gallery at Lutyens Exhibition. Very well displayed but exhibits of architects' work necessarily difficult, for a mass of photographs becomes boring. But furniture and objects interspersed. I can't take those early Lutyens Great West Road suburban villas with half-timbered gables and inglenooks. His versatility and maverick qualities were a weakness I think. Upstairs an exhibition of paintings of the old Sickert. Marvellous full-length of Edward VIII in Welsh Guards uniform, carrying bearskin, stepping out of Buck Palace with harassed, still youthful face. The usual number of coruscating mud canvases. A smiling full-length of Gavin Faringdon descending stairs, and a horrifying one of ghastly Lord Castlerosse.[*] Richard told story of Lady Astor[†] meeting Castlerosse at a party, tapping his stomach and saying, 'If that were on a woman what would they be saying?' To which C. replied, 'It was on a woman last night. And what *were* they saying?'

Ros lunched with me at Como Lario. Usual table. She told me something which upset me very much, namely that, two years ago,

---

[*] Valentine Browne, Viscount Castlerosse (1891–1943); son and heir of 5th Earl of Kenmare (whom he s. as 6th Earl, 1941); gossip columnist.

[†] Nancy Langhorne (1879–1964); m. (2nd) 1906 Waldorf, 2nd Viscount Astor; campaigner for Christian Science and other causes, and the first woman MP to take her seat in the House of Commons.

A. wrote an accusing letter to M. which he immediately took to Ros for advice on how to answer. She emphatically said that she dictated his reply, which was to the effect that he was not behaving in a way which could possibly harm her marriage and saw no reason not to continue seeing me. I said to Ros, 'But this is awful. Most young men of 26 would have been terrified away. It is a miracle that he still does see and correspond with me.' On my return to Badminton I found A. suffering much from bronchitis, but so upset was I that I fear I could not be as affectionate and solicitous as I should have been.

Monday, 30 November

Selina Hastings, who knows Brian Masters well, told me his life story. He is the illegitimate child of a barmaid in Whitechapel. The father a bus driver. The mother saw from the first that the child wanted to learn. She managed to send him to a good grammar school. He got the required grades and did well. He managed to meet Gilbert Harding* who took to him, practically adopted him and taught him how to speak. Hence his almost perfect accent. To Harding he owes nearly everything, probably also a small legacy. For he owns a house in Kensington where he takes in lodgers in an inefficient way. There is a woman who is in love with him, and a Spanish waiter with whom Brian is in love – the unshaven, dark, silent youth we met at Peggy Munster's. He is terribly jealous of Brian and won't allow his friends to the house. Selina has somehow gained entry. She is fond of Brian who, she is sure, is a masochist. Brian always wanted to mix with society people in high life, something he has achieved. They like him and he likes them.†

---

* Gilbert Harding (1907–60), the first British television star, famous for his sparkling wit and his belligerent manner. In private life, he was notorious for his rudeness, drunkenness and homosexuality.
† Brian Masters is content, on literary grounds, for this entry to be published as it was written, but points out that some of its details are inaccurate. He is in fact the legitimate son of a family in domestic service in Camberwell; it was his father who was the illegitimate son of a bus driver. He received no legacy from Harding.

Tuesday, 8 December

Went to tea with Hilary Spurling* in Ladbroke Grove, walking there from Notting Hill station as I used to years ago. For the first time since Jamesey's death saw his No. 9. It is still empty, very melancholy, sinister in fact, with a For Sale board between the windows. Walked up the Grove to No. 48. Thought this mid-Victorian house seemed familiar. It was Dame Una Pope-Hennessy's.† She moved there on the General's death in the war, as an impoverished widow. Yet she lived in the whole house. Now the Spurlings have two floors. Mrs Spurling has had three children since I last saw her and she published Vol. I of her Ivy Compton-Burnett book. Her immediate interest now is Margaret Jourdain. Margaret was the daughter of a poor parson. It was expected of her to become a governess. Family disapproval alienated her. Lived for years with old mother, earning perhaps £40 a year writing articles. Always wanted to be a writer even after she had won renown as a furniture expert. Happily she met Ivy just after Great War. Ivy had some money. Thereafter she was free of money worries. Hilary went to see Joan Evans, sent by me. Joan told her why she detested Ivy. Reason that Ivy took Margaret from her and poisoned M.J. against Joan, who apparently, though younger, expected M.J. to live with her. There must have been strong latent lesbian tendencies among these bluestocking ladies, though Hilary S. is sure that I.C.-B. and M.J. were never lovers in the rude sense.

Saturday, 12 December

A severe spell of cold weather. Much snow and frost. Tony Mitchell was to have taken me to Kingston Lacy‡ yesterday but decided it was unwise. Today a beautiful morning with sun and we risked it. Roads all right, but severely cold. Spent afternoon in house. Of course the

---

* Writer and critic (b. 1940).
† Dame Una Pope-Hennessy (1876–1949); writer, mother of John and James, of whom J.L.-M. had seen much during the 1940s.
‡ House in Dorset, recently left to N.T. together with its contents and park; built by Sir Roger Pratt for Sir Ralph Bankes, 1663–5; cased in stone and altered by Sir Charles Barry, 1835–41.

original, Pratt building quite overlaid by Barry. The Barry work very interesting in its own right, notably the grand staircase. For how much was he himself responsible? Architectural drawings of his survive in the archives room. In the library Tony produced folios of Bankes's* drawings of Egyptian monuments, very good, in colour. An interesting character who might merit a book – Byron's friend and correspondent (much of the correspondence still unpublished), traveller in Middle East, amateur architect, had to leave the country for 'the usual' [*i.e.*, homosexuality]. I am interested. Important pictures in bad condition. In acreage, this is one of the largest properties left to the Trust.

Tuesday, 15 December

We lunched at the French Embassy in Kensington Palace Gardens. Lovely house, huge red and gold reception rooms. Charming Madame de Margerie.† About twenty-four guests. Our names on cards in front hall. I sat between Lady Antonia Pinter and Joan Haslip,‡ who is writing life of Marie Antoinette. Lady A. has beautiful fair complexion and lovely piercing blue eyes. I liked her. Her next book about notable seventeenth-century women. She told me she did not use the services of a researcher, but was once helped by Anne Somerset whom she described as a clever girl. The Stephen Spenders present and friendly. He said he had taken some splendid photographs of me when we met at Rory's for Christmas three years back. We agreed it was a mistake to read reviews of our books.

Dashed away before coffee to N.T. Properties Committee, item which concerned me not yet reached. This was Kingston Lacy. But there was no need for me to raise my voice and plead. Committee agreed without dissent to recommend acceptance.

---

* William John Bankes (1786–1855); art collector, traveller and (until obliged to resign his seat and live abroad) Member of Parliament.
† Hélène Hottinguer; m. 1953 Emmanuel ('Bobbie') de Margerie (1924–91; son of Roland de Margerie – see 3 May 1980), French Ambassador to London, 1981–4, and Washington, 1984–7.
‡ Writer (1912–94); her biography of Marie Antoinette was published in 1987.

Jonathan Guinness* came to Brooks's at 5.30 to talk about Mitfords for his book. Chiefly wanted to know about Tom [Mitford], the mystery figure he barely knew. Said that when he was a child of eight, Tom was deputed to take him for a walk. He made no concessions, treated J. as an adult, did not slacken speed. The child became exhausted and fell behind. When asked on return whether the walk a success, T. replied not really, Jonathan lagged behind and conversation was uninteresting. J. thinks Tom was the lynchpin of the family who kept the sisters together and that only after his death did they drift into camps. Not quite true, for their fanatical and opposing political views were not the cause of their differences. We talked about the two grandfathers, Lord Redesdale and Tommy Gibson-Bowles. I liked Jonathan immensely. He is over fifty, round-faced, a little faded, with bushy, thick hair flying Einstein-like from his brows. Great charm, like all Diana's sons; welcoming, affable. We were talking happily in the Library when at 7 the hall porter approached me with 'Madam is waiting in the car outside.' This 'Madam' nowadays very old-fashioned. Was sorry to part from him. I think I was right to tell him that Tom had a limited sense of humour, was inclined to be morose, moody, caviare-to-the-general, disliked people, but dearly loved his friends to whom his loyalty was touching.

Friday, 18 December

At breakfast A. said to me that during the night she had a vivid dream that Anthony [Chaplin] was dying. She was with him. She was very upset. It is true that Clarissa [Luke] had telephoned yesterday that he had had a relapse. Then at 9 a.m. Clarissa telephoned again to say Anthony had died in the night. A. replied, 'It was at twenty minutes to three?' Clarissa confirmed that that was the time, the very moment A. awoke from her dream. They talked, then poor A. turned away and wept. I wept too. She apologised. I said, 'But it is not wrong, to shed a tear for those we have loved.' Poor Anthony. Never has there been a

---

* Hon. Jonathan Guinness (b. 1930); e.s. of Diana Mosley by her 1st marriage to Bryan Guinness, 2nd Baron Moyne (whom he succeeded as 3rd Baron, 1992); author, with Catherine Guinness, of *The House of Mitford* (1984).

more wasted life. He was gifted, clever, well-informed. But intolerably idle, disorganised, opinionated, unwilling to enter public life. Never took his seat in the Lords where he could have spoken for the causes he had at heart – music, wildlife, botany. He is the last of the Chaplins. He achieved little. I may be wrong for he did compose a cadenza or two for Mozart operas, and he may have discovered some unknown species of creature in the Far East, which discovery may be registered at the Zoo. Not only did he play the piano very well, but he painted birds with talent. He could have achieved so much; that is what is so sad. He was one of those endowed with that fatal charm. The last time I saw him he was exercising it. 'How is our wife', he asked, 'which art in Heaven?' How well did he know that within a month he would be there himself? For I am sure he will go there after a minimum of purgatory.

Sunday, 27 December

Spent our usual Christmas at Parkside with the Droghedas. Derry, Alexandra and Burnet [Pavitt] present. The Moores not getting on well with the parents; little tearful scenes and misunderstandings. On Christmas Day we went to St George's Chapel. This time we were given seats in the front row of the nave, I on the end seat of the central gangway, next to the inserted stone with inscription recording the Duke of Windsor's lying-in-state on that spot. When the Royal Family left by the West Door I was within spitting distance. Queen wearing hideous turquoise blue dress, Prince of Wales with scar on left cheek, Duke of Edinburgh shorter than I had supposed, and lined. Princess Pushy of Kent, as they call her, in hideous hat. Prince Michael's beard a mistake. Princess of Wales sweet. Old Duchess of Gloucester a sweet, shrunken old lady. After chapel we had a drink at Adelaide Cottage with Sir John Johnston and his wife. He a good-looking, frank, decent sort of chap. She has a vocal chord missing. Daughter of Alec Hardinge of Penshurst. These royal posts are hereditary, which is quite right for they are born to courtiership. She collects nineteenth-century photograph frames. Has forest of them, mostly filled with present-day royalties. Adelaide Cottage built by Nash, *cottage orné* all right with bargeboards and verandah. Pretty outside. Nothing left inside.

On Boxing Day Sir Robin Mackworth-Young, wife and handsome doctor son came. Sir Robin asked me what I was writing next. This gave me the opportunity to remind him what he had forgotten, namely the snub he administered to me when I asked for permission to see the Stuart papers. He excused himself by saying that they had to be particular not to let random writers have access to the Queen's papers, but I would be a different matter, etc. So now I have only to write to him formally. Have written all this to M. who will consider me a traitor.

Joan, I fear, is verging on senility. She hears badly and cannot concentrate. Is too intent on being agreeable, appearing to be responsive while not listening to what one is saying. So sad when I remember how bright and on the spot she used to be. She has become like Anne Rosse.

On our return the telephone rang. A. answered and told me that a Mr Haines wanted to speak to me. At once I guessed what had happened. He said, 'I have some bad news to tell you, Sir. Mother passed away on Christmas Eve.' Poor old darling, she was ninety-two. As Audrey says, that is the last link with Wickhamford broken. And if they do go ahead with the outrageous scheme of wrecking the manor we need never go near the place again. Unfortunately I love the church. Sad though I am at Mrs H's death, having known her all my life – she was a housemaid at the manor when I was born – I was made sadder by reading of the death of Patrick O'Donovan. He was in my company in the Irish Guards, likewise a platoon commander. He was the only friend I had in those dismal, wretched days. Ten years younger than I, he was gay, amusing, amused, very bright and clever, always with a smile and giggle. A pious Catholic, yet ready to laugh at his religion. He really was adorable, and as queer as a coot in those days. I remember him telling me that, while he stood at the salute of the King and Queen at the Victory Parade, the upper part of his body out of his tank, his soldier servant was fellating him below. He married very happily soon after I believe. Poor Paddy, he was entrancing with his ugly, jolly face, his gallantry, piety, humour and good brain. He became a very successful journalist. I remember his worry about what to do when the war was over, and his delight when the *Observer* took him on. He hadn't a penny then.

This year has been a fairly productive one. *Harold Nicolson* Vol. II has been published. So have my contribution to *Places*, edited by Ronald Blyth, my entry on Nancy Mitford for the *DNB*, which I shall not live to see, my piece on Henry Green for an American magazine, my article on Worcestershire for the *Illustrated London News*, and several reviews for *Book Choice* and *Apollo*. Also I have written three books in a manner of speaking – *Images of Bath* for Bamber Gascoigne's series, *An Anthology of Country Houses* for OUP, and a third volume of my diaries, to be called *Caves of Ice*, 1946 and 1947, for Chatto's. I think it is far less entertaining than the previous diaries; lacks sparkle, contains too many pedestrian descriptions of houses visited for the National Trust, with in-filling of gossip about people met. Then there are the occasional items of a private nature. How much should I disclose? I feel they may embarrass A. Besides, is it of interest to mention that one went to bed with so-and-so thirty-five years ago without an account of the affair or even of the actual experience? And I was not in love during these two years. That is the difference. Love is one thing to write about, lust another, and the latter is uninteresting unless the circumstances are amusing, horrifying or titillating, my affairs having been none of these things.

1982

1982

On the way to Mrs Haines's funeral, I kept thinking incongruously of Anthony Chaplin. He has been dead three weeks and is already forgotten. One short succinct account of his life in *The Times*. No follow-up, no appreciation of his musical talents by Lennox Berkeley or William Glock. And Anthony was a thinker, not a doer. What did he think about? He pondered as Shakespeare must have done the awful destinies of life and death, without conviction, without faith. His love and understanding of animals, his discoveries of their means of living and dying, are unrecorded. It is as if he had never been.

Then I reached the Cheltenham Crematorium, that ghastly place where I attended services of my father, my mother, and old Haines himself. I had been thinking so deeply about Anthony that I failed to leave the motorway at Gloucester, went on to Tewkesbury and had to return to Prestbury. Anyway I was in time, and joined Simon* who came over. We entered that empty, hospital-like waiting room, boiling hot from radiators hidden, no furniture or pictures, only seats and a central table with copies of *The Casket*, such jolly reading under the circs. I rootled out an undertaker to whom I gave my sorry wreath made in Wotton, some mimosa and chrysanthemum tied with yellow ribbon. Then we were called as though to enter Concorde at Heathrow. The previous funeral was over, its cortège driving to the far end of the cemetery for burial. No burial for Mrs Haines. Simon and I followed a handful of mourners of this 92-year-old woman and sat in a back pew, or rather bench of yellow pitchpine. All clinically clean. On the bench in front of mine was a small, screwed-up handkerchief of floral pattern, left by a mourner at the previous ceremony.

---

* J.L-M's nephew Simon Lees-Milne.

A whirring noise was of scented disinfectant from the roof, probably needed since poor Mrs H. died a fortnight ago. Service sheets much thumbed and soiled, protruding from hideous plastic covers. 'The Lord is my Shepherd' of course, intoned by parson and congregation alternately. Only I raised my voice and answered responses. Then the clergyman, a nice man, gave a short address, or rather read out basic facts about Mrs Haines – born 92 years ago, daughter of a Badsey market gardener, lived all her life at Wickhamford, her husband chauffeur of L.-M. family. He praised her sense of duty, her knitting garments for troops in both wars, her public spirit, her friendliness, her charity. When I remember how uncharitable the dear old thing was to her neighbours, refusing to speak to the nice Leathers family who for twenty years lived in the other part of her semi-detached cottage at Wickhamford. We filed out. Jackie Haines has developed a nice, rather good face, but his sister Peggy, whom I remember as the prettiest, most blooming girl, is now tiny and wizened with bad false teeth. Shook hands with them all, murmured words of sympathy, received murmured words of thanks, and that will be all. Shall I ever see them again? Mrs H. has left me Barraclough's portrait of my mother which I shall have to fetch one day.

Wednesday, 13 January

Unable to motor to Bath, the road still absolutely blocked. I resent not being able to work. Yet am paralysed with cold. We have experienced one of the coldest spells ever known. One night the temperature dropped to minus forty. Twice the pipes in my bathroom burst. One evening in London I walked to the Berkeleys' in Warwick Avenue and arrived suffering, I believe, from hypothermia. I could not speak, and did not know where I was; felt almost in a state of coma. I have learnt since that this happens to the old who ought always to keep extremities warm.

Sunday, 24 January

I seem to have unconsciously told myself that I cannot live much longer and therefore should not bother to try cures for my arthritis and deafness. I will just manage to last out. Whereas twenty years ago I would bother lest I became totally crippled before old age set in. Similarly I cannot be bothered to learn things which twenty years ago I would have considered worth the effort. For instance, the typewriter shop where I have my machines serviced pressed me to use an electric machine and even gave me one to take away on trial. But I could not manage it. Am too accustomed to banging away. The touch required for the electric is so light that the keys depress themselves almost before one fingers them. This machine is of course easier and more satisfactory and less tiring if one can learn to master it, but I cannot be bothered.

Thursday, 28 January

Last night I had two dreams which I remembered, a rare thing. One was that I had broken my wrist watch. The whole of the works had fallen out. Only a fragment of glass still stuck to the rim. This distressed me very much until I remembered that I had a spare watch. The other was that I was abroad and realised with horror that I had another fortnight before I could return home, and hated being away. Both dreams are concerned with M., I think. For yesterday I went to London to see him and hand him my diaries to read. I booked a table at a Jermyn Street restaurant and waited. A message came that he would be twenty minutes late. By the time he arrived the restaurant had become extremely noisy and hot. I felt uncomfortable and could not hear. He ate little and drank nothing and left after an hour, saying he had to see his publishers. I paid the bill and walked to the London Library, feeling very unhappy. This meeting is the first unsatisfactory one we have had. Through his sensitive politeness I detected boredom. He said he would telephone today. He hasn't, which is unlike him. I ask myself what this relationship is bringing either of us. If we are only to have infrequent meetings in uncomfortable and noisy restaurants, it may be better not to meet at all but only write and telephone. What I think upset me most yesterday was the information that he is going to Paris again next week. I rebuked him for waltzing off at this moment when his publishers are clamouring for his manuscript, but my rebukes do not irk him.

Sunday, 31 January

Of course the dear reliable creature telephoned two days running. On the second occasion he said he had read one-third of my new diary and liked it. This has cheered me. Strange how much I depend on him, how much I love him with a love which is totally unphysical and wholly platonic.

I motored Audrey yesterday to Wickhamford to tea with Jack Haines and wife, both charming. In spite of Jackie's success in life as centre-forward for England, he still addresses me as Sir or Mr Jim, and Audrey as Miss Audrey or Madam. Audrey and I later agreed we were embarrassed by such address today, but in this particular case thought it best not to invite them to address us by our christian names, which might embarrass them. Anyway, Audrey and Jack embraced warmly on parting. I asked Audrey how well she knew her son-in-law James Sutton, who stays four nights a week with her. She said she didn't think she really knew anyone. 'And I don't suppose I know you really,' she added rather sadly.

Wednesday, 10 February

June and Jeremy Hutchinson told us they had dined at 10 Downing Street, Mrs Thatcher having expressed a wish to meet the heads of the various national museums and galleries, Jeremy being Chairman of the Tate. Jeremy went with an open mind, prepared to like Mrs T. although disapproving of her policy. But it was difficult to do so. She was like a steam-roller. He wished to ask some questions, but she never drew breath or gave him an opportunity of putting them. After dinner she conducted them round the house and showed them her private apartments. Even there she interrupted relentlessly the moment he tried to speak. Jeremy says she totally lacks charm, though Mr T. does have some – he stood with his right hand behind his back motioning to a waiter to put a fresh glass of whisky into it. And Alex Moulton who likewise has recently been to 10 Downing Street, and is a fervent supporter of Mrs T., admitted she was charmless. But he admired her grasp of the matter – in this case, design in industry – for in taking the chair she knew her stuff exactly and what she wanted to get from the meeting. Above all he was impressed by her patriotism.

Gervase Jackson-Stops lunched with me at Brooks's yesterday. He thinks it an admirable idea that I should write a biography of W. J. Bankes. From the latter's letters to his father which he has seen in the library of Kingston Lacy he believes him to have had a fascinating mind. Gervase also asked me to write an introduction to a book about how writers have been influenced by their houses and vice versa. Must be N.T. properties of course. He is getting John Lehmann to write on the Woolfs and Monk's House, Tony Powell on Kipling and Bateman's, Lord Blake on Disraeli and Hughenden, David Cecil on Coleridge's house, etc.

Saturday, 20 February

On Tuesday last A. and I motored to London for the day. I had my [N.T.] Properties Committee in the afternoon, and Johnnie Churchill to lunch with me beforehand at Brooks's. He was very sweet and affectionate, much calmer, drinking less, and a little pitiable in that he does not make much money from his painting and has not received much acclaim. But is resigned and philosophical. Talked of old days, his father and mother. Says his father was always supposed to be the son of some Edwardian called Jocelyn. So, said J., I ought really to be the 10th Earl of Roden. After the Committee I slipped away in order to see a German film at the ICA* called *Taxi zum Klo*, strongly recommended by Alex [Moulton]. John Cornforth left the meeting at the same time and *would* stick to me like a leech. I had to pretend I was going to the Travellers. Finally shook him off and descended Duke of York's steps to ICA premises. The film was appalling – about a queer Berlin schoolmaster and his doings off-duty. Nothing left to the imagination. When it came to the anti-hero being examined for syphilis by a hospital doctor I thought I would be sick. Left and fled to Brooks's. There met Giles Eyre† and told him of my experience. He had also been to see it and

---

* The Institute of Contemporary Arts in the Mall, showing *avant-garde* films.
† Dealer in watercolours and art critic (1922–2006).

reacted exactly as I had done. Gave me a stiff whisky and soda to recover. Am I being oversensitive, hypocritical, prudish? I felt degraded, debased and embarrassed. I am, all things considered, a romantic. When I told M. over the telephone of my disgust over the film he said, 'I told you not to go to it. Why do you never do what I tell you?'

Sunday, 7 March

On Friday two young men came to see me about the early days of the Georgian Group – John Martin Robinson and Gavin Stamp.[†] Apparently I am the last living person to have attended the first committee meeting in 1937.[‡] They are devoting a whole issue of the *Architect's Journal* to the Group and asked me dozens of questions about my colleagues. Both tremendous admirers of Robert Byron and regard me as a phenomenon for having known him so well. They *would* take photographs of me. I hate it, and put on a self-conscious face, try as I may not to.

Saturday, 13 March

Rory Cameron told A. this story. Friends of his in New York went out to dinner, leaving their son, aged 12, behind in their apartment. They said to him, 'If anyone rings the bell, do not open the door.' Within an hour the doorbell rang. The 12-year-old opened it. An 18-year-old entered and said, 'Hand me the keys to the safe.' 'All right,' said the 12-year-old, who opened a drawer, drew out his father's revolver and shot the 18-year-old dead. Then telephoned his parents who had left their number with him. He said, 'Mummy, I have shot a man.' She replied, 'What nonsense, go back to bed.' The parents' hosts said, 'Perhaps you had better return to see what has happened.' On their return they found that the 18-year-old was the son of their hosts.

---

[*] Architectural historian (b. 1948).

[†] The Group (which still flourishes) had been founded in 1937 under the aegis of the Society for the Protection of Ancient Buildings. J. L.-M. was not in fact the last survivor of the original committee: two others, John Betjeman and John Summerson, were then still alive.

Wednesday, 17 March

At six went to New Zealand House in Haymarket for Hatchards' Authors-of-the-Year Party, which the Queen and Prince Philip attended. Lovely view over London at dusk from topmost floor, walls of which are of glass. But too hot, so I dared not drink. Knew few people there, but Mark Bonham Carter[*] most friendly. For Collins apparently own Hatchards. I stood next to a man who greeted me and said, 'I saw quite a lot of you at Rainbirds when we produced your St Peter's book. My name is . . .', which I didn't hear. I said brightly, 'Of course I remember you well,' and we talked. Then I said, 'Do tell me, does John Hadfield still have anything to do with Rainbirds? Is he even alive?' 'But I am John Hadfield,' he answered. I tried to pass it off by explaining that I was extremely deaf.

We stood in a circle, the Queen brought round. She spoke to little groups. When my turn came Mark Bonham Carter mentioned my name which meant nothing to her. She said, 'Are you an author? I thought I was to meet authors and most of those I have talked to don't seem to be.' I said, 'Yes, I suppose I can call myself one, Ma'am.' 'And what books, what are you . . .?' she began. So seeing she needed help I explained that I had recently written a biography of Sir Harold Nicolson. 'Such an interesting man,' she said, 'but it must have been an uphill struggle?' 'It wasn't so much a struggle as rather onerous,' I replied, 'because of the quantity of letters the Nicolsons wrote to each other, all of which I had to read through.' Then we talked about letters. She asked if I kept them. I said I kept a great many, and couldn't bear to throw away ones I thought might be interesting or amusing. Then Mark B. C. joined in, 'And do you keep letters, Ma'am?' 'Oh yes, a lot,' she said; and to me, 'But do you re-read them?' I said I seldom did because I found it sad work. 'Oh, I don't find it sad,' she said. And I, rather cheekily, 'Well, Ma'am, you are so much younger than I am. But most of the letters I have kept are from dead friends.' Then a few more *politesses* and she passed on. But what I found was that, far from being stuffy or awkward, she was bright, extremely natural, and rather funny.

---

[*] Mark Raymond Bonham Carter (1920–94); Liberal politician, publisher, and first Chairman (1966–70) of Race Relations Board; cr. life peer, 1986.

I would far prefer to sit next to her than the Q. Mother. There is none of that sugary insincerity in the Queen. She is absolutely direct. V. dignified notwithstanding. Face to face she is good-looking, with that wonderful complexion. Was wearing a purple two-piece with high collar of black velvet, pearls and diamond brooch. I have a great 'up' on her.

Did not enjoy party otherwise, and hastened away as soon as the royal couple left.

Monday, 29 March

To London for the night to dine with Elizabeth [Cavendish] and John Betj[eman]. Lately I have had a hunch that John will not last long. Indeed tonight I was shocked by his condition. When I arrived, he was sitting in his usual chair under the window of No. 19, his belly swollen and prominent. Not his usual self, but quieter than usual. No guffaws of laughter, and when amused he gave a funny little half-snigger, half-grunt as though it were painful for him to laugh outright. But I tried to cheer him. He began by reciting a new poem he was writing: 'Sir Christopher Wren/ Was dining with some men/ He said "If anyone calls/ Say I'm building St Paul's." '* 'No, you have not got it right, love,' said Elizabeth. Moving him to table for dinner was a great effort. She walked backwards, holding his outstretched hands. He groaned, as though with pain, and moved to the table in a kind of dancing movement like an old bear. It was rather piteous. Talked of Gavin Stamp. I said how nice he was and clever. J. said he was a very good writer and had a column in *Private Eye* on architecture, under assumed name. J. said he (John) was only interested in young men. Wanted to go to bed with them. This did make him laugh outright. I said, 'We must get used to the fact that this is impossible now.' Talked of David Linley,† Feeble's godson. A true Messel, he is a craftsman who designs and makes furniture with his own hands. Thinks of nothing else. This is good.

---

* Garbled version of well-known lines by E. Clerihew Bentley.
† David Armstrong-Jones, Viscount Linley (b. 1961); o.s. of Princess Margaret and 1st Earl of Snowdon; furniture designer; m.1993 Hon. Serena Stanhope.

Talked of the Parsons family. I told them that Lady de Vesci was to be a hundred this year and she ought to be recorded on telly or radio. They thought this an excellent idea. Discussed who should interview her. Feeble instantly telephoned John Julius [Norwich] who said I should do it because I had known all of them; but I said I would not be good. Had no experience of such a thing. Someone needed who could egg on. Agreed it must be a gent who understood the world Lady de V. came from. At ten John became silent. I realised I should go but stayed on. So much to say to them both. At 10.15 John said he must go to bed. So I sprang up and left. They are off to Cornwall for six weeks. I would not be surprised if he did not return.

Tuesday, 30 March

In London Library saw Sachie [Sitwell] sitting in reading room browsing through periodicals. I told him he looked well which did not please. 'I am very depressed,' he said, 'and sit here until luncheon time. It is as good as anywhere else.' Told me he had a volume of poems to be published by Macmillans next month. 'It will be my eightieth book,' he said, 'and my last.' I said I would come and see him in the summer if he liked. He asked me to stay. But I felt he was indifferent to everyone and everything. When I asked Sachie about Roy Campbell* whose biography I have just reviewed for the *Standard*, and who consorted with the Sitwells in the Twenties, he said he could not remember him. I said, 'But he was a swashbuckling, violent sort of man, wasn't he?' 'Perhaps he was,' S. said.

Monday, 5 April

At the shop in Acton Turville, where I had gone to buy some milk, a very old local stopped to talk about what he called 'the war'.† Said he

---

* Poet (1902–57).
† Argentina had invaded and occupied the Falkland Islands on 2 April, and a Royal Navy 'Task Force' was preparing to sail to recapture them. The Argentines surrendered to British forces on 14 June.

knew it was coming. 'My father never would vote because he said if you had a Tory government there will be war, if a Labour government there will be starvation. I don't know which be worst.' It is strange how one cannot take our armada seriously somehow. Yet the situation might provoke a world war – if Argentina succeeds in recruiting all the South American countries; if Russia joins the fray; if (low be it spoken) our assault were to fail. Yet I think the crisis is uniting the people.

Wednesday–Thursday, 7–8 April

The much-deferred two-day tour of Cornwall with Alex [Moulton] in his lovely smooth Rolls-Royce. Agreeable and involved staying the night in a small hotel in Looe. But terribly cold and grey. We visited Lanhydrock, Cothele and Antony. I was impressed by the splendid way these three N.T. houses are kept. An improvement on how they used to be under my jurisdiction. Michael Trinick* has worked marvels. Even the restaurants have good food and the china and tablecloths are pretty. Alex intends to write an autobiographical book on his career, stressing his impulse to advance from one scientific invention to another. He feels his life has been more than moderately successful, and that young engineers must always have an eye on the task ahead.

Tuesday, 13 April

To London for N.T. Properties Committee. In the morning I delivered my diaries to Chatto's, reduced by 7,000 words. I now have four books in the press,† so to speak, but no book on hand, which makes me sad. I wonder if I have the impulse to write another, that spring to which Alex attaches so much importance? Met M. before dinner. He has handed in the final chapter of his Duke of Windsor book, and I accordingly handed him the letter I have been threatening to write him. When it came to writing it I had forgotten some of the

---

* G. E. M. Trinick (1924–94); N.T. land agent, later Historic Buildings Representative, for Cornwall, 1953–84 (of which county he became DL and High Sheriff).

† Apart from *Caves of Ice*, these were a country house anthology for OUP, an illustrated book on Bath for Bamber Gascoigne, and *The Last Stuarts*.

reprimands I had intended to put across. M. very sweet and apologetic for neglecting his friends these months past. It is true he has written me less, but he is as affectionate as ever.

Saturday, 8 May

Spent ten days in Italy with Eardley. We went to Vicenza and Asolo. A great success. Eardley is the ideal traveller. He notices everything, and we invent fantasies about the people we see in restaurants and bars.

Since my return I have within two days written Part I of my novel.* I think it rather good, but then it was easy. The feelings of Rupert and his seduction come easily to me. I got so worked up during the writing that the characters became real to me. It was like writing auto-biography, although totally fictitious. Of course all novels must be wish fantasies.

Went for my cardiac test yesterday. When it was over the print-out was passed to the doctor who read it like a musical score. A long roll of zig-zags, showing the pulse beat. He explained that the downward fall never quite reached the level mark on the roll. He said, 'You have had a small coronary attack during the past three months. Do you remember it?' Now I am not sure whether I do or not. I remember having a pain in my chest once, and there was the occasion when I walked to the Berkeleys' house during the intense cold in London and felt extremely affected by it.† A. thinks that may have been the occa-sion. Anyway doctor suggests no precautionary measures but stresses the importance of my taking exercise. Says coronaries are usually caused either by excessive smoking and drinking, or lack of exercise. Tests have proved beyond argument that bus drivers are more subject to them than bus conductors, postmasters sitting in their offices than postmen on their rounds. This is encouraging. It means that I have no excuse not to accompany Derek [Hill] to Mount Athos.

I wrote to Master yesterday asking if I might illustrate his portrait of the Countess of Albany. He telephoned this morning asking us to

---

* See last entry for 1979.
† See 13 January 1982.

dine tonight which we can't do. Said he can't identify any such portrait in the catalogue. Will I point it out to him? So I went round there and then. Slowly and painfully he and Mary walked up the stairs. We had to go to the top floor. There the portrait was, but it was not labelled Countess of Albany but Princess Stolberg. 'I can't think of any relation of ours called Lady Albany,' he said. Mary hadn't a clue as to who I was, and begged me to come back and see the pictures another time. They have a red carpet up one side of the staircase. She explained that the Queen Mother had said the last time she stayed that, unless they provided a carpet, never again, too slippery. 'We could not afford more than a small strip,' Mary said. They were very friendly and rather pathetic. He much more bent than formerly, his head jutting forward. (I notice that Eardley who will be eighty this autumn is inclined to jut his jaw forward in that enquiring, anxious way the old have. Must avoid doing it myself, if possible.)

Sunday, 9 May

We lunched with Charlie and Jessica Douglas-Home[*] at their mill house, out of doors on the lawn. Delicious hot mutton but cold session. Charlie explained much about the workings of *The Times* that I had always wanted to know. He is an autocrat in that he decides policy entirely. He tells the writer of every leader what he wishes him to say. He has two meetings with his staff each day, at 11.30 a.m. and about 5 p.m., at which they discuss the news of the past twenty-four hours and how it should be reported. He is very pro-Thatcher but says she is faced with, if not a conspiracy, a hotbed of dissent within her ranks from what he terms 'the White's boys', who deeply resent being led by a woman. I asked who were loyal to her. Pym?[†] No, he said. He does not much like Pym. Nor Whitelaw, who is waffly. Keith Joseph[‡]

---

[*] Charles Douglas-Home (1937–85); editor of *The Times*, 1982–5; m. 1966 Jessica Gwynne, artist and stage designer.

[†] Francis Pym (b. 1922), Foreign Secretary, 1982–3 (appointed on resignation of Lord Carrington after Argentine invasion of Falklands); backbench critic of Mrs Thatcher in 1983–7 parliament; cr. life peer, 1987.

[‡] Sir Keith Joseph, 2nd Bt (1918–94); ally of Mrs Thatcher, known as 'the mad monk'; Education Secretary, 1981–6; cr. life peer, 1987.

and Howe* are thoroughly loyal. He evidently has much admiration for Murdoch,† as might be expected. He says Michael Ratcliffe‡ is going. They can't afford to keep him on for he takes a fortnight to write a review, reading all the other books on the subject of the book he is writing about, like Raymond [Mortimer]. Charlie is much concerned by the Falklands trouble. He has written all the leaders on the subject himself. I asked him how long it took him to write a leader. He said he does them very quickly. He has a reliable woman secretary who advises him by confirming or questioning the clearness of his message to the average reader. He is a most sympathetic, jolly and charming fellow, very simple, but quick. He has an awfully responsible task. I hope he sticks it out. When we arrived they were listening to the news and thought we might be about to invade the islands. He thinks that, if Mrs Thatcher wins, she will be more persecuted by colleagues than ever. This does not speak highly for Tory ministers.

Charlie wore an old pair of nondescript trousers and torn woolly jersey. Not the least vain. He has rather lost his looks, but is still charming. Jessica is dark, inscrutable, very fascinating and attractive, her face obscured beneath a fringe of black hair and wide summery hat. Two scruffy little boys, natural and affectionate with parents, playing together with the lock gate of the mill race. Looking at these underfledged chicks I thought of my Rupert. Must make him fifteen I think, not fourteen.

Tuesday, 11 May

Called on Rosamond [Lehmann] before dinner. She is terribly upset by a letter from A. abusing her for being a treacherous friend. In a way this is my fault because, when A. admitted to me that she had written to M. threatening him two years ago,§ I stupidly said that I knew of

---

* Sir Geoffrey Howe (b. 1926), Chancellor of the Exchequer, 1979–83; considered a Thatcher loyalist at this time but contributed to her downfall in 1990; cr. life peer, 1992.
† Rupert Murdoch (b. 1931), Australian media tycoon, whose group had bought *The Times* in 1981.
‡ Literary editor of *The Times*, 1967–72 (b. 1935).
§ See 29 November 1981.

this and did not wish to discuss it. A. instantly jumped to the conclusion that Ros had told me, which indeed she had in an unguarded moment. Most unfortunate, and I hate being involved in this sort of thing and causing R. distress. Afterwards M. dined with me at Brooks's and I stayed with J.K.-B. who was in one of his black moods, his tenants absconding, etc.

Wednesday, 12 May

Lunched with the Bamber Gascoignes at Richmond. Such a nice terrace house right on the river, with only a footway between house and river and that sunk below their terrace. Facing them an island of willow trees and birds. House bare and carpetless, floors cleverly painted to resemble carpets. We lunched out of doors beneath a wisteria in full flower. Salad luncheon, adequate. Afterwards I signed nearly two hundred copies of *Images of Bath*. It took well over an hour. Bamber is extremely methodical, carrying stacks of these heavy books on to a table, providing blotting papers. I am disappointed by the quality of the prints, which is muzzy. The original photographs were very good. The type is excellent and the layout, but for so high a price I think there may well be criticism.

Thursday, 13 May

A. and I motor to Kingston Lacy for day. I look through some of the Bankes papers, but still the Trust has not been given permission to enter the Muniment Room. Unless there are more papers there of a personal nature or about Bankes's travels, I doubt whether I could make much out of accounts and payment for works of art he bought.

Sunday, 16 May

June and Jeremy [Hutchinson] came over to tea in the kitchen. I accompanied Jeremy on foot nearly to Lyegrove down the verge with the dogs on a lead. I said how lucky he was to have known Virginia Woolf, for I have been reading about her friendship with his parents

412

in the latest volume of her diaries. He said he was too young to know her properly. She was very fond of children who loved her because she was such a tease and so funny. Always seemed cheerful to them. Bloomsbury struck him and Barbara as a great joke. They imitated their exaggerated voices with deep emphasis on adjectives, particularly Roger Fry's.* Jeremy a most sympathetic man, but I was a bit distressed by his obvious dislike, if not resentment, of Diana, who he thinks fags June unmercifully. He says D. is very exacting and not good with servants – very Edwardian, in other words. Jeremy hates the aristocracy and is horribly left-wing. At tea, A. refused to discuss Argentina because of their dislike of Mrs Thatcher. 'Let's change the subject,' she said. 'We shall never agree.'

Chiquita [Astor]† and Sally [Westminster] lunched. Chiquita is curiously shy of telephoning her friends in case they don't want to see her, she being Argentinian. She has just returned from there via Madrid. Says Galtieri is not a clever man and is a mere figurehead. The presidency of the country lasts only two years. Nor is the Government the least fascist. It is however a bulwark against Communism, and she is sure the whole Falklands crisis has been engineered by Russia.

Whitsun, 30 May

Selina Hastings and M. came for three nights. A. had to provide food for every meal despite suffering from a bad bronchial cold that made her feel rotten. We both found Selina perfect – amusing, clever, appreciative, getting on with everyone. Each morning she worked in her bedroom on the children's books she writes for Sebastian Walker. M. says he enjoyed himself very much. I took him and Selina to see Eliza Wansborough, who showed us a photograph of Sibyl [Colefax] which is a rarity. And Selina went off with my Eton photograph of Tom [Mitford] for her Nancy biog. A. tells me how much she likes M., but I don't think she finds him wholly her cup of tea. He is too nervous of her. And no wonder.

---

* Bloomsbury artist and art critic (1866–1934).
† Ana Inez Carcano; m. 1944–72 Hon. John Jacob Astor (d. 2000), 4th son of 2nd Viscount Astor.

Tuesday, 15 June

To London. For several days have been in a state over the few words I am to deliver at tomorrow's prize award.* Indeed the prospect upsets me to the point of taking all the savour out of life. I have written out my few words and learnt them by heart.

Dined with Elizabeth and John Betj[eman]. Noticeable declension since my last visit. J. barely spoke. Must have had another little stroke by the slipped look of his face on right-hand side. Enormous blown-up stomach. Movement from his chair to dinner table most painful. Was told not to help. Nice friendly old Anglican monk staying. While Elizabeth supported J's shoulders the monk gently kicked J's feet. Thus they dragged him, bent sideways like a telephone pole half blown over, to the table. I sat beside him. Tried to tease him into amusement. Barely succeeded. Yet yesterday, he was televised sitting in his chair. I said, 'I suppose you were talking about yourself as usual?' He laughed in the old way. He said, 'No. I was catty.' Strange reaction. Asked him how his biography was getting on. He said it was awkward. I have since learnt that Feeble does not like Bevis Hillier† and won't cooperate with him. Left feeling very sad. Cannot believe he will survive the year.

Wednesday, 16 June

The dreaded day. Lunched at Collins with MacLehose,‡ Mark Bonham Carter and my co-prize winner, Jonathan Raban,§ youngish man with charming smile. Did not enjoy it. Mark charmless and embittered. Loathes Mrs Thatcher of course. After meal, MacL. talked about the book they want me to do. To take ten houses of the world (no less) which survive untouched since built. All travelling paid for. I to discuss

---

* J.L.-M's biography of Harold Nicolson had been awarded the Heinemann Prize by the Royal Society of Literature.

† Writer and journalist (b. 1940); sometime editor of *The Connoisseur* and *The Times Saturday Review*; his monumental biography of John Betjeman was published by John Murray in three volumes appearing in 1988, 2002 and 2004.

‡ Christopher MacLehose (b. 1940); publisher.

§ Novelist, travel writer and critic (b. 1942).

their creators and intentions. They say the BBC will do a programme on each house in turn, but only if I am the author. I don't altogether trust these people. I don't know how much I want to do such a book.

Then came the Royal Society of Literature. I walked from Brooks's. Sat through annual meeting, C. M. Woodhouse[*] in chair. Awful tea afterwards. Hundreds of people came up and congratulated. Helen Dashwood embraced me. Joanna Richardson[†] like a huge man-of-war in full sail. The hall was full to the brim. I came first. Woodhouse read out some words about the book, called upon me, presented me with envelope, made me sign a book. Then I turned round and delivered my words. Was not good, but did not disgrace myself. A. sitting below me said it was all right. So did M. who was present, but I don't think they were impressed. Relief that all was over. Then I gave a small dinner at Brooks's – Nigel, Sheila Birkenhead, Charlotte Bonham Carter, A. and M. Ordered champagne. Enjoyed it because I am fond of Charlotte and dearly love Sheila. She told me that she has lost the use of her right hand and cannot write, but she doesn't seem to mind. I cut up her duck for her. Charlotte's head sideways in the plate.

Friday, 2 July

Terrible fork luncheon at Alderley Grange after meeting of [N.T.] Regional Committee there. Lots of old colleagues. I escaped early and stopped car on the hill of the Tresham road. Walked the dogs in Foxholes Wood. Never had I seen a more beautiful landscape. These combes on the edge of the Cotswolds surpass everything. Passed through a field of barley sprinkled with red poppies. Glimpsed through the trees, very decayed and Constablesque, the winding yellow lane to the farmstead, and the prospect of the vale. Just like a Jane Austen drive which phaetons would take for picnics. The Grange is full of lovely things but too expensive, like a Bond Street antique

---

[*] Hon. C. Montagu Woodhouse (1917–2001); academic and politician, sometime Conservative MP for Oxford; author of works on modern Greek history; s. bro. as 5th Baron Terrington, 1998.
[†] Author of historical and literary biographies; FRSL, 1959.

dealer's. One imagines a price ticket discreetly tied to the back of each piece of furniture. Garden lush and much grown since we left. A. complained as we went round that the dear Acloques had made some mistakes in replanting. I could not see this but regretted some of the garden statuary. But what a joy that this is now a family home with children being born and brought up there. They will love it.

Saturday, 10 July

On Thursday Bamber [Gascoigne] gave a party in my Bath library for subscribers to the morocco-bound volumes of *Images of Bath*. Beautiful they are, splashed with gold too. An extraordinary collection of subscribers turned up. No one I had ever seen before, and not rich-seeming. Yet why do they buy these volumes? For Bamber says the leather people, as he calls them, are generally the same for all the volumes in the series. There are two butcher brothers in Richmond who buy two copies of each issue, at £600 a time. Extraordinary.

Yesterday I motored to Kingston Lacy to glance through some more papers of W. J. Bankes. Found one or two personal papers relating to his outlawry but suspect recent members of family may have destroyed compromising letters. Anyway I have decided to defer tackling this subject,* and to do the Rome anthology for Nick [Robinson]† when I have finished my novel.

Monday, 12 July

Yesterday morning I rang up Nick and told him that I had finally decided to do the Rome anthology for him. Then in the evening A. and I went to the Hollands' annual concert in their barn in aid of the National Art Collections Fund. Before the concert I saw Lionel Esher, who said to me, 'You remember that a year ago I told you I had engaged another writer to do my grandfather's biography. It was

---

* J.L.-M. did not return to the project. A biography by Anne Sebba, *The Exiled Collector*, was published by John Murray in 2004.
† He had recently started his own publishing business.

Max Egremont.* He has now backed out, so if you are free I will offer it to you.' I was struck all of a heap, and during the first half of the concert, Howard Shelley playing Schubert and Rachmaninov, could think of nothing else. During the interval I had a further talk with Lionel who said he didn't want a fourth chucker after Philip Magnus, Michael Howard and Egremont. Lionel wonders what it was about his grandfather that put these eminent people off. Each made a different excuse, Egremont's being that he had decided to concentrate on writing novels. I wonder if the reason was that Esher was too stuffy, for the volumes of his letters which M. gave me for Christmas I found extremely boring. Lionel says they were heavily expurgated. Says his grandfather was too grand by half, an outrageous snob. L's father Oliver took against his father because he opposed Oliver's marriage to Antoinette who was not only American but un-grand. When, going through his father's papers on his death, Oliver discovered the truth about his father, he wrote a short but bitter book about him which he decided not to publish. I asked if I might be allowed to read it, but Lionel thought not. I must form my own opinion. No M. to discuss.

Today the Berkeleys lunched on their way from the Cheltenham Festival to Berkeley Castle. Lennox very detached, Freda complaining in front of us that he paid no heed to two things which were worrying her, the dissolute conduct of their youngest son and the notice from their landlords that No. 8 Warwick Avenue must be sold in a few years for £130,000 which they have not got. Lennox just smiled blandly and seemed not to take it in. After luncheon I strolled with him in the park. Conversation proved difficult until I said, 'Lennox, you must have bad days when you can't compose. I have bad days when I can't write, which make me suppose I may never write again. This depresses me inordinately.' This awakened him and he became quite animated. 'Yes,' he said, 'I do have these days and I have these same fears. And it is awful,

---

* Max Wyndham (b. 1948); s. father 1972 as 2nd Baron Egremont and 7th Baron Leconfield; of Petworth House, Sussex (which after negotiations largely conducted through J.L.-M. had been donated to the N.T. by his great-uncle, 1947); writer; m. 1978 Caroline Nelson.

awful.' He lives in a world of his own, music, at which he is as good as formerly. But he shrugs off every other consideration. Lives in a cloud.*

Tuesday, 13 July

Motored to London with A. last night. She stayed with Midi, I with Eardley whom I found low, muddled and losing things. Took my car round to Norah's yard in the morning and was leaving keys at her office when Dirk Bogarde[†] and a friend walked in. A short, well-preserved, still youthful man with dark hair, looking like Angus Menzies. I said, 'I saw you three evenings ago in the best film in the world.' He asked what film that was, and whether I had not mistaken him for Humphrey Bogart. '*Death in Venice*,' I said. 'I've never seen it,' he said. 'You're like me then, I never read my own books.' 'I read mine all the time,' he said. There is something rather camp about him.

Sunday, 18 July

A. and I motored to Calke Abbey [Derbyshire] on Friday to join a small party of members of the Properties Committee to determine whether this property with its large estate, lovely park and the 1703 house is worthy of acceptance through the Treasury in lieu of death duties. A. and I have no doubts whatever of its worthiness. I was last here twenty-eight years ago with Rupert Gunnis[‡] and Hugh Euston. Exterior totally untouched, except for Wilkins's portico which is an improvement, and balustrade. Fine staircase and upstairs saloon, heightened by Wilkins. No great works of art perhaps but every stick of furniture, every content covetable. Nothing thrown away. I opened a trunk in the cook's room over the kitchen, and found it full to the brim with sailor

---

* He was starting to suffer from Alzheimer's Disease.
† Professional name of Derek van den Bogaerde (1921–2000), film actor, becoming known at this time for his novels and autobiographical writings.
‡ Author (1899–1966) of *A Dictionary of British Sculptors, 1660–1851* (1953).

suits and other Edwardian children's clothes. We saw photographs taken in 1880 of rooms which look exactly the same today. Quite extraordinary. The family has been eccentric for 150 years, the late owner and present owner (his brother) no exception. By tradition each owner leaves his predecessor's apartments intact and moves on to the next suite of rooms. In the Gothic church in the park, a late eighteenth-century tablet praises a Mrs Harpur Crewe in these terms: 'Though she was placed far above want herself yet Affluence could never abate her Humanity.' Howard Colvin who has nursed this house ever since Rupert's death was present to receive us. He said that he had peeped into a box which contained Caroline of Anspach's* unpacked bed, its hangings still in pristine condition.

Marion Brudenell present. We went on to Deene to stay with the Brudenells. Large house party. Twenty every meal. Table covered with silver, and delicious food. A very fine house within. Great hall with open roof superb. Excellent collection of family portraits, many bought back by Edmund. The twin sons came on Saturday night, dark, saturnine, well-mannered youths. On Sunday, service was held in a chapel made in the house since we were last there, for the church has been closed down, and memorial busts, one by Pierce very good indeed, removed by Edmund into the house. One of the twins read the lesson. Fellow guests included George Lane† and wife, daughter of Lord Heald. He is a Hungarian with great contempt for the Poles, the Pope and the Church. David Scott came to luncheon on Sunday, aet. 95 and not well. Francis Egerton‡ and I walked from Deene to Kirby Hall, almost getting lost. Impressive ruins but Ministry-kept gardens atrocious. We left after luncheon on Sunday and drove to Northampton to visit Gervase Jackson-Stops, who has broken several limbs in a motor smash. Sitting in bed with one leg on a pulley. Totally naked and looking like a boy of ten were the top of his head not bald. Even this gives him a baby look with his fair, smooth skin.

---

* Queen (d. 1737) of George II.
† George Lanyi (b. 1915); war hero, farmer and businessman; m. (2nd) 1963 Elizabeth Heald.
‡ Chairman of Mallett & Son, antique dealers (1917–2001).

Tuesday, 20 July

Motoring in the dark I ran over a hedgehog and killed it flat. Very distressed. Had seen the poor little thing scuttling across the road. Tried to avoid it so that it might pass under the car between the wheels, but no. A. says its babies would wonder why it had not returned and would die of starvation. I loathe killing things. Could only kill IRA members willingly.

Friday, 23 July

Met Mary Beaufort walking through the gates of the big house. She was wearing blue bedroom slippers, white cotton trousers too short in the leg and a peasant shawl over her head. I asked her where she was going. 'I am going to the Agent to apologise for not keeping an appointment this morning.' Then she said, 'Do you like living in this little cottage?' I said Yes, we did. 'We must arrange for you to come to dinner one night, or do you dislike dining out?' 'Not with you,' I said gallantly. 'Snob!' she replied. A. vastly amused when I told her. I said I hope to God she doesn't invite us, it is such torture. A. said, 'She may say to Master, "Who are those people who live at the lodge?", and he will reply, "I wouldn't bother about them if I were you."'

Saturday, 24 July

I virtually finished my novel yesterday. When I killed Rupert on his bicycle, I wept. Probably a bad sign of sentimental twaddle.

Monday, 2 August

Took train to London for seventy-fifth birthday dinner given for Alec Clifton-Taylor at the Savile Club. Walked from Bond Street Station to Savile with my bag. One of those summer London dog days, stiflingly hot. But dinner in large cool room at head of grand double-flight staircase in this pomposo building, once the London house of the Harcourts, all Frenchified Edwardian and rather splendid.* About thirty guests at three tables joined to form a U. Alec protested that he had known nothing of the feast until he arrived, having been bidden by two old friends and expecting their company only. I was honoured to be put at the top table, between John Julius Norwich and Jasper More,† one away from Alec. Jasper made usual witty speech with jokes at which we laughed. Said Alec had achieved immortality, a thing few of us could claim, with his book on building materials. Alec replied listing the prerequisites for leading a happy life. (1) Health. (2) Money, enough to satisfy modest needs. (3) Interest in and dedication to one's work. (4) Ability to control and come to terms with one's sexual urges. (Surprising coming from him. I never supposed he had any. Turn away from the thought.) (5) Friendships, which to him meant everything. To which he added (6) being able to recognise one's own limitations, stretch them to the utmost, and never to envy the superior ability of others. Rather charmingly put. The moment the meal was over I slipped off to take underground to Islington to stay at Jack Rathbone's.

Tuesday, 3 August

Max Egremont lunched with me at Boodle's. Delightful man, what I would call young middle-aged, with looks of a less handsome Nick Robinson. Yet strange to learn he was born after the war, in 1948. We discussed Reginald Esher. What put him off were the mass of papers and the unsympathetic character of the man. But was not put off by his sexual deviations, not at all. I liked Egremont much. Have since read his *Balfour*, which lacks sparkle. Went to tea with Ros. She is upset by her row with A. and wants me to put things right, but A. will not listen and regards the subject as closed.

---

* The house (69 Brook Street) was designed by the Paris architect Bouwens in 1891 for the American banker Walter H. Burns and his wife, sister of J. Pierpont Morgan. The Burnses' daughter married the politician Lewis (later 1st Viscount) Harcourt, and they moved there after Mrs Burns's death in 1918. Harcourt committed suicide there in 1922 after a sex scandal involving J.L.-M's Eton contemporary Edward James (then aged thirteen). The Savile acquired the building as their clubhouse in 1927.
† Sir Jasper More (1907–87); author of books on Mediterranean countries; Conservative MP for Ludlow, 1960–79; Eton contemporary of J.L.-M.

Wednesday, 11 August

M. has told me that he considers the ending of my novel bad, trite and unacceptable. Am rather put out by this, though pleased by his candour. I had a misgiving that the death of Rupert was too sentimental. I would now like someone else to advise me. M. sees silliness in a 1920s boy's serious attitude towards sexual deviation, and thinks the end should be a *ménage à trois* between Rupert, Ernst and Amy. He does not realise, I tell him, how we had to conceal, be evasive, were fearful.

Friday, 13 August

Hansel Pless* told me this evening that when he was a small boy the Kaiser and retinue came to stay at his father's house in Poland. The men of the house, including Hansel, awaited the Kaiser with their hats in their hands; after His arrival, they put them on again. The Kaiser went up to Hansel and crushed his top hat over his nose and chin. Not only did it hurt, but the boy was deeply offended. The Kaiser roared with laughter, as of course did the courtiers. When I told Pless Diana Mosley's story of how the Kaiser requested the Headmaster of Eton to have a boy swished in front of Him for His benefit, he said that this was another example of His peculiar sense of humour. Pless said the Poles were hopeless like the Irish. They had charm, and liked to tell you what they thought you wanted to hear, but were inefficient and untrustworthy. The Plesses always employed Germans to run their Polish estates.

Monday, 16 August

On Sunday I motored to stay the night with the Droghedas. Garrett full of charm and most welcoming. Joan subdued and memory extremely bad. One has to help her along, reminding her of names and trying to think ahead for her. Barbara Ghika and husband

---

* Henry, Prince of Pless (d. 1984); m. 1958–71 Mary Minchin.

staying.* A very intelligent, liberal-minded, equable woman abounding in good sense, like Fanny Partridge without the political fanaticism. After breakfast I left for Windsor Castle.

Arrived at Henry VIII entrance gate. Police asked me my business. Before admitting me they telephoned the Library. Were given OK and let me through. Then I walked to what is called the Side Door. Police inside. Again they telephone Miss Langton,† who looks after the Archives. An official in morning coat, long tails, took a huge bunch of keys on the end of a long chain and opened the entrance door of the Round Tower. I climbed straight long flights of steps. Smiling Miss Langton at head of stairs. Charming, efficient, helpful spinster. I was shown card catalogue of Stuart documents of which there are about 150,000 in 552 bound files or boxes. Quite impossible to go through all these, but I found the catalogue most useful because the name of the writer and recipient of each letter is listed, with a short description of who each correspondent was. I managed to get through five of the fourteen drawers between 10 a.m. and 5 p.m., with a break (to be polite) for coffee with three ladies on the staff and two other researchers, one of whom 'knew my books'. I calculate that I can complete the work in two more visits. Am always happy working in a library of this sort, being waited on by kindly, helpful people in the quiet of a scholarly atmosphere. No sign of Sir Robin which is rather a relief, he being in Australia. I only looked at three files. One rather interesting letter of 1751 from a Roman tailor to the Cardinal Duke gives estimates for the stuff of liveries, enclosing a sample about four inches square – of rose silk velvet with silver braid border, in mint condition.

Saturday, 21 August

The one hundredth birthday of my uncle Robert Bailey. When I remarked on this to A. at breakfast, she said that her father would probably be one hundred and ten if alive today, so what? But I remember

---

* Barbara Hutchinson (sister of Jeremy, Baron Hutchinson); m. 1st (1933–46) 3rd Baron Rothschild, 2nd 1949 Rex Warner, 3rd 1961 Nico Hadjikyriakou-Ghika, painter (she d. 1989).
† Jane Langton; Registrar, Royal Archives.

my Uncle Robert with reverence and affection, for I was brought up to believe him to have been the gentlest, most saintly scholar and sportsman, the ideal of a pre-1914 English gentleman, adored by his colleagues among the House of Commons clerks, by his friends, by his two sisters, my Mama and Aunt Doreen, and by the working men at whose clubs he taught. I have one memory of him, like a muzzy, rapid shot of an old cinematograph film, chasing me around the yard at Wickhamford. This must have been during his last leave in the First War. He was wearing a black-and-white check suit and stiff collar, with his short hair parted at the side and a smooth, youthful, not quite handsome face. He was in his mid thirties. As a boy I rejoiced when told I resembled him. I feel more in accord with him than with any of my relations.

Friday, 27 August

My third visit to the Royal Archives in the Round Tower at Windsor. Managed to complete my rapid survey of Stuart catalogue entries. I noticed nervousness on the part of Miss Langton. When I mentioned that I saw four boxes of letters labelled *Lord Esher's Correspondence*, she said, charmingly but firmly, 'You would have to get Sir Robin's permission before I could let you see these.' When her back was turned I took one down from the shelf, and tried quickly to open it just to see what was inside. Like Peeping Tom. Discovered folder fastened by press buttons. Opened one, saw nothing inside but a blank sheet of paper, couldn't do up the button and hastily thrust it, not properly shut, back on the shelf.

Monday, 30 August

Have corrected proofs of *Caves of Ice* and have to face up to index when I return from Venice. I left with Norah the draft of my novel, provisionally entitled *Innocence*. She reports that it is too short for a novel and too long for a short story. I must add 15,000 words at least. Claims not to be shocked by the story, but says I need to be 'more subtle with seduction scenes' – which means she does find it too porn-like, I fear.

Sunday, 17 October

If I didn't know the Vicar [Tom Gibson] and merely attended his services I would be an unconditional admirer. He has a splendid, bold voice, and his sermons are superb. Today he spoke about the Church expressing views on unilateral nuclear disarmament. Roundly condemned it for interference in matters it could not judge. We must leave these tricky matters to the Government which receives expert advice. Introduced St Luke, whose feast day tomorrow, as the Intellectual Evangelist. Easy to distinguish his gospel from the others by his keen observation of detail, for he paints a background which the other Es neglect. But the Vicar *will* nobble me in Church. This evening at Acton Turville he regaled me with long story of misbehaviour at Eddie Somerset's* wedding, where one of his most respectable parishioners on going to the loo found two young people 'at it'. Parishioner deeply shocked; Vicar pretended to be also; and so did I, but halfheartedly. I don't think I really mind in the least – good luck to them – but they might have locked the door. Everything is permissible behind locked doors.

Wednesday, 20 October

Was met at Cambridge station by M. who gave me cosy supper in his room at 9 King's Parade, in front of the gas fire. Memories of Oxford *circa* 1930. M. has got me a room in St John's.

Friday, 22 October

All yesterday and today it poured with rain from dawn to dusk and dusk to dawn. Got soaked walking under umbrella to Churchill College, down the main road to Bedford. Beastly building, like enormous public lavatory. Nothing to recommend it except its inhabitants, all nice to me. Charming and helpful archivist, Miss Marion Stewart. They begged me to write Regy Esher's life. Spent from 9.30 to 5 both

---

* Edward Alexander (b. 1958); yr s. of David and Lady Caroline Somerset; m. 1982 Hon. Caroline Davidson.

days glancing at his papers. Appalled by the quantity, but have decided to go ahead, provided the College and Lionel will allow to me to take the papers away. Otherwise impossible. Miss Stewart said she would be glad to get rid of papers until the biography is written. Could easily be sent to me by Securicor van. I suppose I could house the 129 boxes in Bath. It would be my last literary enterprise. I only wish I liked Regy more. Don't positively dislike; am mystified, and interested. Had a talk with Dadie [Rylands] in King's and discussed the question with him. Dear Dadie will be eighty tomorrow. He was very intelligent and wise, and strongly advised me to take it on. So does M.

Much enjoyed staying in St John's. A cloistered existence suits me. But surely Churchill would have been even more appalled by the college named after him than he was by Graham [Sutherland]'s portrait of him.

Sunday, 24 October

A splendid review of M's book in *Sunday Telegraph*. Had to telephone. He of course in bed asleep. Came half-comatose to telephone. When I said, 'Congratulations on having written "a classic of its kind",' he was thrilled, not yet having seen it. Am so glad because he has been a little disappointed by the slowness of reviews.

Tuesday, 26 October

Have corrected the Index to *Caves of Ice*, the best and most complete index I have ever done. Now that book is off my chest. Have written a long letter to Lionel saying I will write Regy's life subject to conditions, the chief one being that I must be allowed to have the papers in Bath. Am now revising my novel. Each time I read through it I find something to correct; but apart from adding or deleting an extra line or two, I have done nothing to 'fluff it out' or to make it more subtle.

Wednesday, 27 October

Dined with Alex [Moulton] last night. A faithful friend who always gives me a hearty welcome and dinner. We gossip about his projects and mine. He is inventing a new bicycle. Tried to explain to me the differences between it and the previous Moulton bicycle, which I failed to understand. When I told him about Regy, he expressed disapproval, saying that I ought to write what he calls books of the imagination. Nice of him, but I haven't any imagination, as recent struggles with novel testify.

All Souls' Eve, Monday, 1 November

When I had tea with Diana Westmorland at Lyegrove on Thursday, she was dreadfully upset by the Doddington[*] debacle. Simon Codrington's[†] last desperate fling at letting part of the park for a funfair has been turned down by the local authorities. On Sunday, Eardley, staying with me, and I dined with the Francis Burnes.[‡] Rosalind Ward[§] and Simon Codrington also present. Lady C. did not come, being I gathered in bed recovering from a nervous breakdown. I liked Simon for the first time. Clearly not bright, but gentle and sympathetic. Seemed sad and left before we finished dinner. Before he left Francis lent across me and gave him advice for a critical meeting to take place next day with the funfair people who were turning nasty. I did not join in conversation beyond saying how sorry I was and wishing him luck. After he had gone Francis told us he owed £400,000, had creditors all round him, could not pay his staff, was utterly broke, without money to buy milk or petrol. Francis had some extraordinary scheme to save Doddington. But Peggy this morning says, 'Did you see Doddington on telly last night?' Apparently the news is all out. The place is to be put into liquidation. Very tragic. This important house is Wyatt's last and best classical country house and has the most beautiful park in these parts. Codringtons have lived there for centuries. It is like an eighteenth-century ending, as though an owner gambled away his

---

[*] Doddington Park near Bath, described by J. L.-M. on 10 May 1953 as a 'disappointing' house constructed of 'shoddy' materials and gone to seed.

[†] Sir Simon Codrington, 3rd Bt (b. 1923); m. (3rd) 1980–8 Sally Gaze.

[‡] Of Wick Manor, Avon; friends of Eardley Knollys.

[§] Rosalind Lygon (b. 1946); granddaughter of 7th Earl Beauchamp and heiress to Madresfield Court, Worcestershire.; m. 1st Gerald John Ward, 2nd 1984 Sir Charles Morrison, MP for Devizes.

wife and estate at Brooks's in a night. Landowners go broke all around us, and have to leave or sell; but seldom is the owner driven to live in the kitchen by a paraffin stove, of which the paraffin is given him by friends.

Tuesday, 2 November

Drove with dogs all the way to Stokesay Court near Craven Arms [Shropshire] to lunch with Philip Magnus, some 90 miles. Beastly dank and grey day, with fog patches. Lady Magnus-Allcroft did not appear. Has had two strokes and lives with a female keeper upstairs in a separate wing, from which Philip is happy to descend I fancy. We lunched alone, good country fare, mutton chops with currant jelly and claret. He is a nice old boy, two years my senior and looks eighty-six. Purpose of visit to discuss Regy [Esher], for he had intimated that I should not write this biog. As it was we talked about the project but I derived little that was useful. However he did warn that the task would be formidable because of the quantity of material; that I would find the papers on Army and Navy Reform very boring; and lastly, that I would be so fascinated by the private life that I would concentrate on this to the exclusion of all else. He added, 'It is not a good thing for people with your tastes and mine to write about such matters.' I replied that being seventy-four I no longer cared what people thought or said about me. He asked if I saw M. still. Such a nice, good-looking boy. I remarked that Regy liked a good-looking boy. 'Who doesn't?' he said. There is something sad about this ageing man with non-compos sick wife living in huge, mid Victorian house which should be full of children and life. I find it fascinating and would like to browse around on my own.

Wednesday, 3 November

I had just got to Bath rather later than usual, having called on Dr King, when the telephone rang. There was a 'Hold on, please', from which I deduced a foreign call. Not M. Then a voice said, 'I am John Julius [Norwich] speaking from Jerusalem.' My heart sank to my knees. I thought, Alvilde is ill, or dead. He said, 'You are not to be alarmed. Alvilde has had an accident. She fell into a hole while sight-seeing at some monument. She has had to have stiches in her head and has injured the bottom of her spine. Luckily the cruise doctor was present.' She is to fly back with the others on Sunday, will stay the night at the hotel at Gatwick, and I am to meet her there on Monday with a large car in which she can stretch out. J.J. admitted she was in considerable pain. I hardly knew what to say, was so shocked. I asked if I should come out. He said on no account. For the rest of the day I was unable to work or concentrate on anything. Felt deeply concerned. Caroline [Somerset] offered to lend me her car.

Thursday, 4 November

This afternoon I had my four remaining front teeth out. I dreaded the operation. Local anaesthetic. At first I felt the digging and begged him to give me some more. Felt like the Duke of Monmouth being executed, begging the executioner to finish him off. As it was, the digging, the wrenching, the crunching, the hammering, the explosions of broken teeth as of rocks, were very disturbing. I felt quite faint and tearful for a minute. Then I walked to the car, went shopping, and took the dogs for the usual walk around the golf course. So can't be too bad. Sally had promised me slops for dinner but it turned out to be pheasant, not minced but shredded.

Monday, 8 November

Caroline lends me her car which is large enough for A. to stretch out in, and Sally arranges for Bob Parsons to drive me in it to Gatwick. We find A. in Hilton Hotel at midday. She looks tense and stiff but is shuffling round the foyer. Sits in the back seat curled up which she says is more comfortable than stretched out. Full of aches and pains but nothing broken, thank God. We drive there and back in torrential rain.

Monday, 15 November

My stepdaughter Clarissa came to stay from Tuesday till Sunday, a great help. I have never liked her more. She is full of chat and laughter, a radiant personality, makes light of all adversity.

I have written to congratulate Brian Masters on his excellent book *Great Hostesses*. It is very well-written and readable, a most charitable, perceptive book. He never derides these women, some of whom might have seemed preposterous to a man of his generation and origins. I really think he is a remarkable young man. He has got Emerald [Cunard] perfectly, her gossamer quality and sense of the ludicrous. Many quotations from my published diaries.

Thursday, 18 November

Victoria Glendinning has sent A. the final chapters of her biography of Vita, in which A's relations with V. are referred to. A. handed them to me at breakfast this morning, asking me to read them with a view to discussing them with her this evening. They have come as something of a shock, for although I always supposed V. and A. had a *Schwärmerei*, I did not realise until now how passionately V. was in love with A. Vita was not entirely honest, for in her correspondence with Harold she consistently belittles A., whereas he of course expresses positive dislike of A. Victoria G. expresses no opinion as to A's reciprocation, but the reader must assume she did reciprocate. Indeed, why not – for there was I, an inattentive husband. But our friends will undoubtedly think badly of A. for having made such a tremendous fuss over my affair with J., which began after hers with Vita, about which I had remained quite mum. I don't take credit for my attitude because I didn't mind, or rather was never as jealous of A. as she was of me. I suppose that, when I was writing Harold's biography, Nigel deliberately withheld Vita's diaries for this period. I have always refused to read V's letters to A., though A. has often asked me to do so. Although I am all for honesty, somehow I don't relish these revelations in our lifetime.*

Tuesday, 30 November

Am in a state of depression, not relieved by anxiety about Mackworth-Young. Having received no answer to my letter written

---

* In the finished work, Victoria Glendinning cut out much of what she had originally written about Vita and Alvilde at the request of the latter.

almost three weeks ago [requesting permission to see Esher papers], I telephoned Miss Langton at Windsor. She told me that Sir Robin had received my letter but has to consult the Queen before he can give permission to see royal papers. Why couldn't he at least have acknowledged my letter? It amazes me that the Queen has to be consulted personally. Since she will not have a clue as to who I am (she had no idea at the Hatchards party when I was presented), and presumably has not heard of Lord Esher either, I suppose she will be guided either by Mackworth-Young or her private secretaries. They may well say I am a louche or flippant writer who has published some questionable diaries and appears in the acknowledgements of an embarrassing book about the Duke of Windsor. I rang up Lionel, who was a pillar of calm, and will write to Sir Robin backing me. He confirms I have the consent of Churchill College to have the papers here, and advises me to proceed with my researches and not to worry.

Friday, 3 December

Everything happens at once. I had been feeling miserable after struggling for three days with a review of two architectural books for the *Burlington*, when this morning I received a letter from Miss Langton to say that the Queen has granted me permission to see the Esher papers at Windsor. A great relief. Also a letter from Nicholas Hill asking to do an article on me for *Tatler*. And a message from Chatto's that *Harper's* will publish extracts of *Caves of Ice*. Then an invitation from Rainbird's to do a book on Florence, and one from OUP asking me to write one on changes in manners (both not on). And I have been asked to write the *DNB* entry on Cecil Beaton.

Sunday, 19 December

Yesterday was a bad day. Nicholas Hill came with two assistants from *Tatler*, including a photographer who took a picture of A. and me, she sprawling on my bed, I sitting on a small chair at the foot with Honey on my knee. I thought this was for an article on us alone, but it turned out to be about four couples, the other three unknown to us and I dare say everyone else. N. Hill is Derek's and Heywood's nephew.[*] He knew nothing about either of us but borrowed Freda Berkeley's copy of *Ancestral Voices*, which he read on the way down. We did our best to be friendly and put ourselves out to the extent of giving them a sandwich luncheon. By the time they left, my working day had been ruined, so I went to Westonbirt gardens with the dogs, who ran away. I waited an hour and a half in perishing cold with no book to read. When Honey returned at dusk I picked up some twigs and beat her as hard as I could.[†] She yelled. A busybody lady came up and said, 'What is going on? No wonder the little dog is too frightened to get into your car.' I was in a furious temper and drove off, only to realise it had been Georgina Harford.[‡] Doubtless my choler and cruelty to animals will be the talk of Beaufortshire. Returned home still angry to find the Lukes had come to stay, and was too put out to be nice. Then had a row with the horrid steward of the village club, this time induced by A., who made me go and complain that he had parked his car so that she could not drive into her motor house. He was very impertinent which made me angrier still. I hate this place. I loathe Badminton and always have.

Thursday, 23 December

No carol singers these days. Formerly there used to be at least one group an evening before Xmas. In a way it was a bore having to listen at the door in the cold, or invite them in, and find money, half a crown. This year we have only had the Marshfield Players, who came this evening and played one dreary tune on their brass band outside the village club. A. said, 'Go and give them something.' I went to the gate but they did not approach me. Instead they all trooped into the club for a drink. As they do this for charity I thought their efforts

---

[*] His father was the brother of the artist Derek Hill and his mother the sister of the bookseller Heywood Hill, the two families otherwise being unrelated.

[†] Marginal note added by J. L.-M. on 16 March 1988: 'Poor darling little dead Honey. I hate myself now for what I did.'

[‡] Wife of 'Ben' Harford of Ashcroft, Gloucestershire (whose parents had been neighbours and friends of the L.-Ms at Alderley).

distinctly half-hearted. When we were children at Wickhamford the great excitement on Xmas Eve was the bell-ringers. Numb with cold they came into the hall and to our amazement and admiration six of them played 'Good King Wenceslas'. Then we gave them beer.

Friday, 31 December

Last night the Somersets and Daphne Fielding dined. Alone they are enchanting. One can talk about anything to David, who is an intelligent as well as an amusing man. He told his mother-in-law and me that when he was a boy he had a tutor to coach him in the holidays. David would sit on the sofa with his legs stretched out and the tutor would stroke his thighs, an experience he found delicious. This from the ardently heterosexual David. He also said that Bobby Shaw, Nancy Astor's son, once told him that he had first been seduced by Lord Kitchener.

Today I finished my long introduction to *Writers at Home* and posted it to Gervase. It has taken me a month, and was a great struggle. I was determined to finish it by the end of the year, to clear the decks for Lord Esher in 1983.

1983

1983

Sunday, 9 January

The Powells and Zita and Baby Jungman lunched yesterday. Tony told me that, in bed every night, before turning to whatever book he is reading, he spends the first twenty minutes on Shakespeare or Fletcher. Zita and Teresa lead a strange existence. They go to bed at 4 a.m., have breakfast in bed, lunch at 4 p.m. and dine at 10 p.m. I asked Zita if she belonged to a public library. No, she said, she bought quantities of books but seldom read them. Instead she reads old newspapers. Has stacks of them never thrown away. An extraordinary waste of time it seems to me. Both sisters say they dislike meeting people younger than themselves except for the young who come to question them about their 1920s heyday. Both are devout papists, and although they were once leading Bright Young Things, claim never to have had extra-marital love affairs. Zita said she only learnt her husband was dead when a friend told her weeks after the event. I asked how she missed the announcement in the papers. She said she had not got beyond the papers of 1980 yet.

Thursday, 20 January

Went to see Rosamond [Lehmann]. She reproached me for not communicating with her. Complained that it was always she who had to get in touch with me these days, and assumed I wanted to avoid her because of the incident with A. I tried to assure the dear old thing that this was nonsense. Women like to be aggrieved. She has Diana Mosley coming to see her to talk about Mrs Hammersley.* Ros sits

---

* Violet Hammersley (d. 1963), rich and eccentric widow who had been a friend of the mothers of both Diana Mosley and Rosamond Lehmann.

in the most ungainly manner, on a low armchair, her legs spread-eagled, displaying her not very attractive knickers up to the fork. Strange no one has told her about this. She *will* wear skirts which are too short and too tight. Diana when placed in the visitor's chair facing Ros will be horrified by this apparition. She is the most fastidious person I know.

I gave a small dinner party at Brooks's for M. Consisted of Derek [Hill], Kenneth Rose, recovering from shingles and yellow-visaged, Peter Fleetwood-Hesketh, and Hugh Massingberd who failed to turn up. Successful. Kenneth got on well with M. and told me he little expected so abrasive a writer to be so gentle. Poor Peter has become a bore. Conversation exclusively about people he knew in the past. Looks very extraordinary now. False teeth have altered his expression, giving him a predatory look. He has become smaller and curiously dapper, wearing pale fancy waistcoat with brass buttons and huge gold watch chain, tight jacket and trousers. Looks like Harry Melvill* or Lord Carisbrooke,† an old queen, which he emphatically is not. But very lonely without his Mo.

Sunday, 30 January

Reading Regy's correspondence with his Eton mentor William Cory,‡ I was surprised to find that my great-uncle Fred Lees was a frequent visitor to Halsdon, Cory's Devon house. Cory states that 'dear Fred' is not intellectual and not much of a reader, but very good with animals and an excellent shot. I do not suppose Cory was sexually attracted by him, although I see from a photograph I have of Uncle Fred in the 1860s, wearing an Eton scug cap, that he had a merry, alert face. I have written to his grandson John Poë to enquire if he has any letters written to Uncle Fred from Cory.

---

* Edwardian man-about-town and raconteur.
† Alexander Mountbatten, 1st and last Marquess of Carisbrooke (1886–1960); favourite grandson of Queen Victoria. Visiting him at Kew on 13 July 1947, J.L.-M. was reminded of 'an old spruce hen . . . a typical old queen'.
‡ William Johnson (1823–92); Eton master and poet, author of Eton Boating Song.

Saturday, 5 February

Jessica Douglas-Home is inscrutable, sharp, very intelligent, sluttish, mysterious and extremely attractive. She is frank, and saying little, makes no silly remarks; when she does speak, her point of view is always original. Her encapsulated personality and her sudden affection, for I believe she likes me, excites me. I feel drawn to her. I would say she is not a happy character, but very fond of that dear man, her husband Charlie, who is unwell with a mysterious disease.

Wednesday, 9 February

Michael Adeane,* Queen's late Private Secretary, lunched with me at Brooks's. Just as I remember him at Eton in the distance – round head, small frame. Kind and helpful, though couldn't tell me much about Regy that I didn't already know. Stayed with him as a boy in Scotland, where Regy helped him fish. Told me that his mother remarked on how Regy painted his face, which meant nothing at the time to the young Adeane. He is Stamfordham's† grandson, and his own son is currently Prince Charles's Private Secretary. These court posts are hereditary, and all the better for it. He explained that the Private Secretary is also Keeper of the Royal Archives, Mackworth-Young being only his deputy, and confirmed that the Queen would certainly have been consulted about my request to see Esher papers. Like all English gentlemen, Adeane is extraordinarily modest and apparently simple, whereas if one looks him up in *Who's Who* one sees that he has every honour, and even got a First at university. I suppose shrewd. Said that travelling overseas with the Queen he was always aware that persons they met were sucking up to him because of his position. Nice little man. Liked him much. He advised me to see Regy's granddaughters by Zena Dare.

---

* Lieut-Col Sir Michael Adeane (1910–84); Principal Private Secretary to HM The Queen, 1953–72; cr. life peer, 1972.
† Arthur Bigge, 1st Baron Stamfordham (1849–1931); Private Secretary to George V as Prince of Wales and King.

Sunday, 20 March

On 12 February we left for South Africa and we returned on the 12th of this month. In retrospect I enjoyed it all, and the safari. Returned to a pile of letters reporting good reviews of *Caves of Ice*. Weather here balmy. Was surprised and uplifted to find a bank of primroses in Somerset Place garden when I took the dogs for their matutinal pee. Crocuses and small daffodils to rejoice the heart.

An awful number of friends have died during my month's absence. First Charles Robertson,* who only a few weeks ago took me to look at the new property on the outskirts of Bath on Sham Castle side. He was so charming and gentle that I regretted having fallen out with him over the Bath [Preservation] Trust rows of a year or so ago, and said to A. that we must ask him and his wife to lunch when we got back. Heart failure, I believe. Then Alan Lennox-Boyd,† run over and killed. Boofy Arran gone. Jock Balfour.‡ And now Leigh Ashton,§ who had been shut up in St Andrew's loony bin for the past 25 years so I cannot lament his departure. Boofy not seen for ages. A nervous, jumpy, sharp little man like a bird. Very intelligent and quick, with a staccato voice like David Cecil's¶ and Andrew Devonshire's, he being related to them both. He was a friend at Oxford and used to make long-distance train journeys in order to write his essays, the only way he could manage them, and had fast motor cars. He once made advances to me when I lived in Norfolk Street off Park Lane, after

---

* Businessman and philanthropist, head of jam-making firm; sometime Chairman of Bath Preservation Trust; m. Barbara Fry (sister of Jeremy Fry, inventor and resident of Bath).

† Alan Lennox-Boyd (1904–83); MP (C) Mid-Bedfordshire, 1931–60; Secretary of State for Colonies, 1954–9; cr. Viscount Boyd of Merton, 1960; m.1938 Lady Patricia Guinness.

‡ Sir John Balfour (1894–1983); HM Ambassador to Spain, 1951–4.

§ Sir Leigh Ashton (1897–1983); Director of Victoria and Albert Museum, 1945–55.

¶ Lord David Cecil (1902–86); yr s. of 4th Marquess of Salisbury; historian and writer; Goldsmiths' Professor of English Literature, Oxford, 1948–69; m. 1932 Rachel MacCarthy.

we had wined and dined, and jumped into bed.* It was not a success and neither of us ever referred to the incident again. I had not seen Alan either for some years and suspected he may have been offended by something I wrote in my diaries about him or Chips.† With him too I slept more than once, as indeed with his brother George, but they were not romantic occasions. I knew all four Lennox-Boyd brothers, Francis the youngest being the most mysterious and charming. Elegant, slim and willowy, and addicted to soft clothing and a soft life, he became a parachutist in the war and was shot on landing behind enemy lines. Donald was murdered by the Nazis before the outbreak of war and his ashes handed over to Alan in a little box on his being summoned to Berlin. I suppose a British spy. Altogether a good bunch of brothers. Some mystery about their origins.

Thursday, 7 April

Map in hand, I drove to look round the Sherborne estate [near Cheltenham, Glos.] which has been bequeathed to the N.T. by the late Charlie Sherborne.‡ It was just like the old days when I so often made these inspections. Went first to Lodge Park, not visited by me since 1938, now inhabited by the Sherbornes' housekeeper and husband, nice people. I found myself automatically exercising that old manner which used to endear me to owners.§ They have been given the right to live in the Lodge if they want to. I was amazed that the Sherbornes, who were very rich indeed, lived in such drab

---

* Lord Arran (see 24 April 1972) was best known to the public as the supposedly heterosexual peer who introduced the Sexual Offences Bill which became law in July 1967 and decriminalised homosexual acts between consenting adults in private.
† In *Ancestral Voices*, J. L.-M. describes the unreciprocated passion of Lennox-Boyd ('X.B.') for the American soldier Stuart Preston in 1943, and the fruitless efforts of Lennox-Boyd's brother-in-law, Henry 'Chips' Channon MP, to encourage the affair.
‡ Charles Dutton, 7th Baron Sherborne (1911–82). (The heir to the barony was his distant cousin Ralph Dutton, friend of J. L.-M., on whose death in 1985 it became extinct.)
§ Marginal note added by J. L.-M. in 1988: 'Some pretension.'

surroundings. Lord S. died only three months ago and the rooms are down at heel, paper peeling off walls in bedrooms and bathrooms. Very little furniture or pictures of interest. In one bedroom a stack of portraits, nothing very good I guess. They had a sale about a year ago. Allowed services of porcelain to go piecemeal, some still remaining at Lodge Park. The housekeeper's husband told me they didn't take the slightest interest in their possessions. And Audrey,* with whom I had tea, said that he never went round the estate for years before his death. Estate very broken down. Altogether a depressing property and I don't find the land beautiful. The part on the hill is flat and dreary, the Sherborne brook vale prettier. The large house was sold and is being turned into flats. Ugly car park with asphalt and concrete curb.

Sunday, 10 April

A. had been due to accompany me to lunch with the Eshers today. Instead she was summoned by Rupert Loewenstein to fly in David Somerset's plane with hired pilot to France. Mick Jagger,† the Rolling Stone, having read *The Englishman's Garden*, told Rupert that he wanted Mrs L.-M. to lay out the garden of his château near Tours. So she chucked the Eshers today and I went alone.

Arrived punctually at one o'clock at the tower Lionel has built for himself on Christmas Common, just inside the drive gates to Watlington [Park, Oxfordshire]. Very nice inside. Outside gloomy and without charm. Not strictly speaking a tower, though built on four levels. More like a London town house. Gloomy dusky brick and ugly pitched roof. Pretty wooden ceilings exposed, and much wainscot. Picture windows. View from top bedroom (Christian's) splendid. No garden, some rides cut through the trees. Elms, once thick, now dead and gone. Oaks, both old and seedlings. I returned Oliver's 'secret life' of his father and another book lent me by Lionel. His sister Nancy

---

* J.L.-M's sister Audrey Stevens was a tenant of the Sherborne estate at Windrush Mill.
† Michael Philip 'Mick' Jagger (b. 1943); singer and songwriter, co-founder of Rolling Stones, 1962.

there along with husband Evelyn Shuckburgh,* retired ambassador with beard. Also his cousin Mary Cheyne, daughter of Maurice Brett and Zena Dare.† During luncheon we talked of Regy. Evident that Mrs Cheyne devoted to him. Wouldn't hear a word of criticism by Lionel. As children, after the death of their father, she and her sister lived with their grandmother, Nellie Esher. Said her grandmother was less sympathetic than her grandfather, whom she could tease; he had a sense of humour and was gentle with children.

Heavenly Christian talked about Regy's daughter Dorothy Brett,‡ known as 'Doll' or 'Brett', whom she and Lionel saw in Mexico where she lived the greater part of her life, having gone there with D. H. Lawrence and Frieda. Showed me one of Brett's pictures, full of dancing movement. Christian would like to organise an exhibition to coincide with the publication of her biography this autumn. I suggested she contact Richard Shone. Regy violently disapproved of his daughter's painting. When the Tate acquired some of her work, she said, 'Poor Pupsie must be turning in his grave at the thought of me hanging there.' Through the library window of the big house, I watched Christian's slim dark figure, like an apostrophe in the grey-green landscape, receding as she walked back to the Tower. Seductive.

Sir Evelyn told a story of a young foreigner in the 1930s staying for the first time in a grand English country house. He told the son of the house that he did not think he could keep up with the tradition of drinking quantities of port after dinner. The son said, 'Oh, that's all right. As soon as you feel you've had enough, just slip under the table.' He drank one glass, which satisfied him, then slowly sank under the table. He waited seemingly for hours in an uncomfortable position

---

* Sir Evelyn Shuckburgh (1909–94); diplomatist; aide to Sir Anthony Eden as Foreign Secretary and Prime Minister; HM Ambassador to Italy, 1966–9; m. 1937 Hon. Nancy Brett, dau. of 3rd Viscount Esher.

† As J.L.-M. was to describe in his biography, Reginald Esher had an unusual relationship with his younger son Maurice Brett (1882–1934), whom he bombarded with love letters and whose marriage (1911) to the actress Zena Dare he arranged. Marie (b. 1916), youngest of three children of that marriage, m. 1938 Commander Archibald Cheyne.

‡ Artist (1883–1977); lived in New Mexico, where she had gone with D. H. Lawrence in 1924.

while the other men continued talking. Then he felt a pair of hands clutching his throat. 'Who are you?' he whispered in horror. A small voice replied, 'Only the boy employed to loosen the collars.' Can that be true? Of Regency times perhaps.

Tuesday, 12 April

A. greatly enjoyed her visit to Mick Jagger. He is charming with a huge smiling mouth. Quite unspoilt. Rather touching in that he reads voraciously and has taste and a desire to accumulate beautiful objects. The château he has bought near Amboise is ravishing and she is eager to lay out and plant the garden for him. House still very uncomfortable. Jagger offered to put her and Rupert up in a hotel, but A. said No, she preferred to stay with him. Given a room with no running water and slept on the floor, after a good French dinner with wine. Jagger drinks little. Speaks good French. Has read my book on Beckford. Told her he came from Lees, Lancashire, where his father was church organist. So we have the same origins. Whenever he buys an antique his mother complains, 'But Mick, you can afford to buy something really nice. That's second-hand.'

Tuesday, 19 April

Lunched with David Lloyd* at Franco's in Jermyn Street. He had come up from Hertfordshire for the occasion in spite of illness. His wife Jean had telephoned me at Eardley's last night warning he might not be able to make it; but he did. Luckily he arrived at the restaurant first and waved to me from a table, otherwise I should not have recognised him. An old man supported by a stick. Face shape altered, eyes large and watery, yet unseeing. Only his teeth when he smiled were recognisable. Suffers from emphysema owing to smoking 50 cigarettes a day, also from excessive drinking. I always picture David as a boy at Eton, then young man at Cambridge, in perpetual trouble for

---

* Alexander David, 2nd Baron Lloyd of Dolobran (1912–85); son of George, 1st Baron, for whom J.L.-M. had worked as private secretary, 1932–5; Undersecretary for the Colonies, 1954–7; m. 1942 Lady Jean Ogilvy.

small peccadilloes, who would come to my room in Portman Square and sit on my writing table, begging me to get him out of some scrape, such as having driven his father's car into a ditch when he should have been attending a lecture. He is now very ill. He had asked to see me ostensibly to talk about the future of his father's papers, which are in fact safely lodged at Churchill College. What he really wants is for me to write the biography, but I told him some years ago that I cannot. Today I exhorted him to undertake it himself, knowing that he will not have either the energy, ability or length of life to do so, but feeling it would give him occupation and interest. He was very pitiful, and talked so much that by the time I left for N.T. meeting we had decided nothing. He showed me a letter from a woman who runs 'the Box', ending, 'I wonder if you have had a serious shock within recent years?' David marvelled at this, saying she could not have known how the suicide of his son Charlie had knocked him edgeways. But of course she could have known it. He asked me directly whether his father was homosexual, 'not that I mind a scrap', etc. I said he surely was so by nature, but did not practise that I knew. He told me that Alan Lennox-Boyd, whose junior minister he had been at the Colonial Office, could often not be found at moments of crisis, having gone off with what David called 'Sweetie', *i.e.* Alex Beattie.[*] He suggested that homosexuals were unreliable in that respect. (Indeed, they do seem to have less control over their emotions than other men. Why is this?) I left David feeling sad, and later wrote telling him I would do anything to help with the biography short of writing it.[†]

Wednesday, 20 April

I suffer less from angst these days and more from worry and fuss. Less too from spring fever or restlessness, due to impotence, I suppose. I think how hateful it will be to leave my possessions which I love and cherish. No one will treat them with the affection which I do.

---

[*] Major Alexander Beattie of the Coldstream Guards; friend of Alan Lennox-Boyd.
[†] Partly thanks to J.L.-M's good offices, a biography of George Lloyd by Dr John Charmley, a friend of Michael Bloch, was published in 1987.

Friday, 22 April

Alex Moulton called for me at 10 in his beautiful Rolls. Drove to Devon. Main object of exercise to visit Halsdon House, William Cory's, where Regy and his friends stayed in the 1870s. We found it in the evening, before sunset. It was just as I imagined, and as it must have looked when Cory was living there. Still very remote, approached down high-banked, primrose-studded lanes. We followed the route they must have taken on foot or by wagonette from Eggesford station. Left car in lane and walked through white gate. Smoke rising from a bonfire. No one about. The house seemed empty, except for a Georgian bookcase and a Regency couch which we espied through a cobwebbed window. Building in state of slight decay, garden being attended to just as it would have been by the young men staying with Cory. I thought of Chat,* Uncle Fred Lees and others in this compact, unimportant small squire's seat in the depths of Devon. Forgot to look for Regy's and Chat's carved names on the window sill. Next morning visited an estate agent in Great Torrington who informed me that the house had just been bought, presumably from the Furse family who have owned it since the seventeenth century, by of all people the drummer of the Rolling Stones.† Curious coincidence in view of A's new alliance with Mick Jagger.

Motored to Penzance. Such a storm, the sea so rough we could not cross to St Michael's Mount. Had tea with Lady St Levan. Gave her a copy of *Some People*, just out in paperback. She did not talk a word about Harold. Remarkably fit for eighty-seven. Might be sixty. Not deaf or decrepit, but cold. Don't suppose my visit gave her much pleasure.‡ Alex on the other hand a great success, talking about his new bicycle which interested her much. On return to Badminton I felt so exhausted that I slept for three hours in the afternoon and woke still feeling tired. Alex a sweet companion, taking an interest in all things.

---

* Charles Williamson, Regy Brett's great love at Eton, who later became a Catholic priest, but remained a close friend.
† Charlie Watts.
‡ Lady St Levan's cool reception of J.L.-M. may have owed something to the fact that, in his biography of her brother Harold Nicolson, he had indicated that she had conducted a lesbian affair in the 1930s with her sister-in-law, Vita Sackville-West.

His sole fault is a tendency to over-emphasise and pontificate, using long words which he often gets wrong.

Saturday, 30 April

Delicious day, sun and storm, but the ground is drenched. Took dogs for the usual weekend walk – Cherry Orchard round. It takes me exactly one hour and thirty-five minutes, and I am quite tired after it. Heard my first and probably last cuckoo in the distance. Of all bird calls it still moves me most, more so than the nightingale's, for it truly recalls far-off things and battles long ago. Primroses along the banks of the lane less conspicuous than a fortnight ago because the grass and other foliage has sprung up. Indeed the green has burst, still only into loose bud, not full flower. This is the one moment when I do want to be in England – this and the October moment.

Have just finished Rupert[Hart-Davis]'s fifth volume of correspondence with George Lyttelton.* I can hardly bear the knowledge that there can be but one more, for Lyttelton died in 1962 and we have now reached 1960. He complains of increasing deafness and pains, yet is never self-pitying. Rupert's spryness is a slight irritant, only very slight to me, but definitely to Diana Mosley who complained of the last volume in this respect. Lyttelton's letters are the more fascinating. Yet he complains that, whereas Rupert has so much to tell about the million things he is doing and distinguished folk he is seeing, he has so little, as a retired schoolmaster living in Suffolk. It merely proves my theory that the best diarists and letter-writers are those who see *nobody* and have *nothing* to write about. The learning of both staggers me. I have written to Rupert today suggesting spending a night at the end of May.

A. told me that, at the opera three days ago, Loelia Lindsay approached her with loud complaints of my *Caves*. A. groaned. Loelia said she might be old-fashioned but she was disgusted by my reference to having caught crabs during the war. This upset me because I had wondered whether to leave the incident out, but in the end my determination to be honest decided me to leave it in. Anyway, when I got

---

* Hart-Davis was editing his correspondence with his old Eton housemaster Hon. George Lyttelton (1883–1962) in six volumes (John Murray, 1978–84).

to Bath I began tearing up several pages of unpublished diaries; then desisted.

Wednesday, 11 May

Motored to London to dine with M. and Charles Orwin at Oxford and Cambridge Club. M. is off tomorrow to Spain and Portugal for a month.* Delicious evening. Charles full of engaging chaff, caustic and affectionate. M. on these occasions goes into a slouching daze, speaks little, and then, aroused by some remark, delivers himself of a devastating rejoinder. Charles deprecates his wasting his talent on the Windsors. Alas, I agree. As we parted on the pavement at Pall Mall, C. embraced me on both cheeks, M. on the lips. M. said, 'Ring me up tomorrow morning, please.' I motored off to stay with Eardley, happy. Found E. suffering from lumbago and somewhat depressed. I fear age is affecting his natural gaiety.

Driving from Oxford to London, I marvelled at the beauty of the spring struggling against the desecrations of man. At a new road junction near High Wycombe, bulldozers were tearing up acres of meadows and woods. Amid the chaos, the mangled, torn earth and the exposed chalk, a few remaining hedges of may in blossom and two weeping willows somehow managed to survive. One must now seek beauty no longer in the mass but in the little, and thank God for the diminishing oases of untouched nature. Plants are the only form of life devoid of evil.

Saturday, 21 May

A. and I motored to Simon and Tricia [Lees-Milne]'s newly acquired house by Clifton-on-Teme. Far larger and nicer than the one at Alfrick. In the heart of old, unspoilt Worcestershire; indeed the most lovely country in England, and on approaching it my heart gave a leap – though not as high as it would have been ten years ago, the spring in it having slackened, I fear, like all my emotions. Odd that Simon, who was brought up in Oldham, where we Leeses sprang

---

* He was writing a book on the Duke of Windsor's adventures there in the summer of 1940.

from, should have made his life and home in Worcestershire, where Dick and I were reared. The house they have bought is a rather basic version of Wickhamford – half-timbered wing, but with tall eighteenth-century brick attachment at one end. All steep little staircases and ups and downs. A. said she would rather live in a villa in Worcester. Poor things, they have absolutely no taste. But they are so happy and proud of their acquisition that it is delicious. A happy pair. Gave us excellent luncheon, roast chicken tenderly cooked, and oranges sliced in ginger. A view of Jones's folly at Abberley would have been visible from the house had it not poured with rain all day. Indeed it has rained every day this year. Worst spring ever. Land waterlogged.

On the news this evening announcement of K. Clark's death. Now I have always regarded him as about the greatest man of my generation. I have never known him intimately. Few men have. He did not care for men, and greatly loved women. Was a proud, aloof man with a gracious manner that did not put one at ease. But whenever he gave praise one felt that God Almighty had himself conferred a benediction. I think he may be classed with Ruskin as an intepreter of the arts. He would also have made an admirable dictator had he turned his talents to politics.

Sunday, 22 May

To the Hollands' annual concert at Sheepridge Barn. Freezing. Nearly died of cold eating our snacks in the cloister. I perched on a chair next to Liz Longman, balancing plate and glass, and was photographed by an inquisitive press man. Joan Holland, dressed and painted to kill, swathed in canary silk rustling dress (with, she explained, tweeds underneath), swept A. and me into a tent where Princess Margaret, guest of the evening, was drinking whisky out of a large tumbler. We were presented. She, possibly distracted by meeting so many people within a small enclosed space, was not gracious and a little brash. Said to me, 'Had I known you were a contributor to the Picnic Book, I would not have written my piece.' How does one take this sort of remark? I smiled wryly and said, 'Oh Ma'am, but I so enjoyed yours.' 'Do you like the book?' she asked. 'I liked the jacket,' I said untruthfully. 'I hate picnics,' she said, 'but did you like the book?' – this time to A. as much as me. That was as far as our contact went. How I hate meeting royalty. One gets absolutely nowhere.

Wednesday, 25 May

Attended my first Foyle's Literary Luncheon as a Guest of Honour, to celebrate Fleur Cowles' garden book and Lady Cottesloe's *Duchess of Beaufort's Flower Book*. Master [the Duke of Beaufort] was incongruously in the chair.* I sat between Sally Westminster and Christina Foyle† at the top table. Liked Miss Foyle. Sympathetic woman, slightly bedint which makes for cosiness. Must have been pretty. Told me about her father who started the bookshop in 1904. She has a mass of papers. Has known all the literary people of her time. She entered the shop at nineteen. I said she ought to write her memoirs and the history of Foyle's. Fleur Cowles,‡ wearing dark spectacles to give herself confidence, read her speech. Mrs Callaghan, wife of late PM, gave vote of thanks. Whereas Master and Miss Cowles began their speeches, 'Your Serene Highnesses, My Lords, Ladies and Gentlemen' (don't know who the SHs were), Mrs Callaghan, with what seemed like some deliberateness, began, 'Ladies and Gentlemen, at short notice I have been asked by Lord Beaufort . . .' Was this meant to take the Duke down a peg according to Socialist principles?

Wednesday, 8 June

A. saw Evelyn Woolriche today who told her she was reading *Caves* and asked if I could possibly have a friend left in the world after the things I wrote about them; or were they all dead? Then this evening A. and I planned our trip to Scotland in September, and thought it

---

* Lady Cottesloe and Sally Westminster were both mistresses of the Duke of Beaufort.
† Christina Foyle (1911–99); Managing Director of W. & G. Foyle Ltd, booksellers (founded by her father); started Foyle's Literary Luncheons, 1930; m. 1938 Ronald Batty.
‡ American writer and artist, author of *The Flower Game* (1983).

would be nice to invite ourselves to stay at Tyninghame with the Haddingtons.* Then I remembered that I had written some rather cheeky things about Lady Binning,† who was the mother of Lord Haddington. We both read them through, and agreed that in the circumstances we could not possibly ask ourselves to stay. At times I am overcome with embarrassment at my foolish and impertinent anecdotes and criticisms. Wish I had never published these bloody diaries. Can't think what came over me.

Wednesday, 15 June

Motored Audrey to Bretforton for Harry Ashwin's memorial service in the village church. He died a week ago after being a cabbage in bed for two years. Was a wraith of his former plump self, and barked at visitors who had to be kept away. We strolled in the churchyard and looked at Ashwin headstones dated 1680. Were told later that the family has been here since the 1530s, 450 years in direct descent. Harry the last, no children. His niece, Ruth's daughter, inherits, and will sell the estate. That is the end of an ancient line of small Worcestershire squires of little distinction, the house of no great distinction either. Yet sadness envelopes me when I cast back my memory nets to their furthest limits. For we children adored the Ashwins, the only friends we had. In the school holidays we saw them most days, either at Bretforton or Wickhamford. Rode over on our ponies, or drove in the trap, or bicycled, motor-scooted, motor-cycled or motored. In summer played tennis on the lawn before scrumptious teas, in winter hide-and-seek upstairs in the gloomy passages and bedrooms. My favourite was Clare, tall and plain with a dry sense of humour; she died in 1945 of consumption brought on by

---

* George Baillie-Hamilton, 12th Earl of Haddington (1894–1986), of Tyninghame, Haddingtonshire; son of Brig.-Gen. Lord Binning (d. 1917) and Lady Binning *née* Salting (d. 1952); m. 1923 Sarah Cook.
† J.L.-M. first met Lady Binning in December 1944 and saw her often during the next three years to discuss her bequest of Fenton House, Hampstead, to the N.T. He depicted her as a rather ridiculous old lady, expressing violently pro-Nazi views, but agreeably infatuated with himself.

war-work. Harry always deadly dull, a lump. Mrs Ashwin a dignified, wistful, beautiful, humorous lady of the old school; Mr Ashwin, like a Cavalier in breeches and gaiters, spent all his days in a separate office building on the edge of the shrubbery and stalked into the dining room for meals, graciously acknowledging the presence of us children. Their enormous limousine was all windows like a greenhouse, driven by Robbins, the Plymouth Brethren chauffeur who considered it wicked to go to the pantomime. Shall never forget the unique smell of the hall, musty linseed oil on the black panelling mixed with Mansion polish. The empty drawing room where for long hours Thetis thumped on the piano and resented our interruptions. There was Bobbie, the good-looking, flagrantly pansy brother, whose friends were rotters; he died when he fell out of the back of a car in Piccadilly onto his head. Lamented by his adoring mother, whose first passion was her son Jim: he died of appendicitis at school in 1907, and might have continued the line had he lived. Harry a sort of castrato. We walked from the church through the garden, still so well kept up and tidy – the square dovecote, the barn, the old tennis court which echoed to our childish voices of gaiety, to the pealing church bells on Saturday evenings when the bell-pullers practised. The house so stuffy inside and un-beautiful, yet so continuous, so unchanging [a record] of this family of small squires, of whose 450 years I witnessed certainly 70 and probably more, for there are photographs of us in our perambulators at Bretforton, Harry an enormous baby in frills and a large linen hat, like an inflated balloon. Today I have seen the veil drawn. It is not only the Kedlestons, the Beltons, the Ugbrookes or the Powderhams which are vanishing, but the humbler manor houses of the small gentry. *Eheu!* I am inured to it all now, and hardly care, for the *dégringolade* has gone too far.

Friday, 17 June

Alec Clifton-Taylor and Eardley dined at Brooks's. For once an excellent meal, total bill £40. Alec very affable. Recognition has come to him in old age with his television series on old cities. Said he had realised his three ambitions, which were to get into *Who's Who*, appear on *Desert Island Discs*, and something equally fatuous which I forget.

Said that, when asked which he thought to be the best modern building in Britain, he could not name one. Remarked that the retention of the able seaman's uniform since the eighteenth century was the most sensible thing the Navy had done, it having great sex-appeal for women. Not only women, I opine.

Went this morning to Clarence House, open to members of Georgian Group and SPAB of which the Queen Mother President. A great treat. Handsome house outside though so often altered since Nash's day. Charming inside though architecture of rooms disappointing. Decoration acceptable, unexciting, not too pastellish. Lovely contents, all covetable. Royal portraits on walls along with contemporary artists. Good marks for Queen Elizabeth. Eclectic collection – Duncan Grant, Matthew Smith, Gunn, Monet, Augustus John (of Herself, and Bernard Shaw asleep), Ethel Walker, and of course de Laszlo and Seago. Not up to date; but why should she be, aged 83? A whole room of John Pipers of Windsor Castle, well-framed. Splendid things. Much silver and gold plate and many bibelots, scattered on occasional tables. Innumerable clocks, French and English of first quality, all going and keeping time. A lady supervising said Yes, we have the clock man in twice a week. Footmen standing in passages and rooms (we were allowed upstairs) in scarlet tails, waistcoats with gold braid, white bow ties, somehow not chic.

Friday, 24 June

Two remarks made to me recently have made me ponder. When walking in the garden at Chatsworth with Debo and E. Winn, I said I could not think of any of our friends who had lived a life of unalloyed happiness. Debo said, 'I can think of one – yours.' I said, 'Yes, I have been very lucky.' Nevertheless, mine is not a happy disposition. I have always felt unfulfilled in love and work. And John Smith, when I met him in the Burlington Arcade, said, 'Do you still work in that beautiful Bath library, where you manufacture all those lies?' I laughed at the time, but the more I think about his remark, the more offensive I think it was. I wish I had made a retort which showed my displeasure.

Last weekend we had Selina Hastings to stay for two nights, and during this week Emma Tennant,* who accompanied A. on a [N.T.] Garden Panel expedition to Kingston Lacy. Both these girls are near perfection. Both extremely intelligent and attractive and entertaining. Both are approaching forty. I far prefer the company of this age group to my own. Eardley proposed himself for lunch on Wednesday and I was not a bit pleased to see him. People fail to realise that I need to be left alone to write; and when I am eating I am still thinking of what I am writing, and cannot concentrate on other things.

Thursday, 30 June

To London for the day. Met J[ohn] K[enworthy]-B[rowne] at the Victoria & Albert for snack luncheon at cafeteria. Good food but expensive. A young man playing sentimental music on a harp. J. very sweet and disarming, told me that if I died he would have no incentive to go on living. We looked at the Oliver Messel exhibition, mostly of quick sketches for theatrical décor, not enough portraits which he often did well. Too clichéd, too slick, too Twentyish-sophisticated, but undeniable talent. Standing before one exhibit and telling J. how Tilly Losch† stuck pins into Diana Cooper to get her to move, I noticed a young god behind me attentively listening. As we proceeded we constantly ran into the young man, who smiled sweetly. As we parted, J. said, laughing, 'You have made a conquest.' Went to Museum shop and bought a postcard or two. There was the young god again. We both smiled. I said, 'You and I seem to have the same interests today,' and passed on. Then he came up to me and said, 'Excuse me, Sir' – the 'Sir' is upsetting – 'I could not help overhearing your conversation with your friend. Did you know Messel?' I told him I did. He said he was writing a thesis on Gertrude Lawrence‡ and asked if I had known her.

---

* Lady Emma Cavendish (b. 1943), dau. of 11th Duke of Devonshire; m. 1963 Hon. Tobias Tennant, yst s. of 2nd Baron Glenconner.
† Ottilie Ethel Losch (1907–75); Austrian actress and dancer, lover of Tom Mitford in early 1930s; m. 1st J.L.-M's Eton contemporary Edward James, 2nd (as his 2nd wife) 6th Earl of Carnarvon.
‡ Actress and singer (1898–1952), particularly associated with the musical comedies of Noël Coward.

Alas, I hadn't. But I took his address, and promised that if any ideas came to me I would write. Tall, slim, wearing clean tight jeans, pretty open shirt revealing gold chain, slender throat, fair complexion, head of Dionysus, thick, wavy, flaxen hair.[*]

I was early for tea with Rosamond, so strolled around area near Hereford Square. Saw plaque on house where George Borrow[†] lived. Passed Bina Gardens, and house inhabited by General Allenby, to Wetherby Gardens, where my old friend Violet Gielgud, John's aunt, lived, whom I used to visit for tea in the late Twenties when I first lived in London. An affected but kindly lady. Returned past Ashburnham Gardens, where dear George Chavchavadze[‡] had a room in his poor bachelor days and would play to me, I being transported both by the music and the romance of his being a Georgian prince. I passed some old people on the pavement and wondered if they too had frequented this backwater of London at the time, perhaps being even younger and handsomer than I. I found Ros very 'up', delighted with the filming of her novel which is being done by a first-class team. Yet complained Selina would never finish her biography before she was dead. I told her one ought to be dead before one's biog. was published.

Wednesday, 6 July

Motored to London to dine with John Betj and Feeble. Feeble sweetly welcoming and prepared delicious roast chicken followed by strawberries and cream. John slumped in his armchair watching *Coronation Street* when I arrived, at an angle to the screen, two feet from it. Made signs of recognition. Spoke little. Mouth down at both sides. Difficult to elicit interest or response, yet I think he was fairly pleased to see me. Did not move to the table. Feeble put a board across arms of chair and gave him his helping, tied a bib, gave him a spoon. He toyed with his

---

[*] He was Timothy Morgan-Owen (b. 1958).

[†] Writer, traveller and linguist (1803–81).

[‡] Prince George Chavchavadze, bisexual Russian *émigré* concert pianist; m. the Philadelphia heiress Elizabeth de Breteuil, *née* Ridgeway, who was killed with him in a car crash in 1962.

food like a baby. His trousers loose, not tied to his person by belt or braces. I talked to Feeble at the table. John heard what we said but did not join in beyond a grunt or two. Then his nurse came. 'Do you want to go to bed, darling?' Feeble asked at 8.45. 'Yes, I think so.' The nurse piloted him upstairs. I did not see him again. Talked to Feeble and left at 9.30. She said he was lucky, for he had no pain and was not lonely. Mind clear. Was read to by a young actor every afternoon. Is wheeled to his house each morning where his secretary opens letters and answers them for him. I asked about Bevis Hillier. F. groaned. Said she had not seen him. Did not see how he could write John's biography without mentioning her, yet did not want to be mentioned while she was alive. At least Jock Murray has promised the book won't come out till John is dead.

Saturday, 9 July

Dined with Ian McCallum at American Museum to meet Princess Margaret of Hesse. A delightful old bird, daughter of Lord Geddes and widow of a great-grandson of Queen Victoria. After dinner I sat with her and Robin Warrender. She entertained us by extracting from a wallet several crumpled old bits of paper from which she read apothegms which had tickled her fancy, such as

> With my peas I always eat honey.
> I have done this all through my life.
> I admit that the taste is quite funny,
> But at least the peas stick to the knife

and others of like nature. Then guffaws of laughter, her old teeth wobbling up and down and her head shaking the sparse strands of grey hair. She is very plain, plump, comfortable, genial and good-natured. Told us a long, involved story about a famous Holbein of a Madonna with spread cloak protecting two children, and a pair of donors (Swiss), which came to the Hesse family in the early nineteenth century. Says it is of great beauty and when K. Clark saw it he was moved to tears. At the outbreak of the last war, she and her husband removed it for safety to their castle in Silesia, thinking it would be safe there now the Russians were allies of Germany.

They did this at some risk as the Nazis had ordered all treasures to be kept where they were. Then Silesia was invaded by the Russians. They managed to smuggle picture to Dresden. All the people involved in the smuggle were killed in the Allies' raid, and the lorry carrying it destroyed. Picture remained intact. It returned to the castle in the West where the Hesses were incarcerated, where they kept it hidden under the bed. The castle was turned into a hostel for children. One night the lights failed, and stampeding children trampled over picture. Unharmed. Then Belgian authorities arrived and offered to buy it. The Hesses, deprived of food and every necessity, refused to sell. 'Just think what you could buy with the money we are offering,' said the Belgians. 'I would buy the Madonna,' replied the Prince. She calls it the Miraculous Madonna. She also told us there are to be centenary celebrations at Darmstadt next week in memory of the Tsarina's sister,* who has been canonised by the Orthodox Church. She was buried alive for days in a cave. The Princess has just seen letters written by the Tsarina, her husband's aunt, from Ekaterinburg, describing ordeals so terrible that the mind boggles.

Monday, 18 July

Last week I went on two-day [N.T.] Arts Panel tour to Devon, visiting Knightshayes, Castle Drogo and Killerton. John Julius [Norwich] being away, I was chairman. The first house Victorian, second Edwardian, third Georgian and modern. I was looked after like a delicate parcel that might, unless cherished, come undone. The niceness of these N.T. boys is touching. And they are far cleverer than we lot were. The heat intense, 90 degrees. Stayed in Moretonhampstead Hotel in room like a furnace. Felt shy meeting the Aclands,† for I said some disobliging

---

* Princess Elisabeth of Hesse (1864–1918); m. 1884 Grand Duke Sergei of Russia (1857–1905); henceforth known as Grand Duchess Ella.
† Sir Richard Acland, 15th Bt (1906–90); radical campaigner, at various times MP for Liberal, Common Wealth and Labour Parties; m. 1936 Stella Alford; donated 19,000 ancestral acres in Devon and Somerset to N.T., 1944, including his houses at Killerton near Exeter and Holnicote near Porlock, on condition that stag hunting should be allowed to continue on the land.

things about them in *Caves*.* Lady Acland said to me, 'I read *Ancestral Voices* and was relieved there was no mention of us.' This woman, whom I remember as aggressive and dogmatic, now charming.

Tuesday, 19 July

Attended what should have been my last Properties Committee, but I have been asked to attend the October one at Marcus Worsley's† personal request. Am dreadfully afraid they may give me a present or make a speech of appreciation. I shall not miss these meetings. They give me no pleasure and I contribute little. Nowadays they consist of discussing long, dreary reports, and seldom consider historic houses.

Friday, 22 July

A. and I motor to Chatsworth for weekend. It might have been one of those house parties in a Disraeli novel: Andrew and Debo; Lady Arran (Boofy's widow);‡ Lady Margaret Tennant (called 'Maggots', sister of Lord Airlie and Jean Lloyd); Kitty Mersey;§ Heywood and Anne Hill. To whom were added on Saturday St John Stevas (whom I call Norman), and Lord and Lady Gowrie.¶ The last is Minister for the Arts and not well-equipped for the job, for he seems to know little about music or painting. St John Stevas [his predecessor as Arts Minister] was very bitchy about him before he arrived. In fact

---

* Of a visit which, accompanied by the Harold Nicolsons, he made to the Aclands at Killerton, J. L.-M. wrote on 9 August 1947: 'We all disliked this property, the garden, the ugly shrubs, the ménage, the dogmatic owners, and two plain little boys . . . In the house is established the Workers' Transport Company, people smelling of disinfectant . . . We saw no point in this property which is no more beautiful than the surrounding country.'

† Sir Marcus Worsley, 5th Bt (b. 1925); Conservative MP, 1959–74; Chairman of N.T. Properties Committee from 1980.

‡ Fiona Colquhoun; m. 1937 Hon. Arthur Gore, who s. 1958 as 8th Earl of Arran.

§ Lady Katherine Petty-Fitzmaurice (1912–95), dau. of 6th Marquess of Lansdowne; m. 1933 3rd Viscount Mersey (d. 1979).

¶ Alexander Ruthven, 2nd Earl of Gowrie (b. 1939); Minister for the Arts, 1983–5; Chairman of Sotheby's, 1985–93; m. (2nd) 1974 Countess Adelheid von der Schulenburg.

St J. S. is a second-rate fellow, very pleased with himself, tactless, and as Anne said, 'no oil painting'. He talks big, shoots a line. Rather bedint. Yet friendly enough. Too much 'darling Debo' and name-dropping. Loathes Mrs Thatcher and spoke with utmost contempt of Gowrie for reducing spending on the arts, especially the Theatre Museum, whereas the man was only following orders. Oh, one other guest was Walter Lees.* He and I walked round the pleasure grounds and talked of M. and Charles Orwin, he besotted with the latter. Wonderful food here. The Devonshires' French chef, who left for America where he was offered enormous wages, has returned, saying no one appreciated his cooking there and he preferred to be where he was appreciated.

Sunday, 31 July

The Aids scare is alarming everyone. Last week an article in *The Times* described the symptoms six months after contraction – lethargy, temperature, then swelling of gland nodules, whatever they may be. Then a year's recovery when the patient believes all is well. Then recurrence of temperature etc. and, from whatever complaint thereafter contracted, certain death, owing to immunity to all drugs and treatment. Terror reigns in the minds of all homosexuals.

Wednesday, 3 August

Talked to 'Johnny' Faucigny-Lucinge† last night after dinner with Caroline [Somerset], who had trouble getting his name right in introducing him. He has taken the place of Charles de Noailles in that he stays annually at Sandringham with the Queen Mother and pilots her around France each summer. Told me the difficulty was finding suitable hosts who were rich enough and possessed large houses with rooms enough and servants enough to accommodate her retinue,

---

* Major Walter Lees; sometime Head of Household at British Embassy in Paris; friend of Duke and Duchess of Windsor; then personal assistant to French oil tycoon Pierre Schlumberger.
† Prince Jean-Louis de Faucigny-Lucinge (1904–92).

consisting of himself, Lady Fermoy, the Graftons, 2 maids, 2 valets, 2 detectives. He had just come from Sandringham and said the Q.M. is the only member of the Royal Family one could call cultivated. She has humour, and is never overtly critical. Interested, reads her prep before making visits. He was vastly amused by a little scene in the park. A lot of local old ladies were displaying their pet rabbits. One old lady, very eccentric and untidy, had an awful exhibit, an ancient, bald rabbit like a melon which she adorned with ribbons and furbelows. The other old ladies did their utmost to shield this spectacle from the Queen. But the Q. made straight for her, talked to her only and stroked the animal. When urged by Fortune Grafton to walk on to some other stall she lingered, turning her head towards the proud owner as though most loth to leave. All the other respectable old lady competitors furious of course. This an example of her compelling charm, he says.

Saturday, 6 August

In what does the perennial melancholy of August consist? The sniff of autumn; the lengthening sunbeams; the tiredness of grasses; the persistence of convolvulus in hedgerows; the disappearance from verges of blue geranium; few flowers, yet colour in the garden; bees bustling to accumulate whatever it is that they do accumulate before it is too late; and above all the quiet. This is the only windless month. Mornings and evenings are still. There is an echo in the firmament, for earth and sky become close, like the inside of a glass bell. And my [seventy-fifth] birthday, now recording the winter rather than the autumn of my life. It is mentioned in *The Times* now, a sign of mortality. Strangers send me birthday cards; bores pester me with sentimental, gushing letters. But I feel old; always tired; and for the past six weeks have suffered from arthritis in thumb joints and right shoulder. Shall I be alive next year? Or the next? Does it matter? One is aware of one's utter insignificance.

Sunday, 7 August

Motored to London. After lunching with M. at his flat, and leaving my car on Embankment, I joined an odd expedition. Had always wanted to see Field Place near Horsham where Shelley was born. Once tried and was repulsed by the then owner, Charrington. So I joined organised visit of Keats–Shelley Society, which set out from Embankment station in a bus. Party consisted of egregiously unattractive individuals of the arty-intellectual, raffia-hat and sandals variety. Didn't know a soul. Sat next to GP from Gloucester wearing a radiant chestnut wig. Bus arrived at Field Place at 3.45. We could have seen the house in half an hour, but were obliged to wait for hours. It is empty now, having been bought by a solicitor. Squire's house set in fields rather than park with lake at bottom. Main part late seventeenth-century. An 1840s colonnade connecting the two wings, which Shelley never knew, covers the spot where he sat on his last visit, denied entry by his father Timothy. Of Shelley's time a fine staircase, in well of which the Charringtons constructed a lift, destroying part of the balustrade. This staircase a good example of college-like joinery with thick handrail and stout turned balusters. The owner told me that the bailiff employed by Charrington remembered a quantity of papers fetched from attics, some of it in Shelley's handwriting, being carted away to put on bonfire. We stayed on for a ghastly entertainment, a concert by amateurs, Dowland on harpsichord, bearable, and endless recitations by an affected woman dressed like a Druid, agony. We were due to leave at 8 but I persuaded two old ladies to take me to Horsham and drop me at the station. Finally after much delay reached Embankment at 10 to see our bus drive off, having returned the rest of the party some time earlier.

Tuesday, 9 August

Am at Eton, having arrived on Monday morning for a week. Renting a guest flat in Hodgson's House opposite Upper Chapel graveyard. Adequate, but uglily done up. Have now spent three days working in Royal Library at Windsor Castle, reading through Regy's letters to King Edward VII (mostly to Knollys,[*] the Sec.). Today I was informed that Sir Robin Mackworth-Young would see me at 12.40. Like being

---

[*] Francis, 1st Viscount Knollys (1837–1924); Private Secretary to Edward VII as Prince of Wales and King, 1870–1910.

summoned to headmaster's study. Sir R., smaller than I remembered, sat at large writing-table with back to window, scanning me. I am always at my worst on these occasions and talk too much. I began talking of the Droghedas, assuming he would remember meeting us with them, but he evidently didn't. I said how splendid I found the Sovereigns' Private Secretaries to have been. He said that George III was not allowed to have one, for his ministers were supposed to be his Secretaries; so when he wrote a letter he copied it for filing in his own hand. George IV did have one, for he was lazy. Queen Victoria did not have one before and during her marriage. It was only after the Prince Consort's death that she engaged Grey. Mackworth-Young told me it would be appreciated if I gave a copy of my *Stuarts* to the Queen, inscribing it suitably and sending it to her Secretary. He said that, if she was interested – and she *was* interested in the Stuarts – she might read it herself before sending it to the Library at Windsor. Must remember to do this.

Yesterday evening I walked upstream, looking for Queen's Eyot [islet in the Thames] where I used to tipple on cider on hot summer afternoons with Desmond [Parsons]. Couldn't find it. Wandered through Arches, a rather fine serpentine stretch carrying the railway, where I had unromantic trysts, with Tulloch* *inter alia*. Still the river preserves its sinuous course – they can't take that away – and still it is bordered with willows, shimmering. Couldn't find Athens where we bathed. Now the bank crawling with trippers, much litter and noise. A train or two crossed Arches, an old-fashioned enough rumble as though a concession from the past to the present age. Not so the roar of the motorway, with tall lamps. Nor the aeroplanes, descending every two minutes for Heathrow. Sir Robin said the interval is some-times only 90 seconds. Wonder how on earth the experts manage to control the entry. Judy's Passage unchanged, but the boys' houses are for the most part excessively ugly, untidy and scruffy, nothing to boast about for the world's most exclusive school.

Ghosts at every turn. Tom [Mitford] emerging from Dobbs's, perhaps the prettiest of the boys' houses; Desmond skulking down the narrow passage entry (now removed) to m'tutor's; Rupert

---

* (Lieut-Col) I.D.G. Tulloch.

[Hart-Davis] with his ram's head; Hamish [St Clair Erskine] and David Herbert; old Harry Ashwin at Brinton's; Teddie Underdown, so beautiful and the women's undoing, though Pop bitch in his day.* Yet it is all devoid of sentiment somehow. Too far removed in years. My schooldays in the 1920s were closer in time to my grandfather's in the 1860s than to today.

Thursday, 11 August

There is still a bookshop where Mrs Brown's bookshop once stood, but what a declension! Nothing I wanted, and seemed shrunken somehow. Here I bought a lovely nineteenth-century illustrated book of coloured prints of naked savages, ladies with full breasts and red scarves round their heads, gentlemen with spears. McNeile my tutor found it in my room, took it away and burnt it, informing my father of my unhealthy tastes. I have ever since regretted that book. What would Heywood Hill charge for it now? Mrs Brown looked like Queen Mary – utmost dignity, ramrod straight, busted, waisted, long skirt, grey hair in piles like a toy fortress, bland smile, gentle, yet one could not take liberties with her. Dear lady, where does she rest?

Saturday, 20 August

I have seen all Regy's letters to Kings Edward and George and their admirable Secretaries Knollys and Stamfordham, taking massive notes. Was taken to see the room which Esher is thought to have occupied; but it faces the North Terrace and Eton, not the Long Walk, as he described in his journal for 1901. The kindness, patience and help of Miss Langton and the other good ladies of the Royal Archives is beyond the conventional words of praise expressed in the introductions of books. We had coffee each morning, and discreet gossip about

---

* An allusion to the era when the prettiest boy in the school was traditionally 'available' to the members of the Eton Society or 'Pop' – the privileged, self-electing club of senior boys, clad in fancy waistcoats, who act as school prefects. Edward Underdown (1908–89) became an actor known for his leading roles in Noël Coward plays.

long-defunct royalties. I had two visitors, M. and J., on separate evenings, and walked with them around the playing fields and along the river. Both adorable and affectionate.

On my return to Badminton, I received polite letter from Sir Martin Gilliat* informing me that Queen Mother had no recollections of Regy beyond remembering that he was always 'about', his advice being sought on all kinds of questions, particularly the 'art' ones. Also found A. in state of great excitement because Caroline had telephoned one morning at 10.30 saying she was bringing the Prince of Wales to see the garden. The Prince was charming and took a lively interest, being keen to improve his own garden at Highgrove. He asked where the whippets were. 'They are shut up, Sir, because I didn't want them to give you a nip.' 'I dare say they would prefer to give a nip to a fox, wouldn't they?' he retorted. So that old story has reached him.† Then to her amazement she received a delightful letter of thanks from him in his own hand, referring to her 'magical' garden, and asking her for the names of old-fashioned roses. And 'when you write to me, put "To Himself" on the envelope.' For good manners he earns full marks.

Tuesday, 23 August

On Saturday, A. and I dined at Nether Lypiatt with the Michaels of Kent. Can't make out why we were asked, having only met them once at the Hollands' annual concert four years ago.‡ I reluctant to accept; A. determined. So she put on her finery, necklaces and diamond ear-rings, I my dreary black tie. Bidden for 8, we thought for royalty we should be on time. We were, precisely, and the first guests, except for a couple staying in the house. Climbed the outside steps into the little hall. Greeted by nice lady in semi-maid's uniform. Made to sign gigantic visitors' book with thick nib in our most flowing Edwardian style. Old-fashioned family butler ushered us into

---

* Lieut-Col Sir Martin Gilliat (1913–93); Private Secretary to HM Queen Elizabeth the Queen Mother, 1956–93.
† See 21 May 1979.
‡ See 8 July 1979.

long drawing-room. The Prince gave a kindly welcome. Dressed in white dinner jacket, with trim beard, the very image of his grandfather George V, he is a poor, but very gentle and courteous little mouse. Other couple the Jonathan Aitkens,* he a Tory MP, very go-ahead, very clever, she Yugoslav-born, Swiss-bred, dull. 'Made' conversation over sherry and smoked oysters. With a rush as of Pentecostal wind, *She* appeared, like a gigantic Peter Pan fairy alighting on the stage at the end of a wire, large, handsome, Valkyrian, blond hair over shoulders in straight Alice in Wonderland rays. Effusive, friendly, charming. Wearing white, spotted dress, *décolletée*, no jewelry at all. Then in came Micky Suffolk,† whom I did not recognise at first, along with female whom I took to be reigning wife. Not so; was Lady Bridport. I was introduced as author of 'Ancestral Prophecies'. Of course he had read it? Hadn't. Instead he cried out, 'You are the man to whom I owe the solution of my house, Charlton! I am eternally grateful.' The truth is that I did see him about this years ago, but don't believe I did anything. But did not disabuse him. Then later still the Duke and Duchess of Marlborough,‡ he tall, handsome, pleased with himself, stuck-up. Very *gratin*, jet-settish. Much whispering between hostess and butler at door, she returning to say, 'It looks as though we shan't get anything to eat.' Finally, about 9.30, we went into dining-room. We were ten. A. and I and the Aitkens, being 'rank-less', were put together in the middle, the Duke and Earl and their females on either side of Their Royal Highnesses. So odd this protocol business, nothing to do with distinction or age. I couldn't hear a word either of my women said. Struggled also to bite my way across a piece of beef swathed in grey sauce. Room too hot. This room undeniably pretty, white walls and lovely Dresden plates hanging in each panel, but spoiled by little search-lights put in ceiling. In fact this house is beautifully decorated, but like a town house in

---

* Businessman and Conservative politician (b. 1942); grandson of 1st Baron Beaverbrook; Chief Secretary to Treasury, 1994–5; imprisoned on charges of perjury, 1998; m. 1979 Lolicia Azucki.
† Michael Howard, 21st Earl of Suffolk and 14th Earl of Berkshire (b. 1935); m. (3rd) 1983 Linda *née* Paravicini, formerly wife of 4th Viscount Bridport.
‡ John Spencer-Churchill, 11th Duke of Marlborough (b. 1926); m. (3rd) 1972 Rosita Douglas.

Mayfair. No longer the dark, brown-oak little squire's gem it was when Violet Woodhouse* lived here.

When women left the room, conversation instantly turned to smut by Micky Suffolk, an attractive, jolly rascal. (I always maintain when questioned by women that men on these occasions talk politics and finance.) He had been at a slimming centre, starved and allowed only prunes to nibble. Said the treatment made him randier than he had ever felt in his life. Talked of a horse in his care – is he a trainer? – of incalculable value, millions. Belonged to the Queen or Aga Khan. He thought it had a cold and called in a vet. Vet produced a long thermometer like a parasol, pushed it up the mare's behind. They stood beside mare and talked. After talking looked down, mare still standing, but thermometer completely disappeared. Looked anxiously on ground. Not there. Horrors. Sent for a plumber with a pair of surgical gloves. Terrified lest glass thermometer had broken. Plumber by hideous operation fished the thing out and mare none the worse.

When we rejoined ladies in drawing room, Princess took me by the arm and hand and led me into a corner. Most intimate and cosy. Is flirtatious. I tried not to press her hand back, lest *lèse-majesté*. She told me how these last few years have taught her never to believe anything in the newspapers. Only one-ninth of press reports are accurate. Told me her mother was in prison when pregnant with her, just before end of war. Was released for birth of child. I said, 'Oh Ma'am, but how romantic it would have been for you to be born in prison.' Remark not favourably received. Her father was her mother's second husband who died at ninety. She did not care for him. Was very saddened by the death of her favourite brown Persian cat. Knocked over by a car on road, it tried to walk home but died en route. She said with tears in her eyes that this cat's death meant more to her than the deaths of most of her friends and relations. She is writing life of Queen of Bohemia, but said she had too little time, and must resort to an assistant. At this I trembled,

---

* On 30 March 1944 J.L.-M. wrote that he 'drove . . . to Nether Lypiatt Manor, near Stroud, to lunch at this wonderful little house with Mrs Gordon Woodhouse . . . It is unspoilt late seventeenth century, and perfect in every way. In fact an ideal, if not *the* ideal small country house.' When the house came on the market in the late 1950s, the L.-Ms considered buying it, but were unable to afford it.

but said nothing. Said that hunting gave her most pleasure. Loved the danger. 'If your life consisted for the most part of cutting blue ribbons, wouldn't you want a change of some adventurous sort?' I asked if she had read Kenneth [Rose]'s *George V*. She is half-way through, and said what a *ghastly* man he was. I said he had his points. No, she said, stamp collecting and killing quantities of birds did not redeem him. I pointed out his kindness to Ramsay MacDonald. She shook her head. Said that when she had tiffs with her husband she would tell him he was no better than his grandfather.

It is impossible not to like this un-royal princess, with her beauty, vitality and friendliness. On parting she said how much she hoped to meet us again.

Sunday, 4 September

Poor Alex Moulton has had all his silver stolen. I telephoned to condole. 'Yes,' he said, 'all my cutlery has been taken.' 'What! All your cruets and serviette rings?' 'Yes, all,' he said.

Saturday, 1 October

Selina [Hastings] came to stay for two nights with her mother Margaret Lane, Lady Huntingdon,* who was giving a lecture in Bath. Lady H. is seventy-six and still extremely pretty. There is something faintly bedint about her pronounciation of 'ows' for a woman of her generation, but her appearance and manner are *bien*. I liked her immensely. She was extremely funny. Told us that her husband (still alive) married his first wife, Cristina Casati,† in face of great opposition from his parents, for she was a foreigner, a Communist and a Catholic. The couple decided to make their

---

* Margaret Lane (1907–94); dau. of H. G. Lane, newspaper editor; m. 1st Bryan E. Wallace (son of thriller-writer Edgar Wallace), 2nd 1944 (as his 2nd wife) Francis Hastings, 16th Earl of Huntingdon (1901–90).

† Cristina (d. 1953), dau. of Marchese Casati; m. 1st 1925–43 Viscount Hastings (who s. 1939 as 16th Earl of Huntingdon), 2nd (as his 2nd wife) Hon. Wogan Philipps (later 2nd Baron Milford, who had m. 1st 1928 Rosamond Lehmann).

married life in Australia and his mother, Australian by birth, gave him a large pile of letters addressed to friends there. On opening some of the letters, Jack Hastings discovered that they asked the addressees on no account to give any help or employment to him or his wife, so he pitched them all out of his port-hole. Lady H. was once invited by Vita to Sissinghurst. When she got there, V. seemed very abstracted, and while walking in the garden fell into a bed of roses. Gardeners appeared and carried her away. Lady H. expressed concern, but the gardeners assured her that this quite often happened. It did not occur to Lady H. that V. might have been drunk. She assumed it was heart trouble, and left.

Thursday, 13 October

Called on Diana Cooper this morning, as I was staying with the Berkeleys next door. Was kept waiting while she prepared herself. Finally called upstairs. Diana lying propped up in large bed with everything within reach, doggie on sheets, telephone, books, pencils, paper, cigarettes. Wearing lace cap on back of head. Face white and strained, yet eyes as beautiful as ever, and bosom exposed, broadness thereof beautiful. Rather vague and deaf. Instantly began discussing words which are now out of date – rotter, ripping. Denied that her world ever said 'town' for London. But she is wrong, for it comes repeatedly into Regy's correspondence before 1914. On subject of [Cecil] Parkinson, she said Ministers of the Crown should uphold tenets of Christian faith which is foundation of Conservative Party.* Difficult to converse with her for she introduces a subject and is tenacious. But what a woman! How intelligent and easy! Said she was very unhappy and longed to die in her sleep. Obsessed by her last car accident, and can no longer drive. Chain-smoking in bed. She is still fun.

---

* Cecil Parkinson, widely regarded as the architect of the recent Conservative election victory, had just resigned from the Cabinet following revelations by his former secretary that he had had an affair with and a child by her and broken a promise to marry her. As the widow of a Conservative minister who had been a notorious philanderer, Lady Diana's remark was presumably ironical.

To Faber & Faber to discuss their paperbacking this autumn of *Another Self* and my three volumes of diaries. Very flattering, but they want me to read through and make corrections by end of this month, which will be a painful task. Told me that the N.T. definitely refused to have my diaries in their shops, considering them shocking and in bad taste. I have always suspected this.

Then hurried in pouring rain to K. Clark's memorial service at St James's Piccadilly. Greeted by Alan Clark and wife standing at main door. Found self sitting at back with Janet Stone and daughter, Janet looking distressed. Service lasted unprecedented hour and a half. Alan and John Sparrow read lessons; John Pope-Hennessy over from USA read long address. Could hardly hear a word. An Irish Catholic priest gave another dissertation, claiming that before his death K. sent for him, received Communion according to the proper rites, and said, 'Thank you, Father, that is what I have been longing for.' Very surprising. Declined Alan's invitation to attend a party after service at John Murray's. Instead walked with J.K.-B. to Brooks's where we had tea. He reminded me that we met 25 years ago this month.

Saturday, 19 November

Dined with Somersets. About fifteen. Ali Forbes and Sebastian Walker, who loathe each other. Young William Waldegrave,* formerly of Mrs Thatcher's Think Tank, now Bristol MP. Charming, gentle and unassuming, unlike two previously named. He came up to me while Sebastian was proclaiming the joys of the modern world, and said, 'Anyone who supposes the world is improving must be raving mad.' Ali asked all the men to give their reply to the old-fashioned question which tailors used to ask, 'On what side do you dress, Sir?' I said, 'On the left until I cross the Channel, and I have to reconsider the matter again when reaching the Austrian frontier.' Sebastian confided to me in a whisper his hopeless love for David Ford, but also

---

* Politician (b. 1946), yr s. of 12th Earl Waldegrave; Fellow of All Souls, 1971–86; MP (C) Bristol W. (1979–97); at this time Undersecretary for the Environment; cr. life peer, 1998.

thought he might marry Anne Somerset, sitting opposite. Told him I thought this a non-starter. Shouting down the table, David asked me how it was possible for Harold [Nicolson] to have caught clap from a boy. Ali overcome by his naïveté.

Sunday, 20 November

No Sunday review of *The Last Stuarts*. The book is a flop. I am very depressed, convinced that it is not a bad book, whereas plenty of trash gets recognition and sales. The fact that Kenneth Rose, next to whom I sat last week at a Foyle's luncheon, has received two (deserved) prizes for his *George V* does not make my plight any easier to endure. He was suitably self-deprecatory in receiving praise from all and sundry, yet I detected a smug sense of superiority.

Thursday, 24 November

Derek Hill rang me up yesterday in one of his usual states. Upset that I had not been in touch. Would I lunch with him on 13 December to meet the Queen Mother? She had particularly said she would like me to be there. I replied that I had just accepted an invitation to lunch that day with June Hutchinson to meet Pinkie Beckett.* 'But you must put that off.' No, I replied, I couldn't. Besides which I had no desire to meet the Q.M. I hated being with royalty. They caused constraint. I also privately doubted that the Q.M. had expressed a wish to meet me. She doesn't know me and my name means nothing to her. Derek very cross and petulant. Said he would ring me up again today to find out if I had changed my mind. He did so as soon as I arrived in Bath, this time in dulcet mood. Took it well when I said I had not changed my mind, but was in despair as to when we should ever see each other again. The truth is that I like D. very much but don't particularly want to see him.

---

* Hon. Priscilla Brett (b. 1921), dau. of 3nd Viscount Esher, m. 1941 Sir Martyn Beckett, 2nd Bt.

1983

Wednesday, 30 November

This morning I met David Somerset approaching on foot down the drive. Thought he was talking to me, and tried to reply to what he was saying. Then discovered that he was in fact talking to Michael Tree on some sort of portable telephone.

Thursday, 1 December

A very favourable review of *The Last Stuarts* in today's *Times* by Woodrow Wyatt.* It has cheered me up, for I have had a paucity of notices. At least there is little risk of my committing a sin against the Holy Ghost by becoming too pleased with myself.

Saturday, 3 December

Saturday morning writing letters. Telephone rang. A. answered in the kitchen. Then came to my room to say, 'That was June [Hutchinson]. Diana Westmorland has died in her sleep.' They found her this morning in the exact position in which they had left her, only her eyes closed. Her heart must have given out. Previous evening she had eaten food and smoked a cigarette. June said to her, 'Mum, I really believe you are better. You will be able to see Jim tomorrow.' Yes, she replied, she would love to see Jim. Touching that these were the last words of this nonagenarian darling, whom I so dearly loved. Felt extremely sad, yet glad she went out like this. Life held nothing more for her and she had been wretched these past six months. Ought to have gone after her ninetieth birthday party last May which she greatly enjoyed.

Sunday, 4 December

After Communion at Little Badminton this morning, David Westmorland† said, 'You will write something for *The Times*, won't

---

* Sir Woodrow Wyatt (1918–98); former Labour MP, Chairman of Horserace Totalisator Board; cr. life peer, 1987.
† David Fane, 15th Earl of Westmorland (1924–93).

you?' I have tried, but the result is not good. Difficult to steer between the Scylla of banality and the Charybdis of sentimentality when writing of someone to whom one was very devoted. I shall greatly miss her. She was far and away *my* greatest friend down here.

Beside her mother's bed, June found a little copy of *The Imitation of Christ* inscribed by Mr Gladstone for her Baptism in 1893, to which I have referred in my obit. Also, in emptying her mother's handbag, she found the love letter I had written to her on her ninetieth birthday, which she carried around with her.

Thursday, 8 December

Darling Diana's funeral in the little Papist Church in Chipping Sodbury. A. unable to go, stricken with bronchitis. Pouring with rain. I got there early to find a crowd of friends. Irish priest officiating in that maddening singsong voice, referring to 'our lost sister, Lady Diana', and lamenting the death of the church's best benefactor. Indeed, every year she raised funds by a sale and opened her garden for the church. Liturgy in English; no incense; the usual irritants. I thanked God all the while that I was no longer a Catholic. Some demon gets into me now in a Catholic church. Pathetic little coffin with sprays of half-budding lilies, very pretty and simple, yet so sad, like a child's coffin. I could not look at it when it was pushed past me down the narrow aisle. Had to go to tea at Lyegrove afterwards. Did not stay long, and motored Joanie Altrincham home afterwards. She was present as a girl of fourteen at Diana's first wedding to Percy Wyndham in 1913, which makes Joanie eighty-four.

Junie came over next day, bringing for me as a memento of D. the aforementioned *Imitation of Christ*. Greatly moved.

Tuesday, 13 December

A. and I went to the N.T. [retirement] dinner party given for me at Fenton House [Hampstead]. I was dreading it but had no reason to, for there were no speeches. Beautifully arranged. We were received in the drawing room upstairs where I used to have tea with Lady Binning, and ate in the large dining room. Was given a present before dinner. Saw it was a picture. Opened it upside-down. Had not my specs on. Saw it was the interior of some house. Martin Drury said, 'Don't you recognise it?' It was my library in Bath. A beautiful water-colour sketch by Mrs Gwynne-Jones, widow of the painter. A. of course in the know. Arranged for her to enter the library during weekends when I was not there. Delighted with the present. Now I have to thank countless friends who subscribed to it but did not attend the dinner, like the Graftons (who were not asked and, I later learned from Midi, were distressed). I sat between Dione Gibson,[*] intelligent and sweet, and Francesca Wall.[†] John Cornforth, Jack Rathbone, the [Tony] Mitchells. Both A. and I enjoyed ourselves. Stayed until after midnight. Discovered the house's current custodian was the son of my friend Mrs Jackson, the original custodian who died of cancer years ago. Much pre-historic chat.

Dudley Dodd[‡] going round the rooms with me after dinner said, 'You were responsible for persuading Lady Binning not to leave her porcelain to the V&A with the rest of the Salting Bequest.' 'Was I?' 'Yes, it is all in the files.' I remarked on the charming alcoves, curved and glazed, which displayed the best china. 'You were responsible for those. You designed them and got [Paul] Geddes Hyslop to carry them out.' 'Did I really?' I can't remember such details.

Friday, 23 December

A. said at breakfast that, were it not for me, she would now emigrate to Australia without hesitation. A year ago I would certainly not have contemplated going; but today I would not particularly mind. I agree with A. that the nuclear cloud hanging over Europe is damnably depressing. Furthermore, I now feel I might just as well vegetate in a

---

[*] Elizabeth Dione Pearson; m. 1945 R.P.T. 'Pat' Gibson (1916–2003; cr. life peer, 1975; Chairman of N.T., 1977–86).

[†] Francesca Fummi (b. 1935); niece of 28th Earl of Crawford, Chairman of N.T., 1945–65; m. 1961 Christopher Wall (b. 1929), N.T. Historic Buildings Representative for Thames & Chiltern Region, 1956–94.

[‡] Deputy Historic Buildings Secretary of N.T., 1981–2000 (b. 1947).

pleasant climate as here. For henceforth I shall merely read and listen to music and, I hope, walk. I shall not write any more books after this one; and I have no interests except M. to keep my affections in this country, to which I am absolutely indifferent. So shall we go off together?

In the event, J.L.-M. continued to reside at Badminton for the remaining fourteen years of his life, during which he published ten more books: apart from his life of Lord Esher, which appeared in 1986, these included his novel The Fool of Love, *a biography of the 6th Duke of Devonshire, two works on architecture, two volumes of memoirs and three volumes of diaries.*

Index

Index

Books by JL-M appear as separate entries; books by others are listed under authors.

May 1st Thursday. It is May
trains stopped, workers in the
moustration against the stal
the Ardèche the inhabitan
left London on the morning
7.46 return to Montélimar
a noisy half hour, half ris
waters, to Boulogne. Thence by
Albert Hotel, rue de Hyacin
I found a sweet note of c

E took a female
dined with Stuart Preston
see Stuart's new apartment
the Rue St. Honoré. A.
Tuileries, corner of Louvre
Ball), the Invalides, the
Boul apartment so small
but the only residence of a